gcse geography
edexcel B

teacher's handbook

Series editor:
Bob Digby

Catherine Hurst

OXFORD
UNIVERSITY PRESS

Great Clarendon Street, Oxford OX2 6DP

Oxford University Press is a department of the University of Oxford.
It furthers the University's objective of excellence in research,
scholarship, and education by publishing worldwide in

Oxford   New York

Auckland   Cape Town   Dar es Salaam   Hong Kong   Karachi
Kuala Lumpur   Madrid   Melbourne   Mexico City   Nairobi
New Delhi   Shanghai   Taipei   Toronto

With offices in
Argentina   Austria   Brazil   Chile   Czech Republic   France   Greece
Guatemala   Hungary   Italy   Japan   Poland   Portugal   Singapore
South Korea   Switzerland   Thailand   Turkey   Ukraine   Vietnam

Oxford is a registered trade mark of Oxford University Press
in the UK and in certain other countries

© Oxford University Press 2013

Authors: Bob Digby, Catherine Hurst.

The moral rights of the authors have been asserted

Database right Oxford University Press (maker)

First published 2009, Second edition 2013

All rights reserved. No part of this publication may be reproduced,
stored in a retrieval system, or transmitted, in any form or by any means,
without the prior permission in writing of Oxford University Press, or as
expressly permitted by law, or under terms agreed with the appropriate
reprographics rights organization. Enquiries concerning reproduction
outside the scope of the above should be sent to the Rights Department,
Oxford University Press, at the address above

You must not circulate this book in any other binding or cover
and you must impose this same condition on any acquirer

British Library Cataloguing in Publication Data

Data available

ISBN 978-0-19-839499-0

10 9 8 7 6 5 4 3 2 1

Printed by Bell and Bain Ltd., Glasgow

Paper used in the production of this book is a natural, recyclable product
made from wood grown in sustainable forests. The manufacturing process
conforms to the environmental regulations of the country of origin.

Contents

The Edexcel Geography B specification		4
About this course		6
Matching the specification		7
Using this teacher's handbook		8
About the students' book		9
- Introduction to the exam-style questions		10
The OxBox		11

Unit 1 overview: Dynamic planet — 12

1	Restless Earth	14
2	Changing climate	32
3	Battle for the biosphere	52
4	Water world	70
5	Coastal change and conflict	88
6	River processes and pressures	106
7	Oceans on the edge	126
8	Extreme environments	144

Unit 2 overview: People and the planet — 166

9	Population dynamics	168
10	Consuming resources	190
11	Globalisation	212
12	Development dilemmas	230
13	The changing economy of the UK	248
14	Changing settlements in the UK	268
15	The challenges of an urban world	286
16	The challenges of a rural world	306

17	**Unit 3: Making geographical decisions**	**324**
18	**Unit 4: Investigating geography — Controlled Assessment**	**337**

The Edexcel Geography B specification

About the specification

The Edexcel GCSE Geography B specification is divided into four units. Students study Units 1 and 2 to build their core knowledge and understanding, which is developed further in Units 3 and 4.

Unit 1: Dynamic Planet

This Unit consists of four compulsory topics (Section A) and four options (Sections B and C) of which students study two (one from each section).

SECTION A (Compulsory topics)	SECTION B (Optional topics)	SECTION C (Optional topics)
Restless Earth	Coastal change and conflict	Oceans on the edge
Changing climate	OR	OR
Battle for the biosphere	River processes and pressures	Extreme environments
Water world		

Section A introduces the planet through its four main spheres: the geosphere, the atmosphere, the biosphere and the hydrosphere. Section B considers aspects of the planet at a small scale, while Section C considers larger scale issues.

Assessment

Unit 1 is assessed through a 1 hour 15 minute, tiered, written examination, which contains a mixture of question styles. 78 marks are available, with 48 marks in Section A, 15 marks in Section B and 15 marks in Section C.

Of the 78 marks available, up to 6 marks are awarded for Spelling, Punctuation and Grammar (SPaG).

Unit 2: People and the Planet

This Unit also consists of four compulsory topics (Section A) and four options (Sections B and C) of which students study two (one from each section).

SECTION A (Compulsory topics)	SECTION B (Optional topics)	SECTION C (Optional topics)
Population dynamics	The changing economy of the UK	The challenges of an urban world
Consuming resources	OR	OR
Globalisation	Changing settlements in the UK	The challenges of a rural world
Development dilemmas		

In Section A students are introduced to the main aspects of how people live on our planet. Section B considers how people in the UK interact with different aspects of our planet on a small scale, while section C considers how people interact with different aspects of our planet on a large scale.

Assessment

Unit 2 is also assessed through a 1 hour 15 minute, tiered, written examination, which contains a mixture of question styles. 78 marks are available, with 48 marks in Section A, 15 marks in Section B and 15 marks in Section C.

Of the 78 marks available, up to 6 marks are awarded for Spelling, Punctuation and Grammar (SPaG).

Unit 3: Making Geographical Decisions

Unit 3 assesses students' ability to make decisions about geographical issues and to justify them. It acts as a synoptic unit bringing together students' understanding of the core topics in Units 1 and 2.

The topic for the Unit 3 examination will be different each year. Students will be provided with a resource booklet in the examination. The examination questions will relate to material in the booklet.

Assessment

This unit is assessed through a 1 hour 30 minute, tiered, written examination. 53 marks are available spread across the questions. Of the 53 marks, up to 3 marks are awarded for Spelling, Punctuation and Grammar (SPaG).

Unit 4: Investigating Geography

For Unit 4, students need to complete a fieldwork investigation and report. They must complete one of the tasks provided by Edexcel, on one of the following themes: coastal environments; river environments; rural/countryside environments; town/city environments.

Assessment

This unit is internally assessed. Students complete their fieldwork task and write it up under controlled conditions. The task is marked out of a total of 50 marks across the following areas: planning; methods of data collection; data presentation and report production; analysis and conclusions; and evaluation. The task will be marked internally, and moderated by Edexcel.

About this course

The students' book and teacher's handbook have been revised and updated to meet the requirements of the Edexcel GCSE Geography B specification for first certification in 2014. The students' book has been written to be accessible and engaging, and will hopefully aid in the success of you and your students.

The course components

The students' book

- Revised and updated throughout to match the 2012 specification.
- A single book for the whole course.
- All the content and case studies students will need.
- Coverage of all the core and option topics.
- Each chapter covers one topic, divided into individual sections of two pages.
- Sections begin with a clear objective and include:
  - activities which practise a range of geographical skills
  - clearly identified exam-style questions with allocated marks
  - *on your planet* interesting facts and ideas
  - *what do you think?* statements and questions to challenge thinking
  - key vocabulary identified in bold, and explained in key word boxes on the page, or in the glossary.
- Support and guidance for Unit 3 (Making geographical decisions) and Unit 4 (Investigating geography).

The teacher's handbook

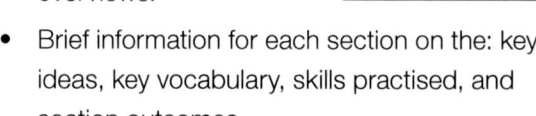

- Specification content matched to the students' book.
- Unit and Chapter overviews.
- Brief information for each section on the: key ideas, key vocabulary, skills practised, and section outcomes.
- Starters, plenaries and homework ideas for each section.
- Answers to the *your questions* from the students' book.
- Mark schemes for the exam-style questions from the students' book, including suggested, differentiated, exam-style questions for Foundation / Higher Tier students.
- Specific guidance for teaching Units 3 and 4.

The OxBox CD-ROM

The OxBox CD-ROM was published to accompany the **first edition** of the students' book. You may still find parts of it useful, but it will not provide an exact match to the second edition of the students' book.

- For more information about the OxBox, see page 11.

Matching the specification

GCSE Geography Edexcel B students' book covers all of the content necessary for Edexcel's Geography B specification for first certification in 2014. Chapters in the students' book are named directly from the related topic, and appear in the order of the specification, to make navigation through the course as straightforward as possible.

Edexcel GCSE Geography B specification — summary of content	*GCSE Geography Edexcel B* — students' book contents
Unit 1 Dynamic Planet *6 topics to be studied* <u>Compulsory</u> Topic 1 Restless Earth Topic 2 Changing climate Topic 3 Battle for the biosphere Topic 4 Water world <u>Options</u> Topic 5 Coastal change and conflict *OR* Topic 6 River processes and pressures *AND* Topic 7 Oceans on the edge *OR* Topic 8 Extreme environments	**Unit 1 overview** *6 chapters to be studied* Ch 1 Restless Earth Ch 2 Changing climate Ch 3 Battle for the biosphere Ch 4 Water world Ch 5 Coastal change and conflict Ch 6 River processes and pressures Ch 7 Oceans on the edge Ch 8 Extreme environments
Unit 2 People and the Planet *6 topics to be studied* <u>Compulsory</u> Topic 1 Population dynamics Topic 2 Consuming resources Topic 3 Globalisation Topic 4 Development dilemmas <u>Options</u> Topic 5 The Changing economy of the UK *OR* Topic 6 Changing settlements in the UK *AND* Topic 7 The challenges of an urban world *OR* Topic 8 The challenges of a rural world	**Unit 2 overview** *6 chapters to be studied* Ch 9 Population dynamics Ch 10 Consuming resources Ch 11 Globalisation Ch 12 Development dilemmas Ch 13 The Changing economy of the UK *OR* Ch 14 Changing settlements in the UK Ch 15 The challenges of an urban world *OR* Ch 16 The challenges of a rural world
Unit 3 Making geographical decisions Assesses students' ability to make decisions about geographical issues and justify them.	**Ch 17 Making geographical decisions** Prepares for Unit 3, with an example of what students might find in the exam resource booklet based on the Christchurch earthquakes. It includes Foundation and Higher Tier exam-style questions.
Unit 4 Investigating Geography A fieldwork investigation and report based on the tasks provided by Edexcel on one of the following themes: coastal environments; river environments; rural/countryside environments; town/city environments.	**Ch 18 Investigating geography** A breakdown of the steps students need to go through in order to complete their controlled assessment.

Using this teacher's handbook

For Units 1 and 2 of the students' book, this teacher's handbook provides:

Unit overviews

- An introduction to each Unit, with the overarching themes and ideas.
- Details on how the unit is assessed.
- Answers to the 'your questions' from the Unit overview pages in the students' book.

Chapter overviews

- The key ideas behind the chapter.
- Matches the key ideas and content from the Edexcel B specification to pages in the students' book.
- The learning outcomes to aim for when teaching the chapter.

Section overviews

- The key ideas, key vocabulary, and skills covered, for each section.
- Learning outcomes i.e. what most students should be able to do by the end of the section.
- Ideas for starters and plenaries.
- Suggestions for further class and homework activities.
- Answers to the 'your questions' and the exam-style questions in the students' book.

Further support and guidance for Unit 3 (Making geographical decisions) and Unit 4 (Investigating geography) can be found in Chapters 17 and 18 of this handbook.

Using starter and plenaries

The starters and plenaries provided in this book can help you to meet your lesson objectives — and with planning, you won't have to rely on sudden inspiration in the classroom. However, you may want to modify them to suit your resources available, your teaching style and your students' needs.

The starters

- Most of the starters provided can be used with the students' book closed, as an introduction to the section. They should then lead easily into the work for that lesson.
- You may wish to combine two starters to provide a more extended activity.
- Starters requiring the use of an atlas can be an excellent way of giving your students atlas practice that's fun.
- Other starters require both mental and physical activity, for example creating a graffiti wall on the board – a great way to get everybody involved.

The plenaries

- Plenaries can be used throughout the lesson – not just at the end – to encourage feedback, assess understanding, and make connections with other subjects and situations.
- Some of those provided are just single questions, and could be combined to make a more extended plenary.
- As with the starters, some of the plenaries will require more preparation than others. These might not be practical for every lesson, but will give a bit of variety to keep your students surprised.

About the students' book

Features of the students' book

Objective statement is clearly displayed to prepare and focus students on the topic of the section.

The 'On your planets' gives interesting, fun or unusual facts, which will (hopefully!) help to hook your students' attention.

Keyword boxes explain key geographical terms from the section, highlighted in bold in the text.

your questions are student activities designed to cater for the full ability range. Opportunities are provided for collaboration, as well as independent work. Answers can be found in this teacher's handbook.

Each section includes an exam-style question (see next page). The mark schemes for these are included in this teacher's handbook.

9

Exam-style questions

In the students' book, exam-style questions are clearly marked within 'your questions' in each section. These provide a regular focus for your students upon exam skills, so that different exam question styles become familiar. Alternatively, save some for revision purposes as the exams approach.

Exam questions mostly reflect the examination for Units 1 and 2:

- Questions for topics in Section A in Unit 1 (chapters 1-4) and Unit 2 (chapters 9-12), carry up to 6 marks, which is the longest response that students will have to give in this Section.
- Questions for topics in Sections B and C in Unit 1 (chapters 5-8) and Unit 2 (chapters 13-16), carry up to 8 marks.
- Questions for Unit 3 reflect the Making Geographical Decisions examination, in that they carry a wider variety of marks; those in chapter 17 vary between 1 and 12 marks.

Mark schemes for these questions are provided within each section in this book.

Using exam questions to prepare students

GCSE students face a daunting task in terms of time demands. In each of Units 1 and 2; 75 minutes are available for earning 72 marks. This should be sufficient, provided that students read the questions fully and know properly in advance which questions they have been prepared for. In spite of this, some students do run out of time; the only way to overcome this is to practise timed answers before the exam.

Your students will gain enormously from the training needed to pass exams. Training should never replace good Geography throughout the course, but as exams approach it is invaluable for focusing students' learning.

The purpose of the exam-style questions is to help prepare your students for the exam. Use this exam guidance to help them to:

- get used to writing in short bursts,
- know and understand what they need to do to achieve top marks,
- understand levelled mark schemes, and how to develop a range of points.

Early in the GCSE course, show students mark schemes when they prepare answers, so that they see the range of possible points and how to develop these. As the exam season approaches, use these after they have written timed answers as part of your feedback.

How long should exam answers take?

Timing is crucial to exam success; students have little more than a minute per mark. Help them to practice. Begin timing them on questions liberally e.g. 4 marks in 6-8 minutes. As students' progress, their answers should become quicker and more succinct. Timed practice helps students to write more quickly, and to focus. By the time they take the exam, they should be able to write a 6 mark answer in 6 minutes. Help students by timing them until they can replicate what is needed in the exam.

The OxBox

The *GCSE Geography Edexcel B OxBox CD-ROM* was published to accompany the **first edition** of the students' book. You may still find parts of it useful, but it will not provide an exact match to the second edition of the students' book.

The OxBox includes an extensive bank of teaching resources, assessment materials and lesson plans.

Customisable

- Many of the resources on the OxBox are provided in a customisable format, so they can be adapted and developed.
- The OxBox also provides a place on your school's network where you can easily save your own resources, plans and assessments, and share them with your department.

User management

- The user management facility allows you to import class registers and create user accounts for your students. Students can directly access any resources or assessments that you make available to them.

Resources

Image collections

- Every photo, map and illustration from the first edition of the students' book is available in a PowerPoint presentation.
- You can display the images on a whiteboard, or extract them for use in your own worksheets and presentations.

Interactive activities

- An interactive activity is included for each section of the first edition of the students' book.
- They could be used as starters or plenaries that can involve the whole class.

Assessment

Interactive formative assessments

- There is a formative assessment for every topic in Units 1 and 2 of the first edition of the students' book.
- Interactive formative assessments are answered on-screen, with feedback after every question and auto-marked results.

Interactive summative assessments

- There is one summative assessment for Units 1 and 2 for the first edition of the students' book.
- Interactive summative assessments are answered on-screen, with auto-marking and feedback at the end of the assessment.

Exam practice and self-assessment

- Exam-style questions, at higher and foundation level are available for Units 1 and 2, complete with assessment criteria and a reflection activity.
- Self assessment forms, including space for peer and teacher review, allow students to review and analyse their own work.

Planning

- The Oxbox provides a lesson plan to support every section in Units 1 and 2 of the first edition of the students' book, which can be customised, and added to, to suit the needs of your class.
- The OxBox lesson player helps you run your lessons with ease. Attach your resources to your lesson plan, then use the player to launch each resource in turn from a simple toolbar.
- You can save your existing plans into the OxBox and adapt those that have been provided.

Unit 1 Dynamic planet

Unit overview
Unit 1, Dynamic planet, introduces the four main spheres of our planet: the atmosphere, hydrosphere, biosphere, and geosphere. Students will look at key issues, such as climate change and sustainable use of the spheres.

The topics
Four compulsory topics are studied in Section A:

Section A
Restless Earth (chapter 1)
Changing climate (chapter 2)
Battle for the biosphere (chapter 3)
Water world (chapter 4)

Two option topics are also studied, one from Section B (small-scale aspects of the spheres) and one from Section C (large-scale aspects). The topics are:

Section B
Coastal change and conflict (chapter 5)
River processes and pressures (chapter 6)

Section C
Oceans on the edge (chapter 7)
Extreme environments (chapter 8)

Assessment
This unit is assessed through a 1 hour 15 minute, tiered, written examination, which contains a mixture of question styles. 78 marks are available: 48 marks in Section A; 15 marks in Section B; and 15 marks in Section C.

Of the 78 marks available, up to 6 marks are awarded for Spelling, Punctuation and Grammar (SPaG).

Assessment support
Each section (double-page spread) in the students' book includes an exam-style question. A full mark scheme for each exam-style question is included in in this teacher's handbook. In most cases; where questions are aimed at Higher Tier students, a differentiated version is provided for Foundation Tier students, and vice versa.

In addition, the OxBox — published to accompany the **first edition** of the students' book includes:

- one interactive summative assessment per unit in different option combinations;
- an interactive formative assessment for each chapter;
- an exam-style question for each chapter in the first edition.

Dynamic planet

answers

1. The atmosphere is the layer of gases that make up the air around us.
   The hydrosphere is the layer of water – seas, rivers, lakes, groundwater and ice – found on the Earth's crust.
   The biosphere is the thin layer of living things – plants, animals and people – found living on the Earth's crust.
   The geosphere consists of the rocks of the Earth's crust and deeper into the Earth towards the core.

2. Students could give a range of answers about how they have used the four spheres, e.g:
   - atmosphere – breathed in oxygen
   - hydrosphere – used water in a variety of ways (washing, drinking)
   - biosphere – eaten food produced from plants and animals on the biosphere
   - geosphere – travelled in a vehicle running on petrol/diesel (a fossil fuel).

3.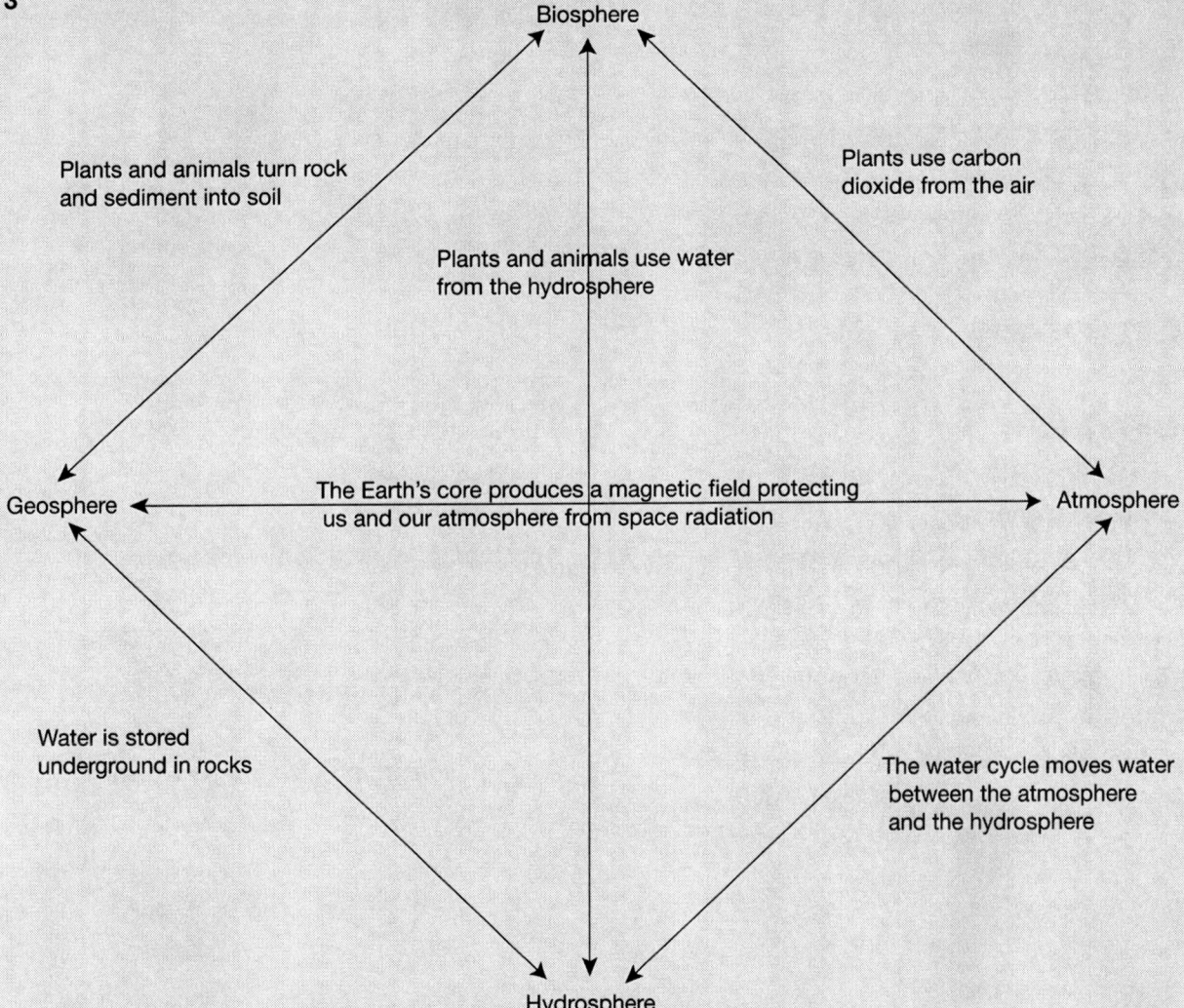

   Students may come up with other links.

4. Students should give four ways in which humans might be harmed by the spheres. The following are given in the text: earthquakes, volcanic eruptions, tsunami, floods, hurricanes, storms and tornadoes.

5. Student responses will vary, but could include the following:
   - Atmospheric pollution with carbon dioxide is causing climate change.
   - Continued and increasing use of fossil fuels means they will run out and we will need to find alternative energy sources.
   - Deforestation, farming and pollution will cause increasing levels of extinction and a loss of biodiversity.
   - Misuse and over-use of water is leading to pollution of supplies and supplies drying up.

1 Restless Earth

About the chapter

These are the key ideas behind the chapter.

- The Earth's interior has a layered structure. The layers have a different composition and physical properties.
- The Earth's core generates heat, which creates convection currents which drive the process of plate tectonics.
- There are three main types of plate boundaries: constructive, destructive and conservative.
- Conservative, destructive and constructive plate boundaries have characteristic volcanic and earthquake hazards associated with them.
- Volcanic hazards can affect people in different ways in developed and developing countries.
- Earthquakes and volcanic eruptions have both primary and secondary, economic and social impacts.
- Volcanic hazards can be predicted but earthquakes cannot.
- Management of tectonic hazards ranges from immediate responses and relief, to long-term planning, prediction and preparation.

Chapter outline

Use this outline to provide your students with a brief roadmap of the chapter.

1.1 Inside the Earth
Learning about the interior of the Earth.

1.2 Earth's heat engine
How the Earth's core drives the process of plate tectonics.

1.3 Plate tectonics
About plate boundaries and how the Earth's tectonic plates have moved in the past.

1.4 Boundary hazards
Which tectonic hazards happen at different plate boundaries.

1.5 Volcanoes in the developed world
The impact of volcanoes on developed countries.

1.6 Developing world volcanic hazards
How volcanoes can have devastating consequences for people in the developing world.

1.7 Earthquake!
How earthquakes are measured, and their power.

1.8 Earthquakes in the developing world
The impacts of earthquakes on developing countries, and how people respond to them.

Restless Earth

How is the specification covered?

This chapter covers Topic 1, Unit 1 Dynamic Planet.

1.1 How and why do Earth's tectonic plates move?

1.2 What are the effects and management issues resulting from tectonic hazards?

Key ideas	Detailed content	Pages in students' book
1.1a The Earth's interior has a layered structure, with different composition and physical properties; the Earth's core generates heat and convection currents drive plate motion.	Interpret a cross-section of the Earth, with details (temperature, density, composition, physical state) of layered structure (including the asthenosphere); using rock samples to contrast continental and oceanic crust.	8-9
	Examine the core's internal heat source (through radioactive decay) and how this generates convection, which drives plate motion and generates the Earth's magnetic field.	10-11
1.1b There are conservative, constructive and destructive plate boundaries, each with characteristic volcanic and earthquake hazards.	Explain the distribution of the three plate boundary types, and identify major plates.	12-13
	Examine the causes of contrasting volcanic (volcano type, magma type and explosivity) and earthquake (shallow versus deep, magnitude) hazards, including tsunami, at contrasting example locations, e.g. Iceland and Indonesia.	14-15, 16-17, 20-21
1.2a Volcanic and earthquake hazards affect people in different ways and at contrasting locations.	Investigate the primary and secondary impacts of earthquakes in two named locations, e.g. the 2005 Kashmir, versus 1989 Loma Prieta, earthquakes. To include reasons for contrasting Impacts on property and people.	20-21, 22-23
	Examine the primary and secondary economic and social impacts of one volcanic event.	16-17, 18-19
1.2b Management of volcanic and earthquake hazards, at contrasting locations, ranging from short term relief to long-term planning, preparation and prediction.	Examine the role of prediction, warning and evacuation in relation to volcanic and earthquake hazards. Contrasting hazard-resistant design in the developed and developing world.	16-17, 18-19, 20-21, 22-23
	Evaluate the role of immediate response and relief efforts linked to a named tectonic hazard event, for example the Izmit earthquake in 1999.	18-19, 22-23

Chapter outcomes

By the end of this chapter, students should be able to:

- Draw a cross-section of the Earth, and annotate it to show the layers, their composition, density, temperature, and physical state.
- Explain why and how tectonic plates move.
- Identify tectonic plates which are moving apart, colliding, sliding past each other — and name the plate boundaries at which this happens.
- Describe the volcanic and earthquake hazards associated with conservative, constructive and destructive plate boundaries.
- Compare and contrast the primary and secondary impacts of earthquakes in developed and developing countries.
- Describe the primary and secondary, economic and social, impacts of a volcanic eruption.
- Explain, using examples, how volcanic eruptions can be predicted, and what precautions can be taken in relation to volcanic and earthquake hazards.
- Evaluate the role of immediate responses and relief efforts linked to a named tectonic hazard event.

1.1 Inside the Earth

Section in brief

This section looks at the structure of the Earth and how it is divided into different layers. It looks at the characteristics of the different layers, and the evidence we can use to tell us about them.

In the activities, students:

- draw a cross-section of the Earth and label the layers with their characteristics;
- describe the differences between the lithosphere and asthenosphere;
- answer an exam-style question to describe the differences between oceanic and continental crust.

Key ideas

- The Earth is composed of layers with distinguishing characteristics.
- The Earth's crust is made up of continental and oceanic crust.
- The asthenosphere is the top layer of the mantle which acts as a lubricating layer below the lithosphere.
- We can use direct and indirect evidence to help us understand the Earth.

Key vocabulary

lithosphere, tectonic plates, asthenosphere, continental crust, oceanic crust, mantle, core, meteorites

Skills practised

Geographical skills: drawing and labelling a diagram of the structure of the Earth; describing differences between the lithosphere and asthenosphere, and oceanic and continental crust

Section outcomes

By the end of this section, most students should be able to:

- define or explain the terms in 'Key vocabulary' above;
- describe the characteristics of the Earth's layers;
- describe some of the evidence we can use to help us understand the Earth's structure;
- understand the difference between direct and indirect evidence.

Ideas for a starter

1. Ask students to draw and label a cross-section of some circular objects, e.g. an apple, an orange, or a peach to show the different layers within them.

2. Tell students that in February 2013 a meteorite hit Russia injuring 1200 people. It created a 6m wide crater where it hit the ground. It contained about 10% iron. Ask students how meteorites might help us to understand the Earth's structure.

Ideas for plenaries

1. Have a quick-fire test. Use the Key vocabulary terms and call out a student's name and a definition for one of the key terms. Allow the student 5 seconds to give you the correct term.

2. Ask students to identify three key points from today's lesson.

Further class and homework activity

Ask students to find out how convection currents in the mantle can move tectonic plates on the Earth's surface.

Restless Earth

answers

1 Students should draw a cross-section of the Earth divided into layers. Each layer should be labelled using the data from the table on page 9 of the students' book.

2 The main differences are temperature, density and composition:
- The lithosphere is the uppermost part of the Earth, comprising the crust and very top of the mantle. It is cool and brittle with a maximum temperature of 900 °C. It is solid.
- The crust is made up of two types – continental and oceanic composed of granite and basalt.
- The asthenosphere is the top part of the mantle. It is below the lithosphere and is partly molten. It has temperatures of 900–1600 °C and has a higher density than the lithosphere.

---

3 Exam-style question *Describe the differences between the oceanic and continental crust. (4 marks)*

This question is point marked and looks for 4 comparative points. Cap students at 2 marks who make four non-comparative statements e.g. 'oceanic crust is heavy' – though note that students who make simple comparative statements e.g. 'oceanic crust is heavier' should be fully credited.

Correct comparisons include:
- Oceanic crust is thinner (1), denser / heavier (1), basaltic (1), lower in silica content (1), makes up most ocean or sea areas of the world (1).
- Continental crust is thicker (1), rich in silica content (1), lighter / less dense (1), granitic (1), makes up most land areas of the world (1).

1.2 Earth's heat engine

Section in brief

This section looks at the Earth's heat source. It examines how internal heat is generated, and the link between the resulting convection currents and the movement of tectonic plates. It explains how the Earth's magnetic field is linked to flows in the outer core.

In the activities, students:

- explain why the centre of the Earth is so hot;
- describe the effect of the convection cells set up in the mantle;
- find out why Mars is a 'dead' planet, with no plate tectonics;
- explain their choice of odd-one-out from sets of words;
- answer an exam-style question to describe the different layers of the Earth's interior.

Key ideas

- We have evidence to prove that the inside of the Earth is very hot.
- Geothermal heat generated inside the Earth is produced by the radioactive decay of elements in the core and mantle.
- Convection cells in the mantle are strong enough to move tectonic plates on the Earth's crust.
- Plumes are concentrated zones of heat bringing magma to the Earth's surface.
- The Earth is surrounded by a magnetic field caused by movements in the outer core.

Key vocabulary

geothermal, radioactive decay, convection currents, plumes, magma, lava, constructive plate boundaries, hot spots, magnetosphere

Skills practised

Geographical skills: interpreting diagrams; explaining the movement of tectonic plates

PLTS: independent enquiry

Section outcomes

By the end of this section, most students should be able to:

- define or explain the terms in 'Key vocabulary' above;
- explain why the centre of the Earth is so hot;
- describe and explain the formation of convection currents in the mantle;
- describe what can happen when plumes rise to the Earth's surface;
- describe how the Earth's magnetic field is generated.

Ideas for a starter

1. Using a stopwatch, give students one minute to recall and write down five facts about the structure of the Earth from section 1.1.
2. Show students a diagram of a pan of water on a stove. Ask: 'What is going to happen to the water as it boils?' This will encourage students to start thinking about convection currents.

Ideas for plenaries

1. Use question 4 from page 11 of the students' book as a plenary activity.
2. Ask students to complete a pyramid review of this lesson. They should write down the following in the shape of a pyramid:
   a. one question they have
   b. two points they are not sure about
   c. three points they have learned.

Further class and homework activity

Give students a diagram which shows convection currents in the Earth, similar to the one on page 10 in the students' book, but minus the labels. Ask students to label the diagram, and to explain how convection currents can cause tectonic plates to move on the Earth's surface.

Restless Earth

answers

1. The heat at the centre of the Earth is produced by the radioactive decay of elements such as uranium and thorium in the core and the mantle. Atoms of these elements release particles from their nuclei and give off heat.

2. The crust begins to move.

3. Mars is known as the dead planet because it is no longer active volcanically, although there is evidence of past volcanic activity. The interior is believed to be rigid and cold, so there is no heat to create convection currents and cause plate movement.

4. *Crust* is the odd one because the others refer to the interior of the Earth.

   Northern lights is the odd one because they occur in the atmosphere, not inside the Earth.

   Uranium is the odd one out. The others are all related to volcanic activity.

---

5. **Exam-style question** *Describe the different layers of earth's interior. (4 marks)*

   This question is point marked and looks for two developed points. Look for two named layers, plus two descriptive points. Cap students who simply list the different layers without any description at 2 marks. Students who give one well-developed descriptive point i.e. with two characteristics, can be credited with a maximum of 3 marks.

   Correct layers and descriptions include, from the centre outwards:

   - The core (1), the densest part of the earth (1), plus (1) if identifies two different layers within it (inner and outer), probably consists of heaviest metals (1).
   - The mantle (1), plus (1) if identifies two different layers within it (inner and outer), probably liquid (1), where many convection currents thought to occur (1).
   - The crust (1), plus (1) if identifies continental and oceanic types within it, solid (1), cool (1).
   - Plus other correct points on merit.

1.3 Plate tectonics

Section in brief

This section looks at plate boundaries and how the Earth's tectonic plates have moved in the past. It introduces students to the three main types of plate boundaries, and locates them on a world map. It explains how new oceanic crust forms at constructive plate boundaries and how old oceanic crust is destroyed at destructive plate boundaries.

In the activities, students:

- describe how India has moved since the time of Pangea;
- answer questions based on a map of tectonic plates;
- answer an exam-style question to explain why tectonic plates move.

Key ideas

- The continents were once all joined together in a supercontinent called Pangea.
- Plate tectonics has moved the continents to their present position.
- There are three main types of plate boundaries — constructive, destructive and conservative.
- New oceanic crust forms constantly at constructive plate boundaries.
- Old oceanic crust is destroyed at destructive plate boundaries.

Key vocabulary

Pangea, tectonic plates, constructive plate boundary, destructive plate boundary, conservative plate boundary, subduction

Skills practised

Geographical skills: comparing maps; interpreting a map of plate boundaries; explaining why tectonic plates move

Section outcomes

By the end of this section, most students should be able to:

- define or explain the terms given in 'Key vocabulary' above;
- describe what happens at constructive, destructive and conservative plate boundaries;
- locate at least one example of each type of plate boundary on a world map and name the associated plates;
- explain why continental crust is so much older than oceanic crust;
- explain why tectonic plates move.

Ideas for a starter

1. Recap the key vocabulary from the last lesson. Give students the initial letter(s) only and ask them to complete the term.
2. Tell students that every year the distance between the UK and the USA grows by about 2cm. Can anyone explain why this is?

Ideas for plenaries

1. Use question 2 from page 13 of the students' book as a plenary activity.
2. Create a 'living world' in the classroom if there is enough space. Divide students into two groups, or pairs. Give each group or pair the names of several plates. When you call the names of two plates, students should move together and collide, or must move apart, depending on the type of boundary those two plates form.

Further class and homework activity

Ask students to find out about one recent volcanic eruption and one recent earthquake in preparation for the next lesson. They should find out when it happened, where it happened and the impacts it had.

Restless Earth

answers

1. India has moved north eastwards, to its current position.
2. a. The UK is on the Eurasian Plate.
   b. Iceland is split by two plates.
   c. The Eurasian and North American Plates are moving apart, as are the African and South American Plates, and the Nazca and the Pacific Plates.
   d. Two plates that are colliding are the Nazca and the South American, and the Indo-Australian and the Eurasian.

3. **Exam-style question** *Explain why earth's tectonic plates move. (6 marks)*

   This question is marked using levels. The key to this question is the command word 'explain' – which is a Higher Tier command word. Remember, therefore, that purely descriptive points by Higher Tier candidates get no marks. If you wish to differentiate, you can give Foundation Tier students the question:

   'Describe three different ways in which the earth's tectonic plates move'.

   In this case, replace the term 'explanations' in the level descriptions below with 'descriptions'.

   In each case, students can get to 6 marks with either three developed or two well-developed points.

   Correct reasons include:
   - Temperature differences between the crust and the interior — plus development e.g. 'which mean that heat currents move from the centre outwards'; extended to well-developed e.g. 'causing convection currents', 'causing movement of plates above them'.
   - Differences in movement between different convection currents — plus development e.g. 'for example, converging currents'; extended to well-developed 'which causes plates to collide / causes destructive margins'.
   - Similarly, credit developed points to describe diverging currents (leading to constructive margins) and parallel currents (leading to conservative margins).

Level	Descriptor
0	No rewardable content
1 (1-2 marks)	Simple or very basic explanations using little or no subject vocabulary. May consist of simple unconnected statements e.g. 'it is hotter below the crust so the plates move'. (1 mark).
2 (3-4 marks)	Generalised explanations but with some use of geographical terms e.g. 'differences in heat cause convection currents'. Up to 2 developed statements as shown by examples above.
3 (5-6 marks)	Detailed statements with clear explanations using geographical terms. e.g. 'differences in heat between the crust and core lead to convection currents, which cause movement of tectonic plates on the crust'. Three developed or two well-developed points as shown by examples above.

1.4 Boundary hazards

Section in brief

This section looks at the relationships between different types of tectonic hazards (earthquakes and volcanic eruptions) and different plate boundaries.

In the activities, students:

- decide which type of plate boundary is most dangerous for humans;
- match words relating to plate boundaries and tectonic hazards into pairs;
- use the San Andreas fault to explain why plates can 'lock' at conservative plate boundaries;
- answer an exam-style question to compare the physical features and tectonic hazards of constructive and destructive plate boundaries.

Key ideas

Different plate boundaries produce different tectonic hazards (earthquakes and volcanic eruptions). Tectonic hazards are natural events that affect people and property.

- Destructive earthquakes occur at conservative plate boundaries.
- Collision zones are a type of destructive boundary – earthquakes happen on faults.
- Constructive boundaries are characterised by both volcanoes and earthquakes.
- Destructive boundaries are characterised by explosive volcanic eruptions and devastating earthquakes.

Key vocabulary

tectonic hazards, collision zones, basalt, andesite, lava flows, friction, subduction

Skills practised

Geographical skills: matching words; interpreting diagrams; comparing physical features and tectonic hazards of different types of plate boundaries

Literacy skills: explanatory writing

Section outcomes

By the end of this section, most students should be able to:

- define or explain the terms given in 'Key vocabulary' above;
- explain why volcanoes and earthquakes happen at plate boundaries;
- explain the tectonic hazards associated with different types of plate boundary.

Ideas for a starter

1 If students completed the Further Activity from section 1.3, ask several to report back to the class. Locate the eruptions and earthquakes on a world map of plate boundaries and ask what they can deduce from the map.

2 Show students the diagram of convection currents within the Earth from page 10 of the students' book. Ask them to explain what is happening and what might result from the plates' movement.

Ideas for plenaries

1 Show a photo of the San Andreas fault from the air on the whiteboard. (A quick search of Google images will bring up plenty of photos.) Ask students what is happening there and why?

2 Make up five statements about plate boundaries – some true, some false. Ask students to identify which are false and to correct them.

Further class and homework activity

Ask students to describe and explain the formation of either volcanoes or earthquakes, using the information about plate boundaries in this section.

Restless Earth

answers

1. Destructive plate boundaries.

2. Conservative/fault; constructive/fissures; destructive/explosive; collision/landslides.

   - At conservative plate boundaries the plates slide past each other, along faults e.g. San Andreas Fault.
   - At a constructive plate boundary the plates move apart, creating fissures (cracks) in the Earth's crust.
   - Destructive plate boundaries result in devastating earthquakes and explosive volcanic eruptions. As an oceanic plate is subducted below the continental plate, seawater is dragged down creating the explosive eruption.
   - At collision zones, two continental plates collide creating mountain ranges.
   Destructive earthquakes can trigger landslides.

3. Plates lock, due to friction, as they are both moving in the same direction at different speeds.

4. **Exam-style question** *Compare the physical features and tectonic hazards of constructive and destructive plate boundaries. (6 marks)*

   This question is marked using levels. Foundation Tier students may answer the alternative question:

   Describe two ways in which movement of tectonic plates can cause hazards. (6 marks)

   In this case, replace the term 'comparisons' in the level descriptions below with 'descriptions'.

   Cap answers at the top of Level 2 (4 marks) if they do not include:
   - *both* physical features and tectonic hazards
   - *comparisons* of the two types of plate boundaries (Higher Tier question)

   Correct comparisons for **physical features** include:
   - Volcanoes formed on both margins.
   - Shallow-sided volcanoes on constructive margins, compared to steep-sided on destructive margins.
   - Ocean trenches on destructive margins, less deep on constructive margins.
   - Terrestrial mountain ranges / volcanic chains created along destructive margins, whereas often deep sea volcanic ranges along constructive margins.

   Correct points for **tectonic hazards** include:
   - Volcanoes and earthquakes created along both margins.
   - Volcanic eruptions far greater and more severe along destructive margins, while lava flows often associated with constructive margins.
   - Earthquakes are far greater along destructive margins.

Level	Descriptor
0	No rewardable content
1 (1–2 marks)	Simple or very basic description with little or no comparison, using little or no subject vocabulary. May be a list of simple statements e.g. 'there are volcanoes and earthquakes along destructive margins'. (1 mark).
2 (3–4 marks)	Generalised comparisons but with some use of geographical terms e.g. 'volcanoes are steeper and more explosive on destructive margins'. Up to 2 developed statements as shown by examples above.
3 (5–6 marks)	Detailed comparisons using geographical terms e.g. 'destructive margins have far more pyroclastic volcanic eruptions than constructive because of the subduction of rocks and water, leading to explosions'. Three developed or two well-developed points as shown by examples above.

1.5 Volcanoes in the developed world

Section in brief

This section looks at the impact of volcanoes in the developed world. It investigates the primary and secondary effects of volcanic eruptions and uses the volcano Sakurajima in Japan as a case study. It also looks at prediction and protection against eruptions in the developed world.

In the activities, students:

- complete a table to show the effects of Sakurajima's eruptions;
- complete a table to list methods used to protect people from Sakurajima, and methods of prediction;
- answer an exam-style question to explain how volcanic eruptions can be predicted.

Key ideas

- The Volcanic Explosivity Index measures the destructive power of volcanoes.
- Volcanoes create a range of hazards for people.
- Volcanic eruptions have primary and secondary effects.
- Volcanic eruptions can be predicted.
- In developed countries tectonic hazards have greater economic, rather than social costs.

Key vocabulary

Volcanic Explosivity Index (VEI), primary effects, secondary effects, stratovolcano, prediction, evacuate

Skills practised

Geographical skills: identify primary and secondary effects of volcanic eruptions; explaining how volcanic eruptions can be predicted; interpreting diagrams

PLTS: independent enquiry

Section outcomes

By the end of this section, most students should be able to:

- define or explain the terms given in 'Key vocabulary' above;
- classify the effects of eruptions as primary and secondary;
- list the methods used to protect people from volcanic eruptions, and to predict eruptions in Japan.

Ideas for a starter

1. Show a photo of the after-effects of a volcanic eruption. Ask students to write down as many words or phrases as they can related to the eruption.
2. Search the internet for a video clip of a volcanic eruption and show it on the interactive whiteboard (the more dramatic the better). Ask students what impacts the eruption could have. Record their ideas as a spider diagram.

Ideas for plenaries

1. Ask students to name three ways in which volcanoes such as Sakurajima are monitored.
2. Ask students to create an acrostic using the word SAKURAJIMA. Make each letter the first letter of a word or phrase to do with volcanoes or earthquakes.

Further class and homework activity

Ask students to research Mount Nyiragongo. They should find out where it is, what type of volcano it is, and when it last erupted.

Restless Earth

answers

1

	Benefits	Problems
Primary effects	Ash and lava create fertile soil.	The volcano emits volcanic bombs, pyroclastic flows and ash every year. It emits poisonous gases which are dangerous for people.
Secondary effects	Hot springs and lava flows attract tourists.	Poisonous gas causes acid rain which kills plants.

2

Protection	Prediction
Concrete shelters protect against the volcanic bombs and ash	Aircraft measure the amount of gas given off by the volcano
Concrete lahar channels divert dangerous mudflows	Tiltmeters detect when the volcano swells
Evacuation routes are clearly signposted	Boreholes measure increases in groundwater temperatures
People have regular evacuation drills	Hot springs are monitored
	Seismometers in the volcano measure any increase in earthquake activity

3 **Exam-style question** *Using examples, explain how volcanic eruptions can be predicted. (4 marks)*

This question is point marked. The key to this question is the command word 'explain'. If you wish to differentiate, you can give Foundation Tier students the question:

Describe two ways in which volcanic eruptions can be predicted.

Rather than four listed points, this answer looks for two developed points, i.e. two points which are expanded in some way. Correct points – all of which are worth additional marks if developed – include:

- Aircraft measure the amount of gas the volcano gives off (1) – plus 1 for development e.g. 'which means any change could mean an eruption will happen' (1)
- Tiltmeters are used to detect when the volcano swells up (1) as it fills with magma (1)
- Use of seismometers (1) – plus 1 for development e.g. to monitor earthquakes which increase as magma rises (1) – plus 1 for further development e.g. 'so scientists can predict an eruption' (1)
- Boreholes measure water temperature (1) – plus 1 for development e.g. because magma heats up groundwater. (1)
- Evacuation plans drawn up (1) so that people know where to go and what to do if a volcano erupts (1).

1.6 Developing world volcanic hazards

Section in brief

This section looks at the effects of volcanic eruptions on people in the developing world. It uses the eruption of Mount Nyiragongo (in 2002) in the Democratic Republic of Congo as a case study.

In the activities, students:

- explain what is meant by 'aid' and 'relief effort';
- complete a table to show the effects of Mount Nyiragongo's eruption;
- assess the success of the relief effort;
- think about why people still live in the area;
- answer an exam-style question to explain the economic and social impacts of a volcanic eruption.

Key ideas

- In developing countries people are at a greater risk from tectonic hazards than those in developed countries.
- Mount Nyiragongo sits on top of a constructive plate boundary.
- The eruption of Mount Nyiragongo had social and economic impacts.
- A volcanic explosion in a developing country requires a huge relief effort from around the world.
- Mount Nyiragongo poses a continual threat, yet many people continue to live in the area.

Key vocabulary

social impacts, economic impacts, refugees, relief effort, aid

Skills practised

Geographical skills: identifying primary and secondary effects; assessing the success of the relief effort; empathising with people

PLTS: independent enquiry; creative thinking

Literacy skills: writing a newspaper article

Section outcomes

By the end of this section, most students should be able to:

- define or explain the terms given in 'Key vocabulary' above;
- classify the effects of an eruption as primary and secondary;
- compare the eruptions of Mount Nyiragongo and Sakurajima;
- explain why developing countries need major relief efforts following a tectonic event;
- explain why people still want to live in high risk areas such as around Mount Nyiragongo.

Ideas for a starter

1. Recap the impacts of a volcanic eruption in a developed country from section 1.5. Which are greater – economic or social impacts?
2. Show a video clip (it could be a news report) of a volcanic eruption, without the sound. Ask students to write a commentary for the video clip.

Ideas for plenaries

1. Remind students about the short-term aid given after the eruption of Mount Nyiragongo. What long-term aid would people affected by the eruption need?
2. Give students three answers concerning the eruption of Mount Nyiragongo. Ask them: 'What are the questions?'

Further class and homework activity

Ask students to write a newspaper article to describe the impact of the volcanic eruption on Goma. They should include what happened, why it happened, and how the outside world helped. They could also include interviews with local people and aid agency workers.

Restless Earth

answers

1 *Aid* — money or help given to a country in need.

Relief effort — organised help given by countries and international aid agencies, e.g. Oxfam.

2 a Primary effects: *Benefits* — lava creates fertile soil. *Problems* — river of lava destroyed villages; people died from poisonous gas and getting trapped in lava; eruption triggered earthquakes and buildings collapsed; many people became refugees; poisonous gases caused acid rain affecting farmland and cattle.

Secondary effects: *Problems* — 120 000 people became homeless and could not afford to rebuild their homes; little clean water and food; diseases e.g. cholera could spread quickly.

b Mount Nyiragongo has far greater social impacts — people left without food, water and shelter; disease spread rapidly; homes were destroyed.

3 The relief effort was partly successful. 400 000 people had been evacuated, but many were left with very little. Short-term relief e.g. food rations and vaccinations were given quickly. However, it was several months before some roads were cleared, the water supply returned, and people could start building new homes.

4 The area around the volcano has fertile soil — good for growing crops; there is a long history of settlement in the area; people are too poor to move to another area.

---

5 Exam-style question *Using a named example, explain the economic and social impacts of a volcanic eruption. (6 marks)*

Foundation Tier students may answer the alternative question:

Using examples, describe the impacts of a volcanic eruption on people. (6 marks)

In this case, replace the term 'explanations' in the level descriptions below with 'descriptions'.

Cap answers at the top of Level 2 (4 marks) which do not include:

- named examples e.g. Mount Nyiragongo;
- explanation of *both* economic and social impacts (Higher Tier only).

Correct explanations for **economic impacts:**

- Cost of re-building caused by river of lava — developed with example e.g. 14 villages destroyed — well-developed if further details are given e.g. 1000 metres wide / destruction of the city of Goma.
- Cost of re-homing people — e.g. Mount Nyiragongo left 120 000 homeless in Goma.
- Further costs caused by earthquakes triggered by eruption — developed if consequence is identified e.g. buildings collapsed.

Correct explanations for **social impacts:**

- Deaths caused by poisonous gas — developed with examples e.g. 100 people died in the eruption of Mount Nyiragongo.
- Eruption of lava and associated earthquakes caused destruction of homes — developed with data e.g. 12 500 homes destroyed by Mount Nyiragongo.
- Risk of disease brought by collapse of health services — developed with example e.g. vaccination against measles.

Level	Descriptor
0	No rewardable content
1 (1-2 marks)	Simple or very basic unsubstantiated statements using little or no subject vocabulary.
2 (3-4 marks)	Generalised statements but with some (not always fully explained) development and use of geographical terms Up to two developed statements as shown by examples above.
3 (5-6 marks)	Detailed developed statements with clear located explanations using geographical terms. Three developed or two well-developed points as shown by examples above.

1.7 Earthquake!

Section in brief

This section looks at earthquakes – what they are, how they are measured, and how destructive they can be. Two earthquakes are compared, Kobe 1995 and Haiti 2010. This section also explains how long-term planning can help survival, and how tsunami form.

In the activities, students:

- explain why distance from the epicentre reduces earthquake damage;
- look at the link between earthquake magnitude and death toll;
- list the stages in the formation of a tsunami;
- classify earthquake impacts as social and economic;
- answer an exam-style question to compare the social and economic impacts of two earthquakes.

Key ideas

- Earthquakes happen when tectonic plates push past each other and pressure is released.
- The magnitude of an earthquake is measured using the Richter scale.
- Earthquakes of the same magnitude may have very different effects.
- Long-term planning can reduce the impact of earthquakes.
- Earthquakes below the sea bed can generate devastating tsunami.

Key vocabulary

energy, faults, focus, epicentre, magnitude, seismometer, Richter scale, Moment magnitude scale, prediction, tsunami

Skills practised

Geographical skills: interpreting diagrams; identifying stages in formation of tsunami; classifying and comparing earthquake impacts

PLTS: independent enquiry; creative thinking

Numeracy skills: using logarithmic scale (Richter Scale)

Section outcomes

By the end of this section, most students should be able to:

- define or explain the terms in 'Key vocabulary' above;
- explain how earthquakes happen;
- classify earthquake impacts as social and economic;
- compare the social and economic impacts of earthquakes in contrasting locations;
- describe the main methods of earthquake management;
- list the stages in the formation of a tsunami.

Ideas for a starter

1. Ask students to locate Japan and Haiti on a blank map of the world. What can they tell you about the two countries?
2. Show students a photo of the impacts of the earthquake in Haiti in 2010. How many words can they come up with to describe the impacts in two minutes?

Ideas for plenaries

1. Give students a partially completed mind map of the effects of the two earthquakes. Ask them to finish it.
2. Working in pairs, one student should choose a key term. Their partner then has to ask questions to identify the term.

Further class and homework activity

Ask students to find out what Haiti is like now. (The chances are it will take Haiti many years to recover from the devastating earthquake.) What conditions are people living in? What is life like in Port-au-Prince? Has Haiti's infrastructure been rebuilt?

Restless Earth

answers

1 The epicentre is directly above the focus – the point where the energy is most concentrated. With increasing distance from the epicentre, the energy is dissipated through the Earth's crust.

2 c Students should find that there is not a clear link between magnitude and fatalities, as some earthquakes of the greatest magnitude are found in sparsely populated areas or offshore.

3
1. Earthquake causes the seabed to jolt upwards.
2. Water is forced upwards.
3. Tsunami waves spread out in all directions.
4. Tsunami waves slow down and wavelength drops as they reach the coast, but wave height increases dramatically.

4 a Social impacts – 5000 people died; 26 000 injured; bridges, roads, train lines damaged; fires broke out; homelessness; disrupted schooling; increased stress.

Economic impacts – bridges, roads and train lines damaged disrupting transport and communication links; £100 billion of damage caused to roads, houses, factories and infrastructure; businesses affected for many weeks due to rebuilding disruption; unemployment.

b Either – many people were affected either directly or indirectly, but the economic costs were enormous.

---

5 Exam-style question *Using named examples, compare the social and economic impacts of two earthquakes. (6 marks)*

Foundation Tier students may answer the alternative question:

Using a named example, describe the social and economic impacts of an earthquake.

In this case, replace the term 'comparisons' in the level descriptions below with 'descriptions'.

Cap answers at the top of Level 2 (4 marks) which do not include:

- a comparison of two named earthquakes;
- a comparison of *both* social and economic impacts.

Examples drawn from Kobe, Haiti and Sichuan suit this question very well.

Economic impacts comparisons include:

- Infrastructure damage e.g. energy / gas pipes in Kobe compared to water supply in Haiti – developed if social impacts outlined e.g. a cholera outbreak;
- Cost of economic rebuilding – developed if costs given for Kobe – further developed if compared to destruction of the port in Haiti.

Social impact comparisons include:

- Deaths and injuries comparing Kobe (5000 died, 26 000 injured) with Haiti (316 000 died, 300 000 injured).
- Causes of death – building collapse in Haiti – developed if explanation includes poverty and poor-quality slum housing, compared to fires in Kobe – developed if explanation includes gas pipes and failure of infrastructure.
- Further comparison could include earthquake-proofing of buildings in Kobe and link to GDP compared to Haiti.

Level	Descriptor
0	No rewardable content
1 (1-2 marks)	Simple or very basic statements using little or no subject vocabulary.
2 (3-4 marks)	Generalised comparisons but with some (not always fully explained) development and use of geographical terms. Up to 2 developed comparisons as shown by examples above.
3 (5-6 marks)	Detailed developed statements with clear explanations using geographical terms. Three developed or two well-developed comparisons as shown by examples above.

1.8 Earthquakes in the developing world

Section in brief

This section looks at the impacts of the earthquake which hit Sichuan, China, in 2008. It investigates the local and international responses to the earthquake, and also how buildings can be made to withstand earthquakes in developing countries.

In the activities, students:

- explain why the Sichuan earthquake happened;
- identify and classify the social and economic effects of the earthquake;
- compare the impacts and explain the differences between the eruptions and earthquakes studied in this chapter;
- answer an exam-style question to explain why earthquakes happen on destructive plate margins.

Key ideas

- The Sichuan earthquake happened at the collision zone between the Indian Plate and the Eurasian Plate.
- The Sichuan earthquake had devastating social and economic impacts.
- Local responses in China included a huge rescue effort, and international responses included money, materials, and rescue teams.
- Buildings can be made to withstand earthquakes in developing countries.
- Aftershocks can kill and injure people and destroy buildings.

Key vocabulary

aftershocks

Skills practised

Geographical skills: classifying earthquake effects as social and economic; comparing impacts of tectonic events and explaining differences; drawing a diagram of a destructive plate margin

PLTS: independent enquiry

Section outcomes

By the end of this section, most students should be able to:

- explain the term given in 'Key vocabulary' above;
- explain why the Sichuan earthquake happened;
- classify the effects of the Sichuan earthquake;
- describe the local and international responses to the earthquake;
- compare the impacts of earthquakes and volcanic eruptions in contrasting locations.

Ideas for a starter

1. Ask: 'Who can remind me what type of tectonic hazard occurs at collision zones? Who can draw a diagram of a collision zone?'
2. Challenge students to see who can be the first to find Chengdu on an atlas map of China. Ask students to describe its location.

Ideas for plenaries

1. Ask students to identify two key things they have learned today. Then ask for another two things that are interesting but less important.
2. Search the Internet for eyewitness accounts from the Sichuan earthquake. Read one or two out to the class. Ask students how the accounts make them feel.

Further class and homework activity

Ask students to complete the exam-style question for homework.

Restless Earth

answers

1 The Sichuan earthquake was caused by the northward movement of the Indian Plate against the Eurasian Plate. This is a collision zone (a type of destructive plate boundary), where two continental plates push into each other. The massive pressures result in strong earthquakes in the region.

2 a Effects of the Sichuan earthquake include: 70 000 deaths; 375 000 injured; 5 million homeless; 1 million lost jobs; $75 billion of rebuilding costs; landslides; flooding; 420 000 buildings collapsed due to aftershocks; over 700 schools destroyed.

b Social effects: 70 000 deaths; 375 000 injured; 5 million homeless, over 700 schools destroyed; 420 000 buildings collapsed due to aftershocks. **Economic effects**: 1 million lost jobs; $75 billion in rebuilding costs.

3 a Students should compare the impacts of the case studies on people and property by referring back to sections 1.5, 1.6 and 1.7.

b Generally, earthquakes are likely to cause more deaths and damage – because they affect a wider area, and they happen with little warning. However, both volcanoes and earthquakes cause more deaths in developing countries.

In the case of volcanoes: developed countries are better prepared in terms of prediction, and evacuation measures are likely to be in place.

In the case of earthquakes: building design and construction is better in developed countries, so they are less likely to collapse. Damage to property is likely to be more costly in developed countries, because more developed infrastructure is more expensive to repair and replace.

4 Exam-style question *Explain why earthquakes happen on destructive plate margins. You may draw a diagram to help with your answer. (4 marks)*

This question is point marked. Rather than four listed points, this answer looks for at least one developed point or sequence of events. These may either be written or labelled on a reasonably drawn diagram which looks like a destructive margin! Correct labels – all of which are worth additional marks if developed – include:

Destructive margin identified correctly on diagram (1) caused by collision of two plates (1) – plus 1 if correctly identifies continental and oceanic plate – which move suddenly causing earthquakes (1). Different points identified regarding the earthquake (maximum 2) e.g. focus (1), epicentre (1).

2 Changing climate

About the chapter

These are the key ideas behind the chapter.

- Climate has changed in both the recent and distant past.
- The natural causes of climate change include: the eruption theory, asteroid collisions, sunspots and solar output, and the orbital theory.
- Natural climate change in the past affected people and the environment.
- The Earth's atmosphere is being changed as a result of human activity.
- Human activity which results in the production of greenhouse gases has led to an enhanced greenhouse effect - global warming.
- The climate of the UK today is influenced by ocean currents and air masses, and might change in the future.
- The UK might be affected by global warming in different ways, creating costs and benefits.
- Climate change will have economic and environmental impacts on developing countries, such as Egypt.

Chapter outline

Use this outline to provide your students with a brief roadmap of the chapter.

2.1 Past climates
How climate was different in the recent, and distant past.

2.2 The causes of climate change in the past
The natural causes of past climate change.

2.3 Lessons from the past?
Some of the impacts of past natural climate change.

2.4 Climate and the environment
Not only humans, but plants and animals are vulnerable to climate change.

2.5 Changing the atmosphere
How our atmosphere is being changed by human activity.

2.6 The enhanced greenhouse effect
How pollution of the atmosphere with greenhouse gases has led to the enhanced greenhouse effect, also known as global warming.

2.7 The UK climate
The climate of the UK today, and why it might change.

2.8 UK climate futures
How the UK might be affected by global warming.

2.9 Egypt on the edge
Some of the impacts of global warming on the developing world, focussing on Egypt.

Changing climate

How is the specification covered?

This chapter covers Topic 2, Unit 1 Dynamic Planet.

2.1 How and why has climate changed in the past?

2.2 What challenges might our future climate present us with?

Key ideas	Detailed content	Pages in students' book
2.1a Climate has changed in the past through natural causes, on timescales ranging from hundreds to millions of years.	Examine past climate change on different timescales including the 'Ice Ages' in the Quaternary Period and UK climate since Roman times.	24-25
	Explore the natural causes of climate change, including asteroid collisions, orbital changes, volcanic activity and variations in solar output.	26-27
2.1b Natural climate change in the past has affected people and the environment.	Examine the impact of a short-term historical event on people and the environment, e.g. the 'Little Ice Age'.	28-29
	Consider the impact of major climatic changes in geological time, e.g. the mass extinction of megafauna at the end of the Quaternary Period.	30-31
2.2a The climate of the UK appears to be changing as a result of global changes caused by human activity.	Investigate the climate of the UK today, including temperature, rainfall and seasonality, and consider why they might change in the future including reference to ocean currents and air masses.	36-37
	Examine how human activities produce rising levels of carbon dioxide and methane and how these contribute to the enhanced greenhouse effect.	32-33, 34-35
2.2b Future climates are uncertain but likely to present major economic and environmental challenges to the UK and, especially, to people in the developing world.	Consider a range of projections for global temperature change and sea level rise, including reasons for the uncertainty.	38-39, 40-41
	Examine the possible economic and environmental impacts of future climate change for the UK and in one named developing country, e.g. Bangladesh.	38-39, 40-41

Chapter outcomes

By the end of this chapter, students should be able to:

- Use graphs to describe variations in temperature in the past.
- Complete a table to compare the natural causes of past climate change.
- Explain how natural climate change affected the Vikings on Greenland.
- Use examples to describe how animals (e.g. megafauna) were affected by climate change in the past.
- Understand how the greenhouse effect works and that it is a natural process.
- Describe how carbon dioxide levels have risen since the 1950s, and explain how human activity has led to the enhanced greenhouse effect.
- Explain how the UK's climate is influenced by latitude, the North Atlantic Drift, and air masses.
- Use examples to describe how global warming in the UK could have both costs and benefits.
- Identify the economic and environmental impacts of climate change on a developing country, such as Egypt.

2.1 Past climates

Section in brief

This section looks at climates that existed in the past, and evidence to support the idea that climate has changed. It investigates both the distant past, and the more recent past.

In the activities, students:

- describe how the northern hemisphere was affected by the last ice age;
- analyse a graph of temperature and carbon dioxide levels over the last 800 000 years;
- examine the extent of the Arctic ice sheets during the last ice age;
- answer an exam-style question to describe the evidence used to reconstruct past climates.

Key ideas

- There is a difference between weather and climate.
- Scientists use different types of evidence to indicate that climate has changed.
- Ice sheets are a valuable source of information about climate.
- The Quaternary period included warm periods (interglacials) and cold periods (glacials).
- There have been significant changes to climate in the more recent past.

Key vocabulary

climatologist, Quaternary, interglacials, glacials

Skills practised

Geographical skills: map interpretation

PLTS: independent enquiry

Numeracy skills: graph interpretation

Literacy skills: writing longer paragraphs

Section outcomes

By the end of this section, most students should be able to:

- define or explain the terms given in 'Key vocabulary' above;
- compare the climate in the last ice age with today's climate;
- use graphs to examine past climate changes;
- describe the evidence used to reconstruct past climates.

Ideas for a starter

1. Brainstorm: Ask students to define weather and climate. Write down their ideas on the board.'
2. Show students photos and/or videos of recent floods, ice calving and heat waves. Ask them to explain what is happening and the possible causes.

Ideas for plenaries

1. Show students a recent weather forecast. Then ask them to write a weather forecast for the last ice age.
2. Read out definitions for the key vocabulary words – some true, some false. Students should say which are which.

Further class and homework activity

Ask students to research the length of time that the Quaternary ice sheets lingered over Britain.

Changing climate

answers

1 During the last Ice Age ice sheets between 400 and 3000 metres thick extended over parts of North America, Northern Europe and Russia. The sea had large areas of floating sea ice. The Earth's crust sank under the weight of the ice, and sea levels fell as water was locked up in ice sheets.

2 a Over the last 800 000 years, the average temperatures have fluctuated. Comparing temperatures with the average for the last 1000 years, there have been several periods (glacials) when it was much colder. However, in the last 400 000 years there have been five periods when it has been warmer than the average for the last 1000 years (interglacials). At present, temperatures are considerably higher than the average.

b The Earth warms up faster than it cools down.

c Fluctuations in carbon dioxide levels and temperature are closely linked, because they show similar patterns. When carbon dioxide levels fall, there is a fall in temperature. The most recent steep rise in carbon dioxide coincides with a steep rise in temperature.

3 Most of Canada, Alaska and parts of the northern USA were covered by ice in the last Ice Age and are now ice free. The same applies to large areas of Scandinavia, northern Russia and Siberia, together with most of Britain as far south as Norfolk.

---

4 Exam-style question *Describe the evidence that can be used to reconstruct past climates. (4 marks)*

This question is point marked. Rather than 4 listed points, this answer looks for two developed points, i.e. two points which are expanded in some way. Correct points – all of which are worth additional marks if developed – include:

Physical evidence e.g.

- Fossilised animals, plants and pollen (1).
- Landforms left by retreating glaciers (1).
- Samples from ice sheets in e.g. Antarctica (1).

Human evidence e.g.

- Old photographs / drawings / paintings (1).
- Written diaries, books and newspapers (1).
- Dates of harvests, migrating birds and spring / tree blossom (1).

2.2 The causes of climate change in the past

Section in brief

This section looks at the natural causes of climate change in the past. These include the eruption theory, asteroid collisions, sunspots and solar output, and the orbital theory.

In the activities, students:

- explain the effects of big volcanic eruptions on climate;
- compare climate change theories;
- answer an exam-style question to explain how solar output and orbital changes can alter the Earth's climate.

Key ideas

- There are a number of natural causes which can explain why climate has changed in the past.
- A large volcanic eruption can cool the Earth's climate, but the effect is only temporary.
- Large asteroid collisions can have a similar impact to a large volcanic eruption.
- Sunspot activity might explain climate change over a period of several hundred years.
- Climate change over long timescales may be explained by changes in the Earth's orbit.

Key vocabulary

stratosphere, sunspots, Milankovitch Cycles

Skills practised

Geographical skills: explaining changes in climate; interpreting diagrams; comparing theories

Numeracy skills: interpreting a graph

Section outcomes

By the end of this section, most students should be able to:

- define or explain the terms given in 'Key vocabulary' above;
- explain how volcanic eruptions affect climate;
- describe the effect of a large asteroid collision on the Earth's climate;
- compare the natural causes of climate change;
- explain how solar output and orbital changes can alter Earth's climate.

Ideas for a starter

1. Recap section 2.1 about past climates. Ask students what might have caused climate to change in the past.
2. Ask students to write down three questions they would like answered concerning climate change.

Ideas for plenaries

1. Working in pairs, students should ask each other questions about the natural causes of climate change.
2. Ask students to prepare an odd-one-out for their partner on what they have learned today.

Further class and homework activity

Ask students to complete a mind map to summarise the key facts about each theory of past climate change.

Changing climate

answers

1 The emphasis must be on large volcanic eruptions. Both ash and gases given off affect climate. If the explosion is big enough, ash and gases will rise into the stratosphere and be distributed around the world by high level winds. They will reflect the sun's rays back into space, reducing temperatures. Students may use the examples of Mount Pinatubo and Tambora on page 26 of the students' book.

2

	The eruption theory	Asteroid collision theory	The sunspot theory	The orbital theory
Process	Volcanic explosions result in ash and gas entering the stratosphere and prevent the sun's rays from reaching the Earth's surface.	A large asteroid hitting Earth would result in ash and dust entering the atmosphere, preventing sunlight reaching Earth.	An increase in sunspot activity indicates more solar energy being given off by the sun.	If the Earth's orbit changes, the amount of sunlight reaching the Earth, and where the sunlight falls, is affected.
Effect on climate	Cooling of the average temperatures	Climate would cool	Temperatures either increase or decrease.	Some places will become cooler
Example	Mt Pinatubo in 1991	No recent example given	The Little Ice Age relates to a period of low sunspot activity	Possible start or end of the big Ice Ages

3 Exam-style question *Explain how solar output and orbital changes can alter earth's climate.* (6 marks)

This question is marked using levels and asks for two things – solar output and orbital changes, so to get 6 marks, both should be explained. If not, then the answer is capped at the top of Level 2 (4 marks).

Correct points for *solar output* include:

- Sometimes the sun has dark / sunspots — plus development e.g. 'which mean that more solar energy / output is given out towards Earth' — or well-developed e.g. 'so that temperatures increase'.

- Fewer sunspots — plus development e.g. 'which can cause cooling' — or well-developed e.g. 'which could cause an ice age'.

Correct points for *orbital changes* include:

- The Earth's orbit can be oval — plus development e.g. 'which affects angles of sunlight' — or well-developed e.g. 'which therefore means temperatures can change over time'.

- The Earth's axis tilts / wobbles' or 'There are Milankovitch cycles' — plus development e.g. 'which means it changes its angle to the sun' — or well-developed e.g. 'which over thousands of years could start an ice age'.

Level	Descriptor
0	No rewardable content
1 (1-2 marks)	Simple or very basic statements using little or no subject vocabulary.
2 (3-4 marks)	Generalised statements but with some use of geographical terms. Up to 2 developed statements as shown by examples above.
3 (5-6 marks)	Detailed statements with clear explanations using geographical terms. Three developed or two well-developed points as shown by examples above.

2.3 Lessons from the past?

Section in brief

This section looks at how natural climate change has affected people and their lives in the past, and whether we can learn from past events in order to cope with global warming.

In the activities, students:

- assess the effect of climate on Erik the Red's prospects in Greenland;
- explain the changes in Greenland caused by the Little Ice Age;
- examine the lack of adaptability of the Greenland Vikings;
- describe how people in Europe adapted to the Little Ice Age;
- answer an exam-style question to explain how natural climate change in the past affected people and their lifestyles.

Key ideas

- Greenland was able to support a successful agricultural society by 1100 because of the changing climate.
- The Little Ice Age had major impacts across Europe.
- In Europe people adapted to the changing climate.
- In Greenland the Vikings did not adapt and did not survive.

Key vocabulary

There is no key vocabulary in this section.

Skills practised

Geographical skills: explaining events using geographical data

PLTS: creative thinking

Literacy skills: writing a letter; creating a presentation

Section outcomes

By the end of this section, most students should be able to:

- describe the effects of a cooling climate on agriculture and the population;
- evaluate how human actions, as well as natural causes, might impact on the Vikings survival;
- explain how people can adapt to climate change;
- explain how natural climate change affected people and their lifestyles.

Ideas for a starter

1. Ask students to locate Greenland, Iceland and Norway on a map of Europe.
2. Ask students to write down five ways in which climate affects their lives.

Ideas for plenaries

1. Ask students to complete a blank flow chart showing the effects of the Little Ice Age on the Greenland Vikings.
2. Students could match up 'tops and tails' of sentences which summarise the key facts from this section.

Further class and homework activity

Ask students to create a presentation (either a PowerPoint or a poster) to explain the impact of past natural climate change on Europe.

Changing climate

answers

1. When Erik the Red arrived in Greenland, the warmer climate meant that he and his followers were able to establish farms growing fodder for their livestock. They were able to trade by sea with Iceland and Norway, and travel north in summer on hunting expeditions.

2. The letter must include facts about the changes in the climate and how these have had an impact on lifestyle and food production.

3. Students should explain how the Vikings could have changed their way of life, following the example of the Inuit by living in harmony with the climate and environment.

4. Despite some years of famine and many deaths, people did adapt by farming new crops, abandoning farms at higher altitudes, and living with frozen rivers in winter.

5. **Exam-style question** *Using named examples, explain how natural climate change in the past affected people and their lifestyles. (6 marks)*

    This question is marked using levels. The key to this question is the command word 'explain' – a Higher Tier command word. Purely descriptive points by Higher Tier candidates get no marks. Foundation Tier students may answer the same question but with the word 'describe'. In this case, replace the term 'explanations' in the level descriptions below with 'descriptions'.

    This question asks for two things: people and their lifestyles, so to get 6 marks, both should be explained. However, there is likely to be overlap – e.g. 'food supply' affects people and lifestyle – so be flexible in interpreting what students say. If a student explains only one, then the answer is capped at the top of Level 2 (4 marks).

    Correct points for **people** include:

    - Sometimes the sun has dark / sunspots — plus development e.g. 'which mean that more solar energy / output is given out towards Earth' — or well-developed e.g. 'so that temperatures increase'.
    - People ran out of food — with reason e.g. 'because the summers were much colder' — plus development e.g. 'so that crops could not ripen'.
    - There was less sea trade — with reason e.g. 'because the sea was frozen' — plus development e.g. 'which prevented access to land'.
    - Crops changed from wheat to potatoes — with reason e.g. 'because wheat needs warm summers' — plus development e.g. 'potatoes grow better in colder, wet weather'.

    Correct points for **lifestyle** include:

    - People changed their leisure — with reason e.g. 'there were colder winters' — plus development e.g. 'which led to frozen rivers' — or well-developed e.g. 'which led to frost fairs held near icy rivers'.

Level	Descriptor
0	No rewardable content
1 (1-2 marks)	Simple or very basic explanations using little or no subject vocabulary. May be a list e.g. 'it got colder, so there was less to eat'.
2 (3-4 marks)	Generalised explanations but with some use of geographical terms e.g. 'summers were shorter and colder which meant fewer crops'. Up to 2 developed statements as shown by examples above.
3 (5-6 marks)	Detailed statements with clear explanations using geographical terms. e.g. 'summers were shorter and colder which meant crops such as wheat failed, causing famine'. Three developed or two well-developed points as shown by examples above.

2.4 Climate and the environment

Section in brief

This section looks at how climate change can affect the existence of different species. It investigates the extinction of the dinosaurs and the Ice Age megafauna extinction.

In the activities, students:

- explain what an ecosystem is;
- draw a simple food chain;
- analyse a graph of megafauna extinctions;
- answer an exam-style question to describe how the environment and ecosystems were affected by past climate change.

Key ideas

- Plants, animals and the physical environment are interlinked in ecosystems.
- A change to one part of an ecosystem leads to changes elsewhere in the ecosystem.
- Major climatic change in the past has led to mass extinction of some species.
- Human activity has played a part in some extinctions.

Key vocabulary

ecosystems, food chains, extinction, megafauna

Skills practised

Geographical skills: describing the effects of climate change in the past

PLTS: creative thinking

Numeracy skills: analysing graphs; working out percentages

Literacy skills: writing a newspaper article

Section outcomes

By the end of this section, most students should be able to:

- define or explain the terms given in 'Key vocabulary' above;
- explain why the dinosaurs might have become extinct;
- describe and explain the loss of megafauna;
- recognise that human factors, as well as climate change, contribute to changes to ecosystems.

Ideas for a starter

1. Begin a flow chart of the possible effects of climate change in the past. Ask students to complete it.
2. Give students six statements (three true, three false) which recap the causes of past climate change and/or its effects. Students should decide which are true and which are false.

Ideas for plenaries

1. With students' books closed, ask groups or pairs of students to draw a diagram of an ecosystem from memory.
2. Write the key vocabulary words on the board and ask students to explain them.

Further class and homework activity

Ask students to write a newspaper article, as if it is happening now, to report on the extinction of the dinosaurs or the mammoth.

Changing climate

answers

1. An ecosystem is a system where there is interaction between all living things and the physical factors of the environment. Energy is transferred between the different parts of an ecosystem by the food chain.

2. A simple food chain could look like this:

   sun → grass → rabbit → wolf

   Note that bacteria live in the soil and contribute to decomposition, releasing minerals which are absorbed by grass as it grows.

3. a i South America, followed by North America and Australia

   ii Africa, followed by Europe

   b North America = 71%; South America = 81%; Australia = 96%; Europe = 27%; Africa = 5%

4. **Exam-style question** *Using examples, describe how the environment and ecosystems were affected by climate change in the past. (6 marks)*

   This question is marked using levels. The key to this question is the command word 'describe' – a Foundation Tier command word. If you wish to differentiate, you can give Higher Tier students the same question with the word 'explain'. In this case, replace the term 'descriptions' in the level descriptions below with 'explanations'. Remember, therefore, that purely descriptive points by Higher Tier candidates get no marks.

   This question asks for two things – environment and ecosystems, so to get 6 marks, both should be described. However, there is likely to be overlap – for example, forests or reference to species could be considered as either. If a student explains only one, then the answer is capped at the top of Level 2 (4 marks). Students can get to 6 marks with either three developed or two well-developed points.

   Correct points include:

   - Species migrated to new areas where the climate suited them.
   - Difficulty in finding the right plants to eat in new areas — developed with consequences e.g. disrupting food chains, leaving some animals short of food.
   - Climate change weakened megafauna — developed with example.
   - Human migration to new areas — developed with impacts e.g. hunting, resulting in less prey for some species.
   - Some herbivores hunted to extinction — developed with impacts e.g. carnivores have nothing to prey on.
   - If one part of an ecosystem changes, the other parts will also change — developed with an example from an ecosystem or species.
   - Mass extinction — developed with an example of a species which has died out altogether.

Level	Descriptor
0	No rewardable content
1 (1-2 marks)	Simple or very basic description using little or no subject vocabulary. May be a list e.g. 'animals moved because it got colder'. (1 mark).
2 (3-4 marks)	Generalised description but with some use of geographical terms e.g. 'animal migrations took place as the climate got colder in order to search for food'. Up to 2 developed statements as shown by examples above.
3 (5-6 marks)	Detailed statements with clear description using geographical terms e.g. 'animal migrations took place e.g. of woolly mammoth, as the climate got colder, in order to search for food supplies which had disappeared'. Three developed or two well-developed points as shown by examples above. For full marks the answer must include both environments and ecosystems.

2.5 Changing the atmosphere

Section in brief

This section looks at how the atmosphere is being changed as a result of human activity. It investigates the greenhouse effect and greenhouse gas emissions.

In the activities, students:

- list the main greenhouse gases;
- draw a diagram to explain the greenhouse effect;
- list human activities which increase greenhouse gases;
- explain why people in the developing world produce only small amounts of greenhouse gases;
- answer an exam-style question to explain why levels of greenhouse gases in the atmosphere are rising.

Key ideas

- Greenhouse gases in the Earth's atmosphere help to regulate the temperature on Earth.
- The greenhouse effect is a natural process.
- Carbon dioxide is the most common greenhouse gas, and it is increasing as a result of human activity, but methane is more potent and is also increasing rapidly.
- Levels of development and population size affect how much carbon dioxide is produced per person in different countries.
- Scientists are looking at how to reduce emissions of greenhouse gases.

Key vocabulary

atmosphere, the greenhouse effect, greenhouse gas

Skills practised

Geographical skills: drawing a diagram to explain the greenhouse effect

PLTS: creative thinking

Literacy skills: summarising information; writing a news bulletin

Section outcomes

By the end of this section, most students should be able to:

- define or explain the terms given in 'Key vocabulary' above;
- draw a diagram to explain how the greenhouse effect works;
- describe how human activity produces carbon dioxide;
- explain the link between level of development and greenhouse gas emissions.

Ideas for a starter

1. Ask: What is a greenhouse and how does it work?' 'What is the greenhouse effect?
2. Ask students to write down the gases found in the atmosphere. Do they know which are greenhouse gases?

Ideas for plenaries

1. Give students the initial letters of key terms. Ask them to state the key terms and write down definitions for them.
2. Ask students to draw a mind map to show the links between the key ideas identified in this lesson.

Further class and homework activity

Ask students to write a TV news bulletin to explain the greenhouse effect.

Changing climate

answers

1. The main greenhouse gases are carbon dioxide, methane, nitrous oxide, and halocarbons.

2. a. The diagram must include: the sun, the Earth's surface, solar radiation, the atmosphere, and greenhouse gases.

   b. The labels must explain in detail the processes taking place to create the greenhouse effect.

3. a. Human activities include: burning fossil fuels in power stations, in homes, in vehicles and industry; deforestation; cattle farming; rice farming; use of fertilisers; sewage farms; use of solvents and cooling agents.

   b. Due to a lower standard of living, people in the developing world, burn small amounts of fossil fuels. This includes: domestic use; transport; energy use for industry. In some developing countries, deforestation and rice farming contribute to greenhouse gas emissions. The percentage of people living in urban areas is much lower than in developed countries, resulting in lower emissions.

4. **Exam-style question** *Using examples of countries and human activities, explain why levels of greenhouse gases in the atmosphere are rising. (6 marks)*

   This question is marked using levels. The key to this question is the command word 'explain' — a Higher Tier command word. Purely descriptive points by Higher Tier candidates get no marks. Foundation Tier students may answer the alternative question:

   Describe how human activities can lead to increases in greenhouse gases. (6 marks)

   In this case, replace the term 'explanations' in the level descriptions below with 'descriptions'.

   Cap answers at 4 marks if they do not:
   - include at least one named country (Higher Tier question only),
   - relate human activities e.g. driving cars, to specific greenhouse gases e.g. increases in CO_2.

   Correct explanations include tying a specific gas to a cause, with examples:
   - Increased economic development — developed with an example e.g. developed world countries produce up to ten times more greenhouse gases per person, per year, compared to the developing world.
   - Increased CO_2 — developed with a cause e.g. burning fossil fuels — well-developed if examples given e.g. coal, oil and gas.
   - Increased methane — developed with a cause e.g. gas pipeline leaks, rice farming, cattle farming — well developed with consequence e.g. flatulence.
   - Increased nitrous oxide — developed with a cause e.g. aircraft, cars and lorries, fertilisers and sewage farms.
   - Increased halocarbons — developed with a cause e.g. solvents and cooling equipment.

Level	Descriptor
0	No rewardable content
1 (1-2 marks)	Simple or very basic explanation using little or no subject vocabulary. May be a simple list of greenhouse gas emissions.
2 (3-4 marks)	Generalised explanations but with some use of geographical terms e.g. 'more industry usually burns fossil fuels, which give off greenhouse gases'. Up to 2 developed statements as shown by examples above.
3 (5-6 marks)	Detailed explanations using geographical terms e.g. 'more industry results in use of fossil fuels such as oil, which give off CO_2, a greenhouse gas.' Three developed or two well-developed points as shown by examples above.

2.6 The enhanced greenhouse effect

Section in brief

This section looks at how human activity has increased the pollution of the atmosphere, and how this has led to the enhanced greenhouse effect, also known as global warming. It also looks at estimates of how climate might change in the future.

In the activities, students:

- complete a paragraph to explain the enhanced greenhouse effect;
- describe how carbon dioxide levels have risen since the 1950s;
- use data to explain global warming;
- answer an exam-style question to explain why predictions of future global temperatures and sea level are uncertain.

Key ideas

- Human pollution of the atmosphere has led to an enhanced greenhouse effect and global warming.
- Key indicators of global warming are changes in global temperatures and sea level.
- Since 1980 global warming seems to have been happening more quickly.
- It is not possible to be precise about the changes global warming will cause.
- There are different scenarios for the future.

Key vocabulary

the enhanced greenhouse effect, thermal expansion

Skills practised

Geographical skills: describing rise in CO_2 levels; explaining what global warming is

Numeracy skills: graph analysis and interpretation

Section outcomes

By the end of this section, most students should be able to:

- define or explain the terms given in 'Key vocabulary' above;
- describe the recent changes in carbon dioxide in the atmosphere;
- explain what global warming is, and how it has been measured;
- assess problems associated with projecting future changes in global temperature and sea levels.

Ideas for a starter

1 Give students a photo of a shrinking ice sheet or flooded coastal area. Ask: 'What has this picture got to do with global warming?'
2 Recap the greenhouse effect from section 2.5.

Ideas for plenaries

1 Hold a class discussion. Why do some scientists believe that humans are not the main cause of global warming?
2 Ask students to complete a flow chart showing the impacts of global warming.

Further class and homework activity

Ask students to draw a diagram to show how the enhanced greenhouse effect works.

Changing climate

answers

1. The missing words are in the following order: CARBON DIOXIDE, GAS, ATMOSPHERE, WARM, POLLUTE, ENHANCED, GLOBAL.

2. Carbon dioxide levels have risen evenly since the 1950s from 315 ppm to 390 ppm in 2009.

3. Global warming is the increase in mean temperatures across the world. The answer must be supported by data such as: global temperatures rose by 0.75 °C between 1905 and 2005; the 20 warmest years ever recorded have occurred since 1987; 2005 was the warmest year ever recorded.

4. **Exam-style question** *Explain why predictions about future global temperatures and sea level are uncertain. (6 marks)*

   This question is marked using levels. The key to this question is the command word 'explain' – a Higher Tier command word. Remember, therefore, that purely descriptive points by Higher Tier candidates get no marks. If you wish to differentiate, you can give Foundation Tier students the question:

   Describe the predictions that are being made about future global temperatures and sea level.

   In this case, replace the term 'explanations' in the level descriptions below with 'descriptions'.

   This question asks for two things – global temperatures and sea level, so to get 6 marks, both should be explained. However, do watch for the student who ties both together, and credit accordingly. If a student explains only one, then the answer is capped at the top of Level 2 (4 marks).

   Correct points for **global temperatures** include:
   - Population and economic growth could increase — developed with a consequence e.g. greater use of fossil fuel — well developed with examples.
   - An opposite scenario — lower population growth, greater use of renewable energy — developed with a consequence e.g. resulting in lower economic growth and use of fossil fuels.
   - People might increase their use of public transport and therefore reduce the amount of CO_2 produced.

   Correct points for **sea level** include:
   - Correct explanation given of the link between increased temperature and increased sea level — developed with an example e.g. ice caps melting.
   - We don't know the exact link between temperature and sea level — developed with a consequence e.g. so temperatures might rise without a large rise in sea level.
   - Or the reverse — increased temperatures might lead to increased evaporation and cloudiness and therefore greater ice sheets.

Level	Descriptor
0	No rewardable content
1 (1-2 marks)	Simple or very basic statements using little or no subject vocabulary. May be a list of greenhouse gases, or simple statements e.g. 'there's more people so there'll be more greenhouse gases'.
2 (3-4 marks)	Generalised statements but with some (not always fully explained) development and use of geographical terms e.g. 'rising population could lead to more greenhouse gases, which would cause rise in sea levels'. Up to 2 developed statements as shown by examples above.
3 (5-6 marks)	Detailed developed statements with clear explanations using geographical terms e.g. 'rising population and standards of living could lead to more greenhouse gas emissions, causing global warming and melting of ice caps'. Three developed or two well-developed points as shown by examples above. For full marks the answer must link global temperatures to sea levels.

2.7 The UK climate

Section in brief

This section looks at the UK's climate in order that students can understand how it might be affected by global warming in future. It investigates the influence of the North Atlantic Drift and air masses, on the UK's climate.

In the activities, students:

- plot climate graphs for Cambridge and Glasgow;
- explain the differences shown on the climate graphs;
- answer an exam-style question to describe the main features of the UK's climate today.

Key ideas

- The UK has a temperate maritime climate influenced by the North Atlantic Drift.
- The position of the polar front and air masses determine the UK's climate.
- Climate is similar across the UK, but there are regional differences.
- Most scientists believe the UK's climate will change in future due to global warming.

Key vocabulary

maritime climates, continental climates, temperate maritime, polar front, air mass

Skills practised

Geographical skills: interpreting a diagram; explaining reasons for differences in climate; describing features of climate

PLTS: independent enquiry

Numeracy skills: using data to draw climate graphs

Section outcomes

By the end of this section, most students should be able to:

- define or explain the terms given in 'Key vocabulary' above;
- draw climate graphs showing precipitation, temperature and sunshine hours;
- explain the differences between climate graphs for different places in the UK;
- describe the main features of the UK's climate today.

Ideas for a starter

1. Show a climate graph for a place in the UK. Ask students what the graph shows. What do they think influences our climate? Why does it tend to be mild with rainfall all year round?
2. Challenge students to find out the wettest and driest places in the UK. Where are they? Can anyone explain their distribution?

Ideas for plenaries

1. Hold a quick quiz with questions based on this section.
2. Have a class discussion. What could the impacts of global warming be on the UK?

Further class and homework activity

Use questions 1 and 2 from page 37 of the students' book as a homework activity.

Changing climate

answers

1 Students' graphs should look like those here.

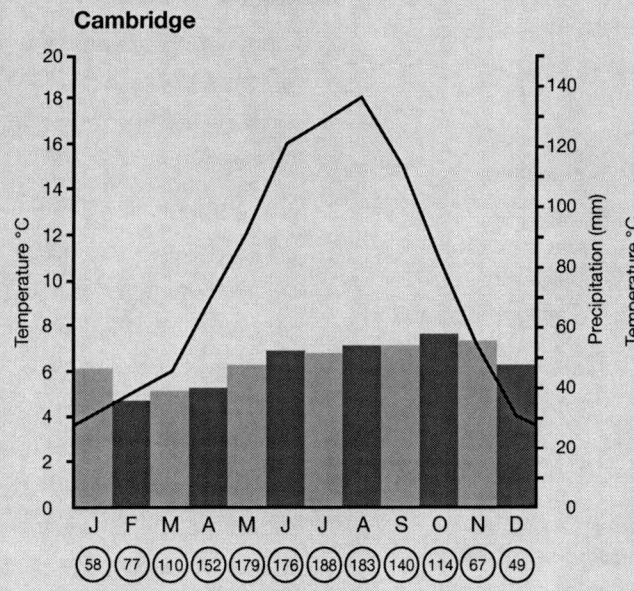

Cambridge

Precipitation values: J 58, F 77, M 110, A 152, M 179, J 176, J 188, A 183, S 140, O 114, N 67, D 49

Glasgow

Key: — = temperature; (34) = average sunshine hours

Sunshine hours: J 34, F 59, M 87, A 131, M 179, J 168, J 160, A 145, S 113, O 81, N 52, D 30

2 In both Cambridge and Glasgow temperatures are higher in summer and lower in winter.

- Cambridge has a similar level of precipitation all year round, but in Glasgow there are distinct seasonal differences, with high precipitation in winter, less in spring and autumn, and least precipitation in summer — although still higher than average precipitation in Cambridge.

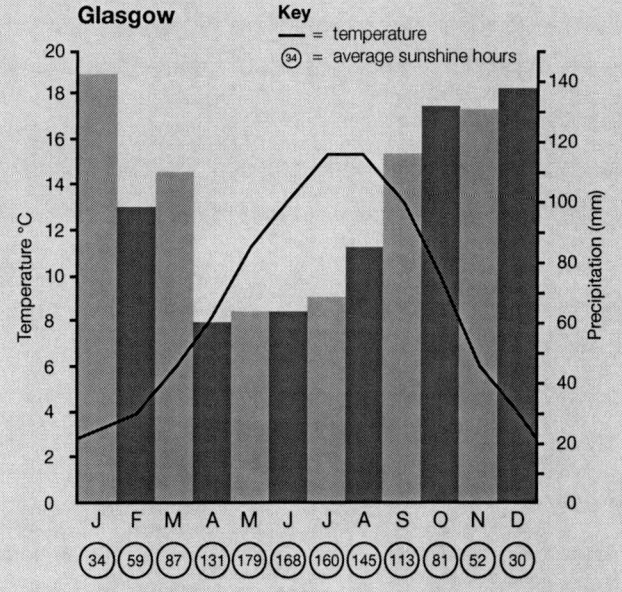

- Glasgow is at a higher latitude than Cambridge so, on average, temperatures are slightly lower in Glasgow.

- In winter the polar front moves south bringing cold polar and arctic air to places like Glasgow. In summer it moves north allowing tropical air masses to warm places like Cambridge.

---

3 Exam-style question *Describe the main features of the UK's climate today. (4 marks)*

This question is point marked. The key to this question is the command word 'describe' – a Foundation Tier command word. If you wish to differentiate, you can give Higher Tier students the same question with the word 'explain'. Remember, therefore, that purely descriptive points by Higher Tier candidates get no marks.

Rather than 4 listed points, this answer looks for two developed points, i.e. two points which are expanded in some way. Correct points – all of which are worth additional marks if developed – include:

- Temperate maritime climate (must be both for 1 mark) (1) — plus developed e.g. mild temperatures (1), rainfall in every month (1).

- Small seasonal difference — plus developed e.g. milder winters and cooler summers (1).

- Influenced by the North Atlantic Drift (1), plus developed e.g. 'which is a warm ocean current' (1).

- Affected by several air masses (1) — plus developed with example and a further mark for its impact e.g. 'the Polar air masses (1) bring cold air in winter' (1).

- Wetter in the western half (1) / drier in the eastern half (award just 1 mark for either).

- Warmer in the southern half (1) / cooler in the northern half (award just 1 mark for either).

47

2.8 UK climate futures

Section in brief

This section looks at the possible impact of global warming on the UK, and what we could do to reduce greenhouse gas emissions.

In the activities, students:

- describe the possible effects of global warming on the UK's climate;
- explain how weather events in the UK could become more extreme;
- explain the 'Stern Review';
- write a letter to suggest ways in which the UK might help to reduce global warming;
- answer an exam-style question to describe how global warming in the UK could have both costs and benefits.

Key ideas

- Global warming could lead to warmer temperatures across the UK, and reduced precipitation, or cooler temperatures and increased precipitation.
- Global warming could lead to more extreme weather events in the UK.
- Global warming will have costs as well as benefits.
- The Stern Review warned that global warming will have economic impacts.
- Greenhouse gas pollution can be reduced if countries work together.

Key vocabulary

There is no key vocabulary in this section.

Skills practised

Geographical skills: map interpretation

PLTS: creative thinking, effective participation

Literacy skills: letter writing; writing an e-mail

Section outcomes

By the end of this section, most students should be able to:

- describe the possible effects of global warming on temperature and precipitation in the UK;
- give examples of the extreme weather which might affect the UK;
- explain what the Stern Review was saying about the economic impacts of global warming;
- describe the costs and benefits of global warming for the UK;
- suggest ways in which individuals, national and international governments can reduce global warming.

Ideas for a starter

1. Ask students to write down five ways in which the UK might be affected by rising temperatures.
2. Give students three minutes to identify and write down the disadvantages of rising temperatures. Ask students to share them with a partner.

Ideas for plenaries

1. Have a class discussion. Should we spend millions of pounds protecting low lying coastal areas from rising sea levels?
2. Ask students: 'Why should we study global warming?' How many reasons can they come up with? Produce a mind map of their responses.

Further class and homework activity

Ask students to imagine that they live on the east coast of England in 50 years' time. They should send an e-mail to a friend describing the problems they are facing.

Changing climate

answers

1. Warmer air from the south could push the Polar Front northwards. Warm tropical air could reach the UK, making summers very hot. Warm air can hold more moisture than cold, so warmer air could mean reduced precipitation.

   Or, the Polar Front could move south causing the UK to become colder. It could cause higher rainfall as warm moist air meets cold Polar air, causing condensation, leading to rainfall.

2. The UK could have more heatwaves, storms, and heavy rain causing flooding.

3. The Stern Review was a report written in 2005 by Sir Nicholas Stern on global warming and its impacts. He suggested that if we do not spend more now to reduce greenhouse gas pollution, there would be increased costs in the future.

4. Possible suggestions: invest in technology; develop alternative sources of energy, e.g. solar power; invest in public transport; increase awareness of international actions, e.g. deforestation.

5. **Exam-style question** *Using examples, describe how global warming in the UK could have both costs and benefits. (6 marks)*

   Cap answers at 4 marks if they do not include costs *and* benefits. Answers which include reference to *global cooling* should also be credited.

   Suitable **costs** for *warming* could include:
   - Increased summer drought / water shortages plus development e.g. 'which could make water cost more' — or if well-developed e.g. 'and affect ecosystems such as rivers or wetlands'.
   - Could be expensive for transport — plus development 'e.g. melting road surfaces'.
   - Negative impact on ecosystems — plus development e.g. in hotter summer temperatures'.

   Suitable **costs** for *cooling* could include:
   - Reduced winter temperatures — plus development e.g. 'which could make energy cost more' — 'and perhaps leave people poorer / increase poverty'.
   - Reduced summer temperatures — plus development e.g. 'which could reduce harvests / crop yields' — e.g. 'and mean that we would have to import more food'.

   Suitable **benefits** for *warming* could include:
   - Lower heating costs / road gritting — plus development e.g. because of warmer winters.
   - Good for the economy — plus development e.g. 'more people take holidays in the UK'.
   - New crops could be grown — plus development e.g. 'creating new opportunities for farmers'.
   - More land farmed at higher altitudes — plus development e.g. 'which could increase the amount of food grown'.

   Suitable **benefits** for *cooling* could include:
   - Reduced summer temperatures — plus development e.g. 'which could reduce health problems caused by summer heat'.
   - Increased winter snow — plus development e.g. 'which could increase winter sports' — e.g. 'leading to more tourist spending and jobs'.

Level	Descriptor
0	No rewardable content
1 (1-2 marks)	Simple or very basic statements using little or no subject vocabulary.
2 (3-4 marks)	Generalised statements but with some development and use of geographical terms. Up to 2 developed statements as shown by examples above.
3 (5-6 marks)	Detailed statements with clear explanations using geographical terms. Three developed or two well-developed points as shown by examples above. For full marks the answer must include both costs and benefits.

2.9 Egypt on the edge

Section in brief

This section looks at some of the possible social, economic and environmental impacts of global warming in a developing country - Egypt.

In the activities, students:

- complete a table to show the economic and environmental impacts of climate change in Egypt and decide which are the greater;
- explain how water could cause conflict between Egypt and other countries;
- answer an exam-style question on the possible impacts of global warming on a developing country.

Key ideas

- Developing countries produce significantly lower greenhouse gas emissions than developed countries.
- Global warming could have a wide range of economic and environmental impacts on Egypt.
- Rising sea levels could create millions of environmental refugees.
- Changes to Egypt's water supply could lead to conflict in future.
- Developing countries are unlikely to be able to afford the costs of coping with global warming.

Key vocabulary

environmental refugees, desertification

Skills practised

Geographical skills: identifying the economic and environmental impacts of climate change

PLTS: independent enquiry

Section outcomes

By the end of this section, most students should be able to:

- define or explain the terms given in 'Key vocabulary' above;
- identify the economic and environmental impacts of climate change on Egypt;
- describe how a reduction in the amount of water reaching Egypt might cause conflict;
- understand that global warming is likely to have different effects on developing and developed countries.

Ideas for a starter

1. Ask students to find out five facts about Egypt and share them with the rest of the class.
2. Give students a photo of a village in the Nile Valley. Ask them to brainstorm how this village contributes to global warming. How do contributions from this village compare with contributions from a village in the UK?

Ideas for plenaries

1. Make up five statements about the possible impacts of global warming on developing countries and read them to the class. Students should say whether they are True or False.
2. Ask students to come up with two questions to ask a partner about today's lesson.

Further class and homework activity

Ask students to complete a spider diagram of the possible effects of global warming on Egypt, on an outline map of the country.

Changing climate

answers

1 a **Economic** impacts of climate change in Egypt include: rising sea levels — causing the flooding of farmland less food being produced (food is needed for Egypt's population and is also an export product); rising temperatures and water shortages leading to falling crop yields.

Environmental impacts of climate change in Egypt include: rising sea levels causing widespread flooding; rising temperatures (to twice the global average at 8°C); rainfall would become more unreliable; desertification; rising sea levels and more frequent storms.

b Students' responses to **a** should show that environmental impacts are greater. They are a response to changes in temperature and rainfall.

2 Egypt is totally dependent on the River Nile, which receives most of its water from rain falling in other countries of East Africa, such as Ethiopia. These countries are building dams and using the Nile's water for HEP and irrigation before it reaches Egypt. Egypt needs to increase its water supply as its population increases, and temperatures rise. Conflict may arise as Egypt's requirements rise, but water supply falls.

3 Exam-style question *Using a named example, examine the possible impacts of global warming on a developing country. (6 marks)*

This question is marked using levels. The key to this question is the command word 'examine' — a Higher Tier command word. Foundation Tier students may answer the alternative question:

Describe the possible effects of global warming on a developing country you have studied.

In this case, replace the term 'explanations' in the level descriptions below with 'descriptions'. Cap answers at the top of Level 2 (4 marks) which do not include a named developing country.

Correct impacts for Egypt, the example used in the students' book, include:

- Rising sea levels — plus development e.g. 'leading to inundation / flooding', and well-developed if identifies a consequence e.g. 'loss of farmland'.
- Temperature rises of 8°C by 2080, — plus development e.g. falling crop yields.
- Less, or more unreliable, rainfall — plus development e.g. leading to drought, failure of crops.
- Desertification — plus development e.g. leading to loss of farmland.
- Heatwaves bringing more illness and death — plus development with example e.g. tropical diseases such as malaria.

Level	Descriptor
0	No rewardable content
1 (1-2 marks)	Simple or very basic statements using little or no subject vocabulary. May be a list e.g. 'the hotter weather could cause starvation'.
2 (3-4 marks)	Generalised statements but with some development and use of geographical terms e.g. 'higher summer temperatures could cause crop failure'. Up to 2 developed statements as shown by examples above.
3 (5-6 marks)	Detailed statements with clear explanations using geographical terms. Three developed or two well-developed points as shown by examples above, e.g. 'summer temperatures could increase by 8°C, leading to crop failure, and eventually famine'.

3 Battle for the biosphere

About the chapter
These are the key ideas behind the chapter.

- Biomes are world-scale ecosystems.
- The distribution of biomes is largely determined by climate, plus local factors.
- The biosphere acts as a life-support system providing goods and services.
- There are a wide range of different demands made on the biosphere which can lead to conflict.
- Human actions, both direct and indirect, are degrading the biosphere.
- The indirect threat of climate change could be the biggest threat to the rainforests.
- There are a range of strategies, at different scales, which we can adopt to conserve rainforests and the biosphere.
- Sustainable environmental and economic management will conserve ecosystems for future generations.

Chapter outline
Use this outline to provide your students with a brief roadmap of the chapter.

3.1 Global biomes
The distribution of global biomes.

3.2 Taking a closer look
The effect of climate and local factors on vegetation.

3.3 A life-support system
The value of the biosphere as a provider of goods and services.

3.4 Conflicts of interest
The different demands made on the biosphere.

3.5 Threats to the biosphere
How rainforests are being degraded by human actions, both directly and indirectly.

3.6 Direct and indirect degradation
Direct threats to the biosphere, and the indirect threat of climate change.

3.7 How can we conserve the biosphere?
Strategies for conserving rainforests.

3.8 Is sustainable management the way ahead?
The sustainable environmental and economic management of ecosystems.

Battle for the biosphere

How is the specification covered?

This chapter covers Topic 3, Unit 1 Dynamic Planet.

3.1 What is the value of the biosphere?

3.2 How have humans affected the biosphere and how might it be conserved?

Key ideas	Detailed content	Pages in students' book
3.1a The distribution of global biomes reflects climate as well as other localised factors.	Define the terms ecosystem and biome, and map the distribution of major biomes across the planet.	42-43
	Evaluate the role of temperature and precipitation in explaining biome location, plus local factors including altitude and soils.	44-45
3.1b The biosphere acts as a 'life support system', and produces a wide range of goods.	Explain how the biosphere regulates the composition of the atmosphere, maintains soil health and influences the hydrological cycle.	46-47
	Investigate how the biosphere provides humans with a range of goods including food, medicines and raw materials.	48-49
3.2a The biosphere is being degraded by human actions.	Consider the role of human activity in the direct destruction of tropical rainforest, including deforestation for timber, mining, conversion to agricultural land.	50-51, 52-53
	Examine how degradation of the biosphere takes place by indirect means including the impact of climate-change on tropical rainforests	52-53
3.2b Management measures, at a variety of scales, are being used to conserve the biosphere and make human use of it more sustainable.	Examine two contrasting examples of biosphere conservation, including one global scale approach e.g. RAMSAR or CITES and one national or local approach e.g. UK National Parks, a tropical rainforest reserve.	54-55
	Examine the challenges of producing sustainable outcomes in economic, social and environmental terms and the possible tensions.	56-57

Chapter outcomes

By the end of this chapter, students should be able to:

- Describe the global distribution of biomes.
- Explain how climatic factors and local factors affect plant growth, and the distribution of biomes.
- Explain how the biosphere regulates the atmosphere, helps to maintain soil, and influences the hydrological cycle.
- Give examples of the goods and services that the biosphere provides.
- Give examples of how the biosphere and rainforests are being degraded by direct human activity.
- Give examples of how the indirect threat of climate change will impact on biomes.
- Describe different strategies for conserving the biosphere.
- Explain how sustainable, environmental and economic management can help to conserve the biosphere.

3.1 Global biomes

Section in brief

In this section students learn what a biome is, and about their global distribution. The location and characteristics of biomes are mainly determined by climate, and biomes change from the tropics towards the poles.

In the activities, students:

- explain the difference between the biosphere and a biome;
- explain how altitude and latitude affect plant growth;
- complete a table comparing marine and continental climates;
- answer an exam-style question to explain the distribution of tropical rainforests.

Key ideas

- The biosphere is the part of the Earth's surface inhabited by living things.
- Biomes are world-scale ecosystems.
- The location and characteristics of biomes are largely determined by climate.
- Biomes change gradually from the tropics towards the poles.
- Other factors affecting vegetation patterns include altitude and distance from the sea.

Key vocabulary

biosphere, biome, biomass, evapotranspiration

Skills practised

Geographical skills: explaining key terms; explaining how factors affect plant growth; comparing climates; explaining the location of biomes

PLTS: independent enquiry

Literacy: writing a long explanatory paragraph

Section outcomes

By the end of this section, most students should be able to:

- define or explain the terms given in 'Key vocabulary' above;
- explain how climatic factors affect plant growth;
- describe the global distribution of biomes;
- explain how altitude and latitude affect plant growth;
- complete a table to compare marine and continental climates.

Ideas for a starter

1. Ask: 'Who can tell me what an ecosystem is? What affects the distribution of large scale ecosystems (biomes)?'
2. Show students a range of photos of different biomes, or ecosystems, e.g. desert, tropical rainforest. If possible, float them onto the whiteboard one at a time. Ask students to describe the vegetation, and see if they can name the biome.

Ideas for plenaries

1. Use the 'On your planet' information on page 43 as the basis for a discussion. Why should we worry if tropical rainforests are disappearing? Why are they of value? Why are temperate forests increasing?
2. Use question 3 from page 43 of the students' book as a plenary.

Further class and homework activity

As a lead in to section 3.2, ask students to find out, and explain in no more than 150 words, how temperature and precipitation affect the global distribution of biomes.

Battle for the biosphere

answers

1 The biosphere is the part of the Earth's surface inhabited by living things. A biome is a large, world-scale, ecosystem.

2 a Altitude is the height of land above sea level Latitude is the distance north, or south, of the Equator. It is expressed in degrees and minutes.

b Altitude affects temperature. Temperature declines by 6.5°C for every 1000 metres in altitude. As temperature falls, so fewer plants can grow. Temperature and precipitation are influenced by latitude. Therefore latitude affects how plants grow. Because the Earth has a curved surface and is tilted, places near the Equator are much warmer than places near the poles, encouraging plant growth. Precipitation is high and constant in a band between the tropics. Along with the high temperatures, this encourages growth of tropical rainforests.

3

Marine climate	Continental climate
Marine climates are found near the coast.	Continental climates are found in central parts of continents away from the coast.
The sea cools nearby land during the hot season and warms it during the cold season.	Away from the moderating effect of the sea, the land heats up in the hot season and cools quickly in the cold season.
This reduces the annual temperature range and increases precipitation.	This increases the annual temperature range and reduces precipitation.

4 Exam-style question *Explain why tropical rainforests are found either side of the equator. (4 marks)*

This question is point marked. Rather than 4 listed points, this answer looks for two developed reasons, i.e. two reasons which are expanded in some way. Correct reasons – all of which are worth additional marks if developed – include:

- It's warm all year (not just 'it's warm') (1) — plus 1 mark if developed e.g. 'because the sun is overhead' (1)
- It rains in every month (not just 'it's wet) (1) — plus 1 mark if developed e.g. 'so plants are always able to grow' / 'and trees need a lot of rain'
- Allow 1 mark max for use of data (temperatures or rainfall) in any part of the answer.

3.2 Taking a closer look

Section in brief

This section looks at how climate (temperature and precipitation) affect vegetation, along with local factors which include altitude, drainage and soils.

In the activities, students:

- match photos of biomes with climate graphs;
- identify biomes shown in photos;
- produce a table to analyse and compare three climates;
- answer an exam-style question to examine how local and global factors influence the distribution of biomes.

Key ideas

- Average temperature is the main factor affecting plant growth.
- The more intense and concentrated the sun's rays are, the better the plant growth.
- Precipitation occurs in low-pressure belts where air masses converge, and air rises.
- Year-round rainfall promotes plant growth.
- Local factors, including altitude, drainage and soils also affect plant growth and ecosystem distribution.

Key vocabulary

pressure belts, converge

Skills practised

Geographical skills: matching photos and climate graphs; identifying biomes from photos; analysing and comparing climates

PLTS: independent enquiry

Numeracy skills: graph interpretation

Section outcomes

By the end of this section, most students should be able to:

- define or explain the terms given in 'Key vocabulary' above;
- understand that temperature is the main factor affecting plant growth;
- explain how latitude affects temperature and rainfall patterns;
- describe how local factors affect ecosystem distribution;
- extract information from climate graphs to compare three different climates.

Ideas for a starter

1. Name this biome. Tell students that it has no real seasons and each day is similar to the next. It is hot and wet all year and the atmosphere is humid. The vegetation appears lush – but appearances can be deceptive. The biome is under threat. What is it, and where do you find it?

2. Ask students what they can deduce about the climate of each place from looking at the photos on page 45 of the students' book.

Ideas for plenaries

1. Ask students to explain to their partner how latitude affects precipitation.

2. Make 10-15 statements based on what students have learned so far in this chapter, some true, some false. Students should hold up True or False cards. Where statements are false ask students to correct them.

Further class and homework activity

As a lead in to section 3.3, ask students to investigate tropical rainforests. They should find out what they provide for local people (thinking about the way they live) and what they provide for the rest of society.

Battle for the biosphere

answers

1 A=X, B=Y, C=Z

2 A= tropical rainforest, B= tropical grassland, C= northern coniferous forest

3

	Tropical rainforest	Tropical grassland	Northern coniferous forest
Maximum temperature	27° C	33° C	20° C
Minimum temperature	26° C	24° C	-41° C
Total annual rainfall	Approx 2800 mm	Approx 600mm	Approx 240 mm
Number of months with rainfall over 50mm	12	3	0

4 Exam-style question *Using named examples; examine how local and global factors influence the distribution of biomes. (6 marks)*

This question is marked using levels. The key to this question is the command word 'examine' – a Higher Tier command word. Purely descriptive points by Higher Tier candidates get no marks. Foundation Tier students may answer the alternative question:

Describe one local and one global factor which can influence vegetation distribution.

In this case, replace the term 'explanations' in the level descriptions below with 'descriptions'.

Cap answers at the top of Level 2 (4 marks) which do not include both a *local* and a *global* factor.

Correct points for **local** include:

- Altitude (which can also be considered a global factor) — plus development e.g. which means that vegetation changes with height, or with an example e.g. rainforest to savannah with height — and well-developed if data are used or impacts explained e.g. 'as temperatures decrease by 6.5°C with every 1000 metres height', 'so it's too cold for tropical forest'.
- Drainage with 1 mark for example e.g. 'it affects vegetation if land is frequently flooded / saturated' —plus developed with a consequence e.g. 'so marsh will develop'.
- Soils with 1 mark about soil type e.g. acid or alkaline — developed if a cause is given e.g. alkali soils develop on chalk / limestone — well-developed if examples of vegetation are given e.g. alkali results in ash / beech trees.

Correct points for **global** include:

- Latitude / distance from Equator — plus development e.g. 'which affects angle of sun's rays' — or well-developed e.g. 'which means that it gets cooler away from the Equator'.
- Continentality / distance from the sea — plus development e.g. 'as climate becomes more extreme / makes it colder in winter / much hotter in summer' — or well-developed e.g. 'because the warming influence of the sea is lost in winter / cooling influence is lost in summer'.

Level	Descriptor
0	No rewardable content
1 (1-2 marks)	Simple or very basic statements using little or no subject vocabulary.
2 (3-4 marks)	Generalised statements but with some use of geographical terms. Up to 2 developed statements as shown by examples above.
3 (5-6 marks)	Detailed statements with clear explanations using geographical terms 'distance from the sea affects temperatures as the ocean cools the land in summer but warms it in winter'. Three developed or two well-developed points as shown by examples above.

3.3 A life-support system

Section in brief

In this section students learn how the biosphere acts as a life-support system by providing us with a wide range of goods and vital services. It explains that different people want to use biomes in different ways, which can result in over-exploitation and unsustainable use.

In the activities, students:

- explain how the biosphere provides vital services;
- explain the differences between how indigenous people and TNCs use the tropical rainforest;
- answer exam-style questions explaining how one biome is threatened by human activities, and what ecosystem goods and services are.

Key ideas

- The biosphere provides a wide range of goods and services.
- Different uses of biomes and over-exploitation can lead to unsustainable use.
- The tropical rainforest biome provides almost everything that indigenous people need.
- Commercial users can destroy the tropical rainforest biome for short-term financial gain.

Key vocabulary

goods, services, sustainable, gene pool, indigenous peoples, transnational companies

Skills practised

Geographical skills: explaining biosphere and ecosystem goods and services

PLTS: independent enquiry: creative thinking

Literacy skills: extended writing about rainforest use

Section outcomes

By the end of this section, most students should be able to:

- define or explain the terms given in 'Key vocabulary' above;
- give examples of the goods and services that the biosphere provides;
- describe the effect of deforestation on the services provided by the tropical rainforest;
- explain why indigenous peoples believe they use the rainforest biome in a sustainable way;
- explain how commercial users can destroy the tropical rainforest biome.

Ideas for a starter

1. Show two photos on the whiteboard – one of indigenous people working in a tropical rainforest, and one of trees being cut down and removed for commercial logging. Create spider diagrams around them showing how the forest is being used, and the effect this has on the biome.

2. If students completed the 'Further activity' in section 3.2 ask a number to feedback their findings to the class.

Ideas for plenaries

1. Use the gene pool information in the 'On your planet' bubble on page 46 of the students' book as the basis for a class discussion on the value of the biosphere.

2. Ask students to write down as many words as they can which refer to the value of the biosphere as a provider of goods and services.

Further class and homework activity

Ask students to look back at the answers they prepared for the 'Further activity' in section 3.2.

a They should classify what the tropical rainforests provide as either 'goods', or 'services'.

b Are tropical rainforests being used sustainably? They must explain their answer.

Battle for the biosphere

answers

1
   a. Forests absorb carbon dioxide from the atmosphere and release oxygen;
   b. Forests trap silt and keep water clean and pure;
   c. Rainforests and reefs provide habitats for a wide range of organisms;
   d. Reefs and rainforests provide attractive scenery for tourists to visit.

2 Students' responses should include the following points:

   a. Indigenous peoples farm using 'slash and burn' — seen as a sustainable form of farming. After 5-6 years a new plot of land is farmed and the old plot recovers; TNCs exploit rainforests resulting in deforestation. Soil is eroded, nutrients are lost, and flooding occurs. Habitats are lost, causing a loss of biodiversity.

   b. TNCs provide resources that people need, e.g. wood, paper, rubber cocoa; Drug companies are searching for new medicines; Companies and governments are providing power in the form of oil and HEP.

3 Exam-style question *Using a named example of a biome, explain why it is threatened by human activities. (6 marks)*

Foundation Tier students may answer the alternative question:

Using examples, describe ways in which a biome can be threatened by human activities.

In this case, replace the term 'explanations' in the level descriptions below with 'descriptions'. Cap answers at the top of Level 2 (4 marks) if they do not include a named example i.e. a specific country, not just 'Africa'.

Correct points include:

- (in rainforests) ranching / logging / farming — plus development e.g. 'which results in clearance of natural forest' / 'which exposes soil to force of rainfall', — or well-developed e.g. 'therefore causing destruction of habitats of named species' / 'which leads to soil erosion'
- mining / urbanisation / construction of dams — with impacts
- pollution — with impacts
- tourism — with impacts

Level	Descriptor
0	No rewardable content
1 (1-2 marks)	Simple or very basic explanations using little or no subject vocabulary.
2 (3-4 marks)	Generalised explanations but with some use of geographical terms Up to 2 developed statements as shown by examples above.
3 (5-6 marks)	Detailed statements with clear explanations using geographical terms. Three developed or two well-developed points as shown by examples above.

4 Exam-style question *Explain what is meant by ecosystem goods and services. (4 marks)*

This question is point marked. Students can achieve 4 marks with separate points, or with 2 developed points, one about goods, and one about services. Both goods and services must be covered for 4 marks; cap students who just name examples of one at 3 marks. Correct points (each worth 1 mark) include:

- **Goods:** food e.g. meat, fish, fruit, nuts; raw materials e.g. hides, timber, fuelwood / biomass for energy, rubber; drinking or irrigation water; potential products e.g. future medicines.
- **Services:** maintaining biodiversity, humus for soil formation, wildlife habitats; water regulation / purification of supply, nutrient cycling; human services e.g. recreation; atmospheric gas / balance; climatic regulation; pollination' for food web/chain; gene pool.

59

3.4 Conflicts of interest

Section in brief

This section looks at the demands made on the biosphere by a range of different players. Different people and organisations have different views about the value of the biosphere. Conflicts can arise between players.

In the activities, students:

- complete drawings of ecological trees for situations where rainforests are destroyed and where they are protected;
- answer an exam-style question explaining the value of a named biome.

Key ideas

- People and organisations (known as players) want to use the biosphere in different ways.
- Different players have different views about the value of the biosphere and can come into conflict.
- The uses of tropical rainforests include: commercial and industrial uses; ecological uses or services, providing for the subsistence needs of local people; and possible genetic uses.

Key vocabulary

players, ecological tree, commercial and industrial uses, ecological uses, subsistence needs, genetic uses

Skills practised

PLTS: independent enquiry; creative thinking

Section outcomes

By the end of this section, most students should be able to:

- define or explain the terms given in 'Key vocabulary' above;
- give examples of the conflicts that can arise between different players over the use and value of the biosphere;
- complete an ecological tree to show what would happen if rainforests were destroyed;
- complete an ecological tree to show what would happen if rainforests were well protected;
- explain the value of a named biome.

Ideas for a starter

1. Brainstorm ideas for the uses of a rainforest. Compare students' responses with the ecological tree in the students' book.
2. Ask students to look at the two photos from page 48 of the students' book. Ask: 'How might these two activities conflict?'

Ideas for plenaries

1. Choose several students to act as Guyanan government ministers. The other students act as reporters and fire (sensible) questions at the ministers about the reasons why they want to develop the rainforest for timber and mining, and the impact of this.
2. Play 'Just a minute'. Students talk for a minute on 'Different demands made on the biosphere' without hesitation or repetition.

Further class and homework activity

Ask students to complete a conflict matrix to show how: a commercial forestry company, a mining company, an ecotourism company, and local people might agree or disagree about deforestation in Rondonia, Brazil.

Battle for the biosphere

answers

1 b Boxes on the tree should include the following:

Possible genetic uses
- No new strains for crops; loss of gene pool for medicines.

Commercial/industrial uses
- Loss of plywood and veneer*; charcoal*; logs*; pulpwood*; industrial chemicals*; gums, resins and oils*. (*Some of these will remain available until all forest has been cleared.)

Ecological uses
- No protection for watershed from soil erosion.
- Flash flooding and landslides will increase.
- Loss of carbon sink would increase global warming.

Subsistence needs
- Loss of: fuelwood and charcoal; fodder and agricultural uses; building materials; weaving materials and dyes; fruit and nuts; green medicine.

c The possible genetic uses, ecological uses, and subsistence uses would remain similar to the ecological tree in the students' book. The rainforest could still have some commercial/industrial uses but in restricted production areas only.

2 Exam-style question *Explain the value of one biome you have studied. (4 marks)*

This question is point marked. Rather than 4 listed points, this answer looks for two developed reasons, i.e. two reasons which are expanded in some way. Students must actually name a biome for the full 4 marks – cap those who do not name one at 3 marks. Correct reasons – all of which are worth additional marks if developed – include:

The *natural* value of the biome e.g.
- As a habitat for animals / plants (1) — plus 1 mark if developed e.g. maintaining biodiversity.
- As a regulator of the atmosphere (1) — plus 1 mark if developed e.g. regulates oxygen / CO_2.
- As a regulator of the quality of water / air quality (1) — plus 1 mark if developed e.g. purification via plants and soil processes.

The *human* value of the biome e.g.
- As a provider of goods / raw materials / foods (1) — plus 1 mark if developed e.g. with named example.
- For the growth and health of crops (1) e.g. pollination by insects of food crops.

61

3.5 Threats to the biosphere

Section in brief

This section looks at how rainforests are being degraded by human actions both directly and indirectly. It examines the threats to rainforests and the impacts they have.

In the activities, students:

- classify the impacts of biodiversity loss as environmental, economic or social;
- explain how far they agree with the view that economic gain is worth the environmental loss of the rainforest;
- answer an exam-style question to explain how demand for resources threatens biodiversity.

Key ideas

- Estimates of the number of species on Earth range from 2 million to over 30 million, but only 1.4 million have been identified.
- Rainforests contain huge numbers of species, but face a number of threats.
- Threats to the world's rainforests can be classified as immediate causes and root causes.
- Most hotspots where biodiversity is endangered are in developing countries.

Key vocabulary

hotspots, biodiversity

Skills practised

Geographical skills: classifying impacts of biodiversity loss

PLTS: creative thinking; independent enquiry

Literacy skills: explaining views in a piece of extended writing

Section outcomes

By the end of this section, most students should be able to:

- define or explain the terms given in 'Key vocabulary' above;
- classify the impacts of biodiversity loss as environmental, economic and social;
- give examples of immediate and root causes of threats to the world's rainforests, and their impacts;
- explain whether the economic gain of deforestation is worth the loss of biodiversity in a tropical rainforest.

Ideas for a starter

1. Show students a photo of any endangered species on the whiteboard. Tell them what it is, where it lives and the threats it faces. Ask why it matters if this species becomes extinct.
2. Brainstorm: 'How do human actions threaten the rainforests?' Record students' ideas as a spider diagram.

Ideas for plenaries

1. If you used starter 2 return to the spider diagram and amend/add to it as necessary.
2. Ask students to tell their partner the biggest insight they gained from this section.

Further class and homework activity

Ask students to research one of the world's biodiversity hotspots. They should find out where it is, what types of plants and animals are found there, and the threats it faces.

Battle for the biosphere

answers

1 Students' table could include the following impacts.

Environmental impacts:
- Deforestation affects rates of flooding, soil erosion and humus formation.
- Deforestation leads to nutrient loss, an increase in CO_2 and global warming.
- Deforestation destroys ecosystems.
- Over-harvesting and over-fishing lead to species extinction and destroys food chains.

Economic impacts:
- Loss of reefs and rainforests mean fewer tourists and less income for local economies.
- Deforestation and mining lead to only short-term economic gain.

Social impacts:
- Loss of mangroves and reefs means less protection from coastal storms for coastal communities, together with less food and fuelwood.
- Deforestation leads to loss of gene pool and possible sources of new medicines.
- Deforestation leads to loss of sources of food, fuel, building materials, etc. for indigenous peoples.

2 Answers will vary.

---

3 **Exam-style question** *Using a named example, explain how demand for resources threatens biodiversity. (6 marks)*

This question is marked using levels. The key to this question is the command word 'explain' — a Higher Tier command word. Purely descriptive points by Higher Tier candidates get no marks. Foundation Tier students may answer the alternative question:

Using examples, describe the human activities that can threaten biodiversity.

In this case, replace the term 'explanations' in the level descriptions below with 'descriptions'.

Cap answers at the top of Level 2 if they do not include:
- a named place or country; not just 'Africa';
- reference to *how* human activities threaten biodiversity.

Correct explanations include linkage to a threat to biodiversity, with examples, include:
- Increased economic development — developed if linked to an example e.g. mining of resources has resulted in the destruction of habitats / deforestation.
- Demand for land for agriculture — developed if linked to an example e.g. cattle ranching has resulted in deforestation and a reduction in biodiversity.
- Root causes such as poverty — developed if linked to an example e.g. to repay foreign debt, rainforests have been destroyed to create more land for food production which is exported.

Level	Descriptor
0	No rewardable content
1 (1-2 marks)	Simple or very basic explanation using little or no subject vocabulary. May be a list e.g. 'there are more people so there is more need for land'.
2 (3-4 marks)	Generalised explanations but with some use of geographical terms e.g. 'increased prosperity leads to demand for resources like wood'. Up to 2 developed statements as shown by examples above.
3 (5-6 marks)	Detailed explanations using geographical terms e.g. 'increased economic development leads to demand for resources such as metals, which lead to opening up and destroying the Amazon rainforest'. Three developed or two well-developed points as shown by examples above.

3.6 Direct and indirect degradation

Section in brief

In this section students learn about direct threats to the biosphere, and the indirect threat of climate change.

In the activities, students:

- describe and suggest reasons for rises and falls in the rates of deforestation;
- explain why rapidly rising temperatures are a problem for plant and animal species;
- answer an exam-style question to explain how the biosphere is threatened by direct and indirect means.

Key ideas

- The biosphere faces direct threats such as deforestation, and indirect threats such as global warming.
- Deforestation in Amazonia has many causes.
- The rate of deforestation in Amazonia has slowed since 2004.
- Global warming is happening too rapidly for many species to adapt to the changing climate.
- Climate stress, such as drought in Amazonia, could accelerate global warming.

Key vocabulary

degradation

Skills practised

Geographical skills: explaining threats to the rainforest

PLTS: independent enquiry; creative thinking

Numeracy skills: describing trends on a graph

Section outcomes

By the end of this section, most students should be able to:

- define or explain the term given in 'Key vocabulary' above;
- suggest reasons for the trends in deforestation;
- explain why rapidly rising temperatures are a problem for many species;
- explain how the tropical rainforest is threatened by direct and indirect means.

Ideas for a starter

1 Brainstorm: 'What threats does Amazonia (the world's largest area of tropical rainforest) face?' Create a spider diagram of students' suggestions. Which do they think is the biggest threat?

2 Tell students that in 2011, Brazil's beef exports were worth $5.4 billion. Ask them what the link is between beef exports and the tropical rainforest.

Ideas for plenaries

1 Hold a class discussion. Do students think deforestation in Amazonia will continue to decline, or is it likely to increase again in the future?

2 Ask students to sum up what they have learned in this lesson in less than 140 characters.

Further class and homework activity

Ask students how far they agree with the following statement. 'Global warming is probably the biggest single threat to the biosphere and the species that live in it.' They should explain their answers.

Battle for the biosphere

answers

1 The overall trend on the graph is downwards (with peaks in 1988, 1995 and 2004).

Reasons for the downwards trend include:

- protection of part of the rainforest and enforcement of the Forest Code law;
- reduced demand for forest resources due to recession and the global financial crisis;
- government crackdown on illegal logging and clearance;
- Brazilians becoming more interested in green issues.

2 Rapidly rising temperatures will create many problems including: biomes shrinking and moving polewards; changes in migration patterns and breeding times; extreme weather events will affect pollination and migration; pests and diseases will thrive and devastate biomes. The rise in temperatures and changes to biomes will occur too rapidly for many species to be able to adapt.

---

3 Exam-style question *Using named examples, explain how the biosphere is threatened by direct and indirect means. (6 marks)*

This question is marked using levels. The key to this question is the command word 'explain' — a Higher Tier command word. Purely descriptive points by Higher Tier candidates get no marks. Foundation Tier students may answer the alternative question:

Using examples, describe different threats to the biosphere.

In this case, replace the term 'explanations' in the level descriptions below with 'descriptions'.

Cap answers at the top of Level 2 (4 marks) which do not include:

- named examples — either place-specific e.g. located threats in Brazil / the Amazon, or examples of specific threats which are un-located,
- inclusion of both direct *and* indirect threats

Correct points for **direct means** include:

- Increased demand for agricultural land — developed if a cause is explained e.g. rising population, GDP, or increased industrialisation.
- Similarly, a demand for urban land — developed with causes.
- Similarly, logging and the demand for timber from developed countries

Correct points for **indirect means** include:

- Changing climate — developed with examples of ways in which this can threaten biomes e.g. increased drought and its impacts.

Level	Descriptor
0	No rewardable content
1 (1-2 marks)	Simple or very basic statements using little or no subject vocabulary. No causes – mostly or all descriptive statements. May be a list of threats, or simple statements e.g. 'rain forests are being cut down'.
2 (3-4 marks)	Generalised statements but with some (not always fully explained) development and use of geographical terms e.g. 'rising population is leading to more logging in rain forests'. Up to 2 developed statements as shown by examples above.
3 (5-6 marks)	Detailed developed statements with clear explanations using geographical terms e.g. 'rising population and increased urbanisation have led to deforestation of rain forests in Brazil, which is destroying natural habitats'. Three developed or two well-developed points as shown by examples above. For full marks the answer must include both direct and indirect means.

3.7 How can we conserve the biosphere?

Section in brief

In this section students explore strategies for conserving rainforests, including conservation strategies at global and national scales.

In the activities, students:

- work in pairs to decide on their priorities for conserving the biosphere;
- map the location of National Parks and Community Forests and design a poster or presentation to explain how National Parks or Community Forests help to conserve the biosphere;
- answer an exam-style question to explain different ways of conserving ecosystems.

Key ideas

- Maintaining the biosphere and reversing devastation requires huge amounts of money and international effort.
- There are a number of questions to consider when deciding which habitats and species to conserve.
- Countries can work together at a global level on conservation issues, but international treaties can be difficult to manage.
- At a national scale, governments can set up protected areas to conserve, manage and restore biodiversity.

Key vocabulary

keystone species, Convention on International Trade in Endangered Species (CITES), RAMSAR Wetlands, Sites of Special Scientific Interest (SSSI), National Parks, Community Forests

Skills practised

Geographical skills: mapping the location of National Parks and Community Forests

PLTS: team-working; creative thinking

Section outcomes

By the end of this section, most students should be able to:

- define or explain the terms given in 'Key vocabulary' above;
- decide on priorities for conserving the biosphere;
- give examples of two different ways of conserving ecosystems;
- design a poster or presentation to explain how National Parks or Community Forests can help to conserve the biosphere.

Ideas for a starter

1 Brainstorm: 'How can we protect and conserve the biosphere?' Record students' ideas as a spider diagram.
2 Ask: 'Who can tell me what a National Park is? Can anyone name one? What are their aims?'

Ideas for plenaries

1 Use the information in the 'On your planet' bubble on page 54 of the students' book as the basis for a class discussion.
2 Ask students to work in pairs to make notes in preparation for answering the exam-style question.

National Parks in Britain have two main aims: to preserve and enhance the natural beauty of the landscape, and to provide a place for recreation and enjoyment. A further aim is protecting the social and economic well-being of people who live/work there.

Further class and homework activity

Why do students think international treaties, such as CITES, are difficult to manage? What interests, or players, are likely to conflict? They should explain their answers.

Battle for the biosphere

answers

1 Responses will depend on students' individual views. They should prioritise how they would spend the $30 billion, decide what they would conserve, and how they would do it.

2 a Check the location of Community Forests and National Parks on students' outline maps of the UK using these websites: www.communityforest.org.uk/ and www.nationalparks.gov.uk/ .

b Students should design a poster or presentation to explain how National Parks or Community Forests help to conserve the biosphere.

---

3 Exam-style question *Using named examples, explain two different ways of conserving ecosystems. (6 marks)*

This question is marked using levels. The key to this question is the command word 'explain' – which is a Higher Tier command word. Remember, therefore, that purely descriptive points by Higher Tier candidates get no marks. If you wish to differentiate, you can give Foundation Tier students the question:

Using named examples, describe two different ways of conserving ecosystems.

In this case, replace the term 'explanations' in the level descriptions below with 'descriptions'.

This question asks for two different ways, so to get 6 marks, two should be identified. However, if the two ways identified are very similar, use discretion in awarding marks. For example, a discussion of creating wildlife protection areas and SSSI can be considered different measures even though they may in some cases be identical areas. However, if a student explains only one, then the answer is capped at the top of Level 2 (4 marks).

Appropriate ways of conserving ecosystems include:

- General strategies e.g. conserve the gene pool and keystone species e.g. bees — developed if extended to explain the impacts on the food web.
- The CITES treaty — developed to explain its aims e.g. listing endangered species — further developed with particular strategies e.g. stopping the trade in animal skin products such as ivory or handbags made from crocodile skins.
- The RAMSAR convention — developed to explain its aims e.g. to protect wetland habitat — further developed with particular details e.g. number of sites, World Wetlands Day, raise the profile of wetlands and areas of very high biodiversity such as coral reefs.
- National scale projects — developed to explain its aims e.g. protect beautiful / special landscapes — further developed with details e.g. creation of National Parks.

Level	Descriptor
0	No rewardable content
1 (1-2 marks)	Simple or very basic statements using little or no subject vocabulary. May be a list of different methods, undeveloped, or simple statements e.g. 'it's important to save insects and plants'.
2 (3-4 marks)	Generalised statements but with some (not always fully explained) development and use of geographical terms e.g. 'RAMSARs are agreements which can help to protect wetlands which are under threat'. Up to 2 developed statements as shown by examples above.
3 (5-6 marks)	Detailed developed statements with clear explanations using geographical terms e.g. 'The RAMSAR convention aimed to protect wetlands e.g. by identifying SSSI which are fully protected from development and allow only limited access to scientists'. Three developed or two well-developed points as shown by examples above.

3.8 Is sustainable management the way ahead?

Section in brief

This section looks at the sustainable environmental and economic management of ecosystems as a way of conserving them for future generations. Kilum-Ijim forest in Cameroon is included as a case study.

In the activities, students:

- draw a table to show the strengths and weaknesses of sustainable environmental management in Kilum-Ijim;
- describe the ways in which the forest is being managed to provide sustainable economic outcomes for the local community;
- explain how far they think the battle to conserve the biosphere has been won;
- answer an exam-style question to explain how sustainable management can help conserve the biosphere.

Key ideas

- Sustainable management conserves ecosystems for future generations.
- The outcomes of sustainable management can be measured in economic, social and environmental terms.
- In the 1980s Kilum-Ijim forest in Cameroon was under pressure from farming and logging.
- Birdlife International started a project in 1987 to create a sustainable forest reserve in the area.
- The project has been a success, but faces challenges in the future.

Key vocabulary

keystone species, Convention on International Trade in Endangered Species (CITES), RAMSAR Wetlands, Sites of Special Scientific Interest (SSSI), National Parks, Community Forests

Skills practised

Geographical skills: interpreting a diagram of a sustainable forest reserve; explaining how sustainable management can help conserve the biosphere

PLTS: independent enquiry

Section outcomes

By the end of this section, most students should be able to:

- define or explain the terms given in 'Key vocabulary' above;
- explain how sustainable management can help to conserve the biosphere;
- identify the strengths and weaknesses of sustainable environmental management in Kilum-Ijim;
- describe the ways in which the forest is being managed to provide sustainable economic outcomes for the local community.

Ideas for a starter

1. Write 'Sustainable management' on the whiteboard. Ask for ideas to create a mind map around the phrase. What is sustainable management in the context of the biosphere? How do students think it could work?
2. One way of conserving ecosystems could be to ban people completely, and close them off. Use this view as the basis for a class discussion.

Ideas for plenaries

1. Opportunities for plenary class discussions include using the 'On your planet' bubble on page 56, and question 3 from the students' book.
2. Give students five minutes to work (in pairs) and write a paragraph on conserving the biosphere.

Further class and homework activity

Give students two blank world maps. Ask them to annotate one with the threats to the biosphere identified in sections 3.5 and 3.6. They should annotate the other map with how the threats can be managed and how the strategies work (use sections 3.7 and 3.8).

Battle for the biosphere

answers

1 Students' tables could include the following impacts of sustainable environmental management in Kilum-Ijim:

- **Strengths:** worked with national organisations as well as local communities; made lists of forest resources; developed rules for sustainable use of forest; managed and monitored the forest; educated communities about replanting trees and safe levels of hunting and logging; forest area has increased by 8% since project began.

- **Weaknesses:** population growth will increase pressure to deforest areas; urban areas, industry and roads could encroach on forest; money and technical support could end; climate change could degrade the forest.

2 The forest has been divided into zones which are used for different purposes and have different levels of protection. The zones include areas of:

- extractive reserves (e.g. rubber and nuts, agroforestry) — where a variety of crops are grown, therefore maintaining biodiversity,
- ecotourism — which provides employment,
- afforestation,
- selective logging,
- hunting — allowed in some zones.

3 Responses will depend on individual views, but clearly the biosphere is still under threat from human activity - in particular from human induced climate change.

4 Exam-style question *Using a named example, explain how sustainable management can help conserve the biosphere. (6 marks)*

This question is marked using levels. The key to this question is the command word 'explain' — a Higher Tier command word. Foundation Tier students may answer the alternative question:

Describe two ways in which sustainable management is being used to conserve the biosphere.

In this case, replace the term 'explanations' in the level descriptions below with 'descriptions'. Cap answers at the top of Level 2 (4 marks) which do not include a named area e.g. Kilum-Ijim or a particular developing country.

Appropriate methods of sustainable management:

- A statement of aims of the example used e.g. conserving forest — developed with the origins of pressures e.g. farming or logging — further developed with details e.g. size of area or nature of the ecosystem.
- Description of strategies e.g. working with local communities to delimit forest reserves — developed with examples of specific resources and rules for the sustainable use of these.
- Methods e.g. setting up an operations unit — developed with its purpose e.g. to manage / monitor the forest.
- Education of communities about afforestation and sustainable levels of hunting / logging.

Level	Descriptor
0	No rewardable content
1 (1-2 marks)	Simple or very basic statements using little or no subject vocabulary.
2 (3-4 marks)	Generalised statements but with some development and use of geographical terms e.g. 'the aim was to save areas of rainforest in Kilum-Ijim from threats such as logging'. Up to 2 developed statements as shown by examples above.
3 (5-6 marks)	Detailed statements with clear explanations using geographical terms e.g. 'the aim was to save areas of rainforest in Kilum-Ijim in Cameroon from threats such as logging, by getting local communities to develop rules about how the forest should be used'. Three developed or two well-developed points as shown by examples above.

4 Waterworld

About the chapter

These are the key ideas behind the chapter.

- Water flows between the atmosphere, oceans and land in a closed system, the hydrological cycle.
- The biosphere and lithosphere act as sub-cycles within the hydrological cycle and help to regulate it.
- Climate change will have a number of impacts on the hydrological cycle.
- People in vulnerable areas are at risk from unreliable and insufficient water supplies.
- Water quality is under threat as a result of human activity.
- Human interference has a range of impacts on the hydrological cycle.
- Large-scale water-management schemes are usually multi-purpose projects and have both costs and benefits.
- Small-scale intermediate technology solutions to manage water supplies are often more sustainable than large-scale schemes.

Chapter outline

Use this outline to provide your students with a brief roadmap of the chapter.

4.1 The Blue Planet
The hydrosphere and the hydrological (water) cycle.

4.2 The global hydrological cycle
The role of the biosphere and lithosphere in the hydrological cycle.

4.3 The effects of climate change
The effects of climate change on the hydrological cycle.

4.4 Living with chronic water shortage
Chronic water shortage in the Sahel, and how climate change may affect water supplies in other parts of the world.

4.5 Threats to water quality
The human threats to water quality.

4.6 Interfering in the hydrological cycle
Some of the impacts of human interference in the hydrological cycle.

4.7 Solutions to the water crisis
Large-scale solutions to managing water supplies.

4.8 Sustainable supplies for developing countries
Small-scale sustainable solutions to managing water supplies.

Water world

How is the specification covered?

This chapter covers Topic 4, Unit 1 Dynamic Planet.

4.1 Why is water important to the health of the planet?

4.2 How can water resources be managed sustainably?

Key ideas	Detailed content	Pages in students' book
4.1a The hydrological cycle regulates water supply and links the atmosphere, biosphere and lithosphere.	Investigate the role of the biosphere and the lithosphere in regulating the hydrological cycle and ensuring water supply.	60-61
	Explain how the hydrological cycle works, as a system of interlinked stores and transfers, including the processes of evaporation, condensation, precipitation and run-off.	58-59, 60-61
4.1b Changes to the hydrological cycle can affect both human and eco-system health.	Examine the impact of climate change on the hydrological cycle, including rainfall reliability and groundwater levels, in areas which already experience aridity.	62-63
	Investigate the impact of unreliable and insufficient water supply on humans, using a case study from a vulnerable area, e.g. the Sahel.	64-65
4.2a There are many threats to maintaining a healthy hydrological cycle.	Consider the consequences of human activities on water quality, including sewage disposal, industrial pollution, and intensive agriculture.	66-67
	Examine located examples of human activities which disrupt water supply, including deforestation, over-abstraction of groundwater, and reservoir construction.	68-69
4.2b There is a range of strategies, at a variety of scales, designed to manage water resources more sustainably using different levels of technology.	Consider the costs and benefits of large-scale water management projects in the developed world and developing world, e.g. The Three Gorges dam and Colorado River.	70-71
	Examine the role of named small-scale intermediate technology solutions, such as water harvesting in the developing world.	72-73

Chapter outcomes

By the end of this chapter, students should be able to:

- Explain why the hydrological cycle is a closed system.
- Describe how the biosphere and lithosphere help to regulate the hydrological cycle.
- Explain how climate change is likely to alter the hydrological cycle.
- Explain how an unreliable water supply affects people in the Sahel.
- Describe the ways in which water quality is threatened by human activity.
- Draw flow diagrams to show how different human activities can affect the hydrological cycle.
- Use examples to explain the costs and benefits of large-scale water-management schemes.
- Give one example of a small-scale sustainable water management project, and explain how it can improve water supplies.

4.1 The Blue Planet

Section in brief

In this section students learn about the hydrosphere and the hydrological cycle. The hydrosphere consists of all the water on the planet: in seas, oceans, rivers, lakes, rocks and soil, in living things, and the atmosphere. Water flows between the atmosphere, oceans and land in a closed system – the hydrological cycle.

In the activities, students:

- label a diagram of the hydrological cycle;
- answer an exam-style question to explain why the hydrological system is a closed system.

Key ideas

- Water makes Earth unique and different from other planets in the solar system.
- The hydrosphere consists of all the water on the planet.
- Water flows between the atmosphere, oceans and land in a closed system – the hydrological cycle.
- Water flows between stores in the hydrological cycle via transfers and this can involve a change of state.
- Water stays in the stores in the hydrological cycle for varying amounts of time.

Key vocabulary

Blue Planet, hydrosphere, hydrological cycle, closed system, stores, transfers, evaporation, condensation

Skills practised

Geographical skills: drawing and labelling hydrological cycle diagram; explaining concepts

Numeracy skills: analysing table of data

Section outcomes

By the end of this section, most students should be able to:

- define or explain the terms given in 'Key vocabulary' above;
- describe the states in which water exists and how it changes from one state to another;
- label a diagram of the hydrological cycle;
- explain why the hydrological cycle is a closed system.

Ideas for a starter

1 Fill a large jug or bucket with 4.5 litres of water (and have a tablespoon handy). Tell students this represents all the water on Earth. Ask them how much they think represents the amount of available freshwater. The answer is one tablespoonful.

2 Ask the students to look at the four photos A-D. Ask: 'What is the link between them?' The answer is that they are all *stores* of water.

Ideas for plenaries

1 Ask students to write down as many bullet points as they can about the work done in this section.

2 With books closed ask students to explain these terms to their partner: hydrosphere, hydrological cycle, closed system, stores, transfers. Then suggest they start a dictionary of key terms for this chapter.

Further class and homework activity

Ask students to find out and write down definitions for these terms: infiltration, percolation, groundwater storage, saturation, water table.

Water world

answers

1 b and c

Students' diagrams should be labelled as follows:

A = evaporation;

B = condensation;

C = trees and vegetation;

D = groundwater;

E = surface runoff (or surface water such as puddles or a river);

F = lake, sea or ocean.

---

2 Exam-style question *Explain why the hydrological system on Earth is a 'closed system'. (3 marks)*

This question is point marked. It requires three sequenced points to offer a fully developed answer for three marks. Correct points include:

- There's a finite amount of water (1) which recycles in the atmosphere (1).
- None leaves or is lost (1).
- It only alters via a change of state within the system (1).
- It exists only in stores and flows (1) — with 1 mark max for examples e.g. lakes, oceans, soil, underground.

4.2 The global hydrological cycle

Section in brief

In this section students find out how the biosphere and lithosphere play a vital role in the hydrological cycle. They act as sub-cycles and help to regulate the hydrological cycle.

In the activities, students:

- complete a copy of a river basin system diagram;
- define terms;
- explain what happens to water from the time it falls as precipitation to the time it reaches the river;
- answer an exam-style question describing how the hydrological cycle links the biosphere, atmosphere and lithosphere.

Key ideas

- Stores of water in the global hydrological cycle are linked by processes which transfer water into, and out of, them.
- The processes of evaporation, evapotranspiration and precipitation regulate the hydrological cycle.
- The biosphere and lithosphere act as sub-cycles within the hydrological cycle.
- The biosphere and lithosphere help to regulate the hydrological cycle.

Key vocabulary

biosphere, lithosphere, river basin system, green water, throughflow, infiltration, percolation, groundwater, groundwater storage, saturation, water table, inputs, outputs, transfers or flows, stores, evapotranspiration

Skills practised

Geographical skills: completing and interpreting a river basin system diagram; defining key words

PLTS: independent enquiry; creative thinking

Section outcomes

By the end of this section, most students should be able to:

- define or explain the terms given in 'Key vocabulary' above:
- complete a diagram of a river basin system;
- explain the passage of water from the time it falls as precipitation to the time it reaches the river;
- describe how the hydrological cycle links the biosphere, atmosphere and lithosphere.

Ideas for a starter

1. Show a diagram similiar to the one on page 60 of the students book, but without the labels, on the whiteboard. Ask students to build up the diagram by adding labels where they can. Work with them, giving them prompts and clues when necessary.
2. Recap section 4.1 – the hydrological cycle and stores of water.

Ideas for plenaries

1. Match key words and definitions. Call out a definition from the text box on page 61 of the students' book and ask students to give you the correct key word.
2. Ask students if they found anything difficult in this section. What was it? Why was it difficult? What would help to make it easier?

Further class and homework activity

Ask students to add the key vocabulary from this section to their dictionary of key terms for this chapter.

answers

1. A = Infiltration,
   B = Percolation,
   C = Groundwater storage

2. Evaporation — the process by which liquid water changes to water vapour (a gas) when it is warmed.

   Evapotranspiration — is the combined process of evaporation and transpiration i.e. the movement of water through a plant, from roots to leaves, and its loss into the atmosphere as water vapour).

3. - Trees intercept precipitation and over half of it is transpired and evaporated.
   - Precipitation drips from vegetation, and reaches the ground by stemflow, where it can be held as surface storage.
   - Water can runoff over the ground surface as overland flow to reach the river, but it may evaporate before it reaches the river.
   - Water infiltrates soil. It can be held within the unsaturated soil or rock as soil moisture storage, move through the soil as throughflow and reach the river, or percolate into groundwater storage.
   - It is then either held in the saturated soil or rock as groundwater storage, or flows as groundwater flow into the river.

4. **Exam style question** *Describe how the hydrological cycle links the biosphere, atmosphere and lithosphere. (4 marks)*

   This question is point marked. It requires linked points to offer a fully developed answer for four marks. Correct points – any 4 of which can be marked correct – include:

   - Biosphere: trees intercept precipitation (1) which then drips or flows down stems (1).
   - Atmosphere: evaporation (1) and transpiration (1) occur.
   - Lithosphere: Infiltration into soil (1) where it flows downhill as throughflow (1) or percolation into rock (1). If underlying rock is permeable (1) can be stored as groundwater (1).

4.3 The effects of climate change

Section in brief

This section looks at the effects of climate change on the hydrological cycle. Climate change will have impacts on precipitation, evaporation, river flow, and therefore drought.

In the activities, students:

- draw the hydrological cycle and change the labels to show how it will change;
- explain why the hydrological cycle will change;
- answer exam-style questions to: describe those parts of the world where rainfall will become more intense and, explain how climate change is likely to alter the hydrological cycle.

Key ideas

Climate change will have a number of impacts on the hydrological cycle:

- Precipitation might increase or decrease, but the most likely impact is an increase in intensity.
- As the atmosphere gets warmer evaporation rates will increase.
- In the northern hemisphere river flow could increase in the spring and reduce in summer.
- Increased temperatures, increased evaporation and reduced river flow is likely to lead to increased drought.

Key vocabulary

water wars, irrigation, precipitation intensity

Skills practised

Geographical skills: interpreting maps of precipitation intensity and drought severity; labelling diagram of hydrological cycle to show changes

PLTS: independent enquiry

Section outcomes

By the end of this section, most students should be able to:

- define or explain the terms given in 'Key vocabulary' above;
- label a diagram of the hydrological cycle to show how it will change as climate changes;
- explain how climate change is likely to alter the hydrological cycle;
- describe those parts of the world where rainfall will become more intense.

Ideas for a starter

1. Recap the global hydrological cycle from section 4.2 of the students' book. Ask students how they think this might change as climate changes.

2. Play students a recording of heavy rainfall to introduce this section. You should be able to find something suitable on www.soundsnap.com. Tell them that increased precipitation intensity is one of the likely impacts of climate change. How do they think this will affect the hydrological cycle?

Ideas for plenaries

1. Play 'Just a minute'. The topic is 'The effects of climate change'. Students have up to one minute to talk on the topic without hesitation or repetition.

2. In pairs, ask students to decide upon one question which they still have about the effects of climate change on the hydrological cycle. Pick suitable questions for students to complete for homework, or extra activities.

Further class and homework activity

Ask students to find out about rainfall and drought in the Sahel in preparation for the next lesson.

Water world

answers

1 Students should label points 1-6 on the diagram of the hydrological cycle as follows: 1 – increase; 2 – increase; 3 – increase; 4 – rain increase, snow decrease; 5 – increase in spring, decrease in summer; 6 – could increase or decrease.

2
- Warmer temperatures cause an increase in *evaporation* from the sea and an increase in *evapotranspiration*.
- Increase in *water vapour* in the air leading to increased condensation.
- Warmer temperatures cause more *precipitation* to fall as rain instead of snow.
- Increased *surface runoff* in spring as warmer temperatures mean mountain snows would melt sooner. Reduced flow in summer as snow has already melted.
- *Infiltration* and *groundwater flow* could increase or decease depending on whether rainfall amounts increase or decrease.

3 Exam-style question *Use the map on the page opposite to describe those parts of the world where rainfall will become more intense. (4 marks)*

This question is point marked. Correct points (1 mark each) include:

- Most of the world will have more intense rainfall.
- The northern hemisphere will have more intense rainfall than the southern.
- Many major mountain ranges will have greater intensity — e.g. Himalayas (1).

4 Exam-style question *Using examples, explain how climate change is likely to alter the hydrological cycle. (6 marks)*

As the command word 'explain' is purely descriptive points by Higher Tier candidates get no marks. Foundation Tier students may answer the alternative question:

Describe how climate change might affect precipitation and evaporation.

In this case, replace the term 'explanations' in the table below with 'descriptions'.

Cap answers at 4 marks which do not include precise explanations of processes. Located examples are not required. Remember that climate change could mean both; a warming, or a cooling, of the climate. Possible explanations could include:

- Increased precipitation — plus development e.g. 'because with warmer temperatures there'll be increased evaporation and therefore condensation' — or well-developed e.g. 'leading to greater cloud and rainfall'.
- Decreased precipitation — plus development e.g. 'because rain-bearing winds could change direction' — or well-developed e.g. 'leading to less rainfall and more drought'.
- Increased evaporation — plus development e.g. 'caused by increased temperatures'.
- Decreased evaporation — plus development e.g. 'caused by increased cloudiness'.
- Credit consequences for river channel flow / surface run-off / groundwater storage.

Level	Descriptor
0	No rewardable content
1 (1-2 marks)	Simple or very basic explanations using little or no subject vocabulary. May be a list without explaining or developing any causes e.g. 'more water will be evaporated'.
2 (3-4 marks)	Generalised explanations but with some use of geographical terms. Up to 2 developed statements as shown by examples above.
3 (5-6 marks)	Detailed statements with clear explanations using geographical terms. Three developed or two well-developed points as shown by examples above.

4.4 Living with chronic water shortage

Section in brief

In this section students find out about chronic water shortage in the Sahel, and how climate change might affect water supplies in other parts of the world.

In the activities, students:

- explain what a graph shows about the amount of rainfall in the Sahel;
- order phrases to show how drought leads to soil erosion;
- explain how farmers can increase the risk of soil erosion;
- answer an exam-style question to explain how an unreliable water supply affects people in a vulnerable region.

Key ideas

- Worldwide, about 780 million people lack a reliable, sufficient, water supply.
- Rainfall in the Sahel is very variable in terms of the total amount, and length of the rainy season.
- Many countries in the Sahel have rapidly growing populations. Drought and water stress causes humanitarian crises.
- The World Bank estimates that by 2025, 50% of the world's population will face water shortages.
- Climate change and population growth will lead to increased water shortages.

Key vocabulary

nomads, subsistence farmers

Skills practised

Geographical skills: explaining a rainfall graph; ordering sentences about soil erosion; explaining impacts of unreliable water supply

PLTS: independent enquiry; creative thinking

Numeracy skills: graph analysis

Section outcomes

By the end of this section, most students should be able to:

- define or explain the terms given in 'Key vocabulary' above;
- interpret a rainfall graph for the Sahel;
- describe how overgrazing makes soil erosion worse;
- describe the impacts of climate change and population growth on future water supplies.

Ideas for a starter

1. If students completed the Further Activity from section 4.3 ask several to feedback what they found out to the class.
2. Show a map of the Sahel on the whiteboard. Ask: 'Who can tell me three facts about the Sahel? Who can tell me some more facts?' Annotate the map with these facts.

Ideas for plenaries

1. Use the two maps on page 65 of the students' book as the basis for a class discussion. How will we cope with the predicted water shortages in 2025?
2. Ask students to put themselves in the shoes of a subsistence farmer in the Sahel. How do they cope with drought and water stress? They should write a 100-word diary entry of a day in their life.

Further class and homework activity

Ask students to create a mind map around the phrase 'Water shortage'. They should use the ideas in this section to complete the mind map.

Water world

answers

1 Until 1970, rainfall was, with one exception, above average. Since 1970, rainfall has often been at least 10% below average, and in some cases up to 25% below average. As rain fails there is a fall in food supply and increasing desertification.

2 The correct order is: drought; grass dies; roots can't hold the soil together; wind blows; soil dries out; soil blows away.

3 As vegetation dies, farmers are forced to graze cattle on what little remains, and on more marginal land. Land becomes overgrazed leading to soil erosion and desertification.

---

4 Exam-style question *Using a named example, explain how an unreliable water supply affects people in a vulnerable region. (6 marks)*

This question is marked using levels. The key to this question is the command word 'explain' — which is a Higher Tier command word. Purely descriptive points by Higher Tier candidates get no marks. Foundation Tier students may answer the question:

Using examples, describe ways an unreliable water supply can affect people. (6 marks)

In this case, replace the term 'explanations' in the level descriptions below with 'descriptions'.

Cap students who do not provide a named example at the top of Level 2 (4 marks). Locations should be at the most at a national scale or river basin (i.e. naming a specific country) and not just 'Africa'. The question also asks for a vulnerable region, so this must be a qualifying factor in validating examples. Interpret 'vulnerable' broadly — it may be an area of drought, or one where vulnerability is brought by human causes e.g. poverty.

Students can get to 6 marks with either three developed or two well-developed points, provided that at least one example is located.

Correct points include:

- Drought causes seasonal rivers and water holes to dry up — developed with a consequence e.g. 'so the water table might fall'.
- Nomads lose grazing land for their animals / subsistence farmers suffer crop losses — developed with consequences e.g. 'which leads to loss of milk or meat from cattle', or well-developed e.g. 'which causes loss of income / poverty'.
- Drought can lead to overgrazing by animals — developed e.g. 'which causes soil erosion and desertification'.

Level	Descriptor
0	No rewardable content
1 (1-2 marks)	Simple or very basic description with little or no explanation, using little or no subject vocabulary. May be a list e.g. 'drought causes crops to fail'. (1 mark)
2 (3-4 marks)	Generalised explanation but with some use of geographical terms e.g. 'drought can cause crop failure which leads to loss of income for subsistence farmers'. Up to 2 developed statements as shown by examples above.
3 (5-6 marks)	Detailed statements with clear explanation using geographical terms e.g. 'drought can cause crop failure which leads to loss of income for subsistence farmers, or milk and meat from cattle, causing poverty'. Three developed or two well-developed explanations as shown by examples above.

4.5 Threats to water quality

Section in brief

In this section students explore the human threats to water quality. The worst sources of pollution are industrial pollution, sewage disposal and intensive agriculture.

In the activities, students:

- classify pollutants and identify the category with the worst impacts;
- draw a spider diagram to show why industries and farmers may resist laws to control and reduce pollution;
- explain why countries such as India and China do not have quality standards for drinking water;
- answer an exam-style question explaining how pollution threatens water quality.

Key ideas

- Water quality is as important as the quantity of water.
- The highest levels of water pollution are often found in countries with rapid rates of economic growth.
- Three main types of water pollution from industrial activity are chemicals, radioactive substances and thermal pollution.
- Sewage disposal in some of the world's rapidly growing cities results in the spread of disease, oxygen depletion, and suspended solids in the water.
- Intensive agriculture causes chemical and solid water pollution.

Key vocabulary

eutrophication, slurry

Skills practised

Geographical skills: classifying pollutants; interpreting graph showing levels of pollution and economic development

PLTS: independent enquiry; creative thinking

Section outcomes

By the end of this section, most students should be able to:

- define or explain the terms given in 'Key vocabulary' above;
- classify causes of pollution;
- describe the link between water pollution and economic growth;
- describe the problems that sewage disposal causes in cities which are growing rapidly;
- give two examples of water pollution caused by intensive agriculture;
- suggest why countries such as China and India do not have quality standards for drinking water.

Ideas for a starter

1. Use the graph on page 67 of the students' book to introduce the idea that the highest levels of water pollution are usually linked to rapid rates of economic growth.

2. Ask the students to look at the photo on page 67 of the students' book. Brainstorm the problems that the children in the photo face in terms of water quality and pollution. Create a spider diagram around the photo in response to students' suggestions.

Ideas for plenaries

1. Hold a class discussion. Ask students: 'Why do countries such as India and China put economic growth before environmental protection?' Students can then answer question 3 from the students' book following on from the discussion.

2. Create an acrostic with WATER QUALITY down one side of the page. Students have to make each letter the first letter of a word, phrase or sentence to do with water quality.

Further class and homework activity

Ask students how far they agree with the view that water quality is just as important as water quantity?

Water world

answers

1. **a** Students' tables could include:
   - **Industrial pollution:** construction; mine waste; industrial discharge; disposal of hazardous waste; deforestation.
   - **Sewage disposal:** sewage treatment plant; municipal sewage discharge.
   - **Intensive agriculture:** livestock waste (slurry); excessive fertiliser use; irrigation; crop spraying.
   - **Others:** salt runoff from roads; siltation in reservoirs; chemical application to parks, lawns and golf courses; landfill.

   b Industrial pollution has the worst impacts e.g. mining, production, waste disposal.

2. Students' spider diagrams could include:
   - Greater focus upon economic growth and industrial development, rather than environmental protection.
   - Increasing crop production may be considered more important than environmental protection.
   - Industrialists and farmers may not consider it their responsibility, or be unable to afford to, protect the environment.

3. Countries such as China and India, are industrialising and developing their energy sources rapidly often putting economic growth before environmental protection. Countries such as Japan had widespread pollution in the 1960s-1980s, but then introduced pollution laws. China and India may do the same in the future.

4. **Exam-style question** *Using examples, explain how pollution threatens water quality. (6 marks)*

   This question is marked using levels. The key to this question is the command word 'explain' — a Higher Tier command word. Purely descriptive points by Higher Tier candidates get no marks. Foundation Tier students may answer the alternative question:

   Describe three ways in which pollution threatens water quality.

   In this case, replace the term 'explanations' in the table below with 'descriptions'. You are looking for three developed statements – the completion of one takes a student to the top of Level 1, and so on.

   Cap students at the top of Level 2 (4 marks), if they do not provide precise examples. These may not be located e.g. industrialisation in developing countries. Cap any student who just lists examples of water pollution at the top of Level 1.

   Correct explanations include:
   - Sewage disposal e.g. the impact of organisms such as bacteria, viruses and river worms, or diseases such as cholera.
   - Industrial pollution e.g. the impacts of chemicals from plastics, oil, pesticides, and PCBs.
   - Intensive agriculture e.g. plant nutrients from fertilisers and eutrophication.

Level	Descriptor
0	No rewardable content
1 (1-2 marks)	Simple or very basic explanation using little or no subject vocabulary.
2 (3-4 marks)	Generalised explanations but with some use of geographical terms e.g. 'chemical pollution from industry can result in toxic chemicals like cyanide being released into rivers'. Up to two developed statements as shown by examples above.
3 (5-6 marks)	Detailed explanations using geographical terms e.g. 'chemical pollution from industry results in toxic chemicals e.g. cyanide being released into rivers which kills most river life and makes water unfit for consumption'. Three developed or two well-developed points as shown by examples above.

4.6 Interfering in the hydrological cycle

Section in brief

This section looks at some of the impacts of human interference on the hydrological cycle — including over-abstraction, reservoir building and deforestation.

In the activities, students:

- draw flow-diagrams to show the knock-on effects of different activities on the hydrological cycle;
- explain which activity has the worst effects on the hydrological cycle;
- answer an exam-style question to show how human activity can disrupt water quality and quantity.

Key ideas

- Some human interventions in the hydrological cycle have positive impacts; others have negative impacts on water supplies.
- Over-abstraction can lead to a drop in river levels, damage to ecosystems, and lowering of the water table.
- Catchment Abstraction Management Strategies (CAMS) are used to manage local water resources.
- Reservoirs can add new stores to the hydrological cycle, but can bring problems.
- Deforestation adversely affects the hydrological cycle.

Key vocabulary

biodiversity, Ramsar Sites, overabstraction

Skills practised

Geographical skills: creating flow diagrams of impacts of human activities

PLTS: independent enquiry

Literacy skills: writing a radio bulletin

Section outcomes

By the end of this section, most students should be able to:

- define or explain the terms given in 'Key vocabulary' above;
- draw flow diagrams to show how deforestation, urbanisation, dam building and over-abstraction affect the hydrological cycle;
- assess which activity has the worst effect on the hydrological cycle;
- give an example of a CAMS and describe how it works.

Ideas for a starter

1. Show a diagram of the hydrological cycle on the whiteboard. Brainstorm: 'How do we interfere with the hydrological cycle?' You are looking for ideas such as deforestation, urbanisation etc.
2. Show a photo of a reservoir, or a dam, on the whiteboard. Ask: 'What benefits can a reservoir provide? What problems can it bring?' Record responses as two separate spider diagrams.

Ideas for plenaries

1. Use questions 1 and 2 as plenaries. Divide the class into groups of four. Each student should be responsible for drawing one of the flow diagrams. The group then decides whether deforestation, urbanisation, dam building or over-abstraction has the worst effects.
2. In pairs, ask students to consider one way in which humans interfere with the hydrological cycle that has not been covered in this section.

Further class and homework activity

Ask students to write a two-minute radio bulletin about how humans interfere in the hydrological cycle.

Water world

answers

1 Flow-diagrams should include the following information.

Deforestation: Reduced evapotranspiration → leads to less rainfall and possible desertification; No interception → raindrop splash washes out finer particles leaving coarser, heavier soil → soil exposed to heat, making it impermeable → increased runoff and flood risk.

Urbanisation: Reduces evapotranspiration; Increase in impermeable surfaces → increased runoff and flood risk.

Dam building: Loss of land including villages and farmland; Drowned vegetation releases methane and carbon dioxide (greenhouse gases).

Over-abstraction: Drop in river flow → some tributaries dry up completely; Increased use of ground water supplies → drop in water table → damages river ecosystem.

2 Answers will vary.

3 Exam-style question *Using named examples, examine how human activities can disrupt water quantity and quality. (6 marks)*

This question is marked using levels. The key to this question is the command word 'explain' — a Higher Tier command word. Purely descriptive points by Higher Tier candidates get no marks. Foundation Tier students may answer the alternative question:

Describe two ways in which human activities can affect water quantity and quality.

In this case, replace the term 'explanations' in the level descriptions below with 'descriptions'.

Cap students at the top of Level 2 (4 marks), if they do not include:

- an example of a specific country or river basin,
- an explanation of *both* water quantity and water quality.

Correct points for **water quality** include:

- Reservoirs — with example e.g. Three Gorges Dam — developed with impacts which disrupt water quality e.g. on siltation; as a source of disease such as malaria; or on vegetation decay.
- Deforestation — with impact e.g. leaching nutrients into river; erosion of soil; leading to siltation.

Correct points for **water quantity** include:

- Over-abstraction — with example e.g. Thames Valley — developed with impacts on river flow e.g. tributary streams dry up — well-developed with causes e.g. rising demand from population growth.
- Deforestation — with example e.g. Amazon rainforest — developed with impacts on water cycle e.g. reduced evapotranspiration so reduced rainfall.
- Climate change — with example e.g. Lake Chad — developed with impacts e.g. lake drying up and reduced water quantity.

Level	Descriptor
0	No rewardable content
1 (1-2 marks)	Simple or very basic statements with little or no explanation, using little or no subject vocabulary.
2 (3-4 marks)	Generalised explanation but with some (not always fully explained) development and use of geographical terms e.g. 'deforestation can affect water quality because soil is eroded into rivers'. Up to 2 developed statements as shown by examples above.
3 (5-6 marks)	Detailed developed statements with clear explanations using geographical terms e.g. 'deforestation affects water quality when soil is eroded into rivers, creating cloudier water and siltation, which can reduce supply or HEP generation'. Three developed or two well-developed points as shown by examples above.

4.7 Solutions to the water crisis

Section in brief

In this section students evaluate large-scale solutions to managing water supplies. They look at the costs and benefits of big dams and investigate the Hoover Dam in the USA, and the South-to-North Water Diversion Project and Three Gorges Dam in China.

In the activities, students:

- complete a table to show the advantages and disadvantages of a big dam;
- explain how far big dams produce economic benefits, but also social and environmental problems;
- discuss as a class whether big dams are sustainable;
- answer an exam-style question to explain the costs and benefits of large-scale water management schemes.

Key ideas

- Large-scale water-management schemes often involve big dams, and are usually multi-purpose projects.
- Large-scale water-management schemes have many economic, social and environmental costs and benefits.
- Dams currently supply 40% of the world's irrigation water, 20% of the world's electricity, and 15% of all blue water.
- The Hoover Dam in the USA supplies water to 8 million people but has some serious problems.
- China has developed major schemes, such as the South-to-North Water Diversion Project and the Three Gorges Project.

Key vocabulary

blue water

Skills practised

Geographical skills: classifying advantages and disadvantages of dams

PLTS: independent enquiry; team-working; effective participation

Literacy skills: extended writing

Section outcomes

By the end of this section, most students should be able to:

- explain the term given in 'Key vocabulary' above;
- complete a table to show the social, environmental and economic benefits and problems of large dams;
- assess whether large dams are sustainable;
- use examples to explain the costs and benefits of large-scale water management schemes.

Ideas for a starter

1 Find newspaper articles about objections to dam building. Show these on the whiteboard. Ask: 'Why do people object to building dams when so many people lack access to clean water?'

2 Ask students, in pairs, to come up with words to do with managing water supplies.

Ideas for plenaries

1 Use question 3 from the students' book – the class discussion.

2 Choose several students (give them advance warning) to act as Chinese government ministers. They take 'hot seats' in front of the class. The class act as reporters and ask sensible questions about the reasons why China is embarking on the South-to-North Water Diversion Project and the impacts it will have.

Further class and homework activity

As a lead in to section 4.8 ask students to research an example of a small-scale project aimed at increasing water supplies in a developing country. They could try these websites:
www.practicalaction.org
www.wateraid.org.

Water world

answers

1.
   - **Social benefits** — increases water supply; scenic asset for recreational use; floods are controlled: **Social problems** — cultural resources submerged; millions of people forcibly relocated; loss of farmland and villages.
   - **Environmental benefits** — provides habitat for water birds: **Environmental problems** — destroys fisheries, wildlife and ecosystems; increases erosion downstream; can reduce river flow downstream.
   - **Economic benefits** — provides electricity (HEP) for industry and economic growth: **Economic problems** — huge costs of building dams; interferes with logging and navigation.

   2 and **3** Answers will vary.

4. **Exam-style question** *Using named examples, explain the costs and benefits of large scale water management schemes. (6 marks)*

   Purely descriptive points by Higher Tier candidates get no marks. Foundation Tier students may answer the alternative question:

   Using a named example, describe the costs and benefits of one large-scale water management scheme.

   In this case, replace the term 'explanations' in the level descriptions below with 'descriptions'.

   Cap answers at the top of Level 2 (4 marks) which do not include:

   - mention of specific location/s — examples should be at least at a river basin scale, or similar e.g. region, locality,
   - an explanation of both costs and benefits.

   Correct points for **costs** include:

   - Depletion of water / river discharge — with named example e.g. Hoover Dam — plus development e.g. Colorado River water now almost entirely used — and well-developed with impacts e.g. bird / fish species have declined in the Colorado estuary.
   - Environmental concerns — with named example e.g. South-to-North Water Diversion Project in China — plus a developed point e.g. the loss of ancient sites; displacement of people.
   - Over-abstraction — with named example e.g. Hoover Dam —plus a developed point e.g. water shortages.

   Correct points for **benefits** include:

   - Water diversion to areas of need with named example e.g. South-to-North Water Diversion Project in China — plus a developed point e.g. transfer water to the drier North China — and well-developed e.g. will divert 45 billion m^3 of water annually.
   - Creation of large reservoirs supplying water with named example e.g. Lake Mead — plus a developed point e.g. water supply for growing cities such as Las Vegas.

Level	Descriptor
0	No rewardable content
1 (1-2 marks)	Simple or very basic explanations using little or no subject vocabulary.
2 (3-4 marks)	Generalised explanations but with some development and use of geographical terms e.g. 'water diversion schemes in China have brought industry to dry areas for farming'. Up to 2 developed statements as shown by examples above.
3 (5-6 marks)	Detailed developed explanations using geographical terms e.g. 'The South-to-North water diversion schemes in China will bring industry and possibly agriculture to dry areas in northern China from wetter areas further south'. Three developed or two well-developed points as shown by examples above.

4.8 Sustainable supplies for developing countries

Section in brief

This section looks at small-scale sustainable solutions to managing water supplies. It investigates the work of non-governmental organisations (NGOs) in setting up low-cost projects using appropriate or intermediate technology.

In the activities, students:

- explain how a hand-dug well works;
- compare the advantages and disadvantages of hand-dug wells and big dams and decide which is more sustainable;
- suggest ways of reducing the amount of water used for different purposes;
- answer an exam-style question to explain how small-scale intermediate technology can improve water supplies.

Key ideas

- NGOs often develop small-scale sustainable solutions to problems of safe and reliable water supplies in developing countries.
- NGOs set up low-cost projects using appropriate or intermediate technology.
- Many NGO projects are in rural areas, but others have been developed to supply clean water in shanty towns in urban areas.
- Intermediate technology is often more sustainable than large-scale schemes.

Key vocabulary

Non-governmental organisations (NGOs), appropriate or intermediate technology, tube wells

Skills practised

Geographical skills: comparing advantages and disadvantages

PLTS: independent enquiry; creative thinking

Numeracy skills: adding percentages

Section outcomes

By the end of this section, most students should be able to:

- define or explain the terms given in 'Key vocabulary' above;
- describe how NGOs involve local communities in projects to develop safe and reliable water supplies;
- give one example of a small-scale sustainable project and explain how it can improve water supplies;
- describe how access to safe water improves people's lives;
- assess whether large-scale schemes or small-scale solutions are more sustainable.

Ideas for a starter

1 Recap section 4.7 – large-scale solutions to managing water supplies.

2 Ask the students to look at the diagram of the rainwater harvester and photo of the hand-dug well on page 72 of the students' book. Tell students that these are examples of small-scale solutions to managing water supplies. Ask students to describe how they differ from the large-scale schemes in section 4.7.

Ideas for plenaries

1 Use the 'What do you think?' on page 73 as the basis for a class discussion.

2 Use the idea in the 'On your planet' bubble on page 72 as the basis for a class discussion. What do students think of this type of idea? Has anyone bought this kind of 'present'?

Further class and homework activity

Ask students to make a set of revision notes about one example of a large-scale water management scheme from section 4.7 and one small-scale scheme from this section. They should make written notes, bullet points, a spider diagram, or whatever works best.

Water world

answers

1. Students' diagrams should be clear and simple.

2. a **Hand-dug wells:** *Benefits* — uses low cost, appropriate/intermediate technology; involves local people; people have easier access to safe, clean water. *Problems* — supply relatively small amounts of water for local community only.

   Big dams: *Benefits* — often multi-purpose i.e. they increase water supply, control flooding, supply energy, attract industry and are used for recreation; provides a habitat for water birds. *Problems* — millions of people removed from homes; cultural resources, farmland and villages submerged; fisheries, wildlife and ecosystems destroyed.

   b The hand-dug well is more sustainable — it benefits far fewer people, but creates fewer social and environmental problems.

3. a/b
   i Personal hygiene (shower, bath, wash basin, washing machine) = 40% — reduce baths and use shower instead.
   ii Sanitation (flushing toilet) = 35% — put a 'brick' in the toilet cistern to reduce water use.
   iii Food and cooking (kitchen sink, dishwasher) = 19% — only use dishwasher for full loads.
   iv Leisure (outside use) = 6% — collect rainwater in water butt or use 'grey' water for gardening.

4. **Exam-style question** *Using named examples, explain how small-scale intermediate technology can improve water supplies. (6 marks)*

   This question is marked using levels. Foundation Tier students may answer the alternative question:

   Using a named example, describe the use of intermediate technology in improving water supplies.

   In this case, replace the term 'explanations' in the level descriptions below with 'descriptions'.

   Cap answers at 4 marks which do not:
   - include a named country or region,
   - describe techniques e.g. 'rainwater harvesting' which improve water supplies.

   Suitable points include:
   - Rainwater harvesting — plus development e.g. 'rainwater is collected in tanks' — and well-developed with link to improving water supplies.
   - Developing gravity-fed piped schemes — plus development e.g. description of the process — and well-developed if the link is made to improving water supplies.
   - Building hand-dug or tube wells for villages — plus development e.g. 'obtained from hand-dug wells using buckets or hand/treadle pumps' — and well-developed if the link is made to improving supplies.

   Credit points which outline how the process of intermediate technology works e.g. cheapness and availability of local materials.

Level	Descriptor
0	No rewardable content
1 (1-2 marks)	Simple or very basic explanations using little or no subject vocabulary.
2 (3-4 marks)	Generalised explanations but with some development and use of geographical terms. Up to 2 developed statements as shown by examples above.
3 (5-6 marks)	Detailed and clear explanations using geographical terms e.g. 'simple rainwater tanks collect water from roofs which can be stored and kept clean for use in the dry season'. Three developed or two well-developed points as shown by examples above.

5 Coastal change and conflict

About the chapter
These are the key ideas behind the chapter.
- Rock type has a major influence on coastal erosional landforms.
- Rock structure influences the shape of the coast and can produce concordant and discordant coasts.
- Constructive waves build up beaches, destructive waves will erode beaches.
- Coastal deposition results in a range of landforms.
- Climate change is likely to result in rising sea levels, an increased flood risk and increased erosion on coastlines.
- Rapid coastal erosion poses a threat to many people.
- Traditional coastal management involves hard engineering, and has both costs and benefits.
- Coasts are now often managed in a more sustainable, holistic way using soft engineering.

Chapter outline
Use this outline to provide your students with a brief roadmap of the chapter.

5.1 Contrasting coasts
The coastal zone, and how rock type influences coastal landforms.

5.2 Geology at the coast
How rock structure influences the shape of the coast.

5.3 Waves
How waves form, and how different types of waves affect beaches.

5.4 Coastal deposition
How coastal processes can create depositional landforms.

5.5 Coastal flood risk
How climate change might increase the risk of erosion and flooding on coastlines.

5.6 Falling into the sea
Why coastal erosion rates vary, and the impacts that erosion has on people.

5.7 Managing the coast
What coastal management is, and looking at the traditional ways of protecting a coast from erosion and flooding.

5.8 Managing the modern way
How coasts are managed in a more holistic, sustainable way.

Coastal change and conflict

How is the specification covered?

This chapter covers Topic 5, Unit 1 Dynamic Planet.

5.1 How are different coastlines produced by physical processes?

5.2 Why does conflict occur on the coast and how can this be managed?

Key ideas	Detailed content	Pages in students' book
5.1a Geological structure and rock type have a major influence on coastal development and landforms.	Investigate the contrasts between a named soft rock coast and a named hard rock coast in terms of cliff profiles, cliff features and erosional landforms.	74-75
	Compare concordant and discordant coasts (headlands and bays), and assess the influence of rock type, joints and faults.	76-77
5.1b Marine processes, sub-aerial processes, mass movement, and climate change are also important.	Investigate how destructive waves, sub-aerial processes and mass movement create a range of erosional landforms including cliffs, wave-cut platforms, caves, arches and stacks and how constructive waves, deposition and longshore drift creates beaches, bars and spits.	78-79, 74-75, 80-81
	Explore the possible consequences of climate change on marine erosion and deposition including an increase frequency of storms and rising sea-level.	82-83
5.2a Physical processes lead to coastal change and retreat, which threatens people and property and generates conflicting views.	Investigate a coastline experiencing rapid coastal retreat, e.g. Holderness, to examine why rates of erosion vary and the threats posed to people and the environment by rapid erosion.	84-85
	Explore the conflicting views of how the case study coastal area should be managed.	86-87
5.2b There is a range of coastal management options from traditional hard engineering to more modern holistic approaches.	For a name coastline, investigate the costs and benefits of traditional hard engineering structures, including groynes and sea walls.	86-87
	Consider the costs and benefits of soft engineering, including beach replenishment and more radical approaches including 'do nothing' and 'strategic realignment' linked to Integrated Coastal Zone Management (ICZM).	88-89

Chapter outcomes

By the end of this chapter, students should be able to:

- Describe the three main types of coastal erosion, and how rock type influences coastal landforms.
- Give examples of concordant and discordant coasts and explain how rock structure has influenced the shape of the coast.
- Explain how waves form and the difference between constructive and destructive waves.
- Explain the process of longshore drift, and describe how coastal processes can create depositional landforms.
- Explain how rises in sea levels, an increased flood risk and increased erosion, could threaten people and the environment.
- Explain why people in vulnerable areas want sea defences to protect the coast.
- Examine the costs and benefits of hard engineering coastal defences.
- Use named examples to explain how coastal management decisions can cause conflict at the coast.

5.1 Contrasting coasts

Section in brief

This section is about the dynamic coastal zone, where land and sea are constantly changing. Erosion is one of the agents of change, and the extent of erosion will depend on the type of rock along the coast. Different coastal landforms are the result of erosion on different rock types, from soft sedimentary rocks to resistant igneous rocks.

In the activities, students:

- make a list of the advantages of living on the coast;
- explain erosion;
- consider the long-term effects of erosion on coastal landforms;
- answer an exam-style question to describe the difference between abrasion and attrition, and explain how cliffs are eroded.

Key ideas

- The coastal zone is a dynamic place which has many advantages for people.
- Some rocks are resistant to erosion, whereas others are more easily eroded.
- Erosion is the process of wearing away and breaking down rocks.
- There are three main types of erosion: abrasion, attrition and hydraulic action.
- Erosion produces characteristic landforms.

Key vocabulary

erosion, wave-cut notch, overhang, wave-cut platform, attrition, abrasion, hydraulic action

Skills practised

Geographical skills: photo analysis and diagram interpretation; explaining geographical terms

PLTS: reflective learning; creative thinking; independent enquiry

Literacy skills: writing an account

Section outcomes

By the end of this section, most students should be able to:

- define or explain the terms given in 'Key vocabulary' above;
- understand that rock type is the most important feature in determining the rate of change in the coastal zone;
- explain the different kinds of erosion;
- describe how erosion can create characteristic coastal landforms.

Ideas for a starter

1. On 6 May 2008, a landslip near Lyme Regis in Dorset caused 400 metres of cliff to collapse onto the beach. Show the BBC series 'Coast' (Series 3 Bournemouth to Plymouth) which looks at landslides in the Lyme Regis region.

2. Ask: 'Does anyone know a particular piece of coast well? Can you describe it?' If the school is on the coast, refer to familiar locations. What are the cliffs and beaches like? Are there significant landforms? How do students think these landforms might have formed?

Idea for a plenary

Ask students to imagine they were one of the two people stranded on the London Bridge Arch in Victoria, Australia, when it collapsed in 1990. Ask them to write an account of what happened and how they felt.

Further class and homework activity

Ask students to find an image of the UK coast which shows some of the landforms they have learned about in this section. They should annotate the image to show how they were formed.

Coastal change and conflict

answers

1. Answers should include: access to the sea for fish and other resources such as oil and gas; good access for trade and for connecting to other places; recreation and tourism opportunities.

2. Erosion is the process of wearing away and breaking down rocks. There are three main types of coastal erosion: hydraulic action, attrition and abrasion.

3.
   a. The large crack will have grown into a cave.
   b. The arch will probably have collapsed, forming a stack.
   c. The stump will have eroded further so that it is only visible at low tide, or is permanently under the water.

4.
   a. **Exam-style question** *Describe the difference between abrasion and attrition. (2 marks)*

   This question is point marked. Correct points, each for 1 mark are:
   - *Abrasion* — the physical process by which rock or sediment grinds down others.
   - *Attrition* — the overall reduction (or 'rounding') of sediment size over time.

   b. **Exam-style question** *Explain how cliffs are eroded. (6 marks)*

   This question is marked using levels. The key to this question is the command word 'explain' – which is a Higher Tier command word. Purely descriptive points by Higher Tier candidates get no marks. If you wish to differentiate, you can give Foundation Tier students the question:

   Describe ways in which cliffs are eroded.

   In this case, replace the term 'explanations' in the table below with 'descriptions'.

   Students can get to 6 marks with either three developed or two well-developed explanations. Correct explanations include:
   - Cliff-foot processes such as abrasion — plus development e.g. 'which involves stones or rocks being thrown at the base of the cliff' — or well-developed e.g. 'and which leads to under-cutting and collapse of the cliff'.
   - Similarly, hydraulic action — plus development e.g. 'which involves air becoming trapped in cliff cracks under pressure' — or well-developed e.g. 'so that small explosions are caused which shatter the rock'.
   - Consequences of these processes such as the continued undercutting of a cliff — plus development e.g. 'which leads to a wave-cut notch' — or well-developed e.g. 'which eventually leads to an overhang and collapse of the cliff'.

Level	Descriptor
0	No rewardable content
1 (1-2 marks)	Simple or very basic explanations using little or no subject vocabulary. May be a list e.g. 'The waves erode the cliff so it wears away'.
2 (3-4 marks)	Generalised explanations but with some use of geographical terms e.g. 'abrasion can lead to stones undercutting the cliff'. Up to two developed statements as shown by examples above.
3 (5-6 marks)	Detailed statements with clear explanations using geographical terms. e.g. 'abrasion can lead to stones undercutting the cliff, which leads to the formation of a wave-cut notch'. Three developed or two well-developed points as shown by examples above.

5.2 Geology at the coast

Section in brief

This section looks at rock structure and the way it influences the shape of the coast. It explains rock strata and describes the difference between concordant and discordant coasts, with examples from Dorset and south west Ireland. It explains how joints and faults in coastal rocks can influence erosion.

In the activities, students:

- draw a sketch of a photo and label it to show the different kinds of rock;
- draw a sequence of diagrams to show how the cliff developed;
- study a photo of Lulworth Cove and put a list of changes into the correct sequence;
- answer an exam-style question to explain the differences between concordant and discordant coasts.

Key ideas

- Rocks are generally found in layers, called strata, with some rocks more resistant than others.
- Rocks can be arranged in different ways to form concordant and discordant coasts.
- Concordant and discordant coasts produce different landforms.
- Erosion of concordant coasts can produce coves.
- Joints and faults are weaknesses which can be eroded.
- A discordant coast is characterised by headlands and bays.

Key vocabulary

concordant, discordant, cove

Skills practised

Geographical skills: photo analysis and interpretation; sketching and labelling a photo; drawing diagrams to show how a cliff developed; analysing a photo and ordering a sequence of events

Section outcomes

By the end of this section, most students should be able to:

- define or explain the terms given in 'Key vocabulary' above;
- explain the differences between concordant and discordant coasts;
- describe the formation of coves along concordant coasts;
- explain how joints and faults in coastal rocks can be eroded;
- recognise the distinctive pattern of headlands and bays that typifies a discordant coast.

Idea for a starter

Show a photo of Lulworth Cove on the whiteboard. Ask students to describe it. Explain that nearby there are examples of headlands and bays. Point out differences found on the coastline on a map.

Idea for a plenary

Tell students that in 2001, part of the Dorset and East Devon Coast was made into a World Heritage Site. It's known as the Jurassic Coast because it is geologically important. Other World Heritage Sites include the Grand Canyon in the USA. Do students think the Jurassic Coast qualifies for the same status?

Further class and homework activity

Ask students to research Lulworth Cove. It has one million visitors a year and sits on a large oil field. It is near an army training range and is a World Heritage Site, but is close to popular seaside resorts. Students should produce a conflict matrix showing the following groups and whether their interests conflict:

a Dorset tourist board,
b British Army,
c an oil company
d a local resident,
e a coastal walker.

Coastal change and conflict

answers

1 Sketches should show that sandstone and ironstone are the most resistant; coal and shale the least resistant.

2 The sequence could start with all strata in the cliff at the same level. The wave action could be shown eroding away the coal and shale strata, leaving sandstone and ironstone protruding.

3 The correct order of the bullet points is: cliffs of resistant limestone; erosion by the sea; forms a break in the cliff; cuts through resistant limestone; less resistant sand and clays are eroded; cove forms; sea reaches resistant chalk; sea can't erode resistant chalk so widens cove.

---

4 Exam-style question *Using named examples, explain the differences between concordant and discordant coasts. (8 marks)*

Like all questions requiring extended writing in the option topics for Higher Tier, this question carries 8 marks, and is marked using levels. Similar questions for Foundation Tier carry 6 marks.
The key to this question is the command word 'explain' — a Higher Tier command word. Purely descriptive points by Higher Tier candidates get no marks. Foundation Tier students may answer the alternative question:

Using examples, describe the landforms along a discordant coast. (6 marks)

In this case, replace the term 'explanations' in the level descriptions below with 'descriptions'.

Answers which do not include a named example should be capped at 6 marks (4 marks for Foundation Tier answers). Locations should be at the scale of a stretch of coast (i.e. naming a county, or bay, or region e.g. 'Jurassic Coast') and not just 'southern UK'.

The question asks for differences. Two separate descriptions, unconnected, are capped at the top of Level 2 (6 marks).

Correct explanations include:

- Concordant coasts – defined correctly as rock strata lying parallel to a coastline with named example e.g. Lulworth Cove — plus development e.g. 'which consists of resistant cliffs into which the sea has cut coves' — or well-developed e.g. 'caused by softer geology'.

- Discordant coasts — defined correctly as rock strata lying at right angles to a coastline — plus development e.g. 'which consists of resistant headlands and bays' — or well-developed e.g. 'caused by softer geology'.

- Causes — such as those involving weaknesses in the cliff along a concordant coast — plus development e.g. 'which are attacked by abrasion / hydraulic action' — or well-developed e.g. 'leading to rapid erosion of softer rock'.

Level	Descriptor
0	No rewardable content
1 (1-3 marks)	Simple or very basic un-developed statements using little or no subject vocabulary. May be a list or simple description e.g. 'this is where the sea erodes rock to form cliffs and headlands'.
2 (4-6 marks)	Generalised explanations but with some use of geographical terms e.g. 'rocks running parallel to a coast get eroded into coves by wave action'. Three developed statements are needed for the top of this level.
3 (7-8 marks)	Detailed statements with clear explanations using geographical terms. e.g. 'rock strata parallel to the coast are opened up by abrasion at weak points such as fault lines to become coves'. At least two well-developed explanations (plus one other developed explanation) are needed for the full 8 marks.

5.3 Waves

Section in brief

This section is about waves, how they form, how they affect the shape of a beach, and how they vary from summer to winter.

In the activities, students:

- measure the fetch of waves across the English Channel, the North Sea and the North Atlantic;
- explain which fetch will produce the biggest waves, and why;
- explain the different shapes of beaches in the summer and winter;
- answer an exam-style question to describe the differences between swash and backwash; and explain how beach formation can depend on different kinds of waves.

Key ideas

- Waves are caused by the friction of wind blowing across the surface of water.
- The size of waves is determined by the strength and duration of the wind, and the length of water across which it blows – its fetch.
- The shape of beaches is a result of how waves break on a beach.
- In summer, constructive, or spilling, waves result in a gently sloping beach profile.
- In winter, destructive, or plunging, waves result in a steep beach profile.

Key vocabulary

beach profile, fetch, swash, backwash, crest, trough, constructive waves, destructive waves

Skills practised

Geographical skills: understanding and interpreting diagrams; explaining how fetch affects size of waves; explaining beach profiles; explaining geographical terms

PLTS: independent enquiry

Section outcomes

By the end of this section, most students should be able to:

- define or explain the terms given in 'Key vocabulary' above;
- describe how waves form;
- explain how fetch can affect the size of waves;
- explain how constructive and destructive waves produce different beach profiles;
- recognise how dangerous plunging waves, and the resultant rip currents, can be for swimmers.

Ideas for a starter

1 Ask: 'Has anyone experienced difficulties from backwash, rip currents or steeply shelving beaches?' Explain that about 170 British holidaymakers die from drowning each year, many due to rip currents.

2 The biggest waves are found in the Southern Ocean at latitudes 40–60° south. These regions are the 'Roaring Forties' and the 'Furious Fifties', where strong winds always blow from west to east. Ask students to locate the region in their atlases. Ask: 'Why are waves so big in these regions?'

Ideas for plenaries

1 Use question 1 from page 79 of the students' book as a plenary activity. Ask: 'Which of the three fetches should be the best one for surfing?'

2 Wave power is a feasible source of renewable energy. If students have completed the Further activity, ask for their views on wave power. What are the advantages and disadvantages of wave power?

Further class and homework activity

Ask students to research the potential of wave power for generating electricity. Discuss, as a class, which type of wave power generation seems most promising.

Coastal change and conflict

answers

1 a about 40 km; about 600 km; about 2200 km

b The west coast of Scotland / **c** — it has the greatest fetch.

2 a The waves in the summer are small, with long wavelengths and low amplitude. They have a strong swash which transports sand up the beach depositing it to create a flat beach.

b The waves in the winter are taller (larger amplitude) and closer together (shorter wavelength). They have a strong backwash which erodes sand creating a steep beach profile.

---

3 a Exam-style question *Describe the difference between swash and backwash. (2 marks)*

This question is point marked. Correct points, each for 1 mark are:

- Swash — waves which advance (or break) up the beach / against the gradient.
- Backwash — waves as they retreat / run back down the beach.

b Exam-style question *Explain how beach formation can depend on different kinds of waves. (6 marks)*

This question is marked using levels. Foundation Tier students could answer the alternative question:

Describe the differences in beaches produced by constructive and destructive waves.

In this case, replace the term 'explanations' in the table below with 'descriptions'. You should ensure that differences are actually stated — cap any student who provides two separate accounts at the top of Level 2.

Correct points for *constructive waves* include:

- Long wavelength, low amplitude / spilling waves — plus development e.g. 'with a strong swash taking sand up the beach' — or well-developed e.g. 'which leads to increased deposition and beach development'.
- Description of beach linked to constructive waves e.g. gentle angle — plus development e.g. 'sloping gradually off-shore'.

Correct points for *destructive waves* include:

- Short wavelength, large amplitude waves — plus development e.g. 'with a strong backwash removing sand from the beach' — or well-developed e.g. 'which leads to beach erosion'.
- Description of beach linked to destructive waves e.g. steep angle — plus development e.g. 'sloping steeply off-shore' — or well developed e.g. 'with off-shore bars'.

Level	Descriptor
0	No rewardable content
1 (1-2 marks)	Simple or very basic un-developed statements using little or no subject vocabulary.
2 (3-4 marks)	Generalised explanations but with some use of geographical terms e.g. 'constructive waves are low waves which lead to deposition and create a beach'. Up to 2 developed statements as shown by examples above.
3 (5-6 marks)	Detailed statements with clear explanations using geographical terms. e.g. 'constructive waves are low amplitude waves which lead to increased deposition and over time develop a wider beach'. Three developed or two well-developed points as shown by examples above.

5.4 Coastal deposition

Section in brief

This section looks at how coastal processes can create depositional landforms. Beach sediment is transported along the coast by longshore drift. Where sediment is deposited, different kinds of landforms are created. Coastal vegetation, like marram grass, can stabilise depositional landforms such as sand dunes.

In the activities, students:

- explain why shingle is usually round;
- explain why spits do not grow right across the mouths of rivers;
- explain how vegetation stabilises depositional landforms at the coast;
- answer an exam-style question to explain the process of longshore drift.

Key ideas

- Beach sediment is the result of erosion by hydraulic action and abrasion.
- Sediment is transported along the coast by longshore drift.
- When sediment is trapped in a bay, it will form a beach.
- As sediment is transported along the coast, landforms are created where it is deposited.
- Vegetation, such as marram grass, can help to stabilise depositional landforms.

Key vocabulary

longshore drift, beach, sand dune, bar, lagoon, spit, recurved end

Skills practised

Geographical skills: interpreting and understanding diagrams; photograph analysis; explaining coastal processes

Section outcomes

By the end of this section, most students should be able to:

- define or explain the terms given in 'Key vocabulary' above;
- explain the process of longshore drift;
- describe how different depositional landforms are created;
- explain how vegetation stabilises depositional landforms at the coast.

Ideas for a starter

1 Use students' experiences of swimming in the sea to explain longshore drift. Students should appreciate how small particles of sediment can easily be swept along.

2 Show students photos of Chesil Beach. The size of the shingle varies from pea-sized at the north-west end, to potato-sized at the south-east end. Smugglers who landed on the beach at night could judge their position by the size of the shingle.

Idea for a plenary

Use the photos on page 81 of the students' book to check understanding of how the features have formed. The top photo shows Slapton Sands. Behind the bar is Slapton Ley National Nature Reserve. The lower photo shows Hurst Castle spit. Behind the spit is the Nature Reserve of the Keyhaven Marshes.

Further class and homework activity

Ask students to research a British depositional landform. Students should produce a poster describing where it is, how it was formed and any unusual features.

Coastal change and conflict

answers

1. Attrition makes sediment smaller and rounder.

2. The spit stops growing when deposition of sand is balanced by erosion from the river.

3. The long roots of the vegetation hold sand in place, and prevent or reduce movement. Marram grass is sometimes deliberately planted as part of coastal defence projects.

4. **Exam-style question** *Explain the process of longshore drift. You may use a diagram to help with your answer. (6 marks)*

   This question is marked using levels. The key to this question is the command word 'explain' – which is a Higher Tier command word. Purely descriptive points by Higher Tier candidates get no marks. Foundation Tier students may answer the alternative question:

   Describe the process of longshore drift. You may use a diagram to help with your answer.

   In this case, replace the term 'explanations' in the level descriptions below with 'descriptions'.

   Do encourage students to develop their skills in using diagrams, though it is not essential to use one for maximum marks. Artistic skill is not required – provided the diagram is clear enough, the labels gain credit. A student who provides only a labelled diagram can also get 6 marks; a separate written account is not needed.

   The skill here is in sequencing the processes. A written account will ideally be sequential – 'A leads to B', and so on – whereas a diagram will need several features to be identified for maximum marks.

   Correct points – written or labelled – include:

   - Waves approach the coast at an angle.
   - Swash runs up the beach at an angle – developed with consequence e.g. 'taking sediment up the beach'.
   - Backwash runs straight down the beach – developed with consequence e.g. 'taking sediment to a new position'.
   - Sediment therefore moves along the beach over time.

   Credit consequences e.g. spit development or sand growth against a feature such as a groyne.

Level	Descriptor
0	No rewardable content
1 (1-2 marks)	Simple or very basic statements using little or no subject vocabulary. May be a list e.g. 'this is where the sea takes sand up and down the beach'.
2 (3-4 marks)	Generalised explanations but with some use of geographical terms e.g. 'waves break at an angle, taking sand up the beach with them'. Up to two developed statements as shown by examples above.
3 (5-6 marks)	Detailed statements with clear explanations using geographical terms. e.g. 'prevailing winds bring waves which break at an angle, taking sand up the beach in the swash'. Three developed or two well-developed points as shown by examples above.

5.5 Coastal flood risk

Section in brief

This section investigates how climate change might increase the risk of erosion and flooding on coastlines. Many people are at risk from sea levels rising as a result of global warming. But the combination of high spring tides, storm surges and rising sea levels will put many more at risk. In the UK sea level rises may render existing sea defences useless.

In the activities, students:

- describe the estimated sea level rise by 2100;
- identify 10 major world cities under threat from rising sea levels;
- explain how a storm surge forms;
- answer an exam-style question to explain how sea level rise could threaten people and their property.

Key ideas

- Global warming may cause sea levels to rise by up to one metre by 2100.
- Many low-lying areas around the world are at risk from rising sea levels.
- A combination of spring tides, increased storm surges and rising sea levels will put more people at risk from flooding.
- Coastal erosion is likely to increase in future.
- Rising sea levels may render existing sea defences useless.

Key vocabulary

storm surge

Skills practised

Geographical skills: using an atlas to identify world cities; explaining formation of storm surges

PLTS: independent enquiry; creative thinking

Section outcomes

By the end of this section, most students should be able to:

- explain the term given in 'Key vocabulary' above;
- give examples of cities at risk from rising sea levels due to global warming;
- explain why storm surges are likely to increase;
- recognise that increased storm surges and high seas may speed up rates of coastal erosion.

Ideas for a starter

1. Discuss the fact that more than 50% of the world's population lives within 60 km of the coast. This could rise to 75% by 2020. Many of the world's poor are crowded into low-lying coastal areas, and vulnerable to rising sea levels. A sea level rise of 1 metre could be catastrophic.

2. Use news reports about Superstorm Sandy, and the size of the storm surge, which struck New York and New Jersey in October 2012, to introduce this section.

Idea for a plenary

Use question 2 from page 83 of the students' book. Ask students to identify their 10 cities.

Further class and homework activity

Ask students to research Venice, which floods regularly. They should find out why the city floods, and then decide whether it is more important to save cities such as Venice from rising sea levels, or small islands such as the Maldives.

Coastal change and conflict

answers

1. The estimates vary from 30cm to 1 metre.
2. Many major cities are vulnerable.
3. Storm surges are caused by falling air pressure (so are often associated with hurricanes and depressions, i.e. low-pressure weather systems). Sea level rises by 10mm for every 1 millibar drop in air pressure.

---

4. **Exam-style question** *Using examples, explain how sea level rise could threaten people and their property. (6 marks)*

   This question is marked using levels. The key to this question is the command word 'explain' – which is a Higher Tier command word. Remember, therefore, that purely descriptive points by Higher Tier candidates get no marks. Foundation Tier students may answer the alternative question:

   Using examples, describe the possible effects of a sea level rise along a stretch of coast.

   In this case, replace the term 'explanations' in the table below with 'descriptions'.

   As the question asks for examples, an explanation of the effects of sea level rise without naming a location is capped at the top of Level 2 (4 marks). Locations should be at the scale of a stretch of coast (i.e. naming a county, bay or region e.g. 'Jurassic Coast') and not just 'southern UK'.

   The question asks for people and property. Cap a response which covers only one of these at the top of Level 2 (4 marks).

   Correct explanations for **people** include:
   - The threat to settlements — plus development e.g. 'which could lead to people having to relocate' — or well-developed e.g. 'and which could lead to whole settlements being lost or abandoned'.
   - Increased cost of protecting a coastline — plus development e.g. 'because hard engineering may be the only way to protect a coast' — or well-developed with examples e.g. 'such as rip-rap or sea walls'.

   Correct explanations for **property** include:
   - Loss of coastal farm / urban / tourist property — plus development e.g. 'which could lead to a loss of farmland' — or well-developed e.g. 'and which might lead to reduced food production'.

Level	Descriptor
0	No rewardable content
1 (1-2 marks)	Simple or very basic statements using little or no subject vocabulary. May be a list e.g. 'rising sea level could threaten people's livelihoods'.
2 (3-4 marks)	Generalised explanations but with some use of geographical terms e.g. 'a rise in sea level could threaten coastal resorts and their hotels, leading to loss of income'. Up to two developed statements as shown by examples above.
3 (5-6 marks)	Detailed statements with clear explanations using geographical terms. e.g. 'a rise in sea level could threaten coastal resorts and their hotels, leading to loss of income and employment and forcing people to migrate elsewhere'. Three developed or two well-developed points as shown by examples above.

5.6 Falling into the sea

Section in brief

This section looks at why coastal erosion rates vary, and the impacts this has on people. It explains that cliffs collapse due to marine processes (erosion), sub-aerial processes (weathering and mass movement) and human action. Christchurch Bay is used as a case study of rapid coastal erosion.

In the activities, students:

- define the term mass movement;
- use a map of Christchurch Bay to describe the type of people who might live and work there;
- draw a spider diagram to show the factors that lead to cliff collapse;
- answer an exam-style question to describe the difference between weathering and erosion, and to explain why coastlines experience rapid erosion.

Key ideas

- Some coastlines in the UK are eroding very rapidly.
- Cliffs collapse as a result of marine processes, sub-aerial processes and human actions.
- The cliffs at Christchurch Bay are eroding by over 2 metres a year.
- Coastal erosion poses a threat to many people.

Key vocabulary

weathering, mass movement, sub-aerial processes, marine processes

Skills practised

Geographical skills: interpreting maps and diagrams; defining geographical terms; drawing a spider diagram to show why cliffs collapse

Section outcomes

By the end of this section, most students should be able to:

- define or explain the terms given in 'Key vocabulary' above;
- explain why some coastal areas of the UK are vulnerable to rapid coastal erosion whereas others hardly change;
- draw a spider diagram to show why cliffs collapse;
- list the types of people affected by coastal erosion;
- explain why people living in vulnerable areas want sea defences to protect the coast.

Ideas for a starter

1. Explain to students that coastal erosion has been going on since the last ice-age ended and sea levels rose as the ice melted. At Happisburgh, in Norfolk, it is estimated cliffs are being eroded at a rate of 8-10m a year. Ask: 'If possible, should we stop coastal erosion?'

2. Show students a photo of a house teetering on the edge of a collapsing cliff. Ask them to imagine that they live there. What could the next storm mean for the cliff and their home?

Ideas for plenaries

1. Show students a selection of images of coastal erosion at Barton-on-Sea. Ask students what they would want done if they lived in the area.

2. Use question 3 from page 85 of the students' book as a plenary. Ask students to compare spider diagrams. Which is the one avoidable factor in the causes of cliff collapse?

Further class and homework activity

Ask students to research a recent cliff collapse. They should explain where and when it happened, and the reasons for the collapse.

Coastal change and conflict

answers

1 Mass movement is the movement of materials downslope, such as rock falls, landslides or cliff collapse.

2 Retired people; owners of second homes; people running/working in hotels, B&Bs, guesthouses, tourist shops; farmers.

3 Students' spider diagrams should include hydraulic action and abrasion (marine processes); weathering and mass movement, rain water saturating permeable rock, eroding the cliff face and flowing through the rock (sub-aerial processes); and human action.

4 a Exam-style question *Describe the difference between weathering and erosion. (2 marks)*

This question is point marked. You can use this as a 2-mark question as shown; if you want to differentiate, you could ask for 4 marks – extension points are shown in italics below.

Correct points, each for 1 mark are:
- Weathering is the breakdown of rocks in situ / where the rock is — *this can be chemical or mechanical.*
- Erosion means is the process of wearing away and breaking down rocks — *this can be abrasion, attrition or hydraulic action.*

b Exam-style question *Using a named example, explain why coastlines experience rapid erosion. (6 marks)*

This question is marked using levels. The key to this question is the command word 'explain' – a Higher Tier command word. Purely descriptive points by Higher Tier candidates get no marks. Foundation Tier students could answer the alternative question:

Using a named example, describe the causes of rapid erosion along a stretch of coast.

In this case, replace the term 'explanations' in the level descriptions below with 'descriptions'.

Answers which do not include a named location should be capped at the top of Level 2 (6 marks). Locations should be at the scale of a stretch of coast i.e. naming a county, or bay, or region e.g. 'Holderness' — and not just 'northern UK'.

Correct explanations include:
- Weak geology — plus development e.g. 'such as boulder clay' — or well-developed e.g. 'which disintegrates easily when attacked by strong waves'.
- A narrow beach — plus development e.g. 'which means that waves can get to the base of a cliff' — or well-developed e.g. 'because none of the energy has been absorbed by friction with the beach'.
- A long fetch — plus development e.g. 'which leads to bigger waves attacking a coast' — or well-developed e.g. 'which means that cliffs can be under-cut easily and collapse'.

Level	Descriptor
0	No rewardable content
1 (1-2 marks)	Simple or very basic statements using little or no subject vocabulary. May be a list e.g. 'weak rocks can't stand up to wave energy'.
2 (3-4 marks)	Generalised explanations but with some use of geographical terms e.g. 'weak geology means that wave action is effective in eroding a cliff'. Up to two developed statements as shown by examples above.
3 (5-6 marks)	Detailed statements with clear explanations using geographical terms. e.g. 'weak geology such as boulder clay means that wave action is effective in eroding a cliff through processes such as abrasion'. Three developed or two well-developed points as shown by examples above.

5.7 Managing the coast

Section in brief

This section looks at what coastal management is and at the traditional approach to coastal management, which involves hard engineering — building structures such as sea walls and groynes. Hard engineering is costly and often unattractive. Whilst solving the problem of erosion in one place they can cause places elsewhere to suffer even greater erosion.

In the activities, students:

- list the various kinds of hard engineering sea defences, in order of cost;
- explain how building sea defences in one place can increase erosion elsewhere;
- answer an exam-style question to examine the costs and benefits of hard and soft engineering coastal defences.

Key ideas

- Coastal management consists of hard and soft engineering.
- Hard engineering is the traditional approach, but it is costly and can be unattractive.
- Several types of sea defences can be used together.
- Groynes help to 'grow' beaches. They are effective but can have negative impacts elsewhere.
- The advantages and disadvantages of hard engineering solutions can lead to conflict.

Key vocabulary

hard engineering, soft engineering, dissipate

Skills practised

Geographical skills: photo analysis; understanding tables of information; explaining how sea defences can increase erosion elsewhere; describing costs and benefits of hard and soft engineering defences

PLTS: independent enquiry

Numeracy skills: listing defences in order of cost

Section outcomes

By the end of this section, most students should be able to:

- define or explain the terms given in 'Key vocabulary' above;
- give examples of hard engineering defences and explain how they work;
- examine the costs and benefits of hard and soft coastal engineering defences;
- describe how groynes can create problems elsewhere.

Ideas for a starter

1. Show students a video clip of waves crashing over a sea wall. Explain that sea walls are just one method of protecting coasts from erosion. How many others can they think of?
2. Ask students; 'Does the beach at Hornsea (page 86) look attractive? What is unattractive about it?'

Ideas for plenaries

1. Look at the photo of Hornsea and ask students to work out the total cost of the different sea defences using the table on page 86. Distance of coast shown is 250 metres, including; rip-rap = 100 metres; sea wall with steps/bullnose = 150 metres; 8 groynes = 25 metres each. Can the class propose a cheaper, more attractive solution?
2. Ask students why people who live on eroding coasts often like hard engineering defences. Who might not be in favour of hard defences?

Further class and homework activity

Ask students to create a poster to show a range of hard engineering defences; including the advantages and disadvantages of each type and a photo from a named location for each.

Coastal change and conflict

answers

1 Sea wall with steps and bullnose; sea wall and groynes (same cost); revetments; rock armour (rip-rap); gabions.

2 Groynes stop longshore drift by trapping sediment preventing transportation and deposition further down the coast. Erosion therefore increases downdrift.

---

3 **Exam-style question** *Using named examples, examine the costs and benefits of hard and soft engineering coastal defences. (8 marks)*

The key to this question is the command word 'examine' – a Higher Tier command word. Purely descriptive points by Higher Tier candidates get no marks. Foundation Tier students may answer the alternative question:

Using examples, describe the benefits and problems brought by hard engineering methods of coastal protection. (for 6 marks)

Cap answers at 6 marks (4 marks for Foundation Tier) which do not include:

- a named example e.g. Jurassic Coast — not just Southern England,
- *both* costs and benefits, and have made a judgment about which of the two is stronger — even if their answer suggests that the two balance each other out.

Correct *costs* include:

- The actual cost of hard coastal protection such as sea walls or rip-rap — plus development e.g. 'which are expensive because of their costly materials and design' — or well-developed e.g. 'but which have the benefit of being very durable'.
- The actual cost of soft coastal protection such as beach nourishment — plus development e.g. 'in order to maintain beach width / reduce wave energy' — or well-developed e.g. 'which may not survive a winter storm'.

Correct *benefits* include:

- The benefits of protecting valuable economic land using hard defences — plus development e.g. 'such as sea walls which can enhance the attraction of a coastal resort' — or well-developed e.g. 'and which can therefore provide jobs and income from tourism to make up for the cost'.
- The benefits of using soft methods such as cliff planting or drainage — plus development e.g. 'which can stabilise cliffs using plant roots' — or well-developed e.g. 'enhancing the natural coastal environment'.

Level	Descriptor
0	No rewardable content
1 (1-3 marks)	Simple or very basic un-developed statements using little or no subject vocabulary. May be a list of defences, or simple statements e.g. 'it costs a lot to protect coasts and people might not think it's worth it'.
2 (4-6 marks)	Generalised statements but with some development and use of geographical terms e.g. 'sea walls are an effective way of protecting coasts and make resorts attractive to tourists'. Up to three developed statements as shown by examples above.
3 (7-8 marks)	Detailed, well developed, statements with clear explanations using geographical terms e.g. 'sea walls are an effective way of using hard engineering to protect coasts and although the most expensive method of protection, can increase jobs and income in resorts from tourists'. At least two well-developed explanations (plus one other developed explanation) are needed for full marks as shown by examples above.

5.8 Managing the modern way

Section in brief

This section looks at the modern way of managing the coast - Integrated Coastal Zone Management. ICZM is a form of holistic management, where soft and hard engineering solutions are applied along a stretch of coast so that solutions in one place will not have an adverse effect elsewhere. Soft engineering is gradually replacing hard engineering because it works with natural processes, and is cheaper and less intrusive.

In the activities, students:

- explain the meaning of 'holistic' coastal management;
- identify who pays for most sea defences;
- answer questions about defending the North Norfolk coastline;
- answer an exam-style question to explain how coastal management decisions can cause conflict.

Key ideas

- Integrated Coastal Zone Management takes into account the needs of different people, economic costs and benefits, and the environment.
- A Shoreline Management Plan is drawn up for long stretches of coast.
- Soft engineering works with natural processes.
- Holistic coastal management means that some places will not be protected from flooding and erosion.
- The UK faces difficult decisions about how best to protect the coast.

Key vocabulary

Integrated Coastal Zone Management (ICZM), Shoreline Management Plan (SMP)

Skills practised

Geographical skills: interpreting map and diagram; explaining how coastal management can lead to conflict

PLTS: independent enquiry

Section outcomes

By the end of this section, most students should be able to:

- define or explain the terms given in 'Key vocabulary' above;
- explain the meaning of holistic coastal management;
- understand the need to draw up a Shoreline Management Plan;
- explain how coastal management decisions can cause conflict.

Ideas for a starter

1. Recap hard engineering coastal defences from section 5.7.
2. Show students photos of stretches of the UK coastline – some of seaside resorts or other urban areas, and others of uninhabited stretches of coast. Ask: 'Should the entire coastline be protected from erosion? How should we decide which parts of the coast to protect?'

Ideas for plenaries

1. Ask students: 'How do you feel about letting nature take its course and leaving parts of our coast to erode naturally?'
2. Ask several students to take on the role of local council members. They will be in the 'hot seat'. The rest of the class can fire reasonable questions at them about the decision to do nothing to protect Happisburgh.

Further class and homework activity

Ask students to research Happisburgh and find out why it is being abandoned – they can use the website www.happisburgh.org.uk/. They should imagine they are a member of the Happisburgh Coastal Concern Action Group and write to the government explaining why they feel their village should be protected.

Coastal change and conflict

answers

1. 'Holistic' management means that a whole stretch of coast is taken into consideration, rather than just one place, e.g. Christchurch Bay rather than Barton-on-Sea.

2. Local Councils — with some money from Central Government or the Environment Agency if there is a flood risk.

3. **a** Some urban areas as well as farmland.

   b Residents in south Mundesley, Happisburgh and Walcott (in the long term) will be affected. These people may work in the towns, or at the gas terminal at Bacton. Farmers will also be affected.

   c Bacton gas terminal is being protected as it brings in vital energy, as well as providing employment.

   d Most inhabitants of villages on this coast will not be happy with the plan, except for the people of Mundesley who may benefit from increased tourism (long term) as the coast becomes a more natural environment.

4. **Exam-style question** *Using named examples, explain how coastal management decisions can lead to conflict at the coast. (6 marks)*

   This question is marked using levels. The key to this question is the command word 'explain' – a Higher Tier command word. Purely descriptive points by Higher Tier candidates get no marks. Foundation Tier students can answer the alternative question:

   Using examples, describe ways in which the decision to manage a coast can lead to conflict.

   Cap answers which do not include a named location, at the top of Level 2 (4 marks). One location is enough, provided that more than one conflict is referred to at this location. Locations should be at the scale of a stretch of coast (e.g. 'Holderness') and not just 'southern UK'.

   Suitable points could include:

   - A decision not to spend further money in protecting farmland along a stretch of coast using hard engineering — plus development e.g. 'such as rip-rap because of its cost' — or well-developed (e.g. 'which can't be justified because the cost would exceed the value of the land being saved'.

   - A decision to spend money in protecting one located stretch of coast rather than another — plus development e.g. 'because commercial property there is worth a lot' — or well-developed e.g. 'which means that residential areas may not be saved as housing is worth less, even though people live there'.

Level	Descriptor
0	No rewardable content
1 (1-2 marks)	Simple or very basic un-developed statements using little or no subject vocabulary e.g. 'it's not worth spending money on farms'. (1 mark).
2 (3-4 marks)	Generalised statements but with some development and use of geographical terms e.g. 'at Holderness there has been conflict over saving Hornsea instead of smaller villages because of the value of tourism there'. Up to two developed statements as shown by examples above.
3 (5-6 marks)	Detailed statements with clear explanations using geographical terms e.g. 'at Holderness there has been conflict about spending money on integrated hard management schemes such as sea walls which protect Hornsea instead of smaller villages, because they earn less from tourism'. Three developed or two well-developed points as shown by examples above.

6 River processes and pressures

About the chapter
These are the key ideas behind the chapter.
- The characteristics of rivers and valleys change from source to mouth.
- Rivers erode their channel in four main ways. River erosion results in characteristic landforms.
- Rivers transport their load in four main ways. Deposition of the load results in landform features.
- The processes of weathering and mass movement take place on the valley sides.
- Storm hydrographs – and how human activity can alter their shape and increase the flood risk.
- River flooding has natural causes, but can be made worse by human activity.
- River flooding has a range of social, economic and environmental impacts.
- Flood management involves both hard and soft engineering methods, which have costs and benefits.

Chapter outline
Use this outline to provide your students with a brief roadmap of the chapter.

6.1 River processes in the upper course
River processes in upland areas.

6.2 River valleys in the upper course
How rivers and their valleys develop in upland areas, and what causes this.

6.3 Rivers and valleys in the middle course
How both the river and its valley change in the middle course.

6.4 Rivers and valleys in the lower course
How both the river and its valley change in the lower course.

6.5 Why does flooding occur?
About storm hydrographs, and how they can help to explain the Sheffield floods.

6.6 Sheffield under water!
How sudden floods affected Sheffield in the summer of 2007.

6.7 Going under!
The impacts of Sheffield's floods in 2007.

6.8 How can flooding be prevented?
How Sheffield has attempted to manage flooding using hard engineering.

6.9 What about soft engineering?
Managing flooding with soft engineering.

River processes and pressures

How is the specification covered?

This chapter covers Topic 6, Unit 1 Dynamic Planet.

6.1 How do river systems develop?

6.2 Why do rivers flood and how can flooding be managed?

Key ideas	Detailed content	Pages in students' book
6.1a River systems develop characteristic landforms and channel shapes along their long profile, from source to mouth.	Explain landform contrasts between the upper courses, mid-courses and lower courses of rivers.	90-91, 92-93, 94-95, 96-97
	Investigate how channel shape and characteristics change along a long profile for a named river, including width, depth, velocity and gradient.	90-91, 94-95, 96-97
6.1b These characteristics result from processes of erosion, transport and deposition, with geology and slope processes also playing a role.	Investigate the role of erosion processes, transport and deposition in river landform formation including meanders, interlocking spurs, waterfalls, floodplains, levees and oxbow lakes.	90-91, 92-93, 94-95, 96-97
	Investigate the influence of geology and slope processes on river valley shape and sediment load.	92-93
6.2a River flooding has natural causes, but flooding may be made worse by human activities, including those causing climate change.	Investigate the factors that cause rivers to flood using hydrographs of two contrasting rivers, one with a short lag time and one with a long lag time.	98-99, 100-101
	Examine how human actions can alter hydrograph shape and increase flood risk through urbanisation and land use change, e.g. deforestation.	98-99
6.2b Flood management involves both traditional hard engineering and more modern, integrated and sustainable approaches.	Investigate the impacts of flooding and effectiveness of flood defences for a case study e.g. Carlisle (2004), York (2002) or River Severn (2007).	102-103, 104-105
	Compare one traditional hard engineering, flood-management scheme, e.g. York, with one soft engineering approach e.g. River Skerne, and assess their respective costs and benefits.	104-105, 106-107

Chapter outcomes

By the end of this chapter, students should be able to:

- Complete a table to show the changes to a river's characteristics, from source to mouth.
- Understand how rivers erode their channels, and draw diagrams to show how erosional landforms are formed.
- List the ways in which rivers transport their load.
- Describe how weathering and mass-movement affect the shape of the river valley.
- Explain how human activity can alter the shape of a hydrograph and increase the flood risk.
- Draw a diagram to show how physical factors led to flooding in Sheffield in 2007, and how human factors contributed to the flood event.
- Classify the effects of flooding as social, economic and environmental.
- Assess the success of Sheffield's hard flood defences, and explain why soft engineering methods are increasingly being used to manage flooding.

6.1 River processes in the upper course

Section in brief

In this section students learn about river processes in upland areas. It begins with the example of Buckden Beck – a small stream which flows into the River Wharfe. It explains how a river carries its load, how a river erodes its channel and how waterfalls are formed.

In the activities, students:

- identify the odd-one-out from terms included in this section;
- explain changes in a river during wet weather;
- answer an exam-style question to explain the processes that lead to the formation of a waterfall.

Key ideas

- A river's upper course has a steep gradient with small rapids and waterfalls.
- In a river's upper course water flows slowly as much of the river's energy is lost through friction with the bed.
- A river carries its load in four ways: in suspension; in solution; by saltation; and by traction.
- A river erodes its channel in four ways: by abrasion; attrition; hydraulic action; and solution.
- In a river's upper course, most erosion is vertical which can lead to the formation of waterfalls.

Key vocabulary

upper course, friction, erosion, channel, gradient, load, suspension, solution, saltation, traction, abrasion, attrition, hydraulic action, solution, waterfall, plunge pool, gorge

Skills practised

Geographical skills: explaining changes in a stream; drawing a diagram to explain how waterfalls form

Section outcomes

By the end of this section, most students should be able to:

- define or explain the terms given in 'Key vocabulary' above;
- explain the features of a river's upper course;
- explain how a river carries its load;
- explain how a river erodes its channel;
- draw and annotate diagrams to show how a waterfall forms.

Ideas for a starter

1. Ask: 'Which is the most important river in the UK? Which is the nearest river to you? What can you tell me about this river?'

2. Ask students to look at the photo of Buckden Beck on page 90 of the students' book, alongside a 1:50 000 OS map extract of the river's upper course. (You will need OS sheet 98). Ask students to describe the photo and describe what the map show about the river's upper course.

Ideas for plenaries

1. Have a quick-fire test to check understanding of key terms in this section. Call out a student's name and a definition e.g for erosion, load etc. The student has five seconds to give you the term.

2. Give students a photo of a waterfall. They have five minutes to sketch it and annotate it explaining how it was formed.

Further class and homework activity

Ask students to draw a cross-section of the upper course of a river from an OS map. Remind them to use the same vertical and horizontal scales.

River processes and pressures

answers

1 a and **b**

- Waterfalls — they are river features.
- Plunge pool — all the others are ways in which a river erodes.
- Gorge — Other terms are related to load and how the river carries its load.
- Hydraulic action — this is a method of erosion, the other terms are ways in which the river carries its load.

2
- Volume of water will increase: increasing the stream's energy.
- Increased energy will increase the stream's ability to erode.
- Less resistant rock is eroded more rapidly, undercutting the resistant rock above. The waterfall may move upstream, leaving a gorge.

3 Exam-style question *Explain the processes that lead to the formation of a waterfall. You may want to use a diagram to help with your answer.*
(6 marks)

This question is marked using levels. The key to this question is the command word 'explain' – a Higher Tier command word. Purely descriptive points by Higher Tier candidates get no marks. Foundation Tier students may answer the alternative question:

Describe the features of a waterfall. You may want to use a diagram to help with your answer.

In this case, replace the term 'explanations' in the level descriptions below with 'descriptions'.

Do encourage your students to develop their skills in using diagrams, though it is not essential to use one for maximum marks. The diagram should be clear with labels to gain credit. A student who provides only a labelled diagram can also get 6 marks; a separate written account is not needed. A written account will ideally be sequential — 'A leads to B', and so on — whereas a diagram will need several features to be explained for maximum marks.

Correct explanations include:

- Explanations focusing on the geology e.g. resistant rock strata — plus development e.g. 'which forms a cap over which the river falls' — or well-developed e.g. 'and which leads to more rapid erosion of weaker rock strata beneath'.
- Similarly, explanations focusing upon river processes e.g. the river's energy picking up stones — plus development e.g. 'which leads to abrasion' — or well-developed e.g. 'so that a plunge pool forms below the waterfall'.
- Consequences of these processes such as the continued undercutting of the waterfall — plus development e.g. 'which leads to collapse' — or well-developed e.g. 'and eventually leads to a steep-sided gorge as the waterfall retreats'.

Level	Descriptor
0	No rewardable content
1 (1-2 marks)	Simple or very basic explanations using little or no subject vocabulary. May be a list e.g. 'The river erodes the rocks under the waterfall'.
2 (3-4 marks)	Generalised explanations but with some use of geographical terms e.g. 'abrasion can lead to undercutting of weaker strata'. Up to two developed statements as shown by examples above.
3 (5-6 marks)	Detailed statements with clear explanations using geographical terms. e.g. 'abrasion can lead to undercutting of weaker strata, which leads to the eventual collapse of the waterfall'. Three developed or two well-developed points as shown by examples above.

6.2 River valleys in the upper course

Section in brief

This section looks at how rivers and their valleys develop in upland areas, and continues to use the example of Buckden Beck. It looks at the features of a river's upper course and the processes of weathering and mass movement.

In the activities, students:

- draw labelled diagrams to explain the features of a valley in the upper course of a river;
- answer an exam-style question to explain how mass movement and weathering affect the shape of river valleys.

Key ideas

- The valley in a river's upper course is V-shaped with interlocking spurs.
- Weathering and mass movement take place on the valley sides.
- Weathering is the physical breakdown, or chemical decay, of rocks exposed at the Earth's surface. It happens in situ.
- Mass movement is the movement of weathered material downhill.
- The valley shape is affected by: the speed of weathering; the speed of mass movement; how quickly a river can remove weathered material.

Key vocabulary

interlocking spurs, weathering (biological, physical and chemical), mass movement, rock outcrops, scree, landslides, soil creep

Skills practised

Geographical skills: drawing labelled diagrams; explaining processes

Section outcomes

By the end of this section, most students should be able to:

- define or explain the terms given in 'Key vocabulary' above;
- describe the shape of a valley in a river's upper course;
- draw diagrams to explain valley features;
- explain how mass movement and weathering affect valley shape.

Ideas for a starter

1. Ask students to look at the photo of Buckland Beck on page 92 of the students' book on. Ask: 'How would you describe the landscape? How are these features formed?'
2. Brainstorm the topic 'weathering'. Ask: 'What is weathering? What different types of weathering are there? What happens?'

Ideas for plenaries

1. Give students five minutes to write a paragraph on rivers in their upper course.
2. Make up 10 statements about rivers in their upper course - some true, some false. Students should hold up True or False cards in response to the statements. Where they are false, ask students to correct them.

Further class and homework activity

Tell students to make a table with these headings: 'Type of weathering', 'What happens'. They should then complete it using the information in this section.

River processes and pressures

answers

1. Students' diagrams should include these explanations:

   - *How scree is formed:* Scree forms as a result of physical weathering, which occurs when physical force breaks rock into pieces. In winter, cracks in the rock fill with rain. This freezes and expands, widening cracks so that more water gets in. This process is known as freeze-thaw. If repeated often enough, pieces of rock break away, and form scree.

   - *Why valley slopes get covered in scree:* Scree has broken away from the cliffs above because of weathering.

   - *Why hedges and stone walls can fall over:* Soil creep is a form of mass movement. Although it is slow (perhaps only 2 cm a year), soil creep can eventually cause hedges and walls to fall over.

   - *How trees can grow out of solid rock cliffs:* Small cracks in the rocks allow plant roots to penetrate in search of water and nutrients. They can grow into trees.

   - *Why stream beds contain large rock fragments:* Weathered material moves downslope as a result of mass movement. If a stream or river does not have enough energy to transport the material, it accumulates in the stream bed.

2. **Exam-style question** *Explain how mass movement and weathering affect the shape of river valleys. (6 marks)*

   This question is marked using levels. The key to this question is the command word 'explain' – a Higher Tier command word. Purely descriptive points by Higher Tier candidates get no marks. Foundation Tier students may answer the alternative question:

   Outline: i) one process of weathering and ii) one process of mass movement — on the sides of a river valley. (6 marks)

   In this case, replace the term 'explanations' in the level descriptions below with 'descriptions'.

   Cap answers at 4 marks which do not include explanations of *both* mass movement *and* weathering, *and* how these affect the shape of the river valley (Higher Tier only).

   Correct points for *mass movement* include:

   - Description of process e.g. slumping, rockfall, landslide — plus development e.g. an explanation of the processes leading to this — and link to valley shape e.g. 'which means that the upper slopes become more vertical' / 'the lower slopes become more gentle.

   Correct points for *weathering* include:

   - Description of process e.g. freeze-thaw, solution, biological processes — plus development e.g. an explanation of the processes leading to this — and link to valley shape e.g. 'which means that the upper slopes become more vertical' / 'the lower slopes become more gentle.

Level	Descriptor
0	No rewardable content
1 (1-2 marks)	Simple undeveloped or very basic statements using little or no subject vocabulary.
2 (3-4 marks)	Generalised explanations but with some use of geographical terms e.g. 'landslips occur when soil becomes saturated during prolonged wet spells'. Up to two developed statements as shown by examples above.
3 (5-6 marks)	Detailed statements with clear explanations, which make links to shape of the valley, using geographical terms. e.g. 'landslips occur on steep land when soil becomes saturated during prolonged wet spells, leading to deposition and a gentler slope in the valley bottom'. Three developed or two well-developed points as shown by examples above.

6.3 Rivers and valleys in the middle course

Section in brief

This section looks at how rivers and their valleys change from the upper to the middle course, using the River Wharfe downstream from Buckden Beck as the example. The river's energy and valley shape change, and meanders are a feature of the middle course.

In the activities, students:

- classify features by whether they are part of a river or valley in its middle course;
- draw and label a sketch of a photo of a river and its valley in the middle course;
- answer an exam-style question to explain the processes that lead to the formation of an ox-bow lake.

Key ideas

- In a river's middle course the increased discharge and velocity provides more energy, and it erodes laterally.
- In the middle course, valleys are U-shaped with a flat valley floor.
- When rivers flood, they create flood plains covered in fertile alluvium.
- Meanders are natural bends in the river.

Key vocabulary

middle course, discharge, velocity, meander, point bar, flood plain, U-shape, alluvium, helical flow, thalweg, river cliff, ox-bow lake.

Skills practised

Geographical skills: classifying river and valley features; drawing and labelling a sketch of a photo; drawing and labelling diagram to show formation of an ox-bow lake

Section outcomes

By the end of this section, most students should be able to:

- define or explain the terms given in 'Key vocabulary' above;
- understand why an increase in discharge and velocity provides more energy for lateral erosion;
- draw and label a sketch of a photo of a river and its valley in the middle course;
- draw diagrams to show the formation of an ox-bow lake.

Ideas for a starter

1 Ask students to look at the photo of the River Wharfe in its middle course on page 94 of the students' book. Ask them to describe the features they can see and suggest how they were formed.

2 Recap. Ask students: 'Where would you find a V-shaped valley and interlocking spurs? Who can tell me three types of weathering and two types of mass movement?'

Ideas for plenaries

1 Use question 2 from page 95 of the students' book as a plenary activity. Students should annotate a sketch of the photo on page 94.

2 Provide students with a suitable OS map. Ask them to identify the middle course of a river, and features typical of the middle course.

Further class and homework activity

Ask students to draw a cross-section of the middle course of a river from an OS map. They should add annotations to their cross-section.

River processes and pressures

answers

1 a River features: lateral erosion; thalweg; ox-bow lake; helical flow; point bar; meander; meander neck.

b Valley features: flood plain; alluvium; U-shape; river cliff.

2 Students should sketch from the photo on page 94 of the students' book. Sketches can be simple, as long as the features are clear and labelled correctly.

3 Exam-style question *Explain the processes that lead to the formation of an ox-bow lake. You may want to use a diagram to help with your answer. (6 marks)*

This question is marked using levels. The key to this question is the command word 'explain' – a Higher Tier command word. Purely descriptive points by Higher Tier candidates get no marks. Foundation Tier students may answer the alternative question:

Describe the stages in the formation of an ox-bow lake. You may want to use a diagram to help with your answer.

In this case, replace the term 'explanations' in the level descriptions below with 'descriptions'.

Do encourage your students to develop their skills in using diagrams, though it is not essential to use one for maximum marks. Artistic skill is not required – provided the diagram is clear enough, the labels gain credit. A student who provides only a labelled diagram can also get 6 marks; a separate written account is not needed.

Correct points – written or labelled – include:

- Water flows around the outer edge of a meander — with development e.g. 'leading to erosion of the outer part of the channel' — and well-developed if particular processes are named e.g. abrasion.

- Water is slower around the inside of a meander — with development e.g. 'leading to deposition of a slip-off slope on the inside of the channel'.

- Further erosion occurs flows around the outer edge of a meander — with development e.g. 'reducing the neck of the meander' — and well-developed if the effects are shown e.g. 'bringing the outer bends of a meander closer together'.

- Breakthrough of the neck occurs — with development e.g. 'leading to a shorter channel' — and well-developed if the effects are shown e.g. 'leaving the former meander as a lake'.

Level	Descriptor
0	No rewardable content
1 (1-2 marks)	Simple or very basic statements using little or no subject vocabulary. May be a list e.g. 'this is where the river flows fast and slow around a meander'.
2 (3-4 marks)	Generalised explanations but with some use of geographical terms e.g. 'the faster river flow around the outer edge of a meander causes erosion there'. Up to two developed statements as shown by examples above.
3 (5-6 marks)	Detailed statements with clear explanations using geographical terms. e.g. 'the thalweg around the outer edge of a meander causes abrasion, leading to a narrower neck in the meander'. Three developed or two well-developed points as shown by examples above.

6.4 Rivers and valleys in the lower course

Section in brief

In this section students learn about how both the river and its valley change in the lower course — characterised by a wide, flat flood plain. Where rivers meet the sea they form mudflats and salt marshes.

In the activities, students:

- complete a table to show how a river's characteristics change from the upper to lower course;
- describe what natural levees are, and explain how they form;
- answer an exam-style question to describe the difference between velocity and discharge, and explain how channel shape and characteristics change along a river's long profile.

Key ideas

- In its lower course a river is wide and deep with a wide, flat flood plain.
- Embankments called lévees, build up beside the river.
- Where the river meets the sea it can form an estuary, with mudflats and salt marshes — a valuable habitat for wildlife, but under threat from industry.
- As a river flows from its source to its mouth, there are changes in its long and cross profiles and in its characteristics.

Key vocabulary

levées, mudflats, bankful, salt marsh, long profile, cross profile

Skills practised

Geographical skills: explaining the formation of lévees; comparing the characteristics of rivers from source to mouth

PLTS: creative thinking; independent enquiry

Literacy skills: writing a report

Section outcomes

By the end of this section, most students should be able to:

- define or explain the terms given in 'Key vocabulary' above;
- describe the features formed where the river meets the sea;
- be aware that estuaries and salt marshes are under threat from industrial development;
- compare the characteristics of a river in its upper, middle and lower courses.

Ideas for a starter

1. Ask: 'What do you know about estuaries and salt marshes? Can you give me some examples?'
2. Show an OS map extract of a river estuary on the whiteboard, e.g. the River Tees. Ask students to describe the features they can see. How is the land used? Could this cause conflict?

Idea for a plenary

Divide the class into two groups. One group should represent environmentalists who want to protect salt marshes from development. The other group should represent industrialists who want to use them for industry. Hold a debate on whether the salt marshes should be developed or preserved. If you want to base this on a real example see the Further activity.

Further class and homework activity

Ask students to investigate the proposal to build a container port at Dibden Bay on Southampton Water, and write a report on their findings. They will need to find out: where Southampton Water is; why Associated British Ports want to build a container port at Dibden Bay; how people have reacted.

River processes and pressures

answers

1. Features which *increase* downstream:
   - River discharge — Streams and tributaries have added to the volume of water in the river.
   - Channel width — River erodes laterally.
   - Channel depth — River also erodes vertically.
   - Velocity — River channel is smoother.
   - Sediment load volume — The river has more energy so can carry a greater load.

   Features which *decrease* downstream:
   - Sediment particle size — Large boulders and rocks are carried in stream in its upper course during periods of wet weather.
   - Channel bed roughness — Larger stones dragged by traction smooth the channel bed.
   - Slope angle — River flowing over almost flat gradient by the time it reaches its lower course.

2. Natural levées are embankments which are found beside a river, formed when the river first floods. As a river reaches bankful (before it spills on to the flood plain) it deposits sand and clay particles where the flow is slower. These build up beside the river as a bank or lévee.

3. a **Exam-style question** *Describe the difference between velocity and discharge. (2 marks)*

   Velocity — speed of a river (1). Discharge is the volume of water in the river channel (1).

   b **Exam-style question** *Explain how channel shape and characteristics change along a river long profile (6 marks)*

   This question is marked using levels. Foundation Tier students may answer the alternative question:

   Describe, i) one change to channel shape and ii) one change to channel characteristics along a river long profile.

   Cap answers which do not include explanations of b*oth*, channel shape *and* characteristics, at the top of Level 2 (4 marks).

   Correct changes to *channel shape* include:
   - Change in cross-section shape e.g. from symmetrical to asymmetrical — plus development with explanation e.g. 'as the river begins to meander more downstream' — or well-developed with further explanation e.g. 'which results in the deepest part of the channel shifting to the outer edge of the bend'.

   Correct changes to *channel characteristics*:
   - Change in pathway from straighter channel in upper course — plus development e.g. 'where volume of water is low but friction high to meandering downstream, — plus development e.g. 'where helical flow causes the river to wind / meander'. Plus any other points from the Bradshaw model.

Level	Descriptor
0	No rewardable content
1 (1-2 marks)	Simple or very basic statements using little or no subject vocabulary.
2 (3-4 marks)	Generalised explanations but with some use of geographical terms e.g. 'the faster river flow around the outer edge of a meander causes the channel to become more asymmetric'. Up to two developed statements as shown by examples above.
3 (5-6 marks)	Detailed statements with clear explanations using geographical terms. e.g. 'the thalweg around the outer edge of a meander causes the river channel to become more and more asymmetric, as abrasion cuts into outer bank more'. Three developed or two well-developed points as shown by examples above.

6.5 Why does flooding occur?

Section in brief

This section looks at why flooding happens – how rain moves into the soil, and how water gets from the soil into rivers. Students learn about storm hydrographs and how human activity can influence the shape of a hydrograph.

In the activities, students:

- match terms to a diagram to show how water reaches a river;
- compare different hydrographs;
- explain how different factors affect the shape of a storm hydrograph;
- answer an exam-style question to describe the meaning of lag time and explain how human activity can increase flood risk.

Key ideas

- Rainfall is intercepted by vegetation.
- Some intercepted water is evaporated into the atmosphere, the rest soaks into the soil by the process of infiltration or flows overground as surface runoff.
- Infiltrated water seeps into the river through the soil (throughflow), or seeps into the solid rock and flows towards the river (groundwater flow).
- A storm hydrograph shows how a river changes as a result of rainfall.
- Different factors (including human activity) can influence the shape of the hydrograph.

Key vocabulary

interception zone, evaporation, infiltration, saturated, surface runoff, antecedent rainfall, permeable, impermeable, transpiration, throughflow, water table, ground water flow, storm hydrograph.

Skills practised

Geographical skills: interpreting storm hydrographs

PLTS: independent enquiry

Section outcomes

By the end of this section, most students should be able to:

- define or explain the terms given in 'Key vocabulary' above;
- list the factors which affect how quickly soil becomes saturated and surface runoff occurs;
- describe what happens to water once it enters the soil;
- explain lag times and peak discharges on different hydrographs;
- explain how human activity can increase the flood risk.

Ideas for a starter

1 Ask students to look at the storm hydrograph on page 99 of the students' book. Ask students what they think this is and why it is useful. Can they explain why hydrographs A and B are different shapes?

2 Write the key terms for this section, and their definitions, each on different sheets of paper. Distribute these around the class. Students take it in turns to hold up the key terms while others hold up the correct definitions.

Ideas for plenaries

1 Give students five minutes to prepare a short report for a local newspaper on how urban areas can increase the flood risk.

2 Ask students to prepare an odd-one-out for their partner using the key terms in this section.

Further class and homework activity

If urbanisation increases the flood risk, what can be done to reduce it? Students should list at least four things and explain their ideas.

River processes and pressures

answers

1 **A** interception zone; **B** infiltration; **C** transpiration; **D** evaporation; **E** throughflow; **F** surface run-off; **G** groundwater flow; **H** river channel.

2 *Hydrograph A* — short lag time i.e. water rapidly reaches the river, and as a result, it reaches peak discharge quickly.

Hydrograph B — long lag time i.e. rainfall takes longer to reach the river. Interception and infiltration of rainfall means that peak discharge is lower and occurs later than in hydrograph A.

3 *Previous rainfall* — soil may already be saturated. Shorter lag time / higher peak discharge.

Vegetation — increased interception and evapotranspiration. Longer lag time / lower peak discharge (less water due to evapotranspiration).

Permeable soil or rock type — absorbs rainfall easily. Longer lag time / lower peak discharge (as water moves more slowly as groundwater flow).

Impermeable soil or rock type — Shorter lag time (unable to infiltrate) / higher peak discharge (water reaches the river more quickly).

4 a **Exam-style question** *Describe what is meant by 'lag time' on a storm hydrograph. (1 mark)*

This question is point marked. The correct definition is: 'the difference between peak rainfall and peak discharge' (1).

b **Exam-style question** *Using examples, explain how human activity can increase flood risk. (6 marks)*

This question is marked using levels. The key to this question is the command word 'explain' — a Higher Tier command word. Purely descriptive points by Higher Tier candidates get no marks. Foundation Tier students may answer the alternative question:

Describe how two human activities can increase the risk of a river flooding.

Answers should be precise in terms of a land use change e.g. 'from farming to urban use' – not just 'building on land'. Examples need not be located.

Correct explanations include:

- Change from woodland to agriculture leads to removal of interception layer — plus development of impact e.g. 'which means that more water reaches the soil more quickly' — or well developed with effect on river e.g. 'which leads to more rapid saturation and surface run-off which increases the flood risk'.

- Change from agricultural to urban land use leads to reduced infiltration — plus development of cause e.g. 'which is caused by greater impermeable surfaces such as concrete' — or well developed with effect on river e.g. 'which leads to rapid run-off via drains into a river and increases the flood risk'.

Level	Descriptor
0	No rewardable content
1 (1-2 marks)	Simple or very basic statements using little or no subject vocabulary. May be a list e.g. 'the river floods more in urban areas'.
2 (3-4 marks)	Generalised explanations but with some use of geographical terms e.g. 'the change from forest to agriculture means lower interception rates and faster saturation of the soil'. Up to two developed statements as shown by examples above.
3 (5-6 marks)	Detailed statements with clear explanations using geographical terms. e.g. 'the change from forest to agriculture means lower interception rates and increased infiltration, which means faster saturation and run-off, leading to a greater flood risk'. Three developed or two well-developed points as shown by examples above.

6.6 Sheffield under water!

Section in brief

This section looks at the floods that affected Sheffield in the summer of 2007. That year saw the wettest May to July period since 1766 when reliable data were first collected. The causes of the Sheffield floods were: prolonged rain; soil saturation; the confluence of several rivers and the physical landscape around Sheffield.

In the activities, students:

- label a hydrograph to show why flooding occurred in Sheffield;
- complete a spider diagram to show how various factors helped to produce Sheffield's floods;
- answer an exam-style question to explain the factors that contributed to a flood event on a named river.

Key ideas

- In summer 2007 several periods of extreme rainfall gave rise to widespread flooding in parts of England and Wales.
- The Sheffield floods were the result of:
  - prolonged rain — June was the wettest month in Yorkshire since 1882;
  - soil saturation — caused localised flooding and surface runoff;
  - the confluence of several rivers — increased the volume of water downstream and caused water to back up and overflow the banks.
  - the physical landscape.

Key vocabulary

saturated, surface runoff

Skills practised

Geographical skills: labelling a hydrograph to show why flooding occurred; identifying how physical and human factors helped to cause the Sheffield flood

Literacy skills: writing a diary entry

Section outcomes

By the end of this section, most students should be able to:

- define the terms given in 'Key vocabulary' above;
- label a hydrograph to show why flooding occurred;
- explain how physical factors helped to cause the Sheffield floods;
- show how human factors helped to cause the floods.

Ideas for a starter

1. Read the newspaper extract on page 100 of the students' book aloud to the class to set the scene.
2. Show students a video clip of a major river flood event from the UK, so that they can grasp how high and fast rivers in flood can flow, and how destructive floods can be.

Ideas for a plenary

Ask students to imagine they are one of the residents of the villages near Rotherham who were forced to leave their homes in case the nearby Ulley Dam collapsed. Ask them to write a 100 word diary entry of the flood event.

Further class and homework activity

Use the Environment Agency website www.environment-agency.gov.uk/ to find out if your area is at risk from flooding. Follow the links for: Flood; Am I at risk of river and sea flooding? Enter your postcode to find a flood map of your area. Identify the risks of flooding in your area and any existing flood defences.

River processes and pressures

answers

1 Labels should relate to the amount of rain which fell (and the period of time it fell in), and how the rivers responded to the rainfall, to explain why the flood occurred.

2 a and **b**

Students' spider diagrams should include:

Prolonged rain — rain fell across South Yorkshire, due to a depression over northern England; June was the wettest month in Yorkshire since 1882.

Soil saturation — saturated soil caused localised flooding (rapid run-off); extreme rainfall overwhelmed rivers and drains.

Confluence of rivers — confluence of the rivers near Hillsborough caused an increase in the volume of water; water backed up in rivers and overflowed the banks.

The physical landscape — Sheffield lies at the foot of the Pennines, where three rivers meet; steep slopes exacerbated run-off.

Human factors — Sheffield was built on the flood plain of the River Don; storage reservoirs and drains were not large enough to cope; bridges restricted river flow.

---

3 Exam-style question *Using an example, explain the factors that contributed to a flood event on a named river. (8 marks)*

This question is marked using levels. The key to this question is the command word 'explain' – a Higher Tier command word. Purely descriptive points by Higher Tier candidates get no marks. Foundation Tier students may answer the alternative question:

Using a named example, describe the causes of one flood that you have studied. (6 marks)

In this case, three developed or two well-developed descriptions are required for 6 marks.

Cap answers which do not include a specific flood, or named location, at 6 marks (4 marks for the Foundation question). Locations should be at the scale of a stretch of river or place e.g. 'Sheffield' or 'River Don', and not just 'in Yorkshire'. Ideally, a date should be given as well.

Correct factors include:

- Intense / prolonged rainfall — plus development with cause e.g. 'a depression over northern England'— well-developed with impacts e.g. 'causing rapid run-off into the city drains which were unable to cope, and over-flowed'.

- River confluence — plus development with details e.g. 'where the rivers Don, Rivelin and Loxley met' — well-developed with impacts e.g. 'causing a back-log of water which was unable to escape, and over-flowed into surrounding residential areas'.

Level	Descriptor
0	No rewardable content
1 (1-3 marks)	Simple or very basic statements using little or no subject vocabulary. May be a list e.g. 'the river flooded in Yorkshire after heavy rain'.
2 (4-6 marks)	Generalised explanations but with some use of geographical terms e.g. 'the rapid run-off of heavy rain caused drains to fill up and over-flow quickly, causing flooding'. Up to three developed statements as shown by examples above.
3 (7-8 marks)	Detailed statements with clear explanations using geographical terms. e.g. 'the rapid run-off, of the heaviest June rain in over a century, caused drains to fill up and over-flow quickly, causing flash flooding'. At least two well-developed points (plus one other developed point) are required for the top of Level 3 as shown by examples above.

6.7 Going under!

Section in brief
This section looks at the devastating impact of the 2007 floods on people working and living in Sheffield. It investigates the impacts of the flooding in four different areas. The flooding was caused by extreme rainfall events which overwhelmed Sheffield's drains, river channels and flood defences.

In the activities, students:
- classify the effects of flooding;
- identify which were the greatest effects;
- answer an exam-style question to examine the impacts of flooding on people and the environment.

Key ideas
- Most of Sheffield's flooding was caused by drains, river channels and flood defences being overwhelmed by extreme rainfall.
- The floods had a devastating impact on people in, and around, Sheffield:
  - two people drowned
  - over 1200 homes were flooded
  - more than 1000 businesses were affected
  - roads were damaged
  - 13 000 people were without power for two days
  - there were fears that the Ulley Dam might collapse.

Key vocabulary
There is no key vocabulary in this section.

Skills practised
Geographical skills: classifying effects of flooding; identifying greatest effects; examining impacts of flooding on people and environment

Section outcomes
By the end of this section, most students should be able to:
- classify the effects of flooding as social, economic, environmental and short, medium and long term;
- identify the greatest effects.

Ideas for a starter
1. Ask students to look at the three photos on pages 102 and 103 of the students' book, along with the photo of the remains of Club Mill Bridge on page 100. Ask students to describe the impacts of the floods from the photos.
2. Ask students to look at the map on page 102 of the students' book, alongside an OS map extract of Sheffield. Recap page 101 – the physical landscape. Ask students to describe the river systems and the topography. Are they surprised that the city flooded?

Ideas for plenaries
1. Meadowhall Shopping Centre's flood defences failed. Why? Discuss as a class.
2. Ask students to work in pairs to write a two minute radio broadcast on the impacts of flooding on Sheffield and South Yorkshire.

Further class and homework activity
Ask students to make a set of revision notes about the 2007 Sheffield floods. They should include the causes of the floods, and the impacts of the flooding.

River processes and pressures

answers

1 The answer below shows the effects of the flooding in just one area: *Hillsborough and north-west Sheffield*.

- Social — *Short-term*: 43% of homes on one estate flooded; health risks from sewage escaped into floodwater. *Medium-term*: Council tenants returned home within 9 months; displaced people suffered stress; some families moved into caravans for the winter. *Long-term*: Some owner-occupiers had to wait longer before they could return home.
- Economic — *Medium-term*: It cost millions of pounds to repair the damage to Hillsborough Football Stadium.
- Environmental — *Short-term*: Raw sewage escaped into the floodwater.

2 Social effects were the greatest, although millions of pounds worth of damage (economic effects) also resulted.

3 **Exam-style question** *Using named examples, examine the impacts of flooding on people and the environment. (8 marks)*

This question is marked using levels. The key to this question is the command word 'explain' — a Higher Tier command word. Purely descriptive points by Higher Tier candidates get no marks. Foundation Tier students may answer the alternative question:

Using a named example, describe the impacts of a flood that you have studied. (6 marks)

In this case, three developed or two well-developed descriptions are required for 6 marks.

Cap answers at 6 marks (4 marks for the Foundation Tier question) which do not include:

- a located flood — locations should be at the scale of a stretch of river or place e.g. 'Sheffield' or 'River Don', and not just 'in Yorkshire'. Ideally, a date should be given as well;
- the impacts of flooding on people *and* the environment.

Correct impacts for *people* include:

- Threat to human life — plus development e.g. 'because of the suddenness of flash-floods' — well-developed with impacts e.g. 'caused by the rapid run-off into drains which over-flowed in a matter of minutes, trapping people'.
- Flooded housing — plus development e.g. 'which meant loss of personal possessions', or with data e.g. '1200 homes were flooded in Sheffield' — well-developed with impacts e.g. 'resulting in people having to be re-housed for several months'.

Correct impacts for the *environment* include:

- Damage to reservoirs — plus development e.g. 'the Ulley Reservoir near Rotherham', or with data e.g. 'meaning the valley bottom and areas of housing were flooded in Whiston' — with well-developed impacts e.g. 'causing the closure of the M1 motorway because of the threat of the dam bursting'.

Level	Descriptor
0	No rewardable content
1 (1-3 marks)	Simple or very basic statements using little or no subject vocabulary. May be a list e.g. 'two people died in Yorkshire in floods'.
2 (4-6 marks)	Generalised explanations but with some use of geographical terms e.g. 'the rapid run-off of heavy rain caused drains to fill up and over-flow quickly, drowning two people'. Up to three developed statements as shown by examples above.
3 (7-8 marks)	Detailed statements with clear explanations using geographical terms. e.g. 'the Ulley reservoir was damaged by intense rainfall, which threatened local settlements such as Whiston, and closed the M1 motorway'. At least two well-developed points (plus one other developed point) are required for the top of Level 3 as shown by examples above.

6.8 How can flooding be prevented?

Section in brief

This section looks at hard engineering solutions to flooding in Sheffield, and how effective they were. There are only a few hard engineering defences in Sheffield — consisting of drains and culverts, and storage reservoirs east of the city. The River Sheaf and the Meadowhall Shopping Centre also have hard defences.

In the activities, students:

- complete a table of the costs and benefits of hard flood protection;
- answer an exam-style question to describe what is meant by hard engineering and explain the costs and benefits of using hard engineering to reduce flood risk.

Key ideas

- Hard engineering solutions are structures built to defend places from flooding.
- Soft engineering solutions adapt to the flood risk and allow natural processes to deal with rainwater.
- Hard defences in Sheffield consist of:
  – drains and culverts;
  – storage reservoirs east of the city;
  – the River Sheaf and Meadowhall Shopping Centre have hard defences.
- Hard engineering solutions have costs and benefits.

Key vocabulary

hard engineering

Skills practised

Geographical skills: explaining the key term; explaining costs and benefits of hard engineering methods

PLTS: team-working; independent enquiry

Section outcomes

By the end of this section, most students should be able to:

- define the term given in 'Key vocabulary' above;
- assess the success of Sheffield's hard defences in 2007;
- complete a table to show the costs and benefits of hard flood protection, and decide which is best.

Ideas for a starter

1. How can we protect places from flooding? Ask: 'Who can come up with five different ways?'
2. If your school is in an area at risk from flooding, ask students to recall any flood events. What flood protection measures are in place already? Are any further flood defences planned as a result of previous floods?

Ideas for plenaries

1. Use the views outlined in the 'What do you think?' on page 104 of the students' book as the basis for a class discussion. Is the Environment Agency right?
2. Write 'Hard engineering' in the middle of the board. Create a mind map around the phrase. How many ideas can students come up with in two minutes?

Further class and homework activity

As a lead in to section 6.9, ask students to find out about different methods of soft engineering related to river flooding. They should describe how two methods work, and their advantages and disadvantages.

River processes and pressures

answers

1 Method of 'hard' protection:
- **Build flood banks** — Costs: increase flood risk downstream — Benefits: fairly cheap to build; increase a river's capacity.
- **Increase size of river channel** — Costs: dredging needs to be done every year; lining with concrete is expensive; increases flood risk downstream — Benefits: speeds up flow of water away from area at risk.
- **Divert river away from city centre** — Costs: very expensive (£14 million for 1km); could cause flooding elsewhere — Benefits: avoids flooding in city centre.
- **Increase size of drains** — Costs: disrupts city whilst being built — Benefits: takes runoff away from city quickly.

2 a **Exam-style question** *Describe what is meant by 'hard engineering' solutions to flooding. (2 marks)*

Correct points are:

'Hard' solutions are structures built to defend areas from flooding (1) — plus additional mark for example e.g. building culverts (1) or flood embankments (1).

b **Exam-style question** *Explain the costs and benefits of using hard engineering to reduce flood risk. (6 marks)*

This question is marked using levels. The key to this question is the command word 'explain' – a Higher Tier command word. Purely descriptive points by Higher Tier candidates get no marks. Foundation Tier students may answer the alternative question: *Describe the costs and benefits of one hard engineering flood management project.*

In this case, replace the term 'explanations' in the level descriptions below with 'descriptions'. Cap answers at 4 marks if both costs *and* benefits are not included.

Suitable *costs* could include:
- High financial cost of some methods — plus development using a described example e.g. 'increasing the size of river channel and lining it with concrete' — well-developed with explanation e.g. 'which is expensive because river sediment can damage it, meaning it has to be repeated each year'.

Suitable *benefits* could include:
- Increasing the size of river channel, which increases the river's capacity before it floods — plus development e.g. 'which means less frequent and less damaging floods' — well-developed with impacts e.g. 'which means that although it is expensive it saves a lot of the costs of a flood, such as re-housing people'.

Level	Descriptor
0	No rewardable content
1 (1-2 marks)	Simple or very basic statements using little or no subject vocabulary e.g. 'there are lots of methods that prevent flooding like flood walls'. (1 mark).
2 (3-4 marks)	Generalised explanations but with some development and use of geographical terms e.g. 'increasing the capacity of a river channel could mean it takes longer before a river floods'. Up to two developed statements as shown by examples above.
3 (5-6 marks)	Detailed statements with clear explanations using geographical terms e.g. 'increasing the size of a river channel and lining it with concrete could speed a river up because there is less friction and its capacity is increased, meaning that it takes longer before flooding occurs'. Three developed or two well-developed points as shown by examples above.

6.9 What about soft engineering?

Section in brief

In this section students learn about soft engineering methods of flood management, including a case study of sustainable management along the River Skerne in Darlington.

In the activities, students:

- label a hydrograph;
- complete a table of the costs and benefits of soft flood protection, and compare them with those for hard engineering;
- answer an exam-style question to explain what is meant by soft engineering and why soft engineering methods are being increasingly used to manage flooding.

Key ideas

- Following the 2007 floods, the Environment Agency decided that soft engineering methods would make flood management more sustainable in Sheffield.
- Soft engineering methods have costs and benefits.
- Alterations to the River Skerne in Darlington in the nineteenth century increased the flood risk.
- The Environment Agency restored 2km of the river – reconstructing meanders, lowering river banks, planting trees and lowering the flood plain.

Key vocabulary

soft engineering

Skills practised

Geographical skills: explaining key term; identifying costs and benefits of soft engineering methods; explaining why soft engineering methods are increasingly used

PLTS: independent enquiry; team-working

Section outcomes

By the end of this section, most students should be able to:

- define the term given in 'Key vocabulary' above;
- complete a table to show the costs and benefits of soft engineering methods;
- decide which flood management strategies have greatest costs and benefits;
- explain why soft engineering methods, such as those made to the River Skerne are increasingly being used to manage flooding.

Ideas for a starter

1 If any students completed the 'Further activity' in section 6.8, ask a number of them to feed back their findings to the class. Record what they found out as a table.

2 Show photos of a variety of flood management methods – some obvious such as flood banks and storage reservoirs – others less so, such as areas of trees, industry/leisure centres built close to rivers. Ask students which are 'hard' methods? How would they describe the others?

Ideas for plenaries

1 In pairs, students should write two paragraphs (one each) on how flooding can be prevented.

2 Create an acrostic. Ask students to write FLOOD MANAGEMENT down one side of the page. They should make each letter the first letter of a word, phrase, or sentence about flooding and flood management.

Further class and homework activity

Students should continue the revision notes on the 2007 Sheffield floods, begun in section 6.7. They should include hard engineering in Sheffield, and the soft engineering methods which could be used to make flood management more sustainable.

River processes and pressures

answers

1 b Hydrograph B is more desirable than Hydrograph A, as the river has a longer lag time, and peak discharge is lower. The flood risk is therefore greatly reduced.

2 a Methods of 'soft' protection:

Flood abatement — Benefits: changing land-use upstream e.g. planting trees reduces peak discharge and delays lag time.

Flood proofing — Costs: expensive to alter existing buildings — Benefits: effective for new builds.

Flood plain zoning — Benefits: fewer people affected by flooding.

Flood prediction and warning — Costs: requires accurate weather forecasting — Benefits: accurate predictions reduce flood damage and allow evacuation.

b Answers will vary.

---

3 a **Exam-style question** *What is meant by 'soft engineering' solutions to flooding? (2 marks)*

Correct points are:

'Soft solutions means using the natural processes in a river basin to reduce flooding (1) — plus additional mark for example e.g. afforestation (1) flood proofing (1).

b **Exam-style question** *Using examples from named rivers, explain why 'soft engineering' solutions are increasingly used to manage flooding. (8 marks)*

This question is marked using levels. Purely descriptive points by Higher Tier candidates get no marks. Foundation Tier students may answer the alternative question:

Using named examples, describe the benefits of using soft engineering to manage the risk of flooding. (6 marks)

In this case, three developed or two well-developed descriptions are required for 6 marks. Cap answers at 6 marks (4 marks for the Foundation Tier question) which do not include:

- a named river e.g. 'River Skerne' — not just 'Darlington' or 'northern England';
- a specific method of soft engineering;
- an explanation as to why these methods are increasingly used (Higher Tier), e.g. because of reasons of cost or effectiveness.

Correct explanations include:

- Cost of hard engineering strategies are expensive compared to softer methods — plus development with an example e.g. 'because they involve using natural processes in the river valley' — well-developed if an example of one strategy is explained e.g. 'such as afforestation which allows increased interception and reduced surface runoff'.
- Soft engineering solutions are just as effective — plus development with an example e.g. 'flood proofing in villages near the River Skerne — well-developed e.g. 'because it helps people to cope with flooding without expense or danger to life'.

Level	Descriptor
0	No rewardable content
1 (1-3 marks)	Simple or very basic statements using little or no subject vocabulary.
2 (4-6 marks)	Generalised explanations but with some use of geographical terms. Up to three developed statements as shown by examples above.
3 (7-8 marks)	Detailed statements with clear explanations using geographical terms. At least two well-developed points (plus one other developed point) as shown by examples above.

7 Oceans on the edge

About the chapter
These are the key ideas behind the chapter.
- Human activities are threatening to destroy marine ecosystems on a global scale.
- The world's coral reefs are under threat from a range of global and local factors.
- A marine ecosystem is a dynamic relationship dependent on physical processes such as food webs and nutrient cycles.
- Climate change has both direct, and indirect impacts on oceans.
- Ocean ecosystems are under pressure, and need to be managed sustainably.
- Sustainable management is needed at local, national, international and global scales to protect oceans and ecosystems.

Chapter outline
Use this outline to provide your students with a brief roadmap of the chapter.

7.1 Bad news
How and why the oceans are threatened with destruction.

7.2 Reefs at risk
The threats to the world's coral reefs.

7.3 Threats to water quality
Physical processes in marine ecosystems and the threats of over-fishing and pollution.

7.4 Climate change and oceans
How climate change impacts directly, and indirectly, on oceans.

7.5 Can we save the ocean's ecosystems?
How ocean ecosystems can be managed sustainably.

7.6 Progress towards sustainable development
The stages of participatory planning.

7.7 Sustainable management can work
Marine Protected Areas and the management of fish stocks in the North Sea.

7.8 Ocean health: It's a 'world thing'
How global actions could help to improve the health of the oceans.

Oceans on the edge

How is the specification covered?

This chapter covers Topic 7, Unit 1 Dynamic Planet.

7.1 How and why are some ecosystems threatened with destruction?

7.2 How should ecosystems be managed sustainably?

Key ideas	Detailed content	Pages in students' book
7.1a Human activities are degrading and destroying marine eco-systems on a global scale.	Investigate the global pattern of either coral reefs or mangrove swamps and how this has changed in the past 50 years.	108-109
	Explain the global threats to this marine ecosystem to explain its changed distribution, through human activities including overfishing, pollution and waste disposal from both land and ocean sources, tourism and coastal development.	110-111
7.1b Unsustainable use of marine eco-systems leads to the disruption of food webs and nutrient cycles and can lead to extinction.	Investigate physical processes in marine ecosystems including marine food webs and nutrient cycles.	112-113
	Examine how these processes can be disrupted through overfishing, eutrophication and siltation, as well as the impacts of climate change including bleaching and species migration.	112-113, 114-115
7.2a The pressure to use marine eco-systems is growing, due to rising populations and resource demand, creating difficult choices for humans.	Investigate the growing local pressures on a named and located marine ecosystem.	116-117
	Examine the conflicting views about how the chosen ecosystem should be managed.	116-117
7.2b Sustainable management is needed locally and globally, if the oceans are to be protected from further degradation.	Compare two located case studies of marine management, e.g. sustainable management in St Lucia, management of fish stocks in the North Sea, marine reserves to establish the tensions between achieving economic and environmental sustainability.	116-117, 118-119, 120-121
	Assess the role of global actions to maintain ocean health, e.g. MARPOL and marine protected areas.	122-123

Chapter outcomes

By the end of this chapter, students should be able to:

- Describe the global distribution of coral reefs and those which are at risk.
- Produce a poster to show the value of the world's coral reefs and describe the threats they face.
- Explain how marine processes can be disrupted by over-fishing, eutrophication and siltation.
- Examine the direct and indirect impacts of climate change on marine ecosystems including coral bleaching and species migration.
- Describe the reasons why St Lucia's marine ecosystems needed protection, the conflicts involved, and how the ecosystems were managed.
- Draw a spider diagram to show how fish stocks in the North Sea could be managed.
- Explain how global actions can help to maintain ocean health.

7.1 Bad news

Section in brief

This section looks at the threats to the world's oceans. Enclosed seas, in densely populated areas, have suffered serious environmental damage. In some places, they have been classified as 'dead zones', where the whole ecosystem has collapsed. Coral reefs have high levels of biodiversity, but many of them are at risk from human activity.

In the activities, students:

- list the uses of coral reefs and rank them in order of importance;
- explain why enclosed seas in densely populated areas are most at risk;
- work in pairs to produce a poster illustrating the value of coral reefs;
- answer an exam-style question to describe and explain the distribution of coral reefs.

Key ideas

- Many of the world's oceans are experiencing serious environmental damage.
- The number of dead zones — where whole ocean ecosystems have collapsed — is increasing.
- Coral reefs have high levels of biodiversity and are very valuable.
- Reefs are under threat from human activity.

Key vocabulary

dead zones, food chains, ecosystems, biodiversity

Skills practised

Geographical skills: analysing maps and describing distributions

PLTS: team-working; effective participation; creative thinking

Section outcomes

By the end of this section, most students should be able to:

- define or explain the terms given in 'Key vocabulary' above;
- list the uses of coral reefs and rank them in order of importance;
- explain why enclosed seas are most at risk from environmental damage;
- produce a poster to show the value of coral reefs;
- identify threats to coral reefs.

Ideas for a starter

1. Use some of the points in the text box 'Think about this' to start a discussion with pupils about the threats facing the world's oceans.
2. Show students the map of environmental damage from page 108 of the students' book. Ask them what they think dead zones are. What causes them? What can explain their distribution?

Ideas for plenaries

1. If you used starter 2, continue your discussion about dead zones with students. Tell them that the good news is that the process is reversible. The Black Sea dead zone, previously the largest in the world, largely disappeared between 1991 and 2001. Fertilisers became too costly to use following the collapse of the Soviet Union, and fishing has again become a major economic activity in the region.
2. Use question 1 from page 109 of the students' book as a plenary activity.

Further class and homework activity

Ask students to find out why the Baltic Sea and the Mediterranean Sea have so many dead zones.

Oceans on the edge

answers

1 Uses of coral reefs include: fishing (to provide food for local communities as well as commercial fishing); shoreline protection; supplying resources for the aquarium trade; tourism; education and research; source of medicine; decorative objects (such as jewellery); and lime (for cement and building). Students should rank the uses in order of importance.

2 Densely populated industrial areas are the most likely to produce high levels of pollution which may be discharged directly into the sea. If the sea is enclosed, e.g. the Mediterranean, there is little tidal flow or exchange of water. Individual species (and then food chains) are most at risk, leading to ecosystem collapse.

3 Students should produce a poster to show the value of coral reefs.

---

4 Exam-style question *Describe and explain the distribution of coral reefs. (6 marks)*

This question is marked using levels. Purely descriptive points should be awarded a maximum of 4 marks. Foundation Tier students may answer the alternative question:

Describe the distribution of coral reefs. (4 marks)

In this case, replace the word 'explanations' in the level descriptions below with 'detailed descriptions'.

Correct *descriptions* include:

- Almost all within the tropics — plus development if exemplified e.g. 'around the coasts of south-east Asia'. Allow just one developed point for a located example.
- The majority are in south-east Asia — plus development if exemplified with the correct name of a country e.g. 'around the coast of Thailand'. Allow just one developed point for a named country.
- Away from river deltas / mouths or 'clear water'
- Shallow waters

Correct *explanations* include:

- Warm temperatures required for continued growth; use any specific temperatures (e.g. 27°C) as evidence of detailed statements qualifying for Level 3.
- Photosynthesis can take place in clear water
- Plus other points on merit.

Level	Descriptor
0	No rewardable content
1 (1-2 marks)	Simple or very basic explanations using little or no subject vocabulary. May be a list of simple undeveloped points e.g. 'Coral reefs need warm water'.
2 (3-4 marks)	Generalised explanations but with some use of geographical terms e.g. 'coral reefs are found in the tropics where temperatures are highest throughout the year'. Up to two developed statements as shown by examples above.
3 (5-6 marks)	Detailed statements with clear explanations using geographical terms. e.g. 'coral reefs are found between the tropics in shallow waters where temperatures are between 24-26°C to enable their survival'. Three developed or two well-developed points as shown by examples above.

Hint: To help you feed back to candidates, and keep track yourself whilst marking, you could use a tick with the letter 'D' for descriptive points, and 'E' for explanatory points. Ideally, descriptive and explanatory points will be combined e.g. 'Most coral reefs are between the tropics (D) because they require warm temperatures all year round for survival (E)'.

7.2 Reefs at risk

Section in brief

In this section students learn about the threats to the world's coral reefs. Coral reefs face increasing risks from local and global threats, which include tourism, fishing and pollution.

In the activities, students:

- consider whether they agree with the statement that the real threats to oceans are land-based activities;
- research a reef tourist destination and consider the costs and benefits of tourism;
- explain why fishing is a threat to ocean ecosystems;
- answer an exam-style question to explain how tourism can damage marine ecosystems.

Key ideas

- The world's coral reefs are under increasing risk from local and global threats.
- Over two-thirds of the coral reefs in the Indian and Pacific Oceans are under threat.
- Tourism benefits local economies, but has many direct and indirect impacts on the reefs.
- Fishing damages reef ecosystems in a number of ways.

Key vocabulary

dead zones, food chains, ecosystems, biodiversity

Skills practised

Geographical skills: researching coral reef tourist destinations and classifying costs and benefits; explaining why fishing and tourism threaten marine ecosystems

PLTS: independent enquiry; creative thinking

Section outcomes

By the end of this section, most students should be able to:

- explain the terms given in 'Key vocabulary' above;
- give examples of the local and global factors affecting coral reefs;
- classify the economic, social and environmental costs and benefits of tourism in coral reef environments;
- explain why fishing is such a threat to reef ecosystems;
- explain how tourism can damage marine ecosystems.

Ideas for a starter

1 Ask students to look at the two photos on page 110 of the students' book. Ask: 'What do you think has caused the bleaching shown in the second photo? What other threats do you think coral reefs face?'

2 Recap the value of coral reefs from section 7.1.

Ideas for plenaries

1 Use question 1 from page 111 of the students' book as the basis for a class discussion.

2 If students have completed question 2 in the students' book in class, ask them which are the greatest costs and benefits. How could the costs be improved? Could ecotourism be the answer?

Further class and homework activity

Ask students to research coral reef ecotourism. They should find out where to go, what to do, and how an ecotourism holiday will help to protect the coral reef ecosystem.

Oceans on the edge

answers

1. 'Activities that happen on land' relates to human activities. Note that this question is about 'the oceans' in general, not just coral reefs, so students could refer back to information in section 7.1 on dead zones and ocean habitats and ecosystems at risk in their answers.

2. Students' responses will depend on their chosen destinations. Some of the costs of tourism are outlined on page 111 of the students' book.

3. Fishing is a threat to ocean ecosystems for a number of reasons:
   - blast fishing (using dynamite) damages coral and kills many species unintentionally;
   - cyanide fishing to collect fish for use in aquariums reduces the fish stock;
   - trawling damages reefs;
   - overfishing reduces fish stock;
   - breeding grounds for fish are being destroyed.

4. **Exam-style question** *Using named examples, explain how tourism can damage marine ecosystems. (6 marks)*

   This question is marked using levels. The key to this question is the command word 'explain' — a Higher Tier command word. Purely descriptive points by Higher Tier candidates get no marks. Foundation Tier students may answer the alternative question:

   Using named examples, describe ways in which marine ecosystems can be damaged. (4 marks)

   In this case, replace the term 'explanations' in the table below with 'descriptions'.

   Cap answers at 4 marks (2 marks for Foundation Tier) which:
   - do not include a named example of a specific threat e.g. 'construction work for hotels' — not just a named location;
   - use generalised terms such as 'pollution', instead of 'sewage pollution'.

   Correct points can be drawn from any of those on page 111 and include:
   - Construction of hotels / tourist services / amenities — plus development e.g. 'which can lead to land clearance and surface run-off' — and well-developed if impacts are explained e.g. 'which mean that sea water becomes cloudier and the corals are unable to survive'.
   - Increased demand for seafood — plus development e.g. 'which can lead to increased fishing on nearby reefs to satisfy demand' — and well-developed if impacts are explained e.g. 'which can lead to over-fishing and species depletion'.

Level	Descriptor
0	No rewardable content
1 (1-2 marks)	Simple undeveloped or very basic statements using little or no subject vocabulary. May be a list of undeveloped points e.g. 'tourists cause damage to the reefs when they go to see them' (1 mark).
2 (3-4 marks)	Generalised explanations but with some use of geographical terms e.g. 'tourists cause damage to the reef when they go snorkelling and break off pieces of coral'. Up to two developed statements as shown by examples above.
3 (5-6 marks)	Detailed statements with clear explanations, using geographical terms. e.g. 'tourists can cause damage to the reef when they go snorkelling by breaking off pieces of coral, which damage fish habitats as well as reducing the coral'. Three developed or two well-developed points as shown by examples above.

7.3 Threats to water quality

Section in brief

This section explores the physical processes in marine ecosystems. It also looks at the threats facing marine ecosystems in the form of overfishing and pollution.

In the activities, students:

- explain the difference between a food web and a nutrient cycle;
- draw a food chain;
- explain some of the links in a food web;
- explain the impacts of increased melting of Arctic ice and over-fishing on the marine ecosystem;
- answer an exam-style question to explain the possible effects of siltation on a marine food web.

Key ideas

- A marine ecosystem is a dynamic relationship – any increase or decrease in species numbers impacts on the whole system.
- The relationships between species in an ecosystem is called a food web.
- The marine food web is at risk from over-fishing.
- Krill are a keystone species.
- Ecosystems rely on nutrient cycles to work.
- Eutrophication and siltation are threatening marine ecosystems.

Key vocabulary

primary producers, consumer, food web, food chain, keystone species, nutrient cycle, eutrophication, siltation

Skills practised

Geographical skills: explaining impacts of increased ice melting and over-fishing on marine ecosystems

Section outcomes

By the end of this section, most students should be able to:

- define or explain the terms given in 'Key vocabulary' above;
- explain the links in a marine food web;
- explain why krill are a keystone species;
- explain the possible impacts of over-fishing on the marine ecosystem;
- describe the effects of eutrophication and siltation on the marine ecosystem.

Ideas for a starter

1 Show photos of krill and whales on the whiteboard. Ask students what the link is between the photos. Use the information on page 112 of the students' book to explain how important krill are and to introduce the term 'keystone species'.

2 Ask students to work in pairs to create a food web for a marine ecosystem. Give them these terms to create the food web: algae, plankton, krill, cod, squid, seal, penguin, whale, polar bear.

Ideas for plenaries

1 Hold a class discussion. Ask students: 'What is the greatest threat to the world's oceans — over-fishing, tourism, global warming or pollution?'

2 Ask students to complete a pyramid review of this lesson. They should write down the following, in the shape of a pyramid:

- one question they would like to ask,
- two points they are not sure about,
- three points they have learnt.

Further class and homework activity

Ask students to research the costs and benefits of fish farming as a way of protecting the marine ecosystem from over-fishing.

Oceans on the edge

answers

1. A food web shows the links between the plants and animals in an ecosystem. A nutrient cycle is the movement of nutrients from one species to another in an ecosystem.

2. Sun's energy → phytoplankton → fish → seals → polar bears

3. **a** Primary producers are things such as phytoplankton. All other creatures in the food chain depend on them, therefore they must be more abundant.

   b Fish (consumers) feed on micro-organisms (producers). So, again, there needs to be more producers than consumers to support the ecosystem.

4. **a** Polar bears hunt seals on the Arctic ice. Increased melting of Arctic ice reduces the hunting season, meaning that polar bears are in danger of extinction, and the seal population would increase.

   b Increased over-fishing will lead to a reduction of certain species in the marine ecosystem. This will alter the balance of the species, and have an impact on food chains within the food web.

5. **Exam-style question** *Explain the possible effects of siltation on the marine food web shown in the diagram. (6 marks)*

   This question is marked using levels. The key to this question is the command word 'explain' — a Higher Tier command word. Purely descriptive points by Higher Tier candidates get no marks. Foundation Tier students may answer the alternative question:

   Describe how siltation can affect marine ecosystems. (4 marks)

   In this case, replace the term 'explanations' in the table below with 'descriptions'.

   Correct effects include:

   - Increased cloudiness can cause damage to a coral reef — developed with effects e.g. 'preventing photosynthesis by phyto-plankton' — and well-developed e.g. 'which means that every other organism feeding on phyto-plankton is threatened'.

Level	Descriptor
0	No rewardable content
1 (1-2 marks)	Simple or very basic statements using little or no subject vocabulary. May be a list e.g. 'sea water becomes cloudy so nothing can survive'.
2 (3-4 marks)	Generalised explanations but with some use of geographical terms e.g. 'increased cloudiness of sea water prevents the survival of phyto-plankton as it prevents sunlight entering seawater'. Up to two developed statements as shown by examples above.
3 (5-6 marks)	Detailed statements with clear explanations using geographical terms. e.g. 'increased cloudiness of sea water prevents the survival of phyto-plankton as it prevents sunlight entering seawater, which in turn affects all other species that feed on phyto-plankton'. Three developed or two well-developed points as shown by examples above.

7.4 Climate change and oceans

Section in brief

This section looks at the impacts of climate change on the world's oceans. The direct impacts of climate change relate to increases in the temperature of oceans, and indirect impacts relate to rises in sea level. This section also looks at how warming oceans are causing marine species to migrate.

In the activities, students:

- explain why sea levels are rising and ocean temperatures are increasing;
- describe the impacts of climate change on the oceans;
- answer an exam-style question to examine the impact of warming oceans on marine species and food webs.

Key ideas

- Climate change is the most serious threat to the world's oceans.
- Direct impacts of climate change relate to increases in temperature.
- Rising water temperature causes coral bleaching.
- Indirect impacts of climate change relate to rises in sea level.
- Warming oceans and seas are causing marine species migration.
- Species migration will affect whole food webs.

Key vocabulary

carbon sink, coral bleaching, alien species

Skills practised

Geographical skills: interpreting maps and a graph; explaining reasons for rising sea levels and ocean temperatures; describing impact of climate change on marine ecosystems

Section outcomes

By the end of this section, most students should be able to:

- define or explain the terms given in 'Key vocabulary' above;
- understand the difference between direct and indirect impacts of climate change;
- give examples of some of the direct impacts of climate change;
- describe the impacts of rising sea levels;
- give examples of the impacts of warming oceans and seas on species migration.

Idea for a starter

Introduce students to the idea of a 'tipping point' beyond which damage to ecosystems is irreversible. In this case a rise in ocean temperatures of 3°C would mean oceans could suffer irreversible damage. What impacts do students think this would have on marine ecosystems? And what would that mean for us?

Ideas for plenaries

1. Ask students to draw a table of the possible impacts of climate change on the world's oceans. They should identify direct and indirect impacts.
2. Tell students that if the Greenland ice cap and West Antarctica ice sheet were to completely melt, sea levels would rise by 12 metres! Point out how much this really is. Before they get too worried, explain that this rise relates to melting over centuries. The 1 metre rise given in the text seems to be the maximum for the year 2100.

Further class and homework activity

Ask students to complete the exam-style question on page 115 of the students' book for homework.

Oceans on the edge

answers

1. Sea levels are rising for two reasons:
   - thermal expansion — warmer water temperatures causes oceans to expand, so sea levels rise;
   - melting glaciers and ice sheets — adding to the volume of water in the oceans.

2. Impacts of climate change on oceans will be direct and indirect:
   - Direct impacts include: changes to ocean ecosystems such as coral bleaching; pollution and siltation — as a result of extreme weather; ocean water could become less salty and less dense, so ocean temperatures could decrease in some places and increase in others; species migration.
   - Indirect impacts (rises in sea level) include: erosion and destruction of coastal ecosystems such as mangrove swamps and salt marshes; flooding of tidal areas.

3. **Exam-style question** *Using named examples, examine the impact of warming oceans on marine species and food webs. (8 marks)*

   This question is marked using levels. The key to this question is the command word 'explain' — a Higher Tier command word. Purely descriptive points by Higher Tier candidates get no marks. Foundation Tier students may answer the alternative question:

   Using named examples, describe ways in which warming oceans can affect marine food webs. (6 marks)

   In this case, three developed or two well-developed descriptions are required for 6 marks.

   Cap answers at 6 marks (4 marks for the Foundation Tier question) which do not include:
   - a specific marine species e.g. 'sardine' – not 'fish', or a specific ecosystem (e.g. coral reefs);
   - an explanation of *both* marine species and food webs (Higher Tier question).

   Correct impacts upon *marine species* include:
   - Change caused by warming waters e.g. species migration — plus development with examples e.g. 'from cod to sardines in the north Atlantic' — or well-developed with further impacts e.g. 'which survive in warmer water and can therefore migrate further north or south from the equator'.

   Correct impacts upon *marine food webs* include:
   - Changing balance of predators and prey — plus development with example e.g. 'where birds such as kittiwake feed on fish which then migrate' — well-developed with impacts e.g. 'which results in complete change in the food web as one species migrates so others that feed on it must migrate too'.

Level	Descriptor
0	No rewardable content
1 (1-3 marks)	Simple or very basic statements using little or no subject vocabulary. May be a list e.g. 'as the oceans warm, so species have to change to adapt'.
2 (4-6 marks)	Generalised explanations but with some use of geographical terms e.g. 'as oceans warm, so species migration occurs, such as cod migrating further north in the Atlantic'. Up to three developed statements as shown by examples above.
3 (7-8 marks)	Detailed statements with clear explanations using geographical terms. e.g. 'as oceans warm, so species migration occurs, such as cod migrating further north in the Atlantic'. Two well-developed points plus other developed statements are required for the top of Level 3 as shown by examples above.

7.5 Can we save the ocean's ecosystems?

Section in brief

This section looks at how ocean ecosystems can be managed sustainably. It uses the example of community-based ecosystem management in St Lucia. The reasons why protection was needed, and the causes of management conflicts, are explained.

In the activities, students:

- explain what is meant by sustainable management of the ocean's resources;
- describe the conflicts that existed in St Lucia over the uses of the sea and its resources;
- explain why healthy marine resources are important to the people of St Lucia;
- answer an exam-style question to explain how ecosystem conservation can cause conflicts with local communities.

Key ideas

- Pressure on marine ecosystems is growing due to rising populations in coastal areas and increased demand for ocean resources.
- Sustainable management is a balancing act between ecosystem conservation and helping local people to make a living.
- St Lucia, in the Caribbean, was the first place to set up a community-based system for managing ecosystems.
- Community participation is essential for such a system to work, and for conflicts to be resolved.

Key vocabulary

finite resources, community-based management

Skills practised

Geographical skills: explaining sustainable management; explaining the importance of marine resources; interpreting a map and diagram

Section outcomes

By the end of this section, most students should be able to:

- define or explain the terms given in 'Key vocabulary' above;
- describe the reasons why St Lucia's marine ecosystems needed protection;
- describe the conflicts that existed in St Lucia over the use of the sea and its resources;
- explain how sustainable management helps ocean ecosystems.

Ideas for a starter

1. Revisit the concept of sustainability i.e. 'meeting the needs of the present without compromising the ability of future generations to meet their own needs'. Then discuss the possible conflicts inherent in any attempt to impose sustainable management on a community.
2. Ask students where St Lucia is. What do they know about St Lucia?

Idea for a plenary

Compare the problems that St Lucia faced with the general problems facing coral reefs described in section 7.2 of the students' book. What are the similarities and differences?

Further class and homework activity

Ask students to plan a five minute video to convince local people to use the ocean's resources in a more sustainable way. They need to think of questions they would ask local people about their use of the ocean, conduct some research into sustainable and unsustainable use of ocean resources and create a storyboard of scenes to use in the video.

Oceans on the edge

answers

1. Sustainable management of the ocean's resources is about maintaining a balance between conserving the ocean's ecosystems, and ensuring that local people can make a living without over-harvesting resources.

2. - In Soufrière the conflicts were between fishermen, divers, snorkelers and yacht owners. Fishermen would throw rocks into the water which would be dangerous for divers and snorkelers. In addition the methods of fishing would damage the coral which divers and snorkelers want to see. Yacht owners would damage the coral with anchors.
   - In Mankòtè the mangrove forest provided resources and services for local people. Spraying with insecticide to eradicate mosquitoes or using it as a site for rubbish disposal would damage the mangrove.

3. Marine resources provide valuable services to the people of St Lucia, including: the protection of the lagoon and coastal area; feeding and spawning area for fish; protecting the coast from erosion and against the effects of severe storms; extracting pollutants from the water; providing wood for charcoal.

4. **Exam-style question** *Using examples; explain how ecosystem conservation can cause conflict with local communities. (6 marks)*

   This question is marked using levels. The key to this question is the command word 'explain' — a Higher Tier command word. Purely descriptive points by Higher Tier candidates get no marks. Foundation Tier students may answer the alternative question:

   Using a named example, describe the conflicts that can arise in local communities from marine conservation. (6 marks)

   Cap answers at 4 marks which do not:
   - name a specific conflict or location e.g. 'St Lucia' or 'Great Barrier Reef' — ideally, including particular interests e.g. fishing communities.

   Correct examples include:
   - Conflicts in Mankòtè between fishing interests, rubbish disposal and mosquito eradication — plus development with explanation of conflicts e.g. 'mosquito eradication used insecticides which polluted the reef' — well-developed with impacts e.g. 'causing run-off into the oceans where coral algae were killed'.

Level	Descriptor
0	No rewardable content
1 (1-2 marks)	Simple or very basic statements using little or no subject vocabulary. May be a list of points rather than conflicts e.g. 'the reefs in St Lucia have been badly affected by tourism'.
2 (3-4 marks)	Generalised explanations but with some use of geographical terms e.g. 'conflicts have arisen because of demands placed by tourists, such as litter, which spoils the beaches for the local people'. Up to two developed statements as shown by examples above.
3 (5-6 marks)	Detailed statements with clear explanations using geographical terms. e.g. conflicts have arisen because of litter left by tourists, which not only spoils the beaches for the local people but may damage the habitat for marine life e.g. plastic bags'. Three developed points or two well-developed points are required for the top of Level 3 as shown by examples above.

7.6 Progress towards sustainable development

Section in brief

This section looks at the process of participatory planning. It considers the Soufrière Marine Management Area (SMMA) in St Lucia, where it has been applied. It looks at the successes of this scheme and the problems that have arisen.

In the activities, students:

- decide what the three biggest successes of the SMMA have been, and why;
- consider why it is essential to involve local people in a scheme like the SMMA;
- answer an exam-style question to explain how marine areas can be managed sustainably.

Key ideas

- In participatory planning the whole community is involved in the development of a scheme.
- The key stages of participatory planning are: assessment, making management decisions, capacity building, and finalising institutional arrangements.
- The SMMA has been successful as a model of sustainability, but there have been problems getting stakeholders to agree.

Key vocabulary

participatory planning, stakeholder, ecotourism

Skills practised

Geographical skills: map interpretation; explaining how marine areas can be managed sustainably

PLTS: team-working; effective participation

Section outcomes

By the end of this section, most students should be able to:

- define or explain the terms given in 'Key vocabulary' above;
- understand that participatory planning is essential for sustainable management schemes to succeed;
- describe the stages of participatory planning;
- describe the problems facing St Lucia in getting the participants of the SMMA to agree;
- decide on the three biggest successes of the scheme.

Idea for a starter

Tourism contributes nearly 50% of St Lucia's annual earnings, but brings with it problems – including those of waste disposal and pollution. How could tourism change to reduce its negative impacts on the island?

Ideas for plenaries

1. Use question 1 from page 119 of the students' book as a plenary. In pairs, ask students to report what they think the three biggest successes of the scheme are, and why. Does everyone agree?

2. Ask students to prepare an argument to persuade local fishermen that setting up a marine conservation area is in their best interests in the long run. Point out that the new boats will help them to fish their designated areas more efficiently – and that fish stocks protected in conservation areas will benefit them eventually.

Further class and homework activity

Ask students to find out about Marine Protected Areas (MPA). They should find out what they are and where they are. They should also find out why Lundy Island, off the coast of Devon, was chosen as an MPA.

Oceans on the edge

answers

1. Successes include:
   - establishment of marine conservation areas means that the numbers, sizes and diversity of fish species have increased;
   - many stakeholders are involved in marine conservation;
   - fees from yacht owners/divers have made the scheme self-financing;
   - local fishermen have been provided with modern boats and a refrigerated ice house;
   - ecotourism has been encouraged;
   - local people have been trained to manage the scheme.

2. Involving local people is essential so that they become stakeholders, rather than having the scheme imposed on them. To be successful, the scheme needs to benefit local people, provide employment and improve their incomes.

3. **Exam-style question** *Using examples, explain how marine areas can be managed sustainably. (6 marks)*

   This question is marked using levels. The key to this question is the command word 'explain' — a Higher Tier command word. Purely descriptive points by Higher Tier candidates get no marks. Foundation Tier students may answer the alternative question:

   Using examples, describe ways in which a marine area is being managed sustainably. (6 marks)

   In this case, replace the term 'explanations' in the level descriptions below with 'descriptions'.

   Cap answers at 4 marks which do not:
   - include named specific examples e.g. Soufrière in St Lucia — not just 'in the Caribbean'.

   Correct examples of sustainable management include:
   - Use of a location and specific management process e.g. land in Mankòtè put aside for woodland growth — plus development e.g. 'to prevent further destruction of mangroves for charcoal' — or well-developed e.g. 'which protects mangroves as breeding grounds for many fish species'.
   - Plus other correct examples from pages 118-119 on merit.

Level	Descriptor
0	No rewardable content
1 (1-2 marks)	Simple or very basic statements using little or no subject vocabulary. May be a list or undeveloped description e.g. 'in Soufrière, they tried to protect fishing'.
2 (3-4 marks)	Generalised explanations but with some use of geographical terms e.g. 'in Soufrière, groups of local fishing and tourist businesses came up with a plan to protect resources that would benefit both'. Up to three developed statements as shown by examples above.
3 (5-6 marks)	Detailed statements with clear explanations using geographical terms. e.g. 'in Soufrière, groups of local fishing and tourist businesses explored the coast with the town council to come up with a plan to protect the coast using different zones (with examples)'. Three developed points or two well-developed points are required for the top of Level 3 as shown by examples above.

7.7 Sustainable management can work

Section in brief
This section looks at the sustainable management of marine ecosystems at a global scale - Marine Protected Areas (MPAs) – and at a regional scale – by looking at the way fish stocks are managed in the North Sea. While a whole ecosystem approach might save North Sea stocks, global warming is an additional factor that is causing problems.

In the activities, students:

- consider why fishing is a difficult industry to manage;
- draw a spider diagram showing the problems facing the North Sea, and solutions to the problems;
- answer an exam-style question to explain how marine areas are managed at a regional scale.

Key ideas
- Sustainable marine management needs to take place at local, national, international and global scales.
- A Marine Protected Area (MPA) is an area of sea or coast where marine life is protected from damage or disturbance.
- Many of the marine hotspots (areas of highest biodiversity) are not currently protected.
- The EU Common Fisheries Policy tries to manage North Sea fish stocks.

Key vocabulary
Marine Protected Area (MPA), marine hotspot, whole ecosystem approach

Skills practised
Geographical skills: interpreting maps; explaining how marine areas are managed at a regional scale

Section outcomes
By the end of this section, most students should be able to:

- define or explain the terms given in 'Key vocabulary' above;
- understand that sustainable marine management needs to take place at a variety of scales;
- describe the problems marine areas face in terms of protection;
- identify the problems facing North Sea fish stocks, and suggest solutions;
- explain how marine areas can be managed at a regional scale.

Idea for a starter
Ask students to look at the map which shows marine hotspots on page 120 of the students' book. The Western Caribbean hotspot includes St Lucia. Explain to students that to ensure that this hotspot has good protection, the efforts currently being put into the SMMA scheme in St Lucia would have to be applied across a much larger area. Is this possible?

Idea for a plenary
Use question 1 from page 121 of the students' book as the basis for a class discussion on how fishing differs from agriculture. Fish are a natural resource as opposed to domestic animals/crops. A farmer can manage crops/animals in a way that the fisherman cannot. Before large-scale commercial fishing, fish stocks replenished themselves naturally; but overfishing means that fishermen have to go further afield and employ more sophisticated techniques which further depletes fish stocks.

Further class and homework activity
Ask students to write a 300-word letter to the UK Fisheries Minister, explaining what they think should be done to save fish stocks.

Oceans on the edge

answers

1 Fishing is like hunting, but on a very large scale. The prey is disappearing rapidly – so the industry has to come up with new ways of catching it. Competition for fish from fishing industries from many different countries increases the problem.

2 and 3
Students should look for evidence of problems in this section and in sections 7.3 and 7.4. Solutions are mostly found in this section under the text on the 'whole ecosystem approach'.

---

4 Exam-style question *Using named examples, explain how marine areas are managed at a regional scale. (8 marks)*

This question is marked using levels. The key to this question is the command word 'explain' — a Higher Tier command word. Purely descriptive points by Higher Tier candidates get no marks. Foundation Tier students may answer the alternative question:

Using a named example, describe the attempts to manage a marine area that you have studied. (6 marks)

In this case, three developed or two well-developed descriptions are required for 6 marks.

Cap answers at 6 marks (4 marks for the Foundation Tier question) which do not:
- include named specific examples at the scale of a small country, or a region of a larger country e.g. the Great Barrier Reef — exceptionally, a region may apply to a group of countries e.g. the Caribbean, or the North Sea within the EU. Judge according to the appropriateness of the management example being explained.

Correct examples of management of a marine area include:
- Attempts to reduce fishing catches by the EU Fisheries Policy because of collapsing fish stocks — plus development e.g. 'which uses methods such as quotas to restrict fish stocks' — well-developed with explanations including detail e.g. 'which protects adult breeding fish and allows them to breed'.
- Plus similarly detailed examples such as MPAs which are explained on pages 120-121.

Level	Descriptor
0	No rewardable content
1 (1-3 marks)	Simple or very basic statements using little or no subject vocabulary. May be a list or descriptive statements without development e.g. 'they have tried to protect declining fish stocks in different parts of the world'.
2 (4-6 marks)	Generalised explanations but with some use of geographical terms e.g. 'The EU has tried to protect fisheries from declining by stopping fishing boats and countries catching more than a certain amount'. Up to three developed statements as shown by examples above.
3 (7-8 marks)	Detailed statements with clear explanations using geographical terms. e.g. 'The EU has tried to protect collapsing fish stock in the North Sea from declining by setting quotas to limit what boats catch, and protect fish breeding grounds'. At least two well-developed points (plus one other developed point) are required for the top of Level 3 as shown by examples above.

7.8 Ocean health: It's a 'world thing'

Section in brief

In this section students learn how global actions could help to improve the health of the oceans and the difficulties of protecting ocean ecosystems.

In the activities, students:

- work in small groups to draw a spider diagram showing reasons why the world's oceans are threatened;
- draw a table to show how two of the problems facing the world's oceans could be solved by the Law of the Sea;
- answer an exam-style question to explain how global actions can help to maintain ocean health.

Key ideas

- The Law of the Sea was developed to prevent nations from taking an unfair share of the ocean's wealth.
- The International Seabed Authority controls the deep seabed area.
- Marpol is a set of standards for the safety and design of ships, and a set of rules to stop ships dumping waste at sea.
- Ocean ecosystems are not as well protected as land-based ecosystems.

Key vocabulary

Law of the Sea, International Convention for the Prevention of Pollution from Ships (Marpol)

Skills practised

Geographical skills: identifying threats to the world's oceans; explaining how global actions can maintain ocean health

PLTS: independent enquiry; team-working; effective participation

Section outcomes

By the end of this section, most students should be able to:

- explain the terms given in 'Key vocabulary' above;
- understand why the Law of the Sea was developed and how it works;
- identify the main threats facing the world's oceans;
- outline what Marpol is, and the successes it has had;
- explain why the world's oceans are still at risk.

Ideas for a starter

1. Ask: 'Have you ever found tar on a beach – or discovered rubbish discarded by ships?' Discuss with the class the sources of ocean pollution and dumping at sea.
2. Tell students that energy companies are constantly looking for new energy resources. Energy exploration puts the ocean environment at risk. Ask how the ocean can be protected.

Ideas for plenaries

1. Use question 2 from page 123 of the students' book. Identify the two biggest problems that the class as a whole agrees about from question 1. Then make a copy of the table and carry out the exercise for these two problems with the whole class.
2. Recap this chapter with the class. Ask: 'Has it all been bad news, or are there grounds for hope for the world's oceans?'

Further class and homework activity

Ask students to find out about the Great Pacific Garbage Patch. They should find out what it is, where it is, the problems it causes, and whether it can be cleaned up.

Oceans on the edge

answers

1. Students should include threats to the world's oceans mentioned on this spread, as well as those mentioned earlier in this chapter.

2. Students' responses will depend on which problems they have chosen, and their own views as to whether the exclusion zones will help to solve the problems.

3. **Exam-style question** *Using named examples, explain how global actions can help maintain ocean health. (8 marks)*

   This question is marked using levels. The key to this question is the command word 'explain' — a Higher Tier command word. Purely descriptive points by Higher Tier candidates get no marks. Foundation Tier students may answer the alternative question:

   Using named examples, describe one global action which has tried to maintain ocean health. (6 marks)

   In this case, three developed or two well-developed descriptions are required for 6 marks.

   Cap answers at 6 marks (4 marks for the Foundation Tier question) which do not include specific projects e.g. Marpol. Examples must be specific and detailed about a particular strategy, but there is no requirement to mention actual places. Mark according to the appropriateness of the management example being explained.

   Suitable global actions could include:

   - UNCLOS, with a brief description of its aim e.g. an attempt to manage the oceans and the rights of countries with coastlines — plus development using a specific example e.g. 'setting territorial rights using 12-mile exclusion zones around every country with a coastline' — well-developed with further explanation e.g. 'which prevents other countries from fishing in, or polluting their waters '.
   - Other examples as shown on pages 122-123.

Level	Descriptor
0	No rewardable content
1 (1-3 marks)	Simple or very basic statements using little or no subject vocabulary. May be a list or descriptive statements without development e.g. 'they have tried to protect coastal waters around countries'.
2 (4-6 marks)	Generalised explanations but with some use of geographical terms e.g. 'Marpol is an international agreement designed to stop ships dumping waste at sea'. Up to three developed statements as shown by examples above.
3 (7-8 marks)	Detailed statements with clear explanations using geographical terms. e.g. 'Marpol is an international agreement of over 150 countries designed to stop ships dumping waste at sea, which has reduced oil spills at sea by 90% since the 1970s'. At least two well-developed points (plus one other developed point) are required for the top of Level 3 as shown by examples above.

8 Extreme environments

About the chapter

These are the key ideas behind the chapter.

- Extreme climates are located in polar regions and hot arid areas – each has different physical characteristics.
- Plants and animals have adapted to the extreme climates in different ways.
- People have to adapt to living in extreme environments in different ways.
- Indigenous people living in extreme environments have a unique culture.
- People and natural systems in extreme environments face a range of threats.
- Climate change could threaten people and natural systems in extreme environments.
- Local actions can help to protect communities against climate change.
- Global action can protect extreme environments from the threat of climate change.

Chapter outline

Use this outline to provide your students with a brief roadmap of the chapter.

8.1 Polar extremes
What polar climates are like and how plants and animals survive there.

8.2 Polar people
The unique lifestyle of polar people.

8.3 Living in the Australian outback
What desert climates are like in Australia.

8.4 How plants and animals survive
How plants and animals survive Australia's desert climate.

8.5 Coping with Australia's extremes
How people cope with living in extreme hot arid conditions.

8.6 Valuing people and culture
Aboriginal culture in Australia and the value of desert cultures.

8.7 Threatened people
The threats facing traditional cultures and natural systems in extreme environments.

8.8 The climate change threat
How climate change threatens polar and hot arid extreme environments.

8.9 Facing up to a changing world
How people can take local actions to help them adapt to climate change.

8.10 Taking action for the future
How local and global actions can protect extreme environments from the threat of climate change.

Extreme environments

How is the specification covered?

This chapter covers Topic 8, Unit 1 Dynamic Planet.

8.1 What are the challenges of extreme climates?

8.2 How can extreme environments be managed and protected from the threats they face?

Key ideas	Detailed content	Pages in students' book
8.1a Extreme climates are located in polar regions and hot arid areas; each one has key physical characteristics and they are fragile environments.	Investigate the climate of polar and hot arid areas including precipitation, temperature range, seasonality and variability.	124-125, 128-129
	Examine why these are fragile environments and how flora and fauna have successfully adapted to the extreme climates, but are also vulnerable to change.	124-125, 130-131
8.1b People adapt to the challenges of extreme environments in a variety of ways.	Investigate the adaptations people make in extreme environments, including farming methods, building styles, clothing, transport, energy use.	126-127, 132-133
	Examine the culture and uniqueness of peoples living in extreme environments, and the value of this culture to others.	126-127, 134-135
8.2a Extreme environments are under threat from a range of processes, including climate change.	Investigate the threats to people and natural systems in extreme environments, including out-migration because of limited economic opportunities, cultural dilution through tourism, pollution through resource exploitation, and land degradation through poor land management.	136-137
	Investigate how climate change could threaten natural systems, including melting of permafrost, loss of sea ice, desertification and species migration and the impact of these on traditional economies.	138-139
8.2b Sustainable management is needed locally and globally, if communities in extreme environments are to survive.	Assess a range of local actions, e.g. intermediate technology and adaptation to changing climates, and assess their effectiveness in achieving a sustainable future for local communities.	140-141
	Assess the role of global actions to protect extreme environments from the threat of climate change.	142-143

Chapter outcomes

By the end of this chapter, students should be able to:

- Draw climate graphs for polar continental and maritime climates and identify the similarities and differences between them.
- Describe and explain how polar and desert plants and animals have adapted to the extreme environments.
- Give examples of the ways people have adapted to extreme polar and hot arid environments.
- Explain why traditional cultures are unique and valuable.
- Describe the threats facing people and natural systems in extreme environments.
- Explain how climate change might affect people and ecosystems in polar and hot arid environments.
- Explain how local action in the Sahel can help to protect people against climate change.
- Assess the achievements and failings of the Kyoto and Copenhagen summits.

8.1 Polar extremes

Section in brief

In this section students learn that polar locations can have either continental or maritime climates, and both are extreme and intensely cold. Few people live in polar regions, and the flora and fauna have adapted to the tough conditions.

In the activities, students:

- draw climate graphs for Svalbard and Inuvik and label the similarities and differences between the two places;
- answer an exam-style question to explain how polar flora and fauna have adapted to the extreme climate.

Key ideas

- Polar regions are found, north of the Arctic circle, and south of the Antarctic circle.
- Polar regions have cold temperatures, polar nights, and days of midnight sun.
- Polar locations can have either continental or maritime climates.
- Plants and animals have adapted to the extreme environment.
- Polar species are vulnerable to global warming.

Key vocabulary

Arctic, Antarctic, polar night, midnight sun, latitude, sunlight (solar radiation), tundra

Skills practised

Geographical skills: identifying similarities and differences between climates of two places; explaining how polar flora and fauna have adapted to the climate

Numeracy skills: drawing and interpreting climate graphs

Section outcomes

By the end of this section, most students should be able to:

- define or explain the terms given in 'Key vocabulary' above;
- explain why polar regions are so cold;
- draw climate graphs and identify similarities and differences between continental and maritime climates;
- describe the differences between the Arctic and Antarctic in terms of geography, countries and people;
- explain how polar flora and fauna have adapted to the extreme climate.

Ideas for a starter

1. Show photos of polar plants and/or animals on the whiteboard. Ask students how they have adapted to the extreme climate.
2. Show students a video clip which shows how plants have adapted to the harsh polar climate. There is a suitable one on the BBC learning Zone. Search for clip 5506.

Ideas for plenaries

1. Hold a quick quiz based on this section. Ask: Where are polar regions found? Why are polar regions so cold? What is the polar night? Who can tell me three differences between the Arctic and the Antarctic? What is the difference between a maritime climate and a continental climate?
2. Ask students to sum up what they have learned in this lesson in no more than 40 words.

Further class and homework activity

Ask students to find out about either: the Inuit, the Nenets, the Aleut. They should find out where they live and about their traditional way of life.

Extreme environments

answers

1 Students climate graphs should look like this:

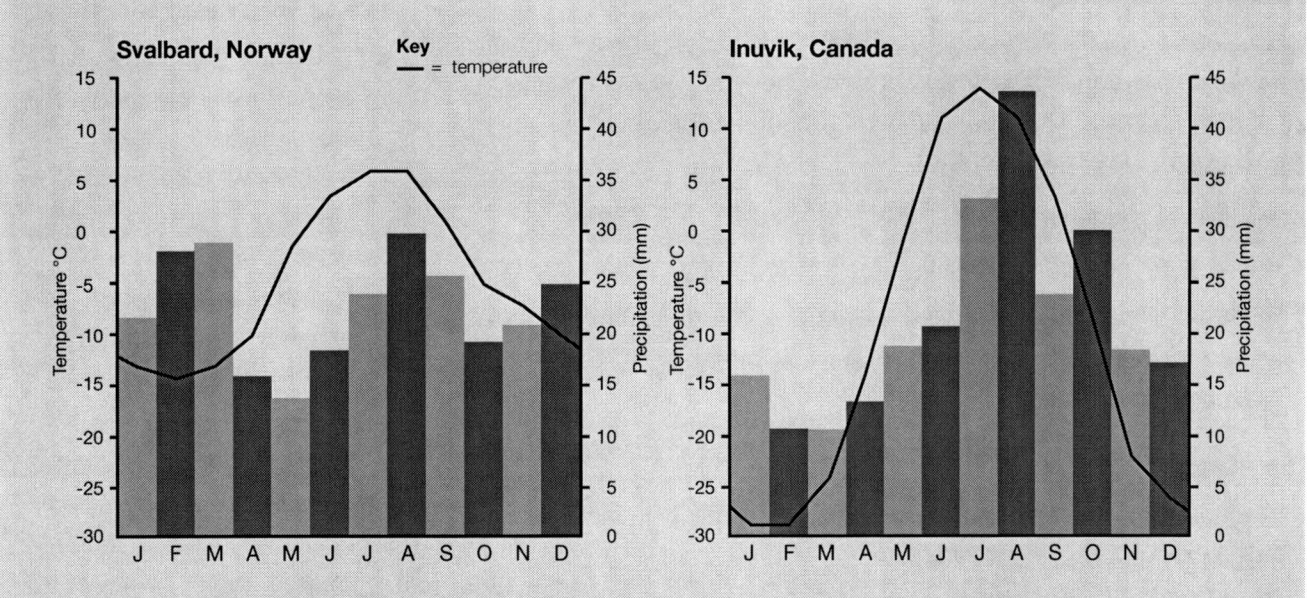

Svalbard, Norway — Key: — = temperature

Inuvik, Canada

Students should label the following on their graphs:

Similarities:

- Both locations have average temperatures below 0°C for 9 months of the year
- Both locations have low precipitation – less than 50mm a year.

Differences:

- Inuvik has wetter summers, but drier winters than Svalbard.
- Inuvik has colder winters, but warmer summers than Svalbard.

---

2 Exam-style question *Explain how polar flora and fauna have adapted to the extreme climate.*
(4 marks)

This question is point marked. It requires two developed points to obtain 4 marks – one on *flora* and one on *fauna*. However, one well developed point on either of these can obtain three marks. Both flora and fauna must be covered – limit any student who explains one only to 3 marks.

Correct points for *flora* include:

- Small leaves (needles) (1) — plus developed reason e.g. to limit water loss (1).
- Evergreen (1) — plus developed reason e.g. so photosynthesis can start early in the growing season (1).
- Trees are cone shape (1) — plus developed reason e.g. to help shed snow (1).
- Plus other adaptations from diagram on page 125.

Correct points for f*auna* include:

- Migrating into the region in spring, but leaving before winter (1) — plus developed reason e.g. to ensure food and survival (1).
- Thick, white fur (1) — plus developed reason e.g. for camouflage against the snow and for warmth (1).
- Creating dens in snow or caves (1) — plus developed reason e.g. for warmth (1).
- Thick blubber (1) — plus developed reason e.g. to act as insulation from cold (1).
- Plus other adaptations on merit.

8.2 Polar people

Section in brief

In this section students learn about the different groups of people who live in the Arctic, the difficulties they face, and how they have adapted to the extreme environment. They also learn a little about the unique culture of different indigenous Arctic people.

In the activities, students:

- explain why permafrost makes building in polar environments a challenge;
- explain why we should value the culture of indigenous people in the Arctic;
- answer an exam-style question to explain how people have adapted to life in extreme environments.

Key ideas

- There are two main groups of people who live permanently in the Arctic – indigenous groups and immigrants.
- People who live in the Arctic face problems of extreme cold, darkness and isolation, and permafrost.
- People have adapted to the extreme polar environment in a number of ways.
- Indigenous Arctic people have unique cultures.

Key vocabulary

indigenous groups, immigrants, permafrost, active layer, Inuit, Nenets, Aleut

Skills practised

Geographical skills: explain how people have adapted to living in the extreme polar environment; explain why we should value the culture of indigenous people in the Arctic

PLTS: independent enquiry; creative thinking

Section outcomes

By the end of this section, most students should be able to:

- define or explain the terms given in 'Key vocabulary' above;
- give examples of the ways in which people have adapted to the extreme polar environment;
- describe the techniques used for building in areas of permafrost;
- explain why we should value the unique culture of indigenous people in the Arctic.

Ideas for a starter

1 Show students a video clip about how indigenous people live in the Arctic. There is a suitable one on the BBC Learning Zone – clip 11945 called 'Living with cold: Narwhal hunting', which explains how Inuit hunters hunt whale.

2 If students completed the Further activity from Section 8.1, ask several to feed back what they found out to the class.

Ideas for plenaries

1 Use question 2 from page 127 of the students' book as the basis for a class discussion.

2 Make up 5-10 statements based on what students have learned so far in this chapter, some true, some false. Students should identify the false statements and correct them.

Further class and homework activity

Ask students to find a map of Australia which shows its deserts. They should also find out why so much of Australia is desert, in preparation for the next section.

Extreme environments

answers

1. Permafrost is permanently frozen ground which can be tens of metres thick. The active layer which is close to the surface freezes in winter but melts in summer. Heat from buildings can melt the active layer and some of the permafrost, which can make buildings unstable. Buildings have to be built on gravel pads or stilts, so that the permafrost is not melted.

2. There are a number of reasons why we should value the culture of indigenous people in the Arctic, including:

   - The Inuit have immense knowledge of Arctic animals and the environment, so they are often the first to know if the environment is changing.
   - The Nenets people respect many elements of the natural environment.
   - The Aleut people use every part of the seals and whales which they kill – nothing is wasted.
   - The implication is that we can learn a great deal from their cultures.

3. **Exam-style question** *Using named examples, explain how people have adapted to life in extreme polar environments. (6 marks)*

   This question is marked using levels. The key to this question is the command word 'explain' — a Higher Tier command word. Purely descriptive points by Higher Tier candidates get no marks. Foundation Tier students may answer the alternative question:

   Using examples, describe ways in which people adapt to life in extreme polar environments. (6 marks)

   In this case, replace the term 'explanations' in the level descriptions below with 'descriptions'.

   Cap answers at 4 marks which do not include examples of specific adaptations — rather than named places.

   Correct adaptations can be drawn from any if those on page 126-27 and include:

   - Housing built on a gravel pad — plus development e.g. 'so heat does not melt permafrost' — or well-developed e.g. 'which means that heat is not lost into the cold ground'.
   - Housing with raised utility services — plus development e.g. 'which make access easier and do not melt permafrost' — and well-developed if impacts are explained e.g. 'which could cause loss of sewage or water supplies'.

Level	Descriptor
0	No rewardable content
1 (1-2 marks)	Simple undeveloped or very basic statements using little or no subject vocabulary. May be a list of undeveloped points e.g. 'houses are insulated against the cold'. (1 mark).
2 (3-4 marks)	Generalised explanations but with some use of geographical terms e.g. 'houses are insulated against the cold by being built out of wood'. Up to two developed statements as shown by examples above.
3 (5-6 marks)	Detailed statements with clear explanations, using geographical terms. e.g. 'houses are insulated against the cold by being built out of wood which prevents heat loss and also prevents melting permafrost'. Three developed or two well-developed points as shown by examples above.

8.3 Living in the Australian outback

Section in brief

In this section students learn what desert climates are like in Australia. More than one-third of Australia is desert - a challenging environment. Australia has so many deserts because of the rain shadow effect of the Great Dividing Range.

In the activities, students:

- identify the benefits and problems of living in Cook on the Nullarbor Plain;
- put phrases in the correct order to explain why Australia's deserts get so little rain;
- answer an exam-style question to describe the climate of a hot arid area.

Key ideas

- More than one-third of Australia is desert with a harsh, challenging environment.
- Australia's outback (desert and semi-desert areas) is one of the world's most barren and least populated places.
- Australia's deserts exist as a result of the rain shadow effect of the Great Dividing Range.
- Hot arid areas have desert or semi-desert climates.
- The Indian-Pacific train which crosses the Nullarbor Plain is a lifeline for people living in the Nullarbor outback.

Key vocabulary

There is no key vocabulary in this section.

Skills practised

Geographical skills: ordering phrases to explain rain shadow effect; describing the climate of a hot arid area

PLTS: team-working; creative thinking; independent enquiry

Section outcomes

By the end of this section, most students should be able to:

- understand why much of Australia is desert;
- explain the rain shadow effect;
- identify the problems and benefits of living in the Australian outback;
- describe the climate of a hot arid area.

Ideas for a starter

1 Ask students what is the hottest place they have ever been to. How hot was it? What did it feel like? Then tell them that the highest temperature recorded in Australia was 50.7°C in January 1960. That's hot!

2 Show students images of Australia's desert environments, or clips from a film such as 'Rabbit proof fence' which show people surviving in the harsh environment. What do the images show about Australia's deserts?

Idea for a plenary

Tell students they are going on a journey – from Perth to Sydney, and will be crossing the Nullarbor Plain. They need to write a 100-word diary entry describing the journey across the Plain.

Further class and homework activity

Ask students to research how animals have adapted to Australia's desert climate, in preparation for section 8.4. They should find out about three animals and give brief information about each one e.g. how big it is, and how it survives in the harsh environment.

answers

1 Students' ideas will vary, but could include the following to a greater or lesser degree for all three groups:

Benefits: space; cheaper housing and land (due to lack of population); few people around; peace and quiet.

Problems: isolation; lack of access to services, particularly for the young and elderly; lack of schools (children have to move away from home and board, or be tutored at home); lack of social activities particularly for families with teenagers; have to provide own water and power supplies; employment is difficult in harsh environment; shopping is difficult.

2 The correct order is:
- on-shore winds from the Pacific
- winds forced to rise
- cooler temperatures
- condensation
- clouds form
- rain falls
- winds descend
- little moisture left
- deserts form

---

3 Exam-style question *Describe the climate of a hot arid area you have studied. (4 marks)*

This question is point marked. It requires two developed points to create a fully developed answer for four marks. You could use this as an opportunity to develop student skills in using data to illustrate points – each extended illustration is worth an extra mark.

Correct points – any four of which can be marked correct – include:

- Temperatures often reach 40°C (1) — plus development e.g. some places such as Marble Bar can experience 50°C (1).
- Even in winter, temperatures may still reach 30°C (1) — plus development e.g. although sometimes it can be as low as 0°C (1).
- Rainfall is often as low as 200 mm per year (1) — plus development e.g. it can also be as high as 700mm (1).
- Plus other points on merit using the graph or text on page 129.

8.4 How plants and animals survive

Section in brief

In this section students look at how Australia's flora and fauna survive the desert climate. Desert plants have adapted to the arid climate in three main ways: succulence; drought tolerance; drought avoidance. The animals which live in the desert have had to evolve to survive.

In the activities, students:

- define the terms succulence, drought tolerance and drought avoidance;
- draw a spider diagram of the ways in which animals, birds and plants survive drought;
- answer an exam-style question to explain how flora and fauna have adapted to the extreme climate in hot arid areas.

Key ideas

- Australia has a unique biodiversity which includes over one million species.
- The three main ways that desert plants have adapted to the arid climate are: succulence; drought tolerance; drought avoidance.
- Succulent species store water in fleshy leaves, stems or roots.
- Drought tolerance means having mechanisms that help to survive drought.
- Most drought avoiders are annuals, surviving only for one season.
- Desert animals have evolved to survive.

Key vocabulary

biodiversity, succulent, drought tolerance, drought avoidance

Skills practised

Geographical skills: defining terms

PLTS: independent enquiry; creative thinking

Section outcomes

By the end of this section, most students should be able to:

- define or explain the terms given in 'Key vocabulary' above;
- describe and explain the three main ways in which desert plants have adapted to the arid climate;
- give one example of a desert animal and explain how it survives drought.

Ideas for a starter

1 If you used the 'Further activity' in section 8.3, ask a number of students to feed back to the class.

2 Show a variety of photos of desert animals e.g. those shown on page 131 of the students' book. Ask the class: 'What have these animals got in common? How have they adapted to their environment?'

Ideas for plenaries

1 With books closed, ask: 'Who can tell me what the terms biodiversity, succulent, drought tolerance and drought avoidance mean?'

2 Give the class five minutes to prepare a 30-second radio bulletin on how plants survive in the desert environment in Australia, as part of a natural history programme. One member of the group will need to read out the final item.

Further class and homework activity

Ask students to choose one plant and one animal. They should produce an A4 sheet to show how they both survive drought. Ask them to include an image and 150 words of text for each one.

Extreme environments

answers

1
- *Succulence* — succulent plants absorb water quickly and store it in fleshy leaves, stems or roots.
- *Drought tolerance* — e.g. shedding leaves during drought; waxy leaves with few stomata; extensive, deep roots; photosynthesise with low leaf moisture levels.
- *Drought avoidance* — adapted to avoid drought e.g. seeds last for years and only germinate when soil moisture is high.

2 Spider diagrams should include the following as a minimum:
- *Plants*: succulence; drought tolerance; drought avoidance.
- *Animals and birds*: settle near watercourses; nocturnal or hibernate; low moisture needs; feed at cooler times of day; burrow or hide to avoid heat.

3 Exam-style question *Using examples from hot arid areas, explain how flora and fauna have adapted to the extreme climate. (6 marks)*

This question is marked using levels. The key to this question is the command word 'explain' — a Higher Tier command word. Purely descriptive points by Higher Tier candidates get no marks. Foundation Tier students may answer the alternative question:

Using examples from hot arid areas, describe the adaptations made by flora and fauna to the cope with extreme climate. (6 marks)

In this case, replace the term 'explanations' in the level descriptions below with 'descriptions'.

Cap answers at 4 marks which do not include examples of specific adaptations to both flora *and* fauna.

Correct adaptations for *flora* include:
- Succulents can absorb water quickly — plus development with explanation e.g. 'through extensive, shallow root systems' — or well-developed e.g. 'which they store for long periods of drought'.
- Stems and leaves have waxy cuticles /surface layers — plus development e.g. 'which make them almost waterproof when their stomata close' — or well-developed e.g. 'so that they minimise loss of moisture by transpiration'.

Correct adaptations for *fauna* include:
- Named animals e.g. the bilby which is nocturnal — plus development e.g. 'sheltering from the daytime heat to avoid dehydration' — or well-developed e.g. 'burrowing for cooler conditions'.
- E.g. the Perenti which digs burrows or hides in deep rock crevices — plus development with example e.g. 'it hibernates May-August to avoid cold' — well-developed with impacts e.g. 'and has low moisture needs'.

Level	Descriptor
0	No rewardable content
1 (1-2 marks)	Simple or very basic statements using little or no subject vocabulary. May be a descriptive or basic list of points e.g. 'many plants and animals can do without water for long periods'.
2 (3-4 marks)	Generalised explanations but with some use of geographical terms e.g. 'animals such as the bilby are nocturnal and feed then because it is cooler'. Up to two developed statements as shown by examples above.
3 (5-6 marks)	Detailed statements with clear explanations using geographical terms. e.g. 'animals such as the bilby live underground in cooler, moist conditions and are nocturnal; because it is cooler and their water needs are less'. Three developed or two well-developed points as shown by examples above.

8.5 Coping with Australia's extremes

Section in brief

This section looks at how people cope with living in extreme hot arid conditions. It looks at the use of water and land for farming and at how building styles, energy use, transport and clothing have adapted to a hot arid climate.

In the activities, students:

- explain why it is difficult to survive in the Australian outback;
- copy a diagram of artesian water, and explain how water gets underground and how it rises to the surface;
- classify the reasons why farming is difficult;
- answer an exam-style question explaining how people have adapted to life in extreme environments.

Key ideas

- People live in Australia's outback, despite the extreme environment.
- Outback farms are enormous, because poor soils means plants are very low in nutrients.
- Farmers have two sources of water: dams/reservoirs, and boreholes which tap into underground artesian water.
- Building styles, energy use, transport and clothing are all adapted for a hot arid climate.

Key vocabulary

boreholes, artesian water, percolates, windpumps

Skills practised

Geographical skills: classifying reasons; explaining artesian water; explaining how people have adapted to live in an extreme environment

PLTS: independent enquiry; creative thinking; team-working

Section outcomes

By the end of this section, most students should be able to:

- define or explain the terms given in 'Key vocabulary' above;
- list and classify the difficulties farmers face in the outback as economic, social and environmental;
- explain why people question whether the use of water and land in the outback is sustainable;
- explain how people have adapted to life in hot arid areas.

Ideas for a starter

1. Search the Internet for stories of people lost in the Australian outback, and read one to the class. In Australia, newspaper headlines and television bulletins regularly report massive searches in remote outback regions for people who have been lost or stranded. Mostly, the searches end in success. Sometimes they don't.

2. Brainstorm: 'How can you find water in a desert?' Record students' ideas as a spider diagram.

Ideas for plenaries

1. Ask students: 'Who can remind me what the term sustainable means? Are the outback's water and land being used sustainably? How could people live more sustainably in the outback?'

2. Ask students to work in pairs to design a sustainable house for the outback. They should think about the use of energy, water and impact on the environment.

Further class and homework activity

Ask students to research the Great Artesian Basin. They should find out:

- where it is,
- why it is important,
- what threats it faces, and how these affect people.

Extreme environments

answers

1 The outback is an extreme environment, subject to: summer temperatures above 40°C; limited rainfall; droughts poor soils; limited grazing.

2 Students should explain that:
  a Rainwater soaks into the desert soil and percolates into the bedrock. Over many years it collects in an aquifer at X.
  b Water will rise to the surface at Y without the need for a pump if it is under enough pressure, as it is below the level of the water table.

3 Farming is difficult in the outback because:
  Economic reasons: difficulties in getting supplies or veterinary assistance; high fuel costs because of distances.
  Social reasons: farms are large – so no close neighbours; isolation; dispersed settlement means few schools — many children learn by radio.
  Environmental reasons: poor soils; plants are low in nutrients; lack of easily available water; drought leads to soil erosion.

4 Exam-style question *Using examples from hot arid areas, explain how people have adapted to extreme environments. (6 marks)*

This question is marked using levels. With 'explain' as the command word, purely descriptive points get no marks. Foundation Tier students may answer the alternative question:

Using examples from hot arid areas, describe the adaptations made by people to cope with the extreme environment. (6 marks)

In this case, replace the term 'explanations' in the level descriptions below with 'descriptions'.

Cap answers at 4 marks which do not include a specific location or adaptation. Locations can be at the scale of a part of country e.g. 'the outback of Australia', or specific places e.g. 'Coober Pedy'.

Correct examples include:

- Using boreholes or reservoirs to obtain / store water — plus developed explanation e.g. 'as there is insufficient rainfall, and very few rivers' — with well-developed explanations e.g. 'in order to provide domestic water or for cattle'.

- Building styles designed for extreme heat / houses have very thick walls — plus developed explanation e.g. 'to keep summer heat out, and winter warmth in — with well-developed explanations e.g. 'and some buildings in Coober Pedy are underground to keep cool'.

Level	Descriptor
0	No rewardable content
1 (1-2 marks)	Simple or very basic statements using little or no subject vocabulary. May be a list of described points rather than explanations e.g. 'house walls are very think as it is hot'.
2 (3-4 marks)	Generalised explanations but with some use of geographical terms e.g. 'distances between places can be very great so that people have to take large amounts of water when travelling to survive a vehicle breakdown'. Up to two developed statements as shown by examples above.
3 (5-6 marks)	Detailed explanations using geographical terms. e.g. 'travelling long distances between places can be dangerous with 40-degree heat and no water, so people have to travel with large amounts of water to survive a vehicle breakdown, or they would suffer heatstroke'. Three developed points or two well-developed points are required for the top of Level 3 as shown by examples above.

8.6 Valuing people and cultures

Section in brief

In this section students learn about aboriginal culture in Australia and the value of desert cultures. Aboriginal people remain hidden in Australia – within cities and in remote outback camps. They face a range of problems. Aboriginal people traditionally survived by hunting and gathering – with a wide ranging and healthy diet.

In the activities, students:

- list how aboriginal people have adapted to Australia's extreme environment;
- list the ways in which the aboriginal lifestyle is unique, and how understanding the lifestyle is valuable;
- research aboriginal food and create a poster or pamphlet;
- answer an exam-style question explaining why traditional cultures are unique and valuable.

Key ideas

- Traditionally, aboriginal people survived by hunting and gathering a wide range of desert food.
- Aboriginal beliefs focus on the land – it is sacred and is to be protected.
- Aboriginal people face problems of low life-expectancy; drug and alcohol abuse; homelessness; and a loss of their traditional lifestyle.
- Traditional cultures in desert and semi-desert regions provide us with valuable insights.

Key vocabulary

hunting and gathering

Skills practised

Geographical skills: explaining why traditional cultures are unique and valuable

PLTS: team-working; effective participation; independent enquiry; creative thinking

Section outcomes

By the end of this section, most students should be able to:

- explain the terms hunting and gathering;
- create a pamphlet or poster to show how aboriginal people use resources for food and medicine;
- describe problems which aboriginal people face;
- explain why traditional cultures are unique and valuable.

Ideas for a starter

1 Read the first paragraph on page 134 of the students' book aloud to students to set the scene for this section.

2 Show photos of the traditional aboriginal diet, such as bush tomatoes, desert limes, wattle seeds, witchetty grubs and kangaroo on the whiteboard – to appear one at a time. Tell students they are all found in Australia. Can they identify them? Ask what they have in common (they all form part of the aboriginal diet).

Ideas for plenaries

1 Ask three students to read out the three bullet points in the text box on page 134 of the students' book. Ask: 'Why they have these problems arisen?'

2 'Is hunting and gathering sustainable?' Discuss this as a class, and then ask students to produce a table showing the ways in which hunting and gathering is, and is not, sustainable.

Further class and homework activity

Ask students to research two aboriginal stories and rewrite them in their own words.

Extreme environments

answers

1. Students' lists should include: desert groups can find a huge range of food; traditional knowledge of what is edible; plants have multiple uses; hunting and gathering creates conditions in which plants and animals survive and grow.

2. Students lists should include the following:
   i. How the aboriginal lifestyle is unique — use and knowledge of a huge range of natural resources; land is sacred and to be protected; aboriginal people see themselves as caretakers of land rather than owners; cultural value of storytelling.
   ii. How understanding the lifestyle is valuable — traditional knowledge leads to a range of plant uses e.g. for food and medicines; hunting and gathering needs to be sustainable; understanding the cultural value of storytelling.

3. Students' pamphlets or posters should focus on how aboriginal people make use of local resources for food and medicine.

4. **Exam-style question** *Using examples from polar and hot arid areas, explain why traditional cultures are unique and valuable. (8 marks)*

   Purely descriptive points by Higher Tier candidates get no marks. Foundation Tier students may answer the alternative question:

   Using examples from polar and hot arid areas, describe ways in which traditional cultures are unique. (6 marks)

   In this case, three developed or two well-developed descriptions are required for 6 marks.

   Cap answers at 6 marks (4 marks for the Foundation Tier question) which do not:
   - include specific examples of both polar and hot arid areas (either located or names of people) e.g. 'Australian aboriginal people' or 'Inuit in Canada's Hudson Bay';
   - clearly state how the aspect of lifestyle is valuable or unique.

   Correct examples of *polar* regions include:
   - Use of a location and specific value / uniqueness e.g. the Nenets people of northern Russia, and their animist religion — plus development e.g. 'respect for natural environments' — or well-developed e.g. 'something that other cultures could learn from'.

   Correct examples of *hot arid* regions include:
   - Use of a location and specific value / uniqueness e.g. 'Australian aboriginal peoples and their knowledge of how to survive in desert environments' — plus development e.g. 'to allow regeneration of plants / seeds' — or well-developed e.g. 'which would ensure the survival of plants on which they depended'.

Level	Descriptor
0	No rewardable content
1 (1-3 marks)	Simple or very basic statements using little or no subject vocabulary. May be a list or undeveloped description e.g. 'Bedouin peoples use water sustainably'.
2 (4-6 marks)	Generalised explanations but with some use of geographical terms e.g. 'Bedouin peoples use water very sparingly as it is scarce and heavy to carry around'. Up to three developed statements as shown by examples above.
3 (7-8 marks)	Detailed statements with clear explanations using geographical terms. e.g. 'Bedouin peoples use water from boreholes or springs very sparingly as it is scarce in the Sahel region and heavy to carry around, so they are experts in knowing where water holes are'. Three developed points or two well-developed points are required for the top of Level 3 as shown by examples above.

8.7 Threatened people

Section in brief

This section looks at the threats facing traditional cultures and natural systems in extreme environments. Extreme environments are popular with tourists, but traditional cultures face cultural dilution as tourist numbers rise. Extreme environments are often fragile. They are at risk from rising numbers of tourists, and from exploitation for their natural resources.

In the activities, students:

- draw a graph to show the increase in tourist numbers at Uluru, and explain the increase;
- explain why traditional cultures of people in extreme environments are of interest to tourists;
- explain why mining and oil drilling are a threat to extreme environments;
- answer an exam-style question examining the threats facing culture and the environment in extreme environments.

Key ideas

- Extreme environments are increasingly popular with tourists.
- Tourism can be a cause of cultural dilution.
- Extreme environments are often fragile and are at risk from rising numbers of tourists and exploitation of natural resources.
- Extreme environments have limited economic opportunities and face out-migration.

Key vocabulary

cultural dilution, out-migration

Skills practised

Geographical skills: describing the threats facing culture and environment in extreme environments

PLTS: creative thinking; independent enquiry

Numeracy skills: drawing a line graph

Section outcomes

By the end of this section, most students should be able to:

- define or explain the terms given in 'Key vocabulary' above;
- suggest why tourist numbers to Uluru have increased so much;
- explain why traditional cultures in extreme environments are interesting to tourists;
- explain why tourism, mining and drilling are a threat to extreme environments;
- explain the reasons for out-migration in extreme environments.

Ideas for a starter

1. Recap section 8.6 — Valuing people and cultures.
2. Ask students to look at the table of increasing visitor numbers to Uluru on page 136. Ask: 'What problems could these visitors bring?'

Ideas for plenaries

1. Ask students to create a mind map around the phrase 'Threats to extreme environments'. How many ideas can they come up with in two minutes?
2. Tell students that in the past tourists liked to climb on Uluru. However, Uluru is sacred and it is against Anangu spiritual beliefs to climb it. Discuss whether tourists should be allowed to climb Uluru.

Further class and homework activity

Ask students to investigate the Uluru-Kata Tjuta National Park. They should find out how culture is preserved within the National Park.

Extreme environments

answers

1 Students should draw a simple line graph to show the increase in tourist numbers. Reasons for increased numbers include: desire to visit extreme environments; cheaper flights to Australia; improved tourist infrastructure.

2 Answers could include: totally different culture and belief system to tourists' own; traditional skills not seen elsewhere; crafts and skills give a sense of history, little understood by visitors.

3 Mining and oil drilling are a threat to the environment because:
- mine waste, soil heaps and infrastructure can scar the landscape;
- mining uses lots of water (a scarce resource) which ends up polluted;
- there is a risk of oil leaks and spills.

4 Young people and indigenous people tend to migrate out of extreme environments due to lack of jobs and educational opportunities.

---

5 Exam-style question *Using examples, examine the threats facing culture and the environment in extreme environments. (8 marks)*

The key to this question is the command word 'explain' — a Higher Tier command word. Purely descriptive points by Higher Tier candidates get no marks. Foundation Tier students may answer the alternative question:

Using examples, describe the threats facing culture and the environment in extreme environments. (6 marks)

In this case, three developed or two well-developed descriptions are required for 6 marks.

Cap answers at 6 marks (4 marks for the Foundation Tier question) which do not include:
- specific examples, ideally located within a region e.g. the Arctic region of Canada;
- threats to both *culture* and the *environment*.

Correct examples of threats to *culture* include:
- Use of a location and specific threat e.g. tourists walking on Uluru / Ayers Rock in central Australia — plus development e.g. 'because it is sacred ground to aboriginal peoples' — or well-developed e.g. 'and cave paintings there are also threatened by tourist interference'.

Correct examples of threats to the *environment* include:
- Use of a location and specific threat e.g. oil and gas extraction from Alaska and Siberia — plus development e.g. 'which threatens landscapes from pollution from oil spills over land' — or well-developed e.g. 'as well as posing threats of an oil spill into the sea when oil is shipped away to markets'.

Level	Descriptor
0	No rewardable content
1 (1-3 marks)	Simple or very basic statements using little or no subject vocabulary. May be a list or descriptive statements without development e.g. 'drilling for minerals is taking place in the Arctic'.
2 (4-6 marks)	Generalised explanations but with some use of geographical terms e.g. 'exploration and drilling for minerals and oil in the Arctic region threatens natural landscapes'. Up to three developed statements as shown by examples above.
3 (7-8 marks)	Detailed statements with clear explanations using geographical terms. e.g. 'exploration and drilling for minerals and oil in the Arctic region of Siberia threatens natural landscapes because of the risk of oil spills and pollution'. At least two well-developed points (plus one other developed point) are required for the top of Level 3 as shown by examples above.

8.8 The climate change threat

Section in brief

In this section students learn about how climate change threatens polar and hot arid extreme environments. Rising temperatures and falling rainfall will affect Australia's outback. In the Arctic, rising temperatures are having a number of impacts, and climate change is affecting people's lifestyles.

In the activities, students:

- describe the impacts of declining rainfall on people in South Australia;
- explain why the reduction in Arctic sea ice is both good and bad for different people;
- answer an exam-style question examining how climate change threatens people who live in extreme environments.

Key ideas

- Rising temperatures and declining rainfall due to climate change will make Australia's outback a more difficult place to live.
- Declining rainfall will increase land degradation in Australia.
- Climate change is already having serious impacts on the Arctic.
- Climate change in the Arctic is affecting people's lifestyles.
- Climate change in the Arctic will have serious impacts on ecosystems.

Key vocabulary

land degradation

Skills practised

Geographical skills: describing the threats facing culture and environment in extreme environments

PLTS: creative thinking; independent enquiry

Numeracy skills: drawing a line graph

Section outcomes

By the end of this section, most students should be able to:

- explain the term given in 'Key vocabulary' above;
- explain how reduced rainfall might affect people in the Australian outback;
- explain how climate change might affect people living in Arctic areas;
- describe changes to Arctic ecosystems as a result of climate change.

Ideas for a starter

1 Ask students: 'What is a drought?' Definitions of drought vary around the world. In the Sahel, a drought is declared when there is below average rainfall for 2 years. In the UK, at least 15 consecutive days without more than 0.2 mm of rain constitutes a drought.

2 Show students a photo of a polar bear on an ice floe. Explain that as Arctic sea ice retreats, bears will find it harder to hunt and may starve. Ask: 'What might happen to other animals in the food web if there are fewer polar bears?'

Ideas for plenaries

1 Ask students to work in pairs to write a paragraph describing how climate change threatens one extreme environment.

2 Use question 2 from page 139 as the basis for a class discussion.

Further class and homework activity

Ask students to research drought in the Murray-Darling Basin in Australia. They should find out:

- where the MDB is, and why it is important;
- the causes of the 'Big Dry' and its impacts.

Extreme environments

answers

1 The overall trend for Marree Station since 1971 has been downwards. Water shortages and bush fires would have been more common; the growth of grass is restricted; animals over-graze, causing soil erosion; farmers may need to leave their land and migrate away from the area.

2 Reduction in sea ice is *good* news for: oil, gas and mineral companies — as exploration becomes easier; shipping companies — the Arctic Ocean will be open to shipping, cutting journey times between Europe and Asia; tourism companies — as the tourist season will lengthen.

Reduction in sea ice is *bad* news for indigenous people — as traditional ice fishing and hunting will decline.

3 **Exam-style question** *Using named examples, examine how climate change threatens people who live in extreme environments. (8 marks)*

This question is marked using levels. The key to this question is the command word 'examine' — a Higher Tier command word. Purely descriptive points by Higher Tier candidates get no marks. Foundation Tier students may answer the alternative question:

Using named examples, describe the ways in which climate change threatens people who live in extreme environments. (6 marks)

In this case, three developed or two well-developed descriptions are required for 6 marks.

Cap answers at 6 marks (4 marks for the Foundation Tier question) which do not:

- include examples of named peoples (e.g. the Inuit) or regions (e.g. the Arctic region of Canada);
- state the specific threat e.g. to food supply, water, or land quality.

Suitable threats could include:

- Increased temperatures in the Australian Outback of 1.4-5.8°C by 2100 — plus development e.g. 'making droughts more frequent and reducing water supply for farmers' — well-developed with further explanation e.g. 'which is likely to prevent farming using animals unless larger, deeper boreholes are built'.
- Increased temperatures affecting the Canadian Inuit — plus development e.g. 'making traditional hunting expeditions harder as permafrost melts' — or well-developed e.g. 'the ground becomes waterlogged in winter making hunting impossible, so people have to relocate'.

Level	Descriptor
0	No rewardable content
1 (1-3 marks)	Simple or very basic statements using little or no subject vocabulary. May be a list or descriptive statements without development e.g. 'the Inuit won't be able to hunt as they used to'.
2 (4-6 marks)	Generalised explanations but with some use of geographical terms e.g. 'The Inuit's traditional hunting grounds will melt more in summer, which will make hunting for seal difficult'. Up to three developed statements as shown by examples above.
3 (7-8 marks)	Detailed statements with clear explanations using geographical terms. e.g. 'The Inuit's traditional hunting grounds will melt more in summer, which will make hunting for seal difficult and force them to search elsewhere for food, or to change their diet'. At least two well-developed points (plus one other developed point) are required for the top of Level 3 as shown by examples above.

8.9 Facing up to a changing world

Section in brief

This section investigates climate change in Africa and how people can adapt to it. It looks at how using intermediate technology has helped to protect people in Burkina Faso against climate change.

In the activities, students:

- use an atlas to identify countries where the climate will change;
- list and explain the problems that countries will face;
- write a speech to persuade people that diguettes are the way forward and draw a poster to show how they work;
- answer an exam-style question explaining how intermediate technology can help people adapt to the changing climate.

Key ideas

- Climate change is already affecting Africa.
- The Sahel depends on monsoon rains, but rainfall varies from year to year.
- The Sahel is one of the poorest regions in the world, and the least able to cope with climate change.
- Climate change threatens the survival of people living in the Sahel.
- Using intermediate technology to build diguettes in Burkina Faso has prevented soil erosion, preserved rainfall, and improved crop yields.

Key vocabulary

diguettes, intermediate technology

Skills practised

Geographical skills: using an atlas; interpreting a rainfall graph

PLTS: independent enquiry; creative thinking

Literacy skills: writing a speech

Section outcomes

By the end of this section, most students should be able to:

- explain the terms given in 'Key vocabulary' above;
- use an atlas to identify countries affected by changes in rainfall;
- explain how climate change threatens the survival of people in the Sahel;
- write a speech, or draw a poster, to explain how diguettes work, and how they improve people's lives.

Ideas for a starter

1 Ask students: 'Who can give me three facts about the Sahel?'

2 Ask students to list the characteristics of intermediate (or appropriate) technology. They can refer back to section 4.8 (page 72-73) if they need to.

Ideas for plenaries

1 Ask students to locate Burkina Faso on a blank map of the Sahel, and to annotate the map with the problems Siguin Voussé faced in one colour, and how the diguettes helped in another colour.

2 Have a quick fire test. Ask:
   - How is rainfall predicted to change in Africa by 2030?
   - How has land been degraded in the Sahel?
   - How does climate change threaten the survival of people in the Sahel?
   - What are diguettes and how do they work?

Further class and homework activity

Ask students to complete question 3b from page 141 of the students' book for homework.

Extreme environments

answers

1 a and b

Students could compare the map at the top of page 140 with an atlas map to identify those countries that will become wetter, and those that will become drier with climate change.

2 Problems faced by countries which will become *wetter* include:

- Rainy seasons likely to be more unreliable – so more rain doesn't help farmers.
- More, heavy rains will wash away soil.
- Increasing rain doesn't mean increased crop production – rain could fall in heavier bursts.

Problems faced by countries becoming *drier* include:

- Less rainfall leads to increased drought and barren land.
- Grassland is under pressure and becomes overgrazed.
- Farming becomes more intensive which reduces soil fertility.
- Grass dies – soil is exposed to wind erosion.

3 a Students' speeches should highlight the problems that Siguin Voussé faced and how diguettes helped.

b Students' posters should include the following:

- a diguette is a line of stones laid along the contours of gently sloping farmland,
- it slows down rainwater and gives it a chance to soak into the ground,
- they trap soil, which builds up behind the stones and reduce soil erosion,
- crop yields can improve.

---

4 Exam-style question *Using a named example, explain how intermediate technology can help people adapt to the changing climate. (4 marks)*

This question is point marked. It requires two developed points to reach four marks, though one well-developed point for 3 marks plus a single point is also acceptable. Three or four single (i.e. undeveloped) points are capped at 2 marks. The example does not get a mark in itself, but validates the rest of the answer to achieve 4 marks; where a general definition of intermediate technology is given without the use of examples, the answer is capped at 3 marks.

Correct points – using the example of diguettes from page 141 – include:

- Cheap because it consists of line of stones (1) – plus development e.g. designed to slow down rainwater and prevent soil erosion (1) – or well-developed with further explanation e.g. and allow rainwater to soak into the ground (1).
- Demands no technical expertise because it involves a structure that everyone can help to build (1) – plus development e.g. because stones and boulders are found everywhere (1).
- Plus other points on merit and depending on the examples used.

8.10 Taking action for the future

Section in brief

This section looks at how local and global actions can protect extreme environments from the threat of climate change. It investigates how local communities can adapt to climate change in areas such as the Sahel, and how global agreements could slow down climate change.

In the activities, students:

- explain how conservation farming might help farmers in the Sahel adapt to a changing climate;
- explain why Africa and the Arctic are vulnerable to climate change;
- list the achievements and failings of the Kyoto and Copenhagen Summits;
- answer an exam-style question to explain why local and global actions against climate change are needed in extreme environments.

Key ideas

- Climate change is a reality in hot arid and polar extreme environments.
- In hot arid regions, such as the Sahel, farmers are adapting farming methods to cope with climate change.
- The Kyoto and Copenhagen Summits developed global agreements to slow down climate change, but with limited success.

Key vocabulary

conservation farming, multi-cropping

Skills practised

Geographical skills: explaining why local and global actions against climate change are needed in extreme environments

PLTS: creative thinking; independent enquiry

Literacy skills: writing a more extensive answer

Section outcomes

By the end of this section, most students should be able to:

- define or explain the terms given in 'Key vocabulary' above;
- explain how conservation farming might help farmers in the Sahel adapt to climate change;
- explain why Africa and the Arctic are vulnerable to climate change;
- assess the achievements and failings of the Kyoto and Copenhagen Summits.

Ideas for a starter

1. Recap how the Sahel has been affected by climate change from section 8.9.
2. Show the map of 'hunger hotspots' in Africa from page 143 of the students' book on the whiteboard. Ask students to describe the pattern it shows. Then show the map of how rainfall is predicted to change from page 140. Ask students to compare the maps.

Ideas for plenaries

1. Give students a blank map of Africa. Ask them to annotate it to show the benefits of conservation farming.
2. People living in polar and hot arid regions only produce about 5% of global CO_2 emissions. Should the countries which emit the most greenhouse gases pay to reduce the impacts of climate change on regions which are likely to be worst affected? Discuss with the class.

Further class and homework activity

'Why is climate change something that all countries should discuss?' Ask students to answer this question for homework.

Extreme environments

answers

1. Conservation farming helps to: trap soil moisture; minimise soil erosion; reduce the risk of crop failure.

2. Students' responses could include: the Sahel is vulnerable as people are poor; the Sahel has huge variations in rainfall from year to year; the Arctic is warming faster than anywhere else on earth; fragile Arctic ecosystems won't be able to adapt.

3. **Kyoto Summit:**

   Achievements — 191 countries had signed by 2011; the UK, France, Germany; Sweden and Poland met targets.

   Failings — many countries signed, but were not set targets (or did not achieve them); the USA, the world's biggest polluter, had not signed by 2008.

   Copenhagen Summit:

   Achievements — agreed to limit global warming to no more than 2°C; China, India and Brazil were involved.

   Failings — no binding targets for reducing greenhouse gas emissions were agreed (a major failing).

4. **Exam-style question** *Using named examples, explain why local and global actions against climate change are needed in extreme environments. (8 marks)*

   Purely descriptive points by Higher Tier candidates get no marks. Foundation Tier students may answer the alternative question:

   Using named examples, describe local and global actions against climate change being taken in extreme environments. (6 marks)

   In this case, three developed or two well-developed descriptions are required for 6 marks.

   Cap answers at 6 marks (4 marks for the Foundation Tier question) which do not:

   - mention *both* local *and* global actions;
   - include the names of specific strategies for global action e.g. Kyoto;
   - include a named location for local actions — though this can be at a broad scale e.g. the Sahel.

   Correct examples of *local* actions include:

   - Conservation farming in the Sahel — plus development e.g. 'which involves inter-cropping so that several crops are planted together' — or well-developed e.g. 'which protects smaller plants from intense heat using shade of taller ones'.

   Correct examples of *global* actions include:

   - A named global action or agreement with brief aim e.g. Kyoto – to achieve cuts in greenhouse gases — plus development e.g. 'to prevent further climate change, or at least slow it down' — or well-developed e.g. 'which has involved most of the world's countries signing-up to cut carbon emissions'.

Level	Descriptor
0	No rewardable content
1 (1-3 marks)	Simple or very basic statements using little or no subject vocabulary. May be a list or descriptive statements without development e.g. 'Kyoto tried to stop climate change'.
2 (4-6 marks)	Generalised explanations but with some use of geographical terms e.g. 'Kyoto was a global agreement designed to cut CO_2 emissions in every country'. Up to three developed statements as shown by examples above.
3 (7-8 marks)	Detailed statements with clear explanations using geographical terms. e.g. 'Kyoto was a global agreement signed by most countries in 1997, which was designed to reduce greenhouse gas emissions in order to slow down the enhanced greenhouse effect'. At least two well-developed points (plus one other developed point) are required for the top of Level 3 as shown by examples above.

Unit 2 People and the planet

Unit overview
Unit 2, People and the planet, introduces the main considerations surrounding the way in which people live. Students will look at key issues, such as the rate of global resource consumption and increasing global population.

The topics
Four compulsory topics are studied in Section A:

Section A
Population dynamics (chapter 9)
Consuming resources (chapter 10)
Globalisation (chapter 11)
Development dilemmas (chapter 12)

Two option topics are also studied, one from Section B (how people interact with the planet on a small scale) and one from Section C (large-scale aspects of how people interact with the planet). The topics are:

Section B
The changing economy of the UK (chapter 13)
Changing settlements in the UK (chapter 14)

Section C
The challenges of an urban world (chapter 15)
The challenges of a rural world (chapter 16)

Assessment
This unit is assessed through a 1 hour 15 minute, tiered, written examination, which contains a mixture of question styles. 78 marks are available: 48 marks in Section A; 15 marks in Section B; and 15 marks in Section C.

Of the 78 marks available, up to 6 marks are awarded for Spelling, Punctuation and Grammar (SPaG).

Assessment support
Each section (double-page spread) in the students' book includes an exam-style question. A full mark scheme for each exam-style question is included in the answers for each section in this teacher's handbook. In most cases; where questions are aimed at Higher Tier students, a differentiated version is provided for Foundation Tier students, and vice versa.

In addition, the OxBox — published to accompany the **first edition** of the students' book includes:

- one interactive summative assessment per unit in different option combinations;
- an interactive formative assessment for each chapter;
- an exam-style question for each chapter in the first edition.

People and the planet

answers

1. Students should list as many resources as they can that they have consumed so far today.
2. Students should list three ways in which they have put pressure on the earth's resources. Some of the resources they have used will be non-renewable (finite) resources, others will be renewable or sustainable.'
3.

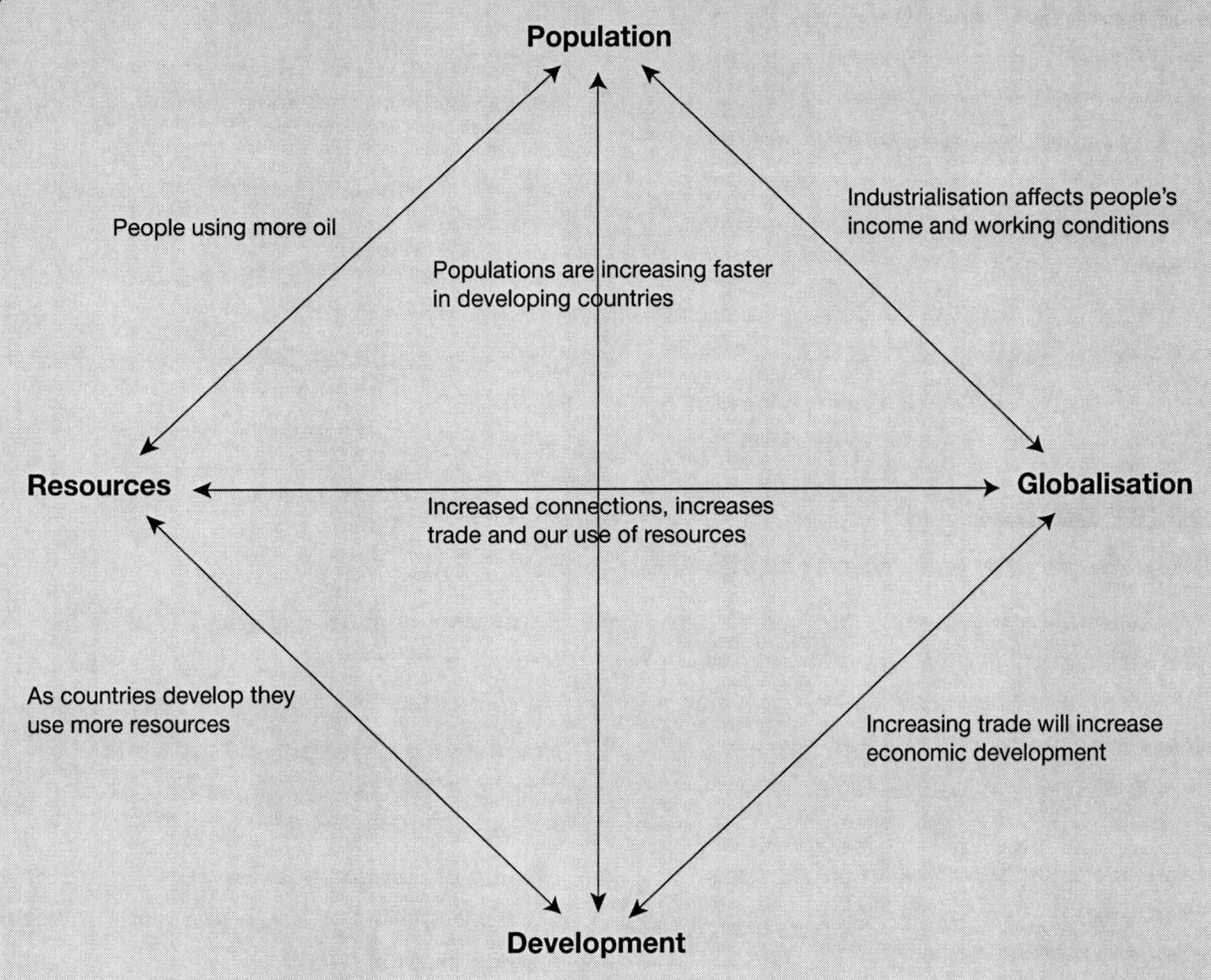

```
                           Population
                              ▲
                            ╱ │ ╲
           People using   ╱   │   ╲   Industrialisation affects people's
           more oil     ╱     │     ╲ income and working conditions
                      ╱   Populations are increasing faster
                     ╱    in developing countries
                    ╱                       ╲
          Resources ◄──────────────────────► Globalisation
                    ╲   Increased connections, increases
                     ╲  trade and our use of resources
                      ╲                     ╱
          As countries develop they       ╱
          use more resources            ╱   Increasing trade will increase
                            ╲         ╱     economic development
                              ▼     ▼
                           Development
```

Students may come up with other links.

4. Students' views may differ, but whatever their view they should be able to explain it.

167

9 Population dynamics

About the chapter
These are the key ideas behind the chapter.
- The world's population was growing exponentially, but is now beginning to slow down.
- Natural population change is the difference between the number of babies born and the number of people who die. It is called the natural increase.
- The Demographic Transition Model helps to explain population change.
- Population change and structure varies between countries at different stages of development.
- Japan's population structure is changing – it is declining, and ageing, creating challenges.
- Mexico's population structure is changing – it is increasing and has a high percentage of young people.
- Many countries have introduced population policies to manage their populations.
- Many countries have policies to control and manage migration flows.

Chapter outline
Use this outline to provide your students with a brief roadmap of the chapter.

9.1 World population growth
The world's population was growing very quickly, but is now beginning to slow down.

9.2 Measuring population change
How to compare population change between countries.

9.3 Understanding how population changes over time
The Demographic Transition Model – how birth and death rates influence how the total population of a country can change over time.

9.4 Variations in population change
Population change is occurring at different rates, in different countries.

9.5 Population change in Japan
Why Japan has a population that is both declining, and ageing.

9.6 Population change in Mexico
Mexico's increasing population, and the country's high percentage of young people.

9.7 Population policies around the world
How governments try to influence population growth in their countries.

9.8 Making population policies work
China's one-child policy.

9.9 Moving around
How the UK tries to control its number of immigrants.

9.10 Migration policy in the USA
How the USA tries to control its number of immigrants.

Population dynamics

How is the specification covered?

This chapter covers Topic 1, Unit 2 People and the planet.

1.1 How and why is population changing in different parts of the world?

1.2 How far can population change and migration be managed sustainably?

Key ideas	Detailed content	Pages in students' book
1.1a The world's population was increasing exponentially but future growth rates are uncertain.	Study an overview of historic trends in global population growth since 1800 and contrasting future projections.	146-147
	Examine the five stages of the demographic transition model to help explain changing population growth rates and structure.	148-149, 150-151
1.1b Population change and structure vary considerably between countries at different levels of development.	Compare two countries at different levels of development to show why their population structure varies, including an assessment of the impact of economic growth, demographic factors, migration and conflict.	152-153
	Investigate different population structures using population pyramids, and explore the issues relating to youthful and ageing populations.	154-155, 156-157
1.2a Different policies attempt to manage change to achieve sustainable levels of population.	Assess the reasons why some countries might wish to manage their populations, including pressure on resources, overcrowding, ageing and skills shortages.	158-159
	Evaluate two contrasting examples of population policies including a pro-natalist (e.g. Singapore) and an anti-natalist (e.g. China).	158-159, 160-161
1.2b Many countries have policies to control and manage migration flows.	Understand why different migration policies develop to either promote or reduce immigration.	162-165
	Evaluate different migration policies including open-door, quotas and skills tests, and the tensions that sometimes arise as a result of these policies.	162-163, 164-165

Chapter outcomes

By the end of this chapter, students should be able to:

- Draw a line graph to show population growth from 1500-2185, and explain what the graph shows.
- Understand how to compare population change between countries.
- Explain how birth and death rates influence the total population at different stages of the Demographic Transition Model.
- Explain the factors that can lead to either population increase, or population decrease.
- Describe the challenges that Japan's declining, but ageing, population creates for the country.
- Describe the changes to Mexico's population structure and give examples of the opportunities that a young population can have for a country.
- Explain why some countries introduce policies to increase their population, while others want to reduce theirs.
- Outline the advantages and disadvantages that immigration has for the UK and USA, and compare the UK and USA's migration policies.

9.1 World population growth

Section in brief

In this section students learn that the world's population has grown very quickly. Up until the 1970s, nearly all countries had an increasing population, but this trend has now changed. Many developed countries are seeing their populations begin to fall, while in some developing countries the number of babies being born is beginning to level off.

In the activities, students:

- draw a line graph to show world population growth;
- calculate and describe past population growth;
- work out and describe future population growth;
- answer an exam-style question to describe different rates of population growth.

Key ideas

- In 2013 the world's population was just over 7.1 billion.
- The world's population has grown exponentially.
- The speed of population growth led to fears of overpopulation and insufficient resources.
- Many developed countries have falling populations.
- In some developing countries the number of babies born is beginning to decrease.

Key vocabulary

demographer, exponential, overpopulated

Skills practised

Geographical skills: interpreting data from a graph and tables; understanding factors which affect population growth

Numeracy skills: drawing a line graph of population growth; calculating population change

Section outcomes

By the end of this section, most students should be able to:

- define or explain the terms given in 'Key vocabulary' above;
- describe changes in world population growth;
- explain why the world's population is still growing, but at a slower rate;
- draw a line graph to show population growth.

Ideas for a starter

1. Show a photo of a class from your school on the whiteboard. Explain to students that this chapter is about real people (like all the students in the photo), who make up the world's population, and how population is changing.
2. Find a world population clock on the Internet and show it on the interactive whiteboard. Use it to demonstrate how fast the world's population is growing.

Ideas for plenaries

1. Give students five minutes to write a paragraph imagining how the world might be in 2185 when there are 10 billion people on the planet.
2. Ask students to prepare five statements for a living graph exercise for their partner, based on the graph they drew for question 1 in the students' book.

Further class and homework activity

Ask students to produce a newspaper report for the birth of the world's 8 billionth person in 2027. Get them to focus on the world's current population growth and the reasons why it is beginning to slow down.

Population dynamics

answers

1 a and b Students should draw a line graph to show world population growth from 1500 to 2185.

c The world's population grew steadily from 1500 to 1900, but it then saw an explosion in growth from around 1930. Projections from the United Nations show that this growth should slow down after 2050, but that the world's population will continue to grow, albeit at a slower rate.

2 a

Year	Number of people	Time taken to add another billion people
1804	1 billion	
1927	2 billion	123 years
1960	3 billion	33 years
1974	4 billion	14 years
1987	5 billion	13 years
1999	6 billion	12 years
2011	7 billion	12 years

b The time taken for the population to increase by another billion people has decreased. It fell from 123 years in 1927, to just 12 years by 1999.

c Exponential — i.e. the bigger the population gets, the faster it grows.

3 a

Year	Number of people	Time taken to add another billion people
2027	8 billion	16 years (since 2011)
2043	9 billion	16 years
2185	10 billion	142 years

b The time taken to add another billion people to the world's population begins to increase again. By 2185 population growth may return to levels last seen in the 1800s.

---

4 Exam-style question *Study the line graph you have drawn for Question 1. Describe the different rates of population growth between 1500 and 2183.*
(2 marks)

This question is point marked. It requires the identification of two stages in the graph. Correct points include:

- it rose slowly to 1927 (1)
- the rate of growth speeded up over time (1)
- it rose rapidly during the 20th century / after 1927 (1)
- the period taken to increase by 1 billion has reduced in almost every decade (1) — with an extra mark if data is used to illustrate e.g. 123 years 1804-1927, 12 years 1987-1999
- geometric progression (1)

9.2 Measuring population change

Section in brief

In this section students learn how to compare population change between different countries. Birth rates and death rates differ between countries and these affect the natural increase of population in a country.

In the activities, students:

- define the terms natural population increase, natural population balance, and natural population decline;
- calculate the natural increase for ten countries, rank them and describe the pattern that emerges;
- calculate birth rates, death rates and natural increase for different countries;
- answer an exam-style question to explain how natural increase is affected by both birth rates and death rates.

Key ideas

- The population of a country is always changing.
- Population change is the difference between the number of babies born and the number of people who die.
- Some countries have population increase, some have population decline, and others population balance.
- Different factors influence birth and death rates in different countries.

Key vocabulary

natural increase, population increase, population decline, population balance, birth rate, death rate, development

Skills practised

Geographical skills: interpreting population data

PLTS: independent enquiry

Numeracy skills: using population information data to calculate natural increase in population, birth rates and death rates

Section outcomes

By the end of this section, most students should be able to:

- define or explain the key terms in the 'Key vocabulary' above;
- calculate the natural increase of population for a given country;
- describe some of the factors that can influence birth rates and death rates in different countries.

Ideas for a starter

1. Show students a news clip about population growth. Ask them to list the factors that could cause a high birth rate and death rate in a country.
2. Give students the birth rate, death rate and natural increase figures for three countries (you could use Denmark, Senegal and Japan from page 148 of the students' book). Ask students how the natural increase has been calculated.

Ideas for plenaries

1. With books closed, ask: 'Who can tell me what the terms birth rate, death rate, and natural increase mean?'
2. Using the 'On your planet' bubble on page 149 of the students' book, get students to calculate how many people have been added to the population in; one minute, one hour, and even one day.

Further class and homework activity

Ask students to find out what the Demographic Transition Model is, and what it shows, in preparation for the next lesson.

Population dynamics

answers

1 a Natural population increase is the number of people added to, or lost from, the population for every 1000 people, in one year.

b Natural population balance is when birth and death rates are almost equal and the population of a country remains constant.

c Natural population decline is when there are more deaths than births in a country and the population falls.

2 a and b

Country	Natural increase %	Rank order
Brazil	1.14	6
Cambodia	1.73	4
China	0.53	=8
Egypt	1.98	3
Haiti	1.62	5
Iraq	2.39	2
New Zealand	0.65	7
Senegal	2.75	1
UK	0.29	10
USA	0.53	=8

c Developing countries have the highest rates of natural increase. Developed countries (New Zealand, USA and UK) have the lowest — all are under 1%. China's rate of natural increase is the same as the USA's as a result of its attempts to limit population growth.

3

Country	Birth rate per 1000	Death rate per 1000	Natural increase per 1000
Austria	8.7	9.9	-1.2
Bolivia	22.4	7.4	15.0
Canada	10.3	7.6	2.7
Thailand	13.6	7.2	6.4
Zambia	40.5	21.3	19.2

---

4 Exam-style question *Explain how natural increase is affected by both birth rates and death rates. (4 marks)*

This question is point marked. It requires some development of points about both birth and death rates to obtain 4 marks. One well developed point on can obtain 3 marks. Both birth and death rates must be mentioned – limit any student who explains only one to 3 marks. However, interpret this liberally – e.g. 'birth rate must exceed death rate for natural increase to occur'.

Correct points include:
- birth rate must exceed death rate for natural increase to occur (1) — plus 1 mark if illustrated using any data in any way;
- where births greatly exceed deaths then the population grows rapidly (1) and vice-versa (1);
- the use of exemplars e.g. 'baby booms cause a rapid increase' (1).

173

9.3 Understanding how population changes over time

Section in brief

In this section students learn how population changes over time as a result of changes in birth and death rates. They are introduced to the Demographic Transition Model and its five stages of population change.

In the activities, students:

- describe what happens to the birth rate, death rate and total population at each stage of the Demographic Transition Model;
- explain how the birth and death rate influence the changing total population at each stage of the model;
- decide which stage of the Demographic Transition Model different countries are at;
- answer an exam-style question to describe how natural increase in population can change as a country's level of development increases.

Key ideas

- The Demographic Transition Model is a simplified representation of how population changes over time.
- The Demographic Transition Model shows how birth and death rates change and influence the total population.
- Countries are at different stages of the Demographic Transition Model.

Key vocabulary

Demographic Transition Model

Skills practised

Geographical skills: analysing changes to birth rates, death rates and total population on the Demographic Transition Model

Section outcomes

By the end of this section, most students should be able to:

- explain the term given in 'Key vocabulary' above;
- describe what the Demographic Transition Model shows;
- explain how birth and death rates influence the total population at different stages of the model;
- describe which stage of the DTM different countries are in, and explain their choice.

Ideas for a starter

1. Ask students: 'Who knows how the UK's population has changed over time? Has it increased? What has happened to the birth rate and death rate in the UK?'
2. If any students completed the Further Activity from section 9.2, ask several to feed back what they found out about the Demographic Transition Model to the class.

Ideas for plenaries

1. Give students a copy of the Demographic Transition Model. Ask them to shade in those areas where population is growing, and those areas where population is declining.
2. Use question 3 from the students' book as a plenary activity.

Further class and homework activity

Tell students that the model has worked quite well for countries such as the UK, which have gone from a rural, poorly educated society to an urban, industrial, well-educated one. Ask them why some poorer countries might not follow all the stages of the model.

Population dynamics

answers

1 a, b, c

	Stage 1	Stage 2	Stage 3	Stage 4	Stage 5
a Birth rate	High	High	Falling	Low	Very low
b Death rate	High	Falling	Falling	Low	Rising
c Total population	Stays low	Increases rapidly	Increases slowly	Little or no increase in population	Population declining slowly

2 **Stage 1** – High death rate cancels out high birth rate, so population stays low.

Stage 2 – Fewer people are dying, but birth rate is still high so population increases rapidly.

Stage 3 – Birth rate is still higher than death rate, so population continues to grow, but it is beginning to slow down.

Stage 4 – Low birth and death rates mean little or no population growth.

Stage 5 – Very low birth rates and rising death rates mean population begins to decline slowly.

3 **China** – Stage 3/4; Low birth and death rates, population still growing.

Italy – Stage 5; Death rate higher than birth rate, so population is declining.

Mexico – Stage 3; Birth rate higher than death rate, population is growing rapidly.

Sierra Leone – Stage 2; Birth rate very high, death rate high (but lower than birth rate), so population rising very rapidly.

Sweden / UK – Stage 4; low birth and death rates, population rising slowly.

---

4 **Exam-style question** *Using examples, describe how natural increase in population can change as a country's level of development increases. (6 marks)*

Cap answers at 4 marks which do not include:

- examples of named countries, or mention of specific population indicators and their relationship to development indicators e.g. GDP, literacy rates, infant mortality;
- an explanation of birth *and* death rates.

Correct changes to *birth rates* include:

- The decline of birth rates as GDP increases — plus development e.g. 'so that families become smaller' — or well-developed with further expansion e.g. 'and women prefer to have fewer children'.

Correct adaptations for *death rates* include:

- The rapid fall in death rates as a country develops — plus development e.g. 'matched by falling infant mortality rates' — or well-developed e.g. 'when more is spent on health care / clean water'.
- Plus other adaptations from page 150-151.

Level	Descriptor
0	No rewardable content
1 (1-2 marks)	Simple or very basic statements using little or no subject vocabulary. May be a descriptive or basic list of points e.g. 'births rates fall as countries get richer'.
2 (3-4 marks)	Generalised explanations but with some use of geographical terms. Up to two developed statements as shown by examples above.
3 (5-6 marks)	Detailed statements with clear explanations using geographical terms. e.g. 'birth rates fall rapidly as countries develop and as GDP increases, together with decreasing infant mortality, are both the result of increases in health spending'. Three developed or two well-developed points as shown by examples above.

9.4 Variations in population change

Section in brief

In this section students look at how the rate of population change varies between different countries. Higher levels of population increase are occurring in low- and middle-income countries, while lower levels of increase, population balance or decline are occurring in high-income countries.

In the activities, students:

- draw a scatter graph to show the relationship between GNI and natural increase, and describe and explain the pattern shown;
- compare the reasons for population change between Russia and Yemen;
- explain how low literacy rates among women can cause high fertility rates;
- answer an exam-style question to explain the factors that can lead to population change.

Key ideas

- Population change is happening at different rates in different countries.
- Higher levels of population increase are occurring in developing (low-and middle-income) countries.
- Lower levels of population increase, balance or decline, mainly occur in developed (high-income) countries.

Key vocabulary

High-income countries (HICs), Middle-income countries (MICs), Low-income countries (LICs), outward migration, fertility rate

Skills practised

Geographical skills: describing and explaining patterns; comparing reasons for population decline and rising population

PLTS: independent enquiry

Numeracy skills: drawing a scatter graph and 'line of best fit'

Literacy skills: researching and writing a case study

Section outcomes

By the end of this section, most students should be able to:

- define or explain the terms given in 'Key vocabulary' above;
- describe the relationship between GNI and natural increase of population;
- compare the reasons for Russia's falling population and Yemen's rising population;
- explain how low literacy rates among women can cause a high fertility rate.

Ideas for a starter

1. Show students a photograph of a Yemeni family. Can students find Yemen on a world map? What do they know about this country? Why do they think Yemen might have a rapidly growing population?

2. Show students the world map showing the global percentage natural increase in population from page 152 of the students' book. Ask them to describe the patterns shown on the map. Why might these patterns exist?

Ideas for plenaries

1. Give students ten minutes to complete the exam-style question. When finished, ask students to work in small groups to see who has produced the best answer. How could other students' answers be improved?

2. Ask students to prepare a 30-second news report from Russia examining the reasons for its declining population.

Further class and homework activity

Ask students to research one example of a country experiencing rapid population increase, and one experiencing population decline. They should produce a short (300 word) case study explaining the reasons for population change in their selected countries.

Population dynamics

answers

1 a–d Students should draw a scatter graph using the data on page 153.

  e The scatter graphs clearly show that, as GNI per person goes up, the % natural increase of population goes down.

  f This pattern means that, as a country gains more wealth (or develops), its rate of population increase will go down. This shows that the wealth, or development of a country, is clearly related to population growth.

2

Reasons for Russia's falling population	Reasons for Yemen's increasing population
A falling life expectancy for men (60 years) caused by industrial disease and alcoholism	Early age of marriage - 48% of women are married by the age of 18
A low fertility rate of 1.2 children per woman	A high fertility rate of 6.7 children per woman
Outward migration of young men and women	A low literacy rate among women
	Increasing life expectancy, especially of children

3 Less educated women are likely to have a higher fertility rate as they: are less likely to delay childbirth due to career commitments; may marry early (and therefore have children earlier) for financial security; may be unable to understand written contraception advice.

---

4 Exam-style question *Referring to examples, explain the factors that can lead to either a natural population increase or a natural population decrease. (4 marks)*

This question is point marked. It requires two developed statements (each worth 2 marks) for 4 marks; exceptionally, award 3 marks for a well-developed statement.

Correct factors for a natural population **increase** include:

- High birth rates due to: early age of marriage (1) — plus development with data e.g. 48% of women in Yemen are married by 18 (1); low levels of female literacy / education (1) — plus development 'which results from leaving school early' (1) — or well-developed e.g. 'which in Yemen leads to a high fertility rate of 6.7 children per woman'.

- Low death rates due to: increasing life expectancy (1) — plus development e.g. 'due to improved child vaccinations' (1) — plus well-developed with further expansion e.g. 'leading to reduced infant mortality'.

Correct adaptations for a natural population **decrease** include:

- Increasing death rates due to: falling life expectancy for men (1) — plus development with example e.g. in Russia — plus well-developed with further expansion e.g. 'caused by industrial disease and alcoholism'.

- Low fertility rates (1) — plus development with example e.g. Russia 1.2 children per woman — plus well developed with further expansion e.g. 'due to outward migration of young men and women i.e. of child-bearing age' (1) — plus development e.g. 'because of economic decline / lack of jobs and people migrate elsewhere for work' (1).

9.5 Population change in Japan

Section in brief

This section looks at the reasons why Japan's population structure is changing, and the impacts this will have. Japan now has the oldest population in the world with the highest average age, as well as a birth rate below the replacement level.

In the activities, students:

- describe and explain the changes in population pyramids for Japan between 1950 and 2050;
- describe the changes in the natural increase in Japan's population since 1950;
- explain why the population of Japan is decreasing and getting older;
- answer an exam-style question to describe what is meant by an ageing population, and outline two problems faced by countries with an ageing population.

Key ideas

- Japan has the oldest population in the world.
- Japan's population is declining as the birth rate remains below the replacement level.
- Japan's population structure is changing because people are living longer and the birth rate is declining.
- The changes in Japan's population structure are creating challenges.

Key vocabulary

replacement level

Skills practised

Geographical skills: describing and explaining changes in population structure; analysing population graph

Section outcomes

By the end of this section, most students should be able to:

- define or explain the term given in 'Key vocabulary' above;
- describe the changes to Japan's population structure since 1950;
- explain why Japan's population is getting older and declining;
- explain how the Japanese government is responding to the changes in the population structure.

Ideas for a starter

1. Ask students to look at the photo and newspaper article on page 154 to introduce this section on Japan's changing population.
2. Show students the three population pyramids for Japan from 1950 to 2050. What do they think they show? How are they changing?

Ideas for plenaries

1. Give students five minutes to draw a quick sketch of a population pyramid for Japan in 2075. How do they think Japan's population will have changed by then?
2. Ask students to complete a pyramid review of this lesson. They should write down the following in the shape of a pyramid:
    - one question they have
    - two points they are not sure of
    - three points they have learnt.

Further class and homework activity

Ask students to research the UK's changing population structure. The US Census Bureau website includes population pyramids for the UK and projections for the future. What challenges will changes to the population structure of the UK present in the future?

Population dynamics

answers

1 a The population pyramid for 1950 has a wide base that narrows towards the top. By 2006 the pyramid appears more egg-shaped, with a narrower base and wider top than previously. The projection for 2050 shows an upside-down pyramid.

b The base of the pyramids for 2006 and 2050 continue to narrow, indicating a falling birth rate; the under 15s in 1950 make up the largest proportion of the population, shown as a bulge in population as they move through the stages of the pyramid.

2 The rate of natural increase has mirrored the fall in live birth rate. A slowly increasing death rate has caused a further fall in the rate of natural increase.

3 a People in Japan are living longer due to a healthy diet (low in fat and salt) and good health and welfare systems.

b Japan's birth rate has fallen below replacement level, partly because the average age at which women have their first child is increasing.

---

4 a **Exam-style question** *Describe what is meant by an 'ageing population'. (2 marks)*

This question is point marked, and requires a developed point for both marks. Correct points include:

- The average age of a population increases (1) — plus a reason e.g. as life expectancy increases / the birth rate declines (1).

b **Exam-style question** *Using a named example, outline two problems faced by countries with an ageing population. (4 marks)*

This question is point marked. It requires two developed points for 4 marks. However, one well developed point on either of these can obtain 3 marks. Two problems must be outlined — limit any student who explains one only to 3 marks maximum.

Correct points include:

- Increasing cost of pensions (1) as more people live longer (1)
- Fewer workers in the economy (1) so higher taxes are needed to fund pensions (1)
- Increase in cost of care in nursing homes (1) and of declining health (1)
- plus other relevant points on merit

9.6 Population change in Mexico

Section in brief

In this section students look at the reasons why Mexico has an increasing population with a high percentage of young people. Mexico's population has grown due to a relatively high birth rate, and low death rate. Mexico's growing population creates challenges and opportunities.

In the activities, students:

- explain why Mexico's population is increasing;
- think about the opportunities that a large youthful population will have for a country like Mexico;
- answer an exam-style question to describe the population pyramids for Mexico and explain the changes between 1985 and 2015;
- answer a second exam-style question to describe changes in birth rates and death rates for Mexico, and to explain how the natural increase in population will have changed.

Key ideas

- Mexico has a large, youthful, and rapidly growing population.
- Mexico's population structure is changing as a result of a low death rate, longer life expectancy, a falling birth rate, and a large percentage of young people.
- A growing population with an increasing percentage of young people creates challenges and opportunities for Mexico.

Key vocabulary

There is no key vocabulary in this section.

Skills practised

Geographical skills: describing and explaining changes in population structure; analysing population graph

Section outcomes

By the end of this section, most students should be able to:

- explain why Mexico's population is increasing;
- describe the changes to Mexico's population structure since 1985;
- give examples of the opportunities that a young population can have for a country.

Ideas for a starter

1. Ask students to look at the population pyramids for Mexico on page 156 of the students' book. Ask them to describe the changes that are happening to Mexico's population structure.

2. Brainstorm: What do students already know about Mexico? Can they locate it on a blank world map? Who can be the first to come up with two more facts about Mexico?

Ideas for plenaries

1. Ask students to share their answers to question 2 from page 157 of the students' book with the rest of the class. Create a table on the whiteboard showing the opportunities that a youthful population will provide for a country such as Mexico.

2. Ask students to sketch a population pyramid for Mexico for 2050. How do they think Mexico's population will have changed by then?

Further class and homework activity

Ask students to find out five facts about migration from Mexico to the USA (in preparation for section 9.10).

Population dynamics

answers

1 The population of Mexico is increasing because it has a large percentage of young people, a relatively high birth rate and a low death rate. More people are being added to the population and life expectancy has increased due to childhood vaccinations and an increase in doctors.

2 Other examples of the opportunities that a young population may provide for a country include:
- a large workforce which could potentially rival South East Asia for mass production;
- the opportunity to create a large highly-skilled workforce with an increase in university educated people;
- a focus on new and emerging technological industries that young people could be part of;
- an increase in tax revenue for the government;
- a boom in education and training companies.

3 **Exam-style question** Look at the population pyramids for Mexico.

  a *Describe the shape of each pyramid. (2 marks)*
  Each of these questions is point marked.
  Correct points include:
  - 1985 – a cone- or triangle-shape / high birth rate and high death rate / broad base and narrow top (1);
  - 2015 – bottle-shape / lower birth and death rate / narrower base and broadening top (1).

  b *Explain the changes over this period. (2 marks)*
  Correct points include:
  - Birth rate fell (1) — plus developed reason e.g. as the country urbanised and family size is lower in cities (1);
  - Death rate fell / life expectancy increased (1) — plus developed reason e.g. as health care developed, lowering infant mortality (1).

4 **Exam-style question** Look at the graph showing the birth and death rates in Mexico.

  a *Describe the changes that the graph shows. (2 marks)*
  This question is point marked.
  Correct points include:
  - Birth rates: a steady / stable period — fluctuating to 1960 (1) — followed by a sharp / steep fall to 1980 (1) — then a stable period (1) — and a slight increase after 2000 (1).

  b *How would the natural increase in population have changed over this period? (2 marks)*
  Correct points include:
  - Likely to have increased rapidly (1) — fastest in 1960s-80s (1) — plus reason e.g. the death rate fell sharply (1) — while the birth rate remained high (1).

9.7 Population policies around the world

Section in brief

In this section students learn how governments try to influence population growth in their countries using anti-natalist, pro-natalist and immigration policies. This section includes examples of these policies, and looks at Singapore's pro-natalist population policy in more detail.

In the activities, students:

- consider the reasons why some countries need to use pro-natalist, and others anti-natalist policies;
- consider other population policies which countries might use;
- discuss Singapore's pro-natalist policy;
- think about the impacts of population policies on people who live in those countries;
- answer an exam-style question to explain why some countries choose to increase their population, while others choose to reduce theirs.

Key ideas

- Many countries around the world have introduced population policies to influence their population size, growth, distribution or composition.
- Pro-natalist policies encourage people to have more children by offering incentives.
- Anti-natalist policies encourage people to have fewer children, by offering different incentives.
- Singapore has developed a pro-natalist policy to balance an ageing and declining population.

Key vocabulary

population policy, pro-natalist policy, anti-natalist policy

Skills practised

PLTS: independent enquiry; creative thinking; team working

Literacy skills: producing a newspaper front page

Section outcomes

By the end of this section, most students should be able to:

- define or explain the terms given in 'Key vocabulary' above;
- explain the reasons why some countries introduce policies to increase their population, while others choose to reduce theirs;
- describe the problems facing Singapore if its pro-natalist policy does not work;
- assess the impacts of population policies on the lives of individuals.

Ideas for a starter

1. Recap section 9.5 on population change in Japan. Remind students that Japan's population is declining, and ageing. Should Japan encourage people to have more children? How could they do this?
2. Ask students to work in pairs. Get them to think about why a country might want to try and limit its population growth, and to list the ways in which a government could reduce the number of babies being born.

Ideas for plenaries

1. Write 'Population policies' in the middle of the board. Ask students to create a mind map around the phrase. How many ideas can they come up with in two minutes?
2. Ask students to work in pairs to write a thirty second sound bite for the radio on Singapore's pro-natalist policy.

Further class and homework activity

Ask students to research population control in Kerala, India, to produce a newspaper front page. They should find out how Kerala has managed to control its population, and the impacts this has had.

Population dynamics

answers

1 Reasons for *pro-natalist* policies include: declining fertility rate (leads to a decrease in the overall population); an ageing population; more workers will be needed in future to keep a country economically competitive.

Reasons for *anti-natalist* policies include: concern that an increasing population might mean a lack of resources/services/facilities in future.

2 Migration policies — to set limits on the number of people allowed to enter a country.

3 a The overall trend in the fertility rate is downwards. By 2040 fertility is predicted to be half what it was in 1900.

b The Baby Bonus scheme is likely to increase the fertility rate — it offers financial incentives to encourage Singaporeans to have children.

c Singapore will have an increasingly ageing population and a smaller working population. The cost of pensions will rise, and those in work will have to pay more in taxes to fund this. Rising numbers of people will need care in nursing homes, and/or additional medical treatment which will be an additional cost for the government and tax payers.

4 Anti-natalist population policies often remove people's freedom to choose how many children they would like to have, sometimes leading to resentment or protests. People are more likely to react positively to policies which encourage them to have children as these can provide financial help towards the cost of raising children.

---

5 Exam-style question *Using named examples, explain why some countries choose to increase their population, but others choose to reduce it. (6 marks)*

This question is marked using levels. Foundation Tier students may answer the alternative question:

Using named examples, describe the ways in which some countries attempt to increase their populations. (6 marks)

In this case, replace references to 'explanations' in the mark scheme with 'descriptions'. Cap answers at the top of Level 2 (4 marks) which do not include named specific countries — and reasons for both *increasing* and *reducing* populations.

Countries choose to **increase** their population:

- To increase the working population — plus development e.g. 'to balance an ageing population' — 'so that there are more people working to support dependents' e.g. Singapore or the UK.
- To ensure there are enough workers for future economic growth — plus development e.g. 'to balance outward migration' — 'so that there are more people paying taxes' e.g Russia.

Countries choose to **reduce** their population:

- To reduce population pressure — plus development e.g. 'because of pressure on housing / health / services' — 'which affects quality of life' e.g. India or China.

Level	Descriptor
0	No rewardable content
1 (1-2 marks)	Simple or very basic statements using little or no subject vocabulary.
2 (3-4 marks)	Generalised explanations but with some use of geographical terms. Up to two developed statements as shown by examples above.
3 (5-6 marks)	Detailed statements with clear explanations using geographical terms. Three developed or two well-developed points as shown by examples above.

9.8 Making population policies work

Section in brief

In this section students learn about China's anti-natalist policy. In 1979 China introduced rules to limit population growth. The policy has successfully prevented millions of births. However, it has had some negative impacts.

In the activities, students:

- describe the changes to China's fertility rate;
- explain why people in China will live longer as they become wealthier;
- describe the problems the 4-2-1 issue will create for people living in China;
- answer an exam-style question to explain how some countries use population policies to limit their population growth.

Key ideas

- China's birth rate, and therefore its population growth, reached unsustainable levels in the 1950s and 60s.
- In 1979 China introduced the one-child policy to limit population growth.
- The one-child policy successfully prevented 300 million births.
- The one-child policy has had a number of negative economic and social effects.

Key vocabulary

one-child policy

Skills practised

Geographical skills: using a graph to describe changes to fertility rate; explaining how countries use population policies to limit population growth

Section outcomes

By the end of this section, most students should be able to:

- explain the term given in 'Key vocabulary' above;
- explain why China introduced the one-child policy;
- describe the changes in China's fertility rate;
- describe the problems that the one-child policy has created.

Ideas for a starter

1. Recap anti-natalist policies from section 9.7. Ask students how governments can reduce the number of babies being born in a country?
2. Tell students some facts about China's population to start this section off e.g. China has the largest population in the world (1.343 billion in 2012); more boys are born than girls; Han Chinese make up 91.5% of the population; 50 000 babies are born every day.

Ideas for plenaries

1. Hold a class debate — 'China's one-child policy should be abandoned'. Some students should be in favour of abandoning the policy, some should be in favour of keeping it.
2. Ask students to work in pairs to write a thirty second sound-bite on China's one-child policy.

Further class and homework activity

Ask students to come up with three questions they would like to ask the Chinese government about its one-child policy. Make this a 'hot seat' activity, with students taking on the roles of the Chinese government to answer the questions.

Population dynamics

answers

1 China's fertility rate peaked in the late 1960s at 5.8 per 1000. It declined rapidly until about 1980 when it reached about 2.7 per 1000. It remained stable until the late 1980s, before falling again to about 1.6 per 1000 by 2010.

2 People in China are expected to live longer as they become wealthier. This is because they will have more money to spend on a healthier, more varied diet and on health care. Taxes paid to the government will see better health and welfare systems set up for the population of the entire country.

3 The 4-2-1 problem will leave *one* member of the family (the 'one-child') possibly having to provide for *two* elderly parents, as well as *four* (much more elderly) grandparents – especially as life expectancy increases. In larger families this burden would have been spread between a number of children.

---

4 **Exam-style question** *Explain how some countries use population policies to limit their population growth. (6 marks)*

This question is marked using levels. Foundation Tier students may answer the alternative question:

Describe the ways in which countries try to limit their population growth.

In this case, replace references to 'explanations' in the mark scheme with 'descriptions'. Cap answers at the top of Level 2 (4 marks) which do not mention specific population policies and the country/countries in which they operate.

Suitable policies could include:

- Ante-natal, with example e.g. China's one child policy — plus development e.g. 'which limits the number of children families can have by law' — with further well-developed explanation e.g. 'and which can be extended by offering tax or cash benefits if you limit family size in this way'.

- Migration controls, with example e.g. strong limits on immigration / skills tests — plus development e.g. 'because of the pressures on housing if the population rises too rapidly' — or well-developed e.g. 'and controlling immigration is one of the ways to prevent young people who might marry and have children from entering the country.

Level	Descriptor
0	No rewardable content
1 (1-2 marks)	Simple or very basic statements using little or no subject vocabulary. May be a descriptive or basic list of points e.g. 'countries reduce populations because there are too many people and not enough housing'.
2 (3-4 marks)	Generalised explanations but with some use of geographical terms e.g. 'India tried to reduce its population using compulsory methods because of pressure on housing and resources such as food'. Up to two developed statements as shown by examples above.
3 (5-6 marks)	Detailed statements with clear explanations using geographical terms. e.g. 'India tried to reduce its population using methods such as compulsory sterilisation because the government thought there would be too much pressure on housing and agriculture in future, and voluntary methods had not worked'. Three developed or two well-developed points as shown by examples above.

9.9 Moving Around

Section in brief

In this section students learn how the UK has tried to control the number of immigrants entering the country. It looks at how immigration has changed the UK's population, at some of the perceived impacts of immigration, and how the UK's migration policy has changed.

In the activities, students:

- explain what is meant by an open-door approach to immigration;
- produce a table showing the positive and negative impacts of migration;
- explain why they think the British government has set limits on the number of immigrants welcome to the UK;
- answer an exam-style question to describe two potential advantages and two potential disadvantages of having a large immigrant population.

Key ideas

- The UK's population has changed as a result of immigration.
- Immigration can have positive or negative impacts, depending on people's point of view.
- Until 2010 the UK operated an open-door policy on migration.
- The UK has now adopted a quota based approach to immigration, and introduced skills tests.

Key vocabulary

one-child policy

Skills practised

Geographical skills: describe the advantages and disadvantages of migration; explain why the government sets limits on immigration

PLTS: independent enquiry; creative thinking

Section outcomes

By the end of this section, most students should be able to:

- define or explain the terms given in 'Key vocabulary' above;
- describe how the UK's population has changed as a result of recent immigration;
- complete a table to show positive and negative aspects of migration;
- explain why the UK government has set limits on the number of immigrants welcome to the UK.

Ideas for a starter

1. Ask students: Why do people migrate? Who is likely to move to the UK, and why? Who is likely to leave the UK, and why?
2. Show students recent newspaper headlines about immigration on the whiteboard. What do students know about migration to the UK? Are there any limits to the number of migrants who can come to the UK?

Ideas for plenaries

1. Hot seat! Ask several students to take on the roles of UK government ministers – they are in the hot seats. The rest of the class should ask them sensible questions concerning the current migration policy, which is based on a quota and skills tests.
2. Hold a class discussion on whether the UK should revert to an open-door policy on migration.

Further class and homework activity

Ask students to find out about Polish migration to the UK. They should find out when large numbers of East Europeans (including Poles) began migrating to the UK; why they came; whether they are still coming in such large numbers.

Population dynamics

answers

1 An open-door approach is when a country encourages migrants to move in, often for economic reasons.

2

Positive impacts of migration	Negative impacts of migration
Promotes tolerance between different groups of people.	Can put a strain on welfare and healthcare systems.
Connects different places around the world.	Local people can find it difficult to compete for jobs.
Boosts the economy.	Immigrants can remain isolated leading to negative stereotypes.
Provides a skilled and well-qualified workforce.	
Contributes to cultural diversity.	
As migrants are often young they balance the population structure.	

3 In order to restrict the numbers of people migrating to the UK the government has introduced a quota system along with skills tests. Students may suggest further arguments based on their own views about why the government has set limits on migrants to the UK.

4 **Exam-style question** *Describe two potential advantages and two potential disadvantages of having a large immigrant population. (4 marks)*

This question is point marked. With 'describe' as a command word, it is suitable for all candidates. You are not looking for any development of points here, simply two listed advantages and disadvantages.

Correct **advantages** include:

- It promotes tolerance / cultural diversity between different groups of people (1)
- It can provide an economic boost to a country with more people to work (1)
- It can prevent labour shortages (1)
- Immigrants contribute more to the economy than they cost (1)
- Helps build a skilled / well-qualified workforce (1)
- Cultural benefits — greater variety of food and music etc. (1)
- Balances an ageing population (1).

Correct **disadvantages** include:

- It can place a strain on welfare / healthcare systems (1)
- Local people can find it difficult to compete in the job market (1)
- Immigrants can often remain isolated and separate from the wider community (1)
- Can create negative stereotypes (1).

9.10 Migration policy in the USA

Section in brief

In this section students learn how the USA tries to control its number of immigrants. The USA has had some form of immigration policy since its inception, and now has 37 million foreign-born residents. The USA sets strict limits on the number of immigrants allowed to enter the country each year. But it is unable to control large numbers of illegal immigrants, particularly from Mexico.

In the activities, students:

- list the reasons why the USA wants to control the number of immigrants entering the country;
- explain the reasons for the 'four aims' of the immigration policy;
- identify peak periods and current trends for immigration;
- identify where migrants to the USA come from;
- answer an exam-style question to explain how some countries try to increase immigration, while others try to reduce it.

Key ideas

- Over 12% of the USA's population is foreign-born.
- The USA's immigration policy sets limits on the number of immigrants allowed to enter the country each year.
- The USA's immigration policy aims to fill skills shortages, reunite families, provide refuge, and increase ethnic diversity in the country.
- There are an estimated 12 million illegal immigrants living in the USA (over 50% are from Mexico).
- Immigration can bring advantages and disadvantages to the USA.

Key vocabulary

There is no key vocabulary in this section

Skills practised

Geographical skills: interpreting a graph

PLTS: independent enquiry; creative thinking

Literacy skills: producing a poster

Section outcomes

By the end of this section, most students should be able to:

- list the reasons why the USA wants to control the number of immigrants entering the country;
- understand the key aims of the US immigration policy;
- describe where migrants to the USA come from;
- list the advantages and disadvantages of immigration for the USA.

Ideas for a starter

1. Brainstorm: Who might want to go and live in the USA, and why?
2. If students completed the Further Activity from section 9.6, ask several to feedback what they found out to the class.

Ideas for plenaries

1. Ask students to annotate a blank map of the USA with the advantages and disadvantages of immigration for the USA.
2. Discuss as a class the problems that illegal immigration can cause for the USA.

Further class and homework activity

Ask students to produce a poster which explains the aims of the US immigration policy to people who might want to move to the USA.

Population dynamics

answers

1 The USA would want to control the number of immigrants entering the country each year because: it ensures that services (e.g. health and welfare) don't become over-stretched; it wants to ensure that immigrants are matched to specific skills shortages; too many immigrants could lead to a reduction in wages for US workers; there may be too much competition for jobs, leaving some migrants unemployed and a possible drain on the welfare system.

2 The reasons are:
- **Aim 1** — To ensure that the USA has a competitive workforce, and to fill gaps in the labour market.
- **Aim 2** — It allows people who have settled in the USA to bring family members over, which is more likely to encourage them to stay and work.
- **Aim 3** — This supports the US Constitution and portrays the USA as the 'Land of the Free'.
- **Aim 4** — Ensures that there continues to be a balanced ethnic mix, something that the USA has prided itself on.

3 a Immigration peaks occurred in: 1880, 1900-1920, mid-1920s and 1990.

b The current trend for immigration is a gradual increase that had a significant spike in 1990, and two smaller spikes more recently.

4 The highest number of migrants come from the West Indies, Guyana, Central America (particularly Mexico), followed by Canada and then northern countries of South America. Pockets of migrants also come from the UK, Eastern Europe, Mongolia and south-east Asia.

---

5 Exam-style question *Using examples, explain how some countries try to increase immigration, whilst other countries try to reduce it. (6 marks)*

This is a Higher Tier question. Cap answers at the top of Level 2 (4 marks) which do not include:
- named specific countries
- examples of how countries both increase and reduce immigration

Countries try to **increase** immigration:
- To expand their pool of skilled labour e.g. Australia — plus development e.g. 'in order to create economic growth' — or well-developed e.g. 'which means a country can develop its industries and provide high-quality services e.g. health and edcuation'.
- To combat an ageing population — plus development e.g. 'as there will be more people to work and pay taxes towards pensions' — or well-developed e.g. 'and if they're young, they'll marry and have more children to balance the population'

Countries try to **reduce** immigration:
- To reduce unemployment amongst a country's population — plus development e.g. 'as immigrants would compete for jobs' — 'especially as they are often prepared to work in menial jobs / work for lower wages'.

Level	Descriptor
0	No rewardable content
1 (1-2 marks)	Simple or very basic statements using little or no subject vocabulary.
2 (3-4 marks)	Generalised explanations but with some use of geographical terms. Up to two developed statements as shown by examples above.
3 (5-6 marks)	Detailed statements with clear explanations using geographical terms. e.g. 'Immigration can help to balance an ageing population, especially if immigrants are younger and then have children, which helps to increase the birth rate and reduce the dependency ratio in the future'. Three developed or two well-developed points are required for the top of Level 3 as shown by examples above.

10 Consuming resources

About the chapter
These are the key ideas behind the chapter.
- Resources can be classified as renewable, sustainable and non-renewable.
- The world's growing population will face a number of challenges regarding resources in the future.
- Malthus and Böserup held different views about the relationship between population and resources.
- Patterns of resource supply and consumption are uneven.
- Oil is a finite resource, but consumption continues to rise.
- The consumption and supply of energy (especially oil) is under pressure due to economic growth and changing international relations.
- There are variations in the consumption and supply of renewable energy.
- Governments can manage resource consumption by education, conservation and recycling.
- Technology and renewable resources could help to resolve resource shortage.

Chapter outline
Use this outline to provide your students with a brief roadmap of the chapter.

10.1 Different types of resources
How resources can be classified into different categories.

10.2 Population and resources
What impacts the world's growing population might have on resources.

10.3 Are there enough resources?
The views of Malthus and Böserup on the relationship between population and resources.

10.4 Patterns of resource supply and consumption
Resource supply and consumption are not evenly spread.

10.5 How much oil is there?
Oil production and consumption, and what the future holds for oil.

10.6 Energy under pressure
Pressures on the supply and consumption of energy.

10.7 Renewable energy
The consumption and supply of renewable energy – in particular, solar power.

10.8 Is there enough food?
How the theories of Malthus and Böserup help to explain global food demand and supply.

10.9 What does the future look like – 1?
Some of the ways in which governments can manage resource consumption.

10.10 What does the future look like – 2?
Whether technology and renewable resources could help to 'fix' future resource use.

Consuming resources

How is the specification covered?

This chapter covers Topic 2, Unit 2 People and the planet.

2.1 How and why does resource consumption vary in different parts of the world?

2.2 How sustainable is the current pattern of resource supply and consumption?

Key ideas	Detailed content	Pages in students' book
2.1a Resources are classified as renewable, sustainable and non-renewable, and this has implications for their supply and consumption.	Define and classify different types of resources including energy, mineral, physical and biological resources.	166-167
	Investigate the changing pattern of global inequalities in the supply and consumption of different types of resource.	168-169, 172-173
2.1b Issues surrounding energy supply and consumption have produced a changing world of 'haves' and 'have nots'.	Examine reasons for variations in the global supply and consumption of one renewable energy resource and one non-renewable energy resource.	174-175, 178-179
	Assess the likely future pressures on both the supply and consumption of the chosen energy resources brought by global economic growth and changing international relations.	176-177, 178-179
2.2a Different theories exist about how far the world can cope with the current consumption of resources.	Investigate the differences between Malthusian and Boserupian theories about the relationship between population and resources.	170-171
	Evaluate these theories by considering the changing relationship between global food demand and supply.	180-181
2.2b The challenges for future resource consumption centre on achieving sustainability.	Identify ways in which governments, both national and local, attempt to manage resource consumption through education, conservation and recycling.	182-183
	Evaluate the potential of renewable resources and the ways in which new technologies e.g. the hydrogen economy, might resolve resource shortages.	184-185

Chapter outcomes

By the end of this chapter, students should be able to:

- Classify resources as renewable, sustainable and non-renewable; including physical, energy, mineral and biological resources.
- Understand that in the future the world's growing population will face a number of challenges regarding resources.
- Explain why some people believe that the world's resources will soon run out, while others think that will not happen.
- Evaluate Malthus' and Böserup's theories by considering the changing relationship between global food demand and supply.
- Describe the differences in the distribution of those countries that export metals and those that import them.
- Describe how the pattern of oil consumption is changing.
- Describe likely pressures on the future global supply and consumption of oil.
- Complete a table to show the advantages and disadvantages of countries obtaining their energy from solar sources.
- Compare the strengths and weaknesses of government policies to manage resource consumption.
- Explain how a hydrogen economy could resolve resource shortages.

191

10.1 Different types of resources

Section in brief
This section looks at how resources can be classified into different categories.

In the activities, students:

- complete a table to classify different resources;
- research one type of energy resource;
- answer an exam-style question analysing a graph of global energy use, and outlining evidence to show that global energy use is not sustainable.

Key ideas

- Resources can be classified as physical, energy, mineral and biological resources.
- Resources can also be divided into renewable (including sustainable) and non-renewable.
- Wind power is an example of renewable energy. In 2012 it provided 5% of California's total energy requirements.
- Bio-gas is a sustainable form of energy providing 57% of India's energy.
- Natural gas in Europe is a non-renewable form of energy, and global gas supplies will fall after 2030.

Key vocabulary
resource, physical, energy, mineral, biological, renewable, sustainable, non-renewable

Skills practised
Geographical skills: classifying resources; describing locations; outlining evidence

PLTS: independent enquiry

Numeracy skills: analysing line graph

Section outcomes
By the end of this section, most students should be able to:

- define the terms given in 'Key vocabulary' above;
- classify resources into different categories;
- use a graph to describe what is happening to global energy use;
- outline evidence to show that the world's energy use is not sustainable.

Ideas for a starter

1. Ask students to look at the photos of the wind turbines, the bio-gas plant and the oil/gas rig on pages 166 and 167. Ask: 'What are these examples of? How can we classify them?'
2. Ask students to look at the graph of global energy use on page 166 of the students' book. Ask: 'Why is global energy use rising so fast?'

Ideas for plenaries

1. Ask students what the advantages and disadvantages of wind power, biogas and natural gas are.
2. Look again at the graph of global energy uses. If oil and gas are non-renewable can we continue to rely on them? What will happen when they run out?

Further class and homework activity

Research the environmental impacts of the three energy resources included in this section.

192

Consuming resources

answers

1 Physical:
Renewable — wave power, wind power, water.
Non-renewable — sand.

Energy:
Renewable — solar power.
Non-renewable — oil, coal, natural gas.

Mineral:
Non-renewable — iron ore, limestone.

Biological:
Renewable — apples, grass, chicken.
Sustainable — vegetable oil, milk, biogas.

Note that some resources may be categorised in more than one column.

2 a and b

Student responses will depend on the type of energy resource they have researched.

---

3 Exam-style question *Look at the graph opposite.*

a *Describe what is happening to global energy use. (3 marks)*

This question is point marked. It requires two statements about global energy use to obtain 2 marks, plus 1 mark for the use of data. Data can either be drawn direct from the graph, or manipulated e.g. a subtraction or percentage increase calculation. The command word is 'describe', so do not credit explanatory points e.g. 'because of industrialisation in China'.

Correct points include:
- all except nuclear sources are increasing (1)
- reference to rate of growth with example e.g. 'oil / natural gas is increasing rapidly' (1)
- any grouping of energies e.g. 'the top 3 energy sources are all increasing' (1)
- other points on merit.

b *Outline two pieces of evidence to show that global energy use is not sustainable. (4 marks)*

This question is point marked. It requires two developed points about global energy use to obtain 4 marks – which can include the use of data. One well developed point can obtain 3 marks, but no more. Sustainability must be implicit e.g. 'these are all finite sources', or explicit i.e. 'these resources will run out eventually'.

Correct points include:
- almost all energy sources / the top three are fossil fuels (1) plus a development of this point e.g. 'which are finite and have a limited life' (1) or use of data (1)
- renewable sources / nuclear make only a small contribution to energy production (1) plus 1 mark for use of data
- other points on merit.

193

10.2 Population and resources

Section in brief

In this section students investigate the impacts that the world's growing population might have on resources, and asks 'Will the world cope?'

In the activities, students:

- use evidence to decide whether they think that food shortages could have severe impacts;
- investigate the impact of China's growing population on resource use;
- look at the challenges created by the world's growing population;
- answer an exam-style question about the countries most affected by resource shortages.

Key ideas

- In 2007 and 2008 there were global protests over food insecurity.
- The causes included a growing global population, shortage of foodstuffs and rising prices.
- The growing global population will face a number of challenges over resources in future.
- The world's growing population faces two possible outcomes:
  - a future where there are not enough resources.
  - a future where people use technology to provide sufficient resources.

Key vocabulary

food security, food insecurity

Skills practised

Geographical skills: using evidence to support views; describing locations and patterns from world map

PLTS: independent enquiry; creative thinking

Section outcomes

By the end of this section, most students should be able to:

- define or explain the terms given in 'Key vocabulary' above;
- describe the causes and effects of food insecurity;
- use evidence to show that food shortages could have severe global impacts;
- state two possible outcomes that the world faces in terms of resource consumption;
- describe the location of countries where food protests took place.

Ideas for a starter

1. Tell students that the world's population is expected to peak at around 10 billion by 2183. What challenges might the world's growing population face? Record students' ideas as a spider diagram.
2. Brainstorm: 'What do these terms mean: food security and food insecurity?'

Ideas for plenaries

1. If you used starter 1 revisit the spider diagram of students' ideas. Add to it, or amend as appropriate, in the light of the work in this section.
2. Ban Ki-Moon, the UN General Secretary in 2012 said that the global food crisis 'could have serious implications for international security, economic growth and social progress'. Ask students to unpick this statement before they attempt question 1 in the students' book.

Further class and homework activity

Ask students to investigate Thomas Malthus in preparation for section 10.3. They should find out when he lived, and his view about the relationship between population and food supply.

Consuming resources

answers

1 The evidence in this section suggests that Ban Ki-Moon was right — i.e. food shortages and rising prices have resulted in street protests, political instability and war; as individuals and governments try to secure supplies. Economic growth and social progress will be hampered.

2 As China's population and economy continue to grow, its consumption of resources is also likely to grow, which could create shortages for other countries.

3 The challenges of a larger world population include: more expensive food and fuel as demand rises; climate change, as more people release more greenhouse gases; water shortages as demand rises; migration — creating further challenges; political instability and conflict — as more people compete for fewer resources.

---

4 Exam-style question *Look at the world map opposite.*

a *Describe the locations of the countries where most of the protests took place. (3 marks)*

This question is point marked. It requires two statements about locations of countries to obtain 2 marks, plus 1 mark maximum for the use of examples. Allow 1 mark maximum for exceptions e.g. an answer which mentions 'the majority are developing countries' and then gives an exception e.g. California.

The command word is 'describe' so do not credit explanatory points e.g. 'these are countries where there has been desertification'.

Cap any candidate who simply lists three or more countries without any attempt to generalise about locations at 2 marks.

Correct points include:

- most are developing countries / low income countries (1) plus 1 mark if illustrated using two countries or more
- half are in Africa (1)
- most riots are about food, with at least one example (1) plus 1 mark for exceptions (1)
- other points on merit.

b *Outline two possible reasons why these countries might be most affected by resource shortages. (4 marks)*

This question is point marked. It requires two developed points about global energy use to obtain 4 marks – which can include the use of data. One well developed point can obtain 3 marks, but no more.

Possible reasons include:

- food production has been made more difficult in many countries (1) plus 1 mark if illustrated with examples, e.g. desertification in the Sahel (1)
- countries where natural disasters have made food distribution difficult (1) plus a developed example e.g. after the earthquake in Haiti in 2010 (1)
- climate change if this includes an illustrated example e.g. 'increased drought in many African countries' (1)
- other points on merit.

10.3 Are there enough resources?

Section in brief

In this section students learn about two different views of the relationship between population and resources – those of Thomas Malthus and those of Esther Böserup.

In the activities, students:

- complete and label a graph of Malthus's prediction, and answer questions on the current situation regarding population growth and food supply;
- describe and explain what a graph of Böserup's view shows;
- answer an exam-style question explaining why people have different views about how long the world's resources will last.

Key ideas

- Malthus believed that population grew exponentially, while food production grew arithmetically, meaning population would eventually outstrip food supply.
- Malthus believed that, whenever population outstripped food supply 'natural checks' would come into play, such as war and disease.
- Böserup believed that, as population grew, people would invent solutions to the problems of resource supply.
- Böserup used the term 'agricultural intensification' to explain how more food can be grown using better techniques and chemical fertilisers.

Key vocabulary

exponentially, arithmetically

Skills practised

Geographical skills: interpreting graphs of Malthus's and Böserup's views

PLTS: independent enquiry; creative thinking

Numeracy: completing graph

Section outcomes

By the end of this section, most students should be able to:

- explain the terms given in 'Key vocabulary' above;
- complete a graph to show Malthus's view about population and food supply;
- explain how Malthus's views influenced the Honourable East India Company;
- describe Böserup's view about population and resource supply;
- explain why some people believe that the world's resources will soon run out, while others think that this will not happen.

Ideas for a starter

1. Recap section 10.2 – the two possible outcomes from consuming resources. Ask students which outcome they think is more likely.
2. Show a world population clock on the whiteboard (do an Internet search for 'world population clock') to show students how fast the world's population is growing. Ask: 'How can we continue to provide enough resources for the growing population?' Record students' ideas.

Ideas for plenaries

1. You could use question 1 or 2 in the students' book as a plenary.
2. Hold a class debate. 'Will the world run out of resources?' Some students should argue for the motion, some should argue against.

Further class and homework activity

Ask students to complete question 3 from the students' book (the exam-style question) for homework.

Consuming resources

answers

1 a and **b** Students' graphs should look like this:

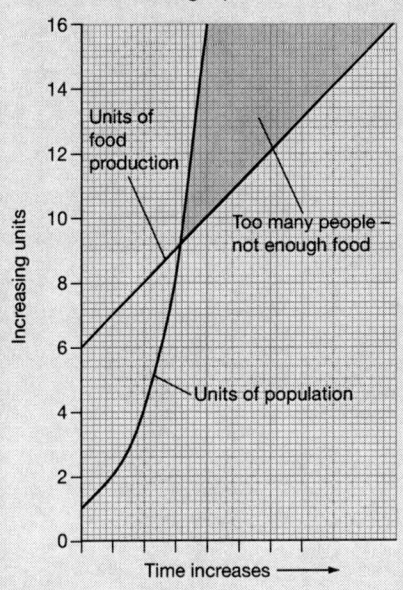

[Graph showing "Units of food production" as a steep exponential curve and "Units of population" as a linear line, with "Too many people – not enough food" labeled in the upper area. Y-axis: Increasing units (0-16). X-axis: Time increases.]

c No. Food comes form a variety of sources and much is imported so there is sufficient food for everyone.

d This is the situation in some parts of the world where growing population outstrips food supply and people suffer from food insecurity.

2 a The graph shows that as population increases, so does the food supply.

b As population grows, people come up with solutions to the problems of food shortages. Böserup used the term 'agricultural intensification' to explain how farmers could grow more food on the same amount of land.

3 Exam-style question *Explain why some people believe that the world's resources will run out soon, while others think that will not happen. (6 marks)*

Cap answers at the top of Level 2 (4 marks) if they do not include *both* viewpoints. Foundation Tier students may answer the alternative question:

Using examples, outline the reasons why some people believe that the world's resources will soon run out. (6 marks)

In this case, replace references to 'explanations' in the mark scheme with 'descriptions'.

Reasons in **support** of the statement include:

- Rapidly increasing demand as global population increases — plus development e.g. 'and industrialisation in some of the world's biggest countries like China' — or well-developed e.g. 'which is placing even greater demand on the world's resources such as oil'.

- The finite nature of some of the world's resources — plus development e.g. 'such as energy, where we rely on fossil fuels' — or well-developed e.g. 'which will eventually run out at some stage, and we have few alternatives'.

Reasons **against** the statement include:

- The invention of alternative sources of raw material in manufacturing / energy — plus development e.g. 'such as timber, which was replaced by coal, and now oil' — or well-developed e.g. 'and now more renewables and nuclear energy might replace fossil fuels'.

- The capacity to recycle and re-use much of what is used or produced if we want to — plus development e.g. 'such as metals, which can be melted down and re-used' — or well-developed e.g. 'or where technology now means you don't need as much material to make something e.g. cars which use less metal'.

Level	Descriptor
0	No rewardable content
1 (1-2 marks)	Simple or very basic statements using little or no subject vocabulary.
2 (3-4 marks)	Generalised explanations but with some use of geographical terms. Up to two developed statements as shown by examples above.
3 (5-6 marks)	Detailed statements with clear explanations using geographical terms. Three developed or two well-developed points as shown by examples above.

10.4 Patterns of resource supply and consumption

Section in brief

This section looks at patterns of resource supply and consumption. It explores the trade in metals, looking at the countries which export metals and those that import them, and the reasons for the rising prices of metals.

In the activities, students:

- describe the distribution of countries exporting metals, and compare this with those importing them;
- analyse a graph of metal consumption;
- explain why the price of silver continues to rise;
- answer an exam-style question to explain how countries will benefit in the future from metal exports, and the problems that the importing countries will face.

Key ideas

- The price of metals is increasing as metals are being used up.
- The distribution of countries importing metals is different from that of countries exporting metals.
- If metals continue to be consumed at current rates, we will have run out of gold, zinc and silver within 50 years.

Key vocabulary

exponentially, arithmetically

Skills practised

Geographical skills: describing and explaining distributions from maps; identifying sources of metals

PLTS: independent enquiry; creative thinking

Section outcomes

By the end of this section, most students should be able to:

- explain or define the terms given in 'Key vocabulary' above;
- explain why the price of metals continues to rise;
- describe the distribution of countries that export metals;
- explain why the distribution of countries importing metals differs from that of countries exporting metals;
- explain how countries that export metals may benefit in the future;
- explain the problems countries that import metals may face in the future.

Ideas for a starter

1. Ask the students to look at the two maps from page 172. If students have not seen this type of map before, explain that they show countries in proportion to the amount of metal and metal products exported (top map) and imported (bottom map). Ask students to describe what the maps show.

2. Show the graph of worldwide metal consumption from page 173. Ask a student to read out the newspaper article on page 173. Ask: 'What is the link between these two items?' (As demand for metals increases, the price rises – hence the theft of catalytic converters.)

Ideas for plenaries

1. Hold a quick fire test to check students' understanding of the work in this section.

2. Ask students to prepare an odd-one-out quiz for their partner about what they have learnt in this section.

Further class and homework activity

Oil is a finite resource. Ask students to find out:

- which ten countries have the largest reserves of oil,
- what 'peak oil' means.

Consuming resources

answers

1 a Mainly found in South America, Africa, Australia, Europe and Eastern Asia.

b Where there are differences in the distribution of importing and exporting countries it is because importers either lack deposits of metal ores, or economies are growing and demanding more metal to support economic growth.

2 a Asia

b South America, Europe, Africa and Australia.

3 The price of silver continues to rise because:
- stocks of silver worldwide have declined
- recycling silver is very difficult
- silver is used in many goods which are in increasing demand e.g. washing machines and mobile phones.

---

4 Exam-style question *In the future, it may be more difficult for countries to obtain the metals needed to make everyday products. Explain:*

a how countries that export metals may benefit from this, and b the problems faced by countries which import metals. (6 marks)

This question is marked using levels. With 'explain' as a command word, purely descriptive points by Higher Tier candidates get no marks. Foundation Tier students may answer the alternative question:

Describe the problems that countries which import metals may face in future. (4 marks)

In this case, the question is point marked, so use the examples below to look for two developed points for 4 marks. Exceptionally, award 3 marks for one well-developed point.

Cap Higher Tier students at the top of Level 2 (4 marks) if they do not explain both *a* and *b*.

a Benefits for countries that **export** metals:
- Increasing global demand for metals such as iron ore — plus development e.g. 'which means that prices will continue to rise' — or well-developed e.g. 'creating more jobs / raising GDP'.
- Increases economic expansion / increases level of development — plus development e.g. 'which creates more income to help develop the economy further / develop infrastructure' — or well-developed e.g. 'or improve health / education services'.

b Problems for countries that **import** metals:
- Rapidly rising global prices for metals such as iron ore — plus development e.g. 'caused by shortages or rising demand' — or well-developed with further expansion e.g. 'which increases the price of everything else such as cars if the price of iron ore increases'.
- Plus other valid points.

Level	Descriptor
0	No rewardable content
1 (1-2 marks)	Simple or very basic statements using little or no subject vocabulary. May be a descriptive or basic list of points e.g. 'countries with iron ore will get a lot richer'.
2 (3-4 marks)	Generalised explanations but with some use of geographical terms e.g. 'demand for metals like silver will go up as the world develops, so it will go up in price and benefit countries which have it'. Up to two developed statements as shown by examples above.
3 (5-6 marks)	Detailed statements with clear explanations using geographical terms. e.g. 'demand for metals like silver will go up as countries such as India develop, so it will go up in price and benefit countries which export it, meaning a higher GDP'. Three developed or two well-developed points as shown by examples above.

10.5 How much oil is there?

Section in brief

In this section students investigate variations in oil production and consumption. Oil consumption has risen dramatically, and is continuing to rise. Saudi Arabia has by far the largest known reserves of oil, but at some point we will reach 'peak oil' - the point at which oil production reaches its maximum level and then declines.

In the activities, students:

- analyse a graph of world oil consumption;
- analyse a map and table of oil reserves;
- explain the problems that countries may face in the future related to oil;
- answer an exam-style question describing the changing pattern of resource consumption.

Key ideas

- Oil is a finite resource which will run out one day.
- Oil consumption continues to rise, but it is predicted that production will not be able to keep up with consumption.
- Peak oil is the point at which oil production reaches its maximum level and then declines.
- Some believe we have reached, or are close to reaching, peak oil.
- Future lack of oil supplies could lead to recession and conflict.

Key vocabulary

black gold, finite resource, peak oil

Skills practised

Geographical skills: analysing a graph of oil consumption; describing the distribution of countries with oil reserves; describing the changing pattern of oil consumption

PLTS: creative thinking

Section outcomes

By the end of this section, most students should be able to:

- define or explain the terms give in 'Key vocabulary' above;
- give reasons why world oil consumption continues to rise;
- describe the distribution of the countries with the largest oil reserves;
- explain the problems that countries will face in the future – both those that rely on oil for energy and transport, and those that were major exporters of oil;
- describe the changing pattern of oil consumption.

Ideas for a starter

1. If students completed the 'Further activity' in section 10.4 ask several students to feed back what they have found out to the class.
2. Start a discussion. Ask: 'How long will our oil last? Who is using it all? Where are the oil reserves?'

Ideas for plenaries

1. Give students five minutes to produce a short newspaper report about the future of oil.
2. Students could work in pairs to write a paragraph with the heading 'How much oil is there?'

Further class and homework activity

Ask students: 'Which is likely to have the greatest impact – climate change or peak oil?' They should explain their answer.

Consuming resources

answers

1 a The most rapid increase in oil consumption has been in countries experiencing rapid industrial and economic growth — especially India and China.

   b The industrialised regions of Europe and North America now account for a smaller proportion of global oil consumption as they industrialised much earlier than developing countries.

2 Six of the countries are in the Middle East or in central and eastern Asia e.g. Russia, Kazakhstan and China; two are in Africa — Libya and Nigeria; and three in the Americas — USA, Canada and Venezuela.

3 a A shortage of oil could lead to price rises, recession and conflict as countries try to secure supplies. They will have to identify alternative sources of energy for transport, heating etc.

   b If countries cannot earn income from oil exports they will have to remodel their economies and identify alternative sources of income.

---

4 Exam-style question *Using examples, describe how the pattern of consumption of one resource you have studied, is changing. (4 marks)*

This question is point marked. It's about an area that students have traditionally struggled with on exam questions; 'consumption' which seem to produce a greater challenge to understanding than 'production'. Direct students to the graph on page 174 to help them think about this, and tell them that 1 mark is available for the use of data directly from the graph, plus an extra mark if they manipulate data in any way (i.e. perform additions, subtractions, working out proportions etc.). The answer requires development of two points to obtain 4 marks, though exceptionally one well-developed point can obtain 3 marks. A named resource must be mentioned – limit any student who explains in general terms only to 2 marks.

Depending upon the resource chosen, correct points for oil could include:

- The industrialised world has increased most in the past (1) — plus development e.g. 'but is changing as demand slows down' (1).
- The developing world is growing rapidly (1) — plus development e.g. 'and growth is getting faster' (1).
- Plus other points on merit.

10.6 Energy under pressure

Section in brief

In this section students find out about pressures on the supply and consumption of energy as a result of global economic growth and changing international relations.

In the activities, students:

- brainstorm the reasons why China and India's economic growth will lead to increased demands for energy and oil;
- assess the energy implications of economic growth in China and India;
- research USA shale gas supplies;
- research a recent dispute over oil or gas supplies;
- answer an exam-style question to describe the likely pressures on the future global supply of either oil or gas.

Key ideas

- Global energy demand is expected to increase by over a third by 2035.
- 'Energy security' means access to reliable and affordable sources of energy.
- The USA has been trying to improve its energy security by increasing its domestic energy production.
- In future, most of the Middle East's oil will be exported to Asia.
- Oil and gas supplies risk being disrupted due to political tension.

Key vocabulary

energy security, energy secure, energy insecure

Skills practised

Geographical skills: interpreting a graph of energy consumption; explaining links between economic growth, energy consumption and security

PLTS: independent enquiry; creative thinking; team-working; self-managing

Literacy skills: extended writing on a poster

Section outcomes

By the end of this section, most students should be able to:

- define or explain the terms given in 'Key vocabulary' above;
- list reasons why economic growth in China and India will lead to greater demands for energy;
- explain why the USA is seeking new energy supplies;
- summarise the risk to oil or gas supplies in an area where there are disputes over energy.

Ideas for a starter

1. Show students the photo of Beijing's streets packed with cars from page 176. Tell them that one thousand new cars arrive on the city's streets every day. Ask: 'Where does all the oil come from which is needed to run all the cars? How fast is China's demand for energy rising? What problems might that create?'

2. Brainstorm: What do students think the term energy security means?' Once you have arrived at a reasonable definition, ask students if they think the UK is energy secure. If not, why not?

Ideas for plenaries

1. Ask students to create a mind map around the phrase 'Energy under pressure'. Give them a two minute time limit to come up with as many ideas as they can from this lesson.

2. Hold a class discussion about the risks Europe faces by relying on Russian gas.

Further class and homework activity

Use either question 3 or 4 from the students' book as a homework activity.

Consuming resources

answers

1 **a** and **b** Answers should include both industrial and domestic demands.

2 Economic growth is: **a** fuelling a growing middle class with money to spend on cars; **b** driving up energy consumption — increasing energy insecurity as China and India become more dependent on imported energy; **c** driving up the global oil demand with China and India accounting for an increasingly large proportion of the demand.

3 and 4 Answers will vary

5 **Exam-style question** *Using examples, describe likely pressures on the future global supply of either oil or gas. (6 marks)*

This question is marked using levels. Cap answers at the top of Level 2 (4 marks) if they do not include reference to:

- named countries or regions, or how specific economic or resource pressures are likely to emerge e.g. 'China's rapid development has led to rising consumption of oil' rather than 'Developing countries are demanding more oil'.
- either oil or gas

Pressures on **oil** could include:

- Economic growth e.g. 'China's economy doubled in size between 2005 and 2012' — plus development e.g. 'Chinese demand for energy now accounts for one sixth of global energy production' — or well-developed with further expansion e.g. growing Chinese car ownership.
- Political pressures on supplies e.g. 'instability in the Middle East' — plus development e.g. 'which has led to conflict and disruption to global supplies in countries such as Iraq' — or well-developed with further expansion e.g. 'which has led to price rises caused by shortages and made petrol expensive in Europe'.

Pressures on **gas** could include:

- Political conflict in Russia e.g. with Ukraine — plus development e.g. Gazprom cutting supplies to Ukraine and Eastern Europe — or well-developed with further expansion e.g. causing the flow of Russian gas through these countries to Western Europe to fall by 40%.
- Political pressures on supplies e.g. 'instability in the Caucasus' — plus development e.g. 'which has led to conflict and disruption to supplies from countries such as Azerbaijan' — or well-developed with further expansion e.g. 'which has led to price rises caused by shortages and made gas expensive in the UK'.

Level	Descriptor
0	No rewardable content
1 (1-2 marks)	Simple or very basic statements using little or no subject vocabulary. May be a descriptive or basic list of points e.g. 'oil will not last forever and developing countries need it more and more'.
2 (3-4 marks)	Generalised explanations but with some use of geographical terms e.g. 'supplies of oil have been disrupted by conflicts in the Middle East, which has led to global price increases'. Up to two developed statements as shown by examples above.
3 (5-6 marks)	Detailed statements with clear explanations using geographical terms. e.g. 'Global oil supplies have been disrupted by conflicts in the Middle East e.g. Iraq, leading to shortages, price increases, and steep increases in petrol prices in the UK'. Three developed or two well-developed points as shown by examples above.

10.7 Renewable energy

Section in brief

In this section students look at the supply and consumption of renewable energy, and solar power in particular.

In the activities, students:

- suggest reasons why solar power is increasing in some countries;
- explain how the development of solar energy offers advantages over oil for countries like Ghana;
- explain how far solar energy has the potential to become the world's number one fuel;
- answer an exam-style question to describe the pattern of the sources of global energy supplies.

Key ideas

- The International Energy Agency predicts that by 2035, renewable energy will be used to produce a third of the world's electricity.
- Solar power generation is growing rapidly.
- Solar energy can be used to heat water, heat and cool living and working spaces, and create electricity.
- Some parts of the Earth have more potential to develop solar energy than others.
- There are a number of advantages for countries in producing their own energy from renewable sources.

Key vocabulary

There is no key vocabulary on this spread.

Skills practised

Geographical skills: describing the pattern of sources of global energy supplies

PLTS: independent enquiry; creative thinking; team-working

Numeracy skills: interpreting a graph and a table of solar power generation

Section outcomes

By the end of this section, most students should be able to:

- describe the pattern of the sources of global energy supplies;
- suggest reasons why solar power generation is increasing;
- list advantages and disadvantages of countries obtaining energy from solar sources;
- explain how far solar energy has the potential to become the world's number one fuel.

Ideas for a starter

1. Ask students to look at the pie chart of the current sources of global energy supplies on page 178 of the students' book. Ask them: Why does solar power provide such a small proportion of global energy supplies?

2. Show students the world map of solar radiation from the students' book. What do they think it shows? Once they have worked it out ask them which countries they think would benefit most from using solar energy as a source of power.

Ideas for plenaries

1. Play 'Just a minute'. The topic is 'Renewable energy'. Students have to talk on the topic, without hesitation, or repetition, for up to a minute.

2. Use question 5 from page 179 as the basis of a class discussion.

Further class and homework activity

Ask students to create a poster on solar energy — including information on: the supply of solar energy; the growth of solar power generation; the uses of solar energy; the advantages of developing solar power.

Consuming resources

answers

1. Most of the growth in solar power generation has taken place in Germany and Italy. Reasons for the increase in solar power generation include: falling costs (e.g. of producing PV panels); rising prices of fossil fuels; government subsidies to support renewable energy projects (including solar power).

2. **Advantages** to countries obtaining more of their energy from solar power: increased energy security; protection from changes in international relations and possible conflicts over energy supplies; more able to drive industrial and economic growth.

   Disadvantages to countries obtaining more of their energy from solar power: high initial investment; requires large land area to produce electricity from solar power; cannot generate electricity at night; requires long periods of sunlight — so not suitable for some countries e.g. Polar regions.

3. a **Industry:**
   For — industry is a major polluter of greenhouse gases, so it would make a real impact on reducing these;
   Against – it would be very expensive to the taxpayer if all industries are to benefit, it would not create enough energy for some industries e.g. a steelworks.

   b **Individual homes:**
   For - would reduce households eco-footprint;
   Against — some people may still not want them or think that solar panels are ugly.

4. a Ghana's economy is growing rapidly. Energy is needed to drive industrial and economic growth.

   b Ghana can increase its energy security by developing solar power, rather than depending on oil which may need to be imported, and which is a finite resource.

5. Students' responses will vary, depending on their point of view. Although solar power generation increased rapidly in 2011, it was from a very low base.

---

6. **Exam-style question** *Describe the pattern of the sources of global energy supplies shown in the pie chart opposite. (3 marks)*

   This question is point marked. It requires three points from the pie chart; one should be reserved for the use of data — used directly or by manipulating data in e.g. calculating total percentages. There is no requirement for developed points.

   Correct points include:
   - Oil is the largest (1) plus 1 mark if illustrated using any data in any way.
   - Any grouping of data e.g. 'fossil fuels make up the vast majority' (1) plus 1 mark for data manipulation.
   - Reference to renewables as a minority with example (1);
   - Other points on merit.

10.8 Is there enough food?

Section in brief

In this section students weigh up the theories of Malthus and Böserup, by considering global food demand and supply.

In the activities, students:

- give reasons why Abu Dhabi is looking to lease land, and whether this is a sustainable solution;
- explain how some countries can be rich in one resource, yet poor in others;
- research GM foods and consider whether they can provide a sustainable food supply;
- answer an exam-style question to describe the rise in calorie consumption and outline the reasons for the rise.

Key ideas

- Abu Dhabi relies on profits from oil to import food.
- Abu Dhabi's search for a sustainable solution to its food security problem has led it to lease farmland in Sudan.
- Food supply has so far kept pace with the growing world population, so Böserup's view would seem more accurate than Malthus's.
- Bio-technology and GM crops may be needed to feed the world's population in future.

Key vocabulary

There is no key vocabulary on this spread.

Skills practised

Geographical skills: describing trends on a graph

PLTS: independent enquiry; creative thinking; self managing

Section outcomes

By the end of this section, most students should be able to:

- give reasons why Abu Dhabi is looking to lease land from other countries;
- explain whether Abu Dhabi's solution to food supply is sustainable;
- assess whether GM crops will provide a sustainable food supply in future;
- outline reasons why the world's food supply has managed to keep pace with the growing population.

Ideas for a starter

1. Tell students: 'There's a problem – a country has a lot of oil but no land suitable for growing food. How can they feed a growing population?' What solutions can they come up with? Record their ideas as a spider diagram.
2. Ask: 'Where is Abu Dhabi? Who can locate it on a map of the Middle East? What can you tell me about Abu Dhabi?'

Ideas for plenaries

1. Choose several students (give them advance warning) to act as members of the Abu Dhabi Fund for Development. They take the 'hot seats'. The class act as reporters, and asks sensible questions about their reasons for leasing land overseas.
2. Use the exam-style question on page 181 of the students' book as a plenary.

Further class and homework activity

The world's population reached 7 billion in 2011, more than doubling from 3 billion in just over 50 years. Ask students: 'Whose view was proved correct regarding population growth and food supply – Malthus or Böserup? Explain your answer'.

Consuming resources

answers

1 a Abu Dhabi is leasing farmland from other countries because it is a desert country with little rainfall or land suitable for growing crops and it wants to produce its own food — given the global food shortage and rises in the price of wheat and grain.

b It will not meet all of Abu Dhabi's food needs — especially as its growing population means that more food will be needed in the future.

2 Abu Dhabi, in the UAE, is a major oil producer — yet its desert environment means it cannot grow crops to feed its population. It therefore uses money gained from the resource that it is rich in (oil), to buy resources that it is poor in (crops/food).

3 Answers will vary.

---

4 Exam-style question *Look at the graph showing calorie consumption levels per day.*

a *Describe the trends shown in the graph. (3 marks)*

This question is point marked. It requires three points from the line graph; one should be reserved for the use of data — used directly or by manipulating data in e.g. calculating totals, percentages etc. There is no requirement for developed points.

Correct points include:
- global total has risen (1) plus 1 mark if illustrated using any data in any way;
- developing countries rising more rapidly than developed (1) and are now very close to developed (1);
- other points on merit.

b *Outline two reasons why the number of calories consumed has continued to increase, despite the world's population continuing to grow. (4 marks)*

This question is point marked. It requires two developed points to obtain 4 marks; exceptionally, award 3 marks (but not 4) for one well-developed point.

Correct points include:
- Growth in food output made possible using fertilisers, irrigation, pesticides etc. (1) — plus 1 mark if developed with examples e.g. 'to gain higher yields in wheat and rice'.
- Continued growth possible because of applied science / technology (1) — plus 1 mark if developed with examples e.g. 'more mechanisation / use of hybrid seed / GM crops.
- Increased area under cultivation (1) — plus 1 mark if developed with examples e.g. 'by clearing rainforests for food production'.
- Other points on merit.

10.9 What does the future look like – 1?

Section in brief

In this section students learn about ecological footprints, and how the global trend in ecological footprints is rising. They find out what local and national governments can do to help reduce resource consumption – through education, conservation and recycling.

In the activities, students:

- calculate their own ecological footprints and consider how they could be reduced;
- complete a table to compare the strengths and weaknesses of government policies to reduce resource consumption;
- design a plan to increase recycling and reduce waste;
- answer an exam-style question to explain how governments try to manage resource consumption.

Key ideas

- An ecological footprint estimates the area needed to supply resources to people to maintain their lifestyle.
- The global trend in ecological footprints is rising.
- National and local governments can help to reduce resource consumption by education, conservation and recycling.
- The UK government offers incentives to reduce energy consumption, and in the past offered subsidies to generate renewable energy.
- Recycling rates in the UK are rising, as local authorities have to meet set targets.

Key vocabulary

ecological footprint

Skills practised

Geographical skills: calculating ecological footprints; comparing strengths and weaknesses of policies to reduce resource consumption

PLTS: independent enquiry; creative thinking; team-working

Section outcomes

By the end of this section, most students should be able to:

- define the term given in 'Key vocabulary' above;
- calculate their own ecological footprint, and suggest how it could be reduced;
- compare the strengths and weaknesses of government policies on education, conservation and recycling;
- design a plan to increase recycling and reduce waste.

Ideas for a starter

1. Brainstorm: 'What does the term ecological footprint mean? How do you measure it?'
2. Show students the graph from page 182 of the students' book. It compares the resources people use and the Earth's ability to provide them. In 2008, we needed 1.25 planets to supply all the resources used. Ask: 'What are the implications of this?'

Ideas for plenaries

1. Hold a class discussion. Remind students that we are using up natural resources faster than the planet can renew them. The UN estimates that continued population and economic growth will cause ecosystems to collapse. Are we are doing enough to manage our resource consumption?
2. Ask students to write down two questions related to what they have learned. Ask other class members to answer them.

Further class and homework activity

Ask students to research the global ecological footprint; how this might change by 2050; and what the impacts of a rising footprint might be. They could use the Global Footprint Network website to help.

Consuming resources

answers

1 a and **b**

Responses may vary depending on the website used, and students' lifestyles.

2
- **Education:** *Strengths* — materials are recycled free, e.g. paper, cans; advice provided on re-using material; bins provided for compostable materials. *Weaknesses* — not target-set, so results cannot be directly measured; advice may not be followed.

- **Conservation:** *Strengths* — grants and loans will encourage resource conservation subsidies; encourage people to use renewable energy, rather than fossil fuels. *Weaknesses* — 100% grants not available to all; loans have to be repaid; subsidies do not encourage people to use less energy.

- **Recycling:** *Strengths* — targets to increase recycling, with financial penalties if targets are not met are likely to increase recycling rates. *Weaknesses* — too much waste e.g. food, is still going to landfill; food waste could be used as bio-fuel which would save oil; recycling plastic bottles would also save oil.

3 Answers will vary.

---

4 Exam-style question *Using examples, explain how governments try to manage resource consumption. (6 marks)*

This question is marked using levels. The key to this question is the command word 'explain' — a Higher Tier command word. Purely descriptive points by Higher Tier candidates get no marks. Foundation Tier students may answer the alternative question:

Using named examples, describe ways in which governments can encourage and discourage people from using resources that might run out.

In this case, replace references to 'explanations' in the mark scheme with 'descriptions'.

Cap answers at the top of Level 2 (4 marks) which do not include examples of named countries / governments or specific strategies which have been used in managing resource consumption e.g. fuel duty, not just 'tax increases'.

Ways of managing resource consumption include:

- Conservation measures / reducing domestic energy consumption — plus development e.g. 'by increasing home insulation' — or well-developed e.g.' which can be achieved by government grants, as in the UK.

- Helping with or offering loans towards home improvements to cut energy consumption — plus development e.g. 'such as secondary glazing' — or well-developed with further expansion e.g. 'or solar panels, where the government guarantees income from any electricity is sold back to electricity companies'.

- Plus other measures from pages 182-183.

Level	Descriptor
0	No rewardable content
1 (1-2 marks)	Simple or very basic statements using little or no subject vocabulary. May be a descriptive or basic list of points e.g. 'the government can help people to save energy by helping with costs'.
2 (3-4 marks)	Generalised explanations but with some use of geographical terms e.g. 'the UK government helps with grants and cheap loans towards the cost of conservation such as secondary glazing'. Up to two developed statements as shown by examples above.
3 (5-6 marks)	Detailed statements with clear explanations using geographical terms. e.g. 'the UK government helps with grants for low-income families or cheap loans towards the cost of conservation such as secondary glazing, or creating benefits for those installing solar panels'. Three developed or two well-developed points as shown by examples above.

10.10 What does the future look like – 2?

Section in brief

In this section students consider whether the use of improvements in technology and the use of renewable resources, including hydrogen fuel, can help to resolve future resource shortages.

In the activities, students:

- explain why hydrogen fuel is a sustainable fuel, and describe some of the ways in which its increased use could create a hydrogen economy;
- explain how a hydrogen economy could reduce ecological footprints;
- outline the advantages and disadvantages of encouraging lower vehicle emissions;
- brainstorm the possible effects of a future hydrogen economy;
- answer an exam-style question to explain how a hydrogen economy could resolve resource shortages.

Key ideas

- Car manufacturers have achieved reductions in fuel consumption and emissions by improving engine technology and developing hybrid cars.
- Hydrogen can be used as an alternative fuel for cars which does not produce harmful emissions.
- The term 'hydrogen economy' refers to the increased use of hydrogen.
- The energy used to separate hydrogen can produce CO_2 emissions.
- There are many advantages to using hydrogen.

Key vocabulary

hydrogen economy

Skills practised

Geographical skills: explain why hydrogen is a sustainable fuel; how its use can reduce ecological footprints, and resolve resource shortages

PLTS: independent enquiry; creative thinking; team-working

Section outcomes

By the end of this section, most students should be able to:

- define the term given in 'Key vocabulary' above;
- describe how vehicle manufacturers have reduced fuel consumption;
- explain how a hydrogen economy could reduce ecological footprints;
- outline the advantages and disadvantages of encouraging lower vehicle emissions;
- explain how a hydrogen economy could resolve resource shortages.

Ideas for a starter

1. Show students the photo of the hydrogen filling station on p185 of the students' book. Ask them what is different about this filling station. How might this help the resource shortages of the future?
2. Brainstorm: How many ideas can the class come up with to either; reduce car use, or reduce cars' fuel consumption? Record students' ideas as a spider diagram.

Ideas for plenaries

1. Create a mind map around the term 'hydrogen economy'. How many ideas can students come up with in two minutes?
2. Ask students: 'Are we working towards a future in which the world depends less on oil as a resource?'

Further class and homework activity

Ask students to research and complete a table of the advantages and disadvantages of hydrogen-fuel-cell vehicles.

Consuming resources

answers

1. **a** Hydrogen fuel is a sustainable fuel compared to fossil fuels, as it is found in water (renewable resource) therefore meeting the needs of people now, without preventing future generations from meeting their own needs.
   b Hydrogen can be used as an alternative to oil for powering vehicles and for heating.

2. **a** Using transport fuelled by hydrogen, would reduce an individual's ecological footprint, because hydrogen is a sustainable resource.
   b If individual ecological footprints fall, so would national ecological footprints.

3. **a** *Advantages for governments*: reduction in carbon emissions; increased energy security. *Disadvantages for governments*: reduction in tax income — as vehicles with low carbon emissions are exempt from Vehicle Licence Duty.
   b *Advantages for individuals*: cheaper running costs; hybrid cars have a longer range and can use both conventional fuel as well as electric power. *Disadvantages for individuals*: the limited range of electric cars; cost of car purchase; availability of hydrogen filling stations.

4. Responses will vary. Students should present their ideas to the rest of the class.

5. **Exam-style question** *Using examples, explain how possible it is that a hydrogen economy could resolve resource shortages. (6 marks)*

    This question is marked using levels. Foundation Tier students may answer the alternative question:

    Using examples, outline ways in which the hydrogen economy could help save resources such as oil. (6 marks)

    In this case, replace references to 'explanations' in the mark scheme with 'descriptions'. Cap answers at 4 marks which do not include:

    - examples from named countries and specific hydrogen technologies e.g. hydrogen cars in the USA,
    - evaluative answers e.g. a judgment about the drawbacks / benefits of hydrogen technologies.

    Suitable explanations include:
    - The low carbon benefits of using hydrogen technology — plus development e.g. for domestic heating or for vehicle fuel — or well-developed with further expansion or qualification e.g. 'although its use of natural gas in separation of hydrogen means that natural gas could still run out quickly'.
    - Reductions in cost could help to produce economic growth / would help poorer consumers — plus development e.g. 'because it's cheap to produce / can be obtained widely — or well-developed e.g. and cutting costs would affect power generation, transport, and low-carbon heating, so would reduce use of resources across the whole economy'.

Level	Descriptor
0	No rewardable content
1 (1-2 marks)	Simple or very basic statements using little or no subject vocabulary.
2 (3-4 marks)	Generalised explanations but with some use of geographical terms e.g. 'hydrogen cars would really help to reduce oil consumption and would be cheaper'. Up to two developed statements as shown by examples above.
3 (5-6 marks)	Detailed statements with clear explanations and evaluation using geographical terms. e.g. 'hydrogen technologies in vehicles and domestic heating would reduce consumption of fossil fuels and would therefore conserve resource, even though natural gas would be used for hydrogen separation'. Two well-developed points which include evaluation about application to resource shortages.

11 Globalisation

About the chapter
These are the key ideas behind the chapter.
- Employment sectors and working conditions vary in countries at different stages of development.
- The Clark Fisher model helps to explain employment structure over time and in countries at different stages of development.
- Countries have become increasingly connected to each other as international trade and foreign direct investment increases.
- There are three main reasons for the rapid rate of globalisation — lower transport costs, TNC growth and mergers and state-led investment.
- Global institutions (including the WTO and IMF) help to create a globalised economy and keep it stable.
- Globalisation has different impacts on men and women in developed and developing countries.
- TNCs operate in different sectors and in different parts of the world, and outsource work in different ways.

Chapter outline
Use this outline to provide your students with a brief roadmap of the chapter.

11.1 Industrialisation – good or bad?
Contrasting different employment and working conditions in Vietnam and Malawi.

11.2 Changing employment
How employment changes, and how the Clark Fisher model can explain this.

11.3 Understanding globalisation
The meaning of globalisation and how countries have become more connected.

11.4 How does globalisation work?
The reasons for the rapid rate of globalisation.

11.5 Keeping the economy afloat
How two global institutions help to keep the global economy stable.

11.6 Globalisation – who wins and loses?
The impacts of globalisation on men and women in Leeds and Bangladesh.

11.7 How TNCs operate – 1 BT
How BT operates in different parts of the world, including outsourcing.

11.8 How TNCs operate – 2 Nike
How Nike operates in different parts of the world, including outsourcing its manufacturing overseas.

Globalisation

How is the specification covered?

This chapter covers Topic 3, Unit 2 People and the planet.

3.1 How does the economy of the globalised world function in different places?

3.2 What changes have taken place in the flow of goods and capital?

Key ideas	Detailed content	Pages in students' book
3.1a The balance between employment sectors (primary, secondary, tertiary and quaternary) varies spatially and is changing.	Use the Clark Fisher model to investigate changing employment structure in countries at different stages of development.	188-189
	Contrast the importance of different employment sectors and working conditions in countries at different stages of development.	186-187
3.1b Globalisation is changing employment sectors both in the developed and the developing world.	Outline the role of global institutions including the World Trade Organisation (WTO), the International Monetary Fund (IMF) and Transnational Corporations (TNCs), in creating a more globalised economy.	194-195
	Evaluate the impact of globalisation on different groups of people, including women as a group, and men as a group, in the developed and developing world.	196-197
3.2a In the past 50 years both international trade and the flow of capital across international borders have expanded rapidly.	Examine the changes in the volume and pattern of international trade and foreign direct investment.	190-191
	Explore the reasons for these changes, including lower transport costs, TNC growth and mergers, state-led investment.	192-193
3.2b Transnational corporations (TNCs) control a substantial part of the global economy, and have created a global shift.	Study one TNC in the tertiary sector to show how it operates in different parts of the world, e.g. administrative work moving overseas, globalisation of products.	198-199
	Study one TNC in the secondary sector to show how it operates in different parts of the world, e.g. HQ location, outsourcing and the global shift in manufacturing.	200-201

Chapter outcomes

By the end of this chapter, students should be able to:

- Complete a table about the advantages and disadvantages of life and working conditions in countries at different stages of development.
- Identify the position of different countries on the Clark Fisher model.
- Describe the changing pattern of global trade since the 1980s.
- Outline the trends which have led to the rapid rate of globalisation.
- Give examples of how the IMF and WTO can help to keep the global economy stable.
- Create tables to show who has gained and lost from employment changes in Leeds and Bangladesh.
- Explain how TNCs operate in different parts of the world.
- Explain how outsourcing can affect different countries in different ways, and the risks and problems for companies who outsource.

11.1 Industrialisation – good or bad?

Section in brief

In this section students contrast different employment and working conditions in Vietnam and Malawi. They consider why Vietnam is booming, and what industrialisation is.

In the activities, students:

- complete a table to compare the advantages and disadvantages of the lives and working conditions of individuals in Vietnam and Malawi;
- explain how industrialisation has boosted Vietnam's GDP;
- answer an exam-style question to identify evidence that Vietnam is more industrialised than Malawi, and outline one benefit and one problem that industrialisation can bring to a country.

Key ideas

- Since 1990 Vietnam has industrialised rapidly and increased its GDP.
- Industrialisation has led to rural-urban migration in Vietnam.
- Companies such as Gap and Nike out-source production to Vietnam to take advantage of the low wages.
- In Malawi (which has not industrialised), the majority of the population live in the countryside, and many are subsistence farmers.

Key vocabulary

globalised, industrialisation, out-source, export, Gross Domestic Product (GDP), subsistence farmer

Skills practised

Geographical skills: identifying evidence from a table of figures; identifying benefits and problems of industrialisation

PLTS: independent enquiry

Section outcomes

By the end of this section, most students should be able to:

- define or explain the terms given in 'Key vocabulary' above;
- explain how industrialisation can increase a country's GDP;
- identify evidence which shows that Vietnam is more industrialised than Malawi;
- outline the benefits and problems that industrialisation can bring.

Ideas for a starter

1 Brainstorm the term industrialisation. Work with students to tease out what this term means.
2 Ask students to locate Malawi and Vietnam on a blank map of the world. What can they tell you about these two countries?

Ideas for plenaries

1 With books closed ask: 'What does industrialisation mean? Who can give me two examples of industrialised countries? When did they industrialise? What can you tell me about them?'
2 Provide students with copies of the lower photo on page 186 of the students' book, and that on page 187 (or similar images). Ask them to annotate the photos with information about the employment sectors and working conditions in Vietnam and Malawi.

Further class and homework activity

Ask students to create pie charts to show where GDP comes from for Vietnam and Malawi, and two more to show the percentage of people employed, by occupation. They should use the information on this spread to explore the differences: a) between the pie charts for each country, b) between the two countries.

Globalisation

answers

1 Dang Thu Hoan (Vietnam): *Advantages* — well paid (for Vietnam); easier than life in the countryside. *Disadvantages* — works in the city which is crowded and floods in the monsoon season; migration of people like Dang Thu Hoan means a shortage of people in rural areas; people in other factories work longer hours for lower wages.

Liena (Malawi): *Advantages* — provides almost all her family's food. *Disadvantages* — only has a small amount of produce to sell so unable to afford better tools and fertiliser; relies on family labour.

2 Vietnam's rapid industrial growth involved setting up factories to turn primary products into manufactured goods (secondary products) e.g. furniture which has more value. Exporting manufactured goods rather than primary products has increased Vietnams' GDP per person.

The majority of Malawi's exports are primary products — tobacco alone makes up 53% of all exports. These have a lower value than Vietnam's manufactured goods. As a result Vietnam has a higher GDP per person than Malawi.

3 Exam-style question

a *Study the table comparing the economies of Vietnam and Malawi. Identify four pieces of evidence to show that Vietnam is a more industrialised country than Malawi. (4 marks)*

This question is point marked. It requires four comparisons. There is no credit for the use of data, but comparisons are essential e.g. 'Vietnam has a higher GDP'. Do not credit negatives, e.g. 'Malawi has a lower GDP', as the focus for the question is Vietnam.

Correct comparisons include the following statements about Vietnam:

- A higher GDP (1).
- A higher proportion of its GDP comes from industry / lower proportion comes from agriculture (do not double-credit these two statements) (1).
- A higher proportion working in industry and services (1).
- It exports mainly manufactured / secondary goods (1).
- The value of its exports is greater, as manufactured goods are worth more (1).

b *Outline one benefit and one problem that industrialisation can bring to a country. (4 marks)*

This question is point marked. It requires two developed points. One well developed point for either can obtain 3 marks maximum. Cap any student at 3 marks who does not include a benefit *and* a problem.

Benefits include:

- Higher value of manufactured goods (1) — plus development e.g. 'which means that GDP will be higher' (1).
- More jobs are created by industries / manufacturing (1) — plus development e.g. 'which creates benefits / higher incomes for people' (1).
- Wages are higher in factories (1) — plus development e.g. 'which means that people will earn and spend more creating even more jobs' (1).

Problems include:

- Long working hours in factories (1) — plus development e.g. 'which gives people little leisure time / time to see families' (1).
- Shortages of people in rural areas caused by migration (1) — plus development e.g. 'meaning that there could be less food produced' (1).
- Pollution in cities e.g. from industries or traffic (1) — plus development e.g. 'which reduced environmental quality of cities' / 'leads to health problems' (1).

11.2 Changing employment

Section in brief

In this section students find out how employment is classified. They look at how employment structures can change over time, and as countries develop — and how the Clark Fisher model can help to explain this.

In the activities, students:

- annotate a copy of the Clark Fisher model to explain the position of Vietnam, the UK, and France, on the model;
- research job vacancies in the local area and overseas, and classify the jobs found;
- answer an exam-style question to identify evidence which shows that France is a high-income country.

Key ideas

- Employment and industry can be classified into four main sectors.
- The balance of employment in different sectors is the employment structure.
- The UK's employment structure has changed over the last 40 years.
- The Clark Fisher model can help to explain changes in employment structure over time.
- The French economy (like many HICs) is changing.

Key vocabulary

primary, secondary, tertiary, quaternary (industry), employment structure, Clark Fisher model

Skills practised

Geographical skills: analysing graph and pie chart of UK's employment structure; classifying jobs; interpreting the Clark Fisher model

PLTS: independent enquiry

Section outcomes

By the end of this section, most students should be able to:

- define or explain the terms given in 'Key vocabulary' above;
- classify jobs as primary, secondary, tertiary and quaternary;
- describe the changes to the UK's employment structure since 1978;
- describe how the Clark Fisher model explains changes in employment structure over time;
- identify the positions of Vietnam, the UK and France on the Clark Fisher model.

Ideas for a starter

1 Show photos of a range of diverse jobs on the whiteboard. Make sure that students understand what the jobs entail. Then ask them to classify the jobs as primary, secondary, tertiary, or quaternary employment.

2 Ask: 'How does employment change over time? What jobs did people do 100 years ago? Do people still do those jobs? What jobs exist now that did not exist even 30 years ago?'

Ideas for plenaries

1 Hold a quick-fire test. Call out a students' name and a definition e.g. for primary industry, secondary industry etc. The student has 5 seconds to give you the term.

2 Ask students how employment is likely to change in future. What jobs do they think they will be doing in 10 and 20 years' time?

Further class and homework activity

Once students have completed question 2 on page 189 of the students' book, ask them to draw two graphs to present the information they have found on the different employment sectors.

Globalisation

answers

1 a Vietnam fits in the industrial sector of the model. It still has a high percentage of people employed in agriculture (48%), but rising percentages in industry (22.4%) and services (29.6%).

b The UK fits in the post-industrial sector of the model. The UK has a very low percentage employed in primary industries (1.4%), declining numbers in manufacturing (18.2%) and rising numbers in tertiary and quaternary employment (80.4%).

c France also fits in the post-industrial sector of the model. It has higher percentage employed in agriculture than the UK (3.8%), and has retained more manufacturing industry than the UK (24.4% of people are employed in industry). It has growing tertiary and quaternary sectors (with 71.8% of people employed in services).

2 Students should classify the jobs they find as primary, secondary, tertiary and quaternary, and describe their findings.

---

3 Exam-style question *Study the table above. Identify three pieces of evidence to show that France is a high income country. (3 marks)*

This question is point marked. It requires three comparisons (1 mark each). There is no credit for the use of data, but comparisons are essential; 'higher', 'biggest' etc.

Correct comparisons include the following statements about France:

- Its GDP is higher than most countries (1).
- Its service sector is by far the biggest (1).
- Its agriculture produces a very small proportion of its wealth (1).
- Very few people work in agriculture (1).
- Very high numbers work in services (1).

11.3 Understanding globalisation

Section in brief

In this section students learn what globalisation means and how countries have become more connected. They find out about China's role in a globalised world, the role of TNCs and changes in the pattern of trade and foreign direct investment.

In the activities, students:

- create a mind map to show how globalisation can benefit China, North America and Europe;
- explain how globalisation has led to enormous increases in exports and global GDP;
- answer an exam-style question to describe the changing pattern of global trade and explain how globalisation has led to greater trade between countries.

Key ideas

- Globalisation refers to the ways in which countries become increasingly connected to each other.
- Increased connection happens through economic inter-dependence, increasing trade, the flow of money (investment) and the spread of technology and culture.
- China has become one of the largest influences in a globalised world.
- Transnational companies have become more influential.

Key vocabulary

globalisation, connectedness, transnational companies (TNCs), inter-dependence, Foreign Direct Investment (FDI)

Skills practised

Geographical skills: identifying the benefits of globalisation; interpreting a map of trade flows, and diagram of changing pattern of global trade; explaining link between globalisation, trade and GDP

PLTS: independent enquiry; team-working

Section outcomes

By the end of this section, most students should be able to:

- define or explain the terms given in 'Key vocabulary' above;
- list the ways in which countries become increasingly connected;
- show how globalisation can benefit China, North America and Europe;
- explain how globalisation has led to an increase in trade and global GDP;
- describe the changing pattern of global trade since the 1980s.

Ideas for a starter

1. Ask students to look at the map on page 190 of the students' book. Tell them that it shows the flow in sea trade from one place to another in 2011. Ask students to describe the trade flows, and why these connections between producers and consumers are important.

2. Show a photo of one of the global products mentioned on page 190 (e.g. Coca-Cola, McDonald's, KFC and Starbucks) on the whiteboard. Tell students that the product is an example of globalisation. Then ask what that term means.

Ideas for plenaries

1. Ask students to work in pairs to produce a 30 second sound-bite on what globalisation is, and how countries are inter-connected.

2. Hold a class discussion: Is globalisation a good thing for everyone?

Further class and homework activity

Ask students how globalisation affects them. They could think about the clothes they wear, the films they watch and the music they listen to, as a start. How many other examples can they come up with?

Globalisation

answers

1 Students' mind maps should include the following benefits:

a China: increase in export markets; increased GDP as a result of increased trade.

b North America and Europe: cheaper production in developing countries; global market for goods; ease of communication with overseas producers; easy to invest in developing countries; culture spreads around the world.

2 The relatively small increase in global population was not a key factor in the huge increases in exports and global GDP. TNC investment in new factories to manufacture goods cheaply e.g. in China and other developing countries), led to a huge growth in exports to North America and Europe. Global GDP increased as a result of the increase in exports.

---

3 Exam-style question

a *Describe the changing pattern of global trade since the 1980s, as shown in the above diagram. (3 marks)*

This question is point marked. The focus is on changes so 3 marks should only be awarded where change is stated, rather than three statements describing individual diagrams. Three changes are acceptable, as is one well-developed change. The command word is 'describe' — so no explanations should be credited.

Correct changes include:

- 1982 — trade used to be between developed countries (1).
- 1982 — raw materials from developing countries to developed (1) in return for manufactured goods from developed countries (1) which has changed so that much trade is now between developing countries (1).
- Manufactured goods are now as likely to flow from developing countries to developed (1) and less from developed to developing (1).
- Plus other changes on merit.

b *Explain how globalisation has led to greater trade between countries. (4 marks)*

This question is point marked. It requires two developed points about trade to obtain 4 marks. One well developed point can obtain 3 marks, but no more. Factors leading to increased trade must be explicit e.g. 'manufactured goods are now made in developing countries so transporting them to developed countries has led to an increase in trade' — not just 'manufactured goods are now made in developing countries'.

Correct points include:

- International trade has increased as TNCs invest in developing countries (1) — plus developed point e.g. 'to manufacture goods which are shipped to markets in North America and Europe' (1).
- US and European TNCs invested in factories in China / increased their FDI (1) — plus developed point e.g. 'because Chinese wages were 90% lower and TNCs could manufacture goods more cheaply' — or well-developed with further expansion e.g. 'leading to a huge growth in Chinese exports and global trade' (1).
- Plus other points on merit.

11.4 How does globalisation work?

Section in brief
In this section students learn about the three main reasons for the rapid rate of globalisation – lower transport costs, the growth of TNCs and state-led investment.

In the activities, students:

- research why a chosen TNC manufactures overseas, and produce a presentation of their findings;
- research brands from different companies and explain how the TNCs have grown;
- answer an exam-style question to explain how the growth of TNCs has led to greater global trade between countries.

Key ideas
- Three trends have made globalisation easier – lower transport costs, the growth of TNCs, and state-led investment.
- Changes in shipping, containerization, and aircraft technology, have reduced the costs of transporting goods.
- TNCs have grown as a result of growth of sales, or mergers with other companies.
- Much of China's economic growth has come from state-led investment by the government.

Key vocabulary
consolidation, conglomeration, state-led investment

Skills practised
Geographical skills: explaining how TNCs have grown; explaining how the growth of TNCs has led to greater global trade between countries

PLTS: independent enquiry; team-working

Literacy skills: creating a PowerPoint presentation

Section outcomes
By the end of this section, most students should be able to:

- define or explain the terms given in 'Key vocabulary' above;
- outline the three trends which have made globalisation easier;
- describe how transport changes have reduced the costs of transporting goods;
- explain how a chosen TNC has grown;
- explain how the growth of TNCs has led to greater global trade between countries.

Ideas for a starter
1. Ask students to look at the photo of the containers by the dockside in China's Pearl River Delta on page 192 of the students' book. Ask students to explain the link between containers and globalisation.
2. Recap globalisation from section 11.3. Ask students what the term globalisation means. How are countries increasingly connected to each other?

Ideas for plenaries
1. Ask students to work with a partner to write an explanation for year 9 students about the three trends which have made globalisation easier.
2. Make up 10 statements based on the work students have done so far on Globalisation. Some should be true and some false. Students should work out which are the false ones, and then correct them.

Further class and homework activity
Ask students to find out the top ten TNCs. They should find out: the name of the company; its country; the type of industry it is, and its revenue.

Globalisation

answers

1 Students can choose any TNC to research. However, if they choose Apple they will find that the reasons Apple manufactures in China include: the cost of the labour force, plus its flexibility and skill; assembly speed and the local supply chain. A significant factor is also the size of the labour force. The factory where iPhones are assembled employs 230 000 workers. Student should create a PowerPoint of their findings to present to the class.

2 Students should research product brands from the following companies and explain how they have grown. The answers to their growth are as follows:
- Whitbread — consolidation. Whitbread is the UK's leading hotel and restaurant group.
- Apple — organic growth.
- Ford — consolidation
- Virgin — conglomeration
- BP — consolidation

3 Exam-style question *Using examples, explain how the growth of TNCs has led to greater global trade between countries. (4 marks)*

This question is point marked. It requires two developed points about trade to obtain 4 marks. One well-developed point can obtain 3 marks, but no more. Factors about the growth in TNCs and increased trade must be explicit, e.g. 'As Apple has expanded, its products are made more cheaply in developing countries and transported to developed countries' — not just 'Apple makes its iPhones in developing countries such as China'.

Correct points include:

- Most TNCs now manufacture in developing countries so that their products are cheaper (1) — plus developed point e.g. 'so that they increase their markets all over the world' (1) — or well-developed with further expansion e.g. 'which has led to a huge increase in global trade of goods made by TNCs' (1).

- As TNCs grow, they make a wider range of products (1) — plus developed point e.g. 'and now operate in almost every country in the world' (1) — or well-developed with further expansion e.g. 'which has led to a huge increase in global trade of goods as they increase market share' (1).

- Plus other points on merit.

11.5 Keeping the economy afloat

Section in brief

In this section students find out about the economic problems faced by Greece, and how global institutions such as the IMF and WTO help to keep the global economy stable.

In the activities, students:

- design a flow diagram to show how Greek debt could lead to problems elsewhere;
- explain how the IMF could intervene in Greece;
- draw a table to show the advantages and disadvantages of cutting tariffs on trade;
- answer an exam-style question to explain how organisations like the IMF and WTO can help the process of globalisation.

Key ideas

- Greece's debt has been rising since the early 2000s.
- Austerity measures have cut spending and jobs.
- Globalisation has meant that economic problems can easily spread.
- The IMF aims to maintain financial stability.
- The WTO aims to get countries to cut duties (tariffs) on goods, and so increase trade.

Key vocabulary

austerity, International Monetary Fund (IMF), World Trade Organisation (WTO), tariffs

Skills practised

Geographical skills: identifying advantages and disadvantages of cutting tariffs; explain how the IMF and WTO can help the process of globalisation

PLTS: team-working

Section outcomes

By the end of this section, most students should be able to:

- define or explain the terms given in 'Key vocabulary' above;
- design a flow diagram to show how Greek debt could lead to problems elsewhere;
- explain how the IMF could help to stop Greece's problems spreading across the EU;
- draw a table to show the advantages and disadvantages of cutting tariffs on trade.

Ideas for a starter

1. Start this section by introducing the IMF to students. Explain what it is, and what it does. Give students current examples of countries the IMF is involved with.
2. Start with a class discussion about the state of the global economy. Which countries have economic problems? How will this affect them? What impact might their economic problems have on other countries?

Ideas for plenaries

1. Use the information on the banana trade as the basis of a class discussion. Is it right that the banana tariff should be cut? Should West Indian farmers be protected from the cheaper bananas produced in Latin America?
2. Ask students if there was anything they found difficult about the work in this section. If so, what was it? Can anyone help to make it easier for them?

Further class and homework activity

Ask students to imagine they are a small banana farmer in the West Indies. They should write an email to the WTO explaining why they want the banana tariff to stay.

Globalisation

answers

1 a–d

Students' flow diagrams should be similar to this:

Greek debt → Cuts in spending and jobs → People and government have less money to spend → Greece can't repay debts → Euro could collapse → Trade with UK declines, so UK economy suffers → Problems in EU and UK affect trade with rest of world.

2 The IMF could intervene at the point where the government has less money to spend. By providing financial help, Greece may be able to repay its debts.

3 Advantages and disadvantages of cutting all tariffs on trade.

	Advantages	Disadvantages
Producers	Sales increase as people buy more because goods are cheaper	Smaller producers lose out to larger, cheaper producers
Consumers	Goods become cheaper	Less choice if smaller producers go out of business

---

4 Exam-style question *Using examples, explain how organisations like the IMF and WTO can help the process of globalisation. (6 marks)*

This question is marked using levels. The key to this question is the command word 'explain' — a Higher Tier command word. Purely descriptive points by Higher Tier candidates get no marks. Foundation Tier students may answer the alternative question:

Using examples, describe how the IMF and WTO tries to help countries develop. (6 marks)

In this case, replace references to 'explanations' in the mark scheme below with 'descriptions'.

Cap answers at the top of Level 2 (4 marks) if they do not include the following:

- named examples — these can include precise ways in which the IMF / WTO assists, or named countries or regions where it works;
- reference to *both* the WTO and IMF — or any other relevant organisation that students may have studied.

Suitable explanations could include:

- To stop financial crises from spreading e.g. 'the IMF is providing Greece with loans — plus development e.g. 'to help it cope with its huge debt so that people aren't affected so badly by austerity' — or well-developed with further expansion e.g. 'and trying to prevent the banking crisis from spreading and causing collapse'.
- To reduce global poverty by helping the world's poorest countries — plus development e.g. 'so that if poorer countries have more money to spend, then global trade will increase' — or well-developed with further expansion e.g. 'and so the whole world will be better off'.

Level	Descriptor
0	No rewardable content
1 (1-2 marks)	Simple or very basic statements using little or no subject vocabulary. May be a descriptive or basic list of points e.g. 'The IMF helps countries develop and sort their debts out'.
2 (3-4 marks)	Generalised explanations but with some use of geographical terms e.g. 'The IMF helps countries in debt with financial help so that their unemployment isn't so high'. Up to two developed statements as shown by examples above.
3 (5-6 marks)	Detailed statements with clear explanations using geographical terms. e.g. 'The IMF helps countries in debt with financial help so that their unemployment is reduced, and to relieve social problems and unrest which can arise as a result'. Three developed or two well-developed points as shown by examples above.

11.6 Globalisation – who wins and loses?

Section in brief

In this section students learn about the impacts of globalisation on men and women, in Leeds and Bangladesh. Globalisation changed the employment structure of Leeds creating both winners and losers in the jobs market. Rapid industrialisation in Bangladesh has also created winners and losers.

In the activities, students:

- complete tables to show who gained and lost from employment changes in Leeds, and from industrialisation in Bangladesh;
- describe how far globalisation benefits different groups of people;
- answer an exam-style question to describe how globalisation can impact on men and women in developed countries, and explain why globalisation can lead to unequal impacts on men and women in developing countries.

Key ideas

- Globalisation led to deindustrialisation in Leeds in the 1980s and changed the employment structure.
- Leeds' changing employment structure has resulted in winners and losers in the jobs market.
- Bangladesh's economy is growing rapidly as large TNCs have moved manufacturing there.
- Bangladesh's clothing industry employs large numbers of people, but has a number of issues.

Key vocabulary

deindustrialisation; Newly Industrialising Country (NIC)

Skills practised

Geographical skills: identify winners and losers from employment changes in Leeds and Bangladesh; describe and explain the impacts of globalisation on men and women in developed and developing countries

Section outcomes

By the end of this section, most students should be able to:

- define or explain the terms given in 'Key vocabulary' above;
- create tables to show who has gained and lost from employment changes in Leeds and Bangladesh;
- describe the issues faced by people working in the clothing industry in Bangladesh.

Ideas for a starter

1 Show the two tables of employment type in Leeds (from 1964 and 2011) from page 196 of the students' book on the whiteboard. Ask students to describe the changes shown on the tables. Why do they think employment changed in Leeds?

2 Find a report about the collapse of a clothing factory in Dhaka, Bangladesh in April 2013, which killed hundreds of workers. Use this to introduce the section on Bangladesh.

Ideas for plenaries

1 Once students have completed questions 1 and 2, use question 3 on page 197 as a plenary activity.

2 Ask students to think back over the lesson and write down two questions related to what they have learned. Ask other class members to try to answer the questions.

Further class and homework activity

Ask students to complete either part a or b of question 4 for homework.

Globalisation

answers

1 Leeds

Men: *Gained* — jobs in financial services, printing, packaging and publishing. *Lost* — jobs in mining, quarrying, engineering and manufacturing; apprenticeships for young people. **Women:** *Gained* — jobs in financial services, printing, packaging and publishing. *Lost* — jobs in clothing factories; apprenticeships for young people.

2 Bangladesh

Men: *Gained* — jobs in transport, distribution and retailing. **Women:** *Gained* — jobs for younger women (though may be in sweatshops). *Lost* — older women returning to work face discrimination.

3 a Younger people — children in Bangladesh can work from the age of 14. Loss of apprenticeships in Leeds means that often only low-paid jobs are available for them.

b Older people — struggled to find new well-paid jobs in Leeds and experience discrimination, in favour of younger women, in Bangladesh.

c Well-qualified women — benefit from new jobs in Leeds (financial and public services) and Bangladesh (clothing industry).

d Well-qualified men — benefit from new jobs in Leeds (financial and public services) and Bangladesh (transport, distribution and retailing).

4 a Exam-style question *Using examples, describe how globalisation can impact on men and women in developed countries. (6 marks)*

This question can be used for all candidates although Higher Tier students could answer question 4b instead. Impacts on men and women could include:

Fewer jobs in manufacturing — plus development e.g. 'as industries close down in developed countries and move overseas' — 'leaving many men unemployed'.

Shift in job sector — plus development e.g. 'as manufacturing declines, men have to seek jobs in the (lowere paid) service sector — 'increasing unemployment among older men as they weren't qualified for those jobs'.

Greater prospects for those who were qualified or well-educated — plus development e.g. 'such as financial industries and banks' — 'creating a bigger gap between rich and poor'.

b Exam-style question *Using examples, explain why globalisation can lead to unequal impacts on men and women in developing countries. (6 marks)*

Foundation Tier students question may answer question 4a instead. Impacts on men and women could include:

More jobs in manufacturing — plus development e.g. 'as industries such as textiles move from developed to developing countries for lower wage costs' — 'increasing employment opportunities for women e.g. in Bangladesh'.

Shift in job sector e.g. 'manufacturing employment increases' — plus development e.g. 'which often results in men leaving villages' — 'so that there are fewer people working in agriculture'.

Poorer working conditions for (young) women — plus development e.g. 'such as textile industries where sweatshops are common' — 'which pays low wages'.

Level	Descriptor
0	No rewardable content
1 (1-2 marks)	Simple or very basic statements using little or no subject vocabulary.
2 (3-4 marks)	Generalised explanations but with some use of geographical terms. Up to two developed statements as shown by examples above.
3 (5-6 marks)	Detailed statements with clear explanations using geographical terms. Three developed or two well-developed points as shown by examples above.

225

11.7 How TNCs operate – 1 BT

Section in brief

In this section students learn how BT operates in different parts of the world, including outsourcing.

In the activities, students:

- research images of Bangalore and produce a presentation to sell the city as an outsourcing location for BT;
- complete a table to show who gains and loses from outsourcing services to Bangalore;
- explain how much Bangalore is gaining and losing from globalisation;
- answer an exam-style question to explain how outsourcing can affect different countries in different ways.

Key ideas

- BT is one of the largest telecommunications companies in the world.
- BT began outsourcing in the 1990s.
- Three main factors have helped Bangalore's growth as an outsourcing centre.
- BT is typical of many companies which are part of the new economy.
- Companies in the new economy are footloose as long as high-quality communication links are available.

Key vocabulary

outsourcing, new economy, footloose

Skills practised

Geographical skills: completing a table to show winners and losers from outsourcing to Bangalore; explaining how outsourcing can affect countries in different ways

PLTS: independent enquiry; creative thinking; team-working

Literacy skills: creating presentation

Section outcomes

By the end of this section, most students should be able to:

- define or explain the terms given in 'Key vocabulary' above;
- complete a table to show who gains and loses from outsourcing services to Bangalore;
- list the factors which have helped Bangalore's growth as an outsourcing centre;
- explain why BT is typical of companies which are part of the new economy;
- explain how outsourcing can affect countries in different ways.

Ideas for a starter

1. Ask: 'What is outsourcing? Who can give me some examples of outsourcing? Why do some companies outsource work elsewhere?'
2. Recap work done on TNCs earlier in this chapter — what they are, how they have grown, and their impact on globalisation.

Ideas for plenaries

1. Ask students to complete questions 2 and 3 from page 199 of the students' book in class. Then choose several students and ask them to read out their answers to question 3. Take a class vote on which is the best answer. Ask class members to explain why it is the best and how the others could be improved.
2. Create a graffiti wall of what students have learnt in this lesson.

Further class and homework activity

Ask students to find out where Nike manufactures its products in preparation for the next section (Google 'Nike manufacturing map'). They should find out about one country - how many factories it has, how many people are employed, and the type of products made there.

Globalisation

answers

1. Students need to research images of Bangalore, and choose ones they feel are suitable to 'sell' Bangalore as a location where a company such as BT should outsource.

2. **BT:** *Gained* — cheaper labour costs; higher profits. *Lost* — skilled labour force in UK; reputation as a company which looks after its workers.

   Bangalore: *Gained* — highly-skilled jobs; graduate opportunities; reputation as a city in which technology develops. *Lost* — dependent on overseas companies for its development, therefore it is always at risk of being undercut by another country which could do the same job for less.

3. a **Gaining:** Bangalore's English speaking university provides science and technology graduates; it offers reduced taxes to attract companies e.g. software development companies, which in turn help to attract other companies such as BT; it has experienced an IT boom which has creates jobs and wealth.

   b **Losing:** The population of Bangalore is rising more rapidly than it can cope with in terms of housing, basic services, and also jobs; as a result there is an increasing divide between well-paid graduates and the poor, with a possibility of social unrest.

4. **Exam-style question** *Using examples, explain how outsourcing can affect different countries in different ways. (6 marks)*

   This question is marked using levels. The key to this question is the command word 'explain' — a Higher Tier command word. Purely descriptive points by Higher Tier candidates get no marks. Foundation Tier students may answer the alternative question:

   Using examples, outline the effects of outsourcing on both developed and developing countries.

   In this case, replace references to 'explanations' in the mark scheme below with 'descriptions'. Cap students at the top of Level 2 (4 marks) if they do not include:

   - examples of named companies, countries or regions — or how specific processes can affect countries e.g. in IT support and India,
   - reference to 'different countries' — ideally developed and developing countries.

   Effects on **developed countries** could include:
   - Loss of employment e.g. 'in support services for companies such as BT' — plus development e.g. 'which can be done more cheaply in India' — 'as wages in the UK may be 10 times what BT would have to pay in India'.

   Effects on **developing countries** could include:
   - Expansion of employment e.g. 'in software development' — plus development e.g. 'which can be done more cheaply in cities such as Bangalore' — 'where there are English-speaking, well-qualified graduates from the university there'.

Level	Descriptor
0	No rewardable content
1 (1-2 marks)	Simple or very basic statements using little or no subject vocabulary. May be a descriptive or basic list of points e.g. 'out-sourcing can mean loss of UK jobs'.
2 (3-4 marks)	Generalised explanations but with some use of geographical terms e.g. 'out-sourcing in IT industries can mean loss of UK jobs where wages are much higher'. Up to two developed statements as shown by examples above.
3 (5-6 marks)	Detailed statements with clear explanations using geographical terms. e.g. 'out-sourcing in IT industries for companies like BT can mean loss of UK jobs and transferring these to India where wages are 90% less'. Three developed or two well-developed points as shown by examples above.

11.8 How TNCs operate – 2 Nike

Section in brief

In this section students learn how Nike operates in different parts of the world including outsourcing its manufacturing overseas.

In the activities, students:

- explain why Nike outsources manufacturing overseas;
- describe the risks for companies outsourcing overseas;
- list the benefits for countries such as Vietnam in attracting TNCs like Nike;
- compare Nike and BT;
- explain how far Nike's attitudes, or campaigns against Nike, affect their own buying habits;
- answer an exam-style question to describe the characteristics of Nike's manufacturing workforce, and explain how TNCs operate in different parts of the world.

Key ideas

- Nike operates and sells in over 140 countries — 46 of these manufacture Nike goods.
- Nike's head office is in the USA - less profitable production work is outsourced.
- Nike employs 40 000 people worldwide - 20 times this number work in factories producing Nike goods.
- Most factories producing Nike goods are in Asia and employ mostly women.
- Many campaigns have been aimed at Nike to encourage them to improve the pay and conditions for factory employees.

Key vocabulary

sweatshop

Skills practised

Geographical skills: identifying advantages and disadvantages of TNCS outsourcing; comparing Nike and BT's operations

PLTS: independent enquiry; creative thinking; effective participation

Section outcomes

By the end of this section, most students should be able to:

- define the term given in 'Key vocabulary' above;
- explain why Nike outsources manufacturing overseas;
- describe the characteristics of Nike's manufacturing workforce;
- explain the risks and problems for companies who outsource like Nike;
- list the benefits for countries which want to attract TNCs like Nike.

Ideas for a starter

1. If students completed the Further activity from section 11.7 ask a number of them to report what they found out to the class.
2. Show students the table from the foot of page 200 of the students' book. Ask them to plot the countries on a world map. Ask them to describe the distribution of countries. Ask them to describe what else the table shows about the workers employed.

Ideas for plenaries

1. Use question 5 from page 201 of the students' book as the basis for a class discussion. How far would either Nike's own attitudes, or the campaigns against Nike, affect students' buying habits? Why?
2. Write 'How TNCs operate' in the middle of the whiteboard. Ask students to create a mind map around the phrase. How many ideas can they come up with in two minutes?

Further class and homework activity

Ask students to complete question 4 from page 201 of the students' book (comparing Nike and BT) as a homework activity.

Globalisation

answers

1. To take advantage of cheap labour.

2. Factories are not owned by them, so they do not have direct control over working conditions, pay or workers' rights. If they use factories where conditions are unacceptable they risk being criticised, or facing a boycott of their goods.

3. Large numbers of jobs; jobs bring money into local and national economy; exports rise – generating more money and encouraging investment from other companies; helps countries to develop.

4.
   a. Nike has a head office (design, marketing, management) in the USA and outsources (manufacturing) to Asia. BT has offices in many countries around the world and outsources (services e.g. sales and software development) to India.
   b. Nike outsources its manufacturing to factories which they do not own.
   c. Most of Nike's outsourced workers are women, aged mid-late twenties, with few qualifications. Most of BT's are English-speaking graduates.
   d. Nike's outsourced jobs are low-paid and low-skilled. Working conditions can be poor. BT's outsourced jobs are comparatively well paid. They help to attract other companies which creates further wealth.

5. Answers will vary.

6. **Exam-style question**

   a. *Using the table below the map, describe the characteristics of Nike's manufacturing workforce. (4 marks)*

   This question requires single and developed points, and the use of data to obtain 4 marks.

   Correct points include:
   - The largest numbers in China, Vietnam and Indonesia (1) — plus use of data (1).
   - In most countries, the majority of workers are female (1) plus exception i.e. Pakistan (1).
   - In all countries, workers are young / in mid-late 20s (1).

   b. *Using examples, explain how TNCs operate in different parts of the world. (6 marks)*

   Replace 'explanations' with 'descriptions' for Foundation Tier students. Cap answers at the top of Level 2 (4 marks) if they do not include:
   - named examples e.g. a TNC or country;
   - reference to different parts of the world i.e. developed and developing countries.

   TNC operations could include:
   - Almost all manufacturing in developing countries — plus development e.g. 'where Nike's wage costs are much lower' — or well-developed e.g. 'which has reduced the price of their products in developed countries where they are sold'.
   - Marketing and product design, are done in the USA — plus development e.g. 'where Nike's company headquarters are located' — 'so all advertising or decisions about products are made there, not where they're made'.

Level	Descriptor
0	No rewardable content
1 (1-2 marks)	Simple or very basic statements using little or no subject vocabulary. May be a descriptive or basic list of points.
2 (3-4 marks)	Generalised explanations but with some use of geographical terms. Up to two developed statements as shown by examples above.
3 (5-6 marks)	Detailed statements with clear explanations using geographical terms. Three developed or two well-developed points as shown by examples above.

12 Development dilemmas

About the chapter
These are the key ideas behind the chapter.
- There are different ways of defining development and different ways of measuring development.
- A global development gap has developed and changed over time.
- Some countries have shown recent development but there are barriers to their further progress.
- Different theories can help to explain why societies develop over time, including Rostow's theory and Frank's dependency theory.
- Levels of development can vary within a country, with core and periphery regions.
- There are different strategies to aid development, including top-down and bottom-up strategies.
- Top-down projects can have different impacts on different groups of people.

Chapter outline
Use this outline to provide your students with a brief roadmap of the chapter.

12.1 Measuring development in Malawi
Different ways of defining and measuring development.

12.2 Other ways of measuring development
How different indicators can give different patterns of development.

12.3 The development gap
The global development gap and how this has changed over time.

12.4 Barriers to progress in sub-Saharan Africa
Recent development in Malawi, and barriers to its progress.

12.5 How do countries develop?
Rostow's theory, and Frank's dependency theory, about how societies develop over time.

12.6 Investigating India
How levels of development vary within India.

12.7 Which way now?
Differences between top-down and bottom-up development.

12.8 A top-down project: the Narmada River scheme
The benefits and problems of a top-down development project.

Development dilemmas

How is the specification covered?

This chapter covers Topic 4, Unit 2 People and the planet.

4.1 How and why do countries develop in different ways?

4.2 How might the development gap be closed?

Key ideas	Detailed content	Pages in students' book
4.1a Definitions of development vary as do attempts to measure it.	Examine contrasting ways of defining development using economic criteria and broader social and political measures.	202-203
	Evaluate different ways of measuring development including GDP per capita, the Human Development Index, and measurements of political freedom and corruption.	204-205
4.1b There remains a large gap between the level of development of the most developed and least developed countries.	Examine the extent of the global development gap and how this has changed over time, using a range of indicators.	206-207
	For one developing country in Sub-Saharan Africa, consider recent social, political and economic development and possible barriers to further progress.	208-209
4.2a Development strategies vary in theory.	Use theories of development to help explain why societies develop over time, including Rostow's modernisation theory and dependency theory.	210-211
	Levels of development may vary within a country with regional differences evident, especially between an urban core and a rural periphery.	212-213
4.2b Types of development vary between top-down and bottom-up strategies.	Compare the characteristics of top-down and bottom-up strategies in terms of their scale, aims, funding and technology.	214-215
	Evaluate the impact of one large top-down project, e.g. a dam on different groups of people in a developing country.	216-217

Chapter outcomes

By the end of this chapter, students should be able to:

- Compare development data for countries at different levels of development.
- Explain why HDI is a better measure of development than GDP.
- Explain how the world has changed in development terms since 1980.
- Describe the barriers that prevent the progress of a country in sub-Saharan Africa.
- Describe Rostow's theory and Frank's dependency theory about development.
- Describe how levels of development vary within India.
- Complete a table to compare the characteristics of a top-down, and a bottom-up development project.
- Complete a table of the economic, social and environmental benefits and problems of the Sardar Sarovar Dam (a top-down project).

12.1 Measuring development in Malawi

Section in brief

In this section students learn about different ways of defining and measuring development, and about what development dilemmas are.

In the activities, students:

- research and complete a table of development indicators for two different countries and compare them with Malawi and the UK;
- explain the reasons for, and impact of, various social indicators on the world's poorest countries;
- answer an exam-style question to describe two indicators which can be used to show a country's level of development.

Key ideas

- Development means economic and social change.
- Development can benefit some people more than others, creating dilemmas for countries.
- When combined, development indicators can give a picture of a country's level of development.
- Development indicators can be economic, social and environmental.

Key vocabulary

development dilemmas, development indicators (economic, social, environmental), level of development, GDP (Gross Domestic Product), poverty line, overseas debt, PPP (Purchasing Power Parity), life expectancy, dependency ratio, infant mortality, maternal mortality, access to safe drinking water, being underfed, literacy rate

Skills practised

Geographical skills: comparing development indicators for different countries; explaining impact of development indicators on poor countries

PLTS: independent enquiry

Section outcomes

By the end of this section, most students should be able to:

- define or explain the terms given in 'Key vocabulary' above;
- describe different indicators which can be used to show a country's level of development;
- research development data for two countries at different levels of development;
- compare their chosen countries with Malawi and the UK.

Ideas for a starter

1. Brainstorm: What do students think the term 'development' means? How can development lead to dilemmas? Use the first paragraph on page 202 to amend students' thinking if necessary.
2. Tell students that in 1973, Malawi was on a list of the world's 25 poorest countries, and it still is today. Ask: 'Who can tell me anything else about Malawi? Where is it? Who can locate it on a map of Africa?'

Ideas for plenaries

1. Hold a quick quiz based on the key vocabulary for this section. Either give students the terms and ask for a definition, or vice versa.
2. Use the exam-style question as a plenary activity. Allow students a maximum of 10 minutes to answer the question.

Further class and homework activity

Ask students to find out about the HDI in preparation for the next section. They should find out: what HDI stands for; what it measures; and the countries ranked in the top 5 for HDI, and those in the bottom 5.

Development dilemmas

answers

1 **a** and **b** Answers will vary.

2

		Reasons for this	The effect of this on the country
a	They have low life expectancy.	Poor countries spend less on health care than richer countries so there are fewer doctors per person. Poor levels of nutrition will also affect life expectancy.	People die before they reach the end of their working life, so fewer people earn less for the country, keeping it poor.
b	They have high maternal mortality.	More people live in rural areas without access to health care. Little spending on health care and very few doctors per person.	More children likely to be looked after by one parent or grandparents, meaning they cannot work and contribute to the economy.
c	They have low literacy rates.	Relatively few years are spent in school (compared with richer countries). Relatively little money is spent on education.	People are not well-educated or well-qualified, so do low-level/low-skilled jobs which means they, and the country, stay poor.
d	They have a high dependency ratio.	A large percentage of the population is too young (aged 0-14) to work.	Fewer people in the working population to contribute to the economy.

3 **Exam-style question** *Describe two indicators which can be used to show a country's level of development. (4 marks)*

It requires two developed descriptions for 2 marks each. Each point should refer to a specific indicator of development. A mark is given not for the indicator itself, but for what it means, and how it shows a country's level of development.

Either social or economic indicators are acceptable, as shown below.

Examples of indicators include:

- GDP / GNI (including 'per capita'): means the value of all goods and services produced in a country (per capita = divided by the number of people) (1) — which shows how high incomes / wealth are in a country (1).
- Working population in each sector: means the % of people in industry / agriculture / services (1) — which shows how well developed industry is, as developed countries have more industry and services (1).
- Literacy: means the proportion / percentage of adults able to read and write / who have completed at least primary schooling (1) — which shows how much a country can afford to spend on education (1).
- Plus other indicators on merit.

12.2 Other ways of measuring development

Section in brief

In this section students learn that different indicators can give different patterns of development. It looks at: the issue of corruption and development; the contribution of women to development; HDI — which can provide a better measure of development than GDP.

In the activities, students:

- describe the strengths and weaknesses of GDP and HDI as indicators of development;
- explain why wealth is needed to improve health and education;
- research development indicators for one country and write a report to describe how developed it is;
- answer an exam-style question to describe features of the countries with the highest HDI, and suggest why countries with the lowest HDI score poorly.

Key ideas

- Corruption can affect a country's economic development.
- Economic indicators of development often ignore the contribution of women.
- Some countries with high GDP have a very unequal distribution of wealth.
- The HDI is used to measure development — there is a close link between GDP and HDI.

Key vocabulary

Human Development Index (HDI)

Skills practised

Geographical skills: identifying strengths and weaknesses of development indicators; researching development indicators; describing development in a chosen country

PLTS: independent enquiry; team-working

Literacy skills: extended writing

Section outcomes

By the end of this section, most students should be able to:

- define the term given in 'Key vocabulary' above;
- explain why HDI is a better measure of development than GDP;
- explain the link between wealth, health and education in terms of a country's development;
- research and write a report on a chosen country's level of development.

Ideas for a starter

1. If any students completed the Further Activity from section 12.1, ask them to report their findings to the class.
2. Show students either of the two maps on page 204 to start this lesson. Work with them to tease out what the map shows and how this can impact on development.

Ideas for plenaries

1. Ask students to work in pairs to write a paragraph on measuring development.
2. Ask students:
   - What is the HDI?
   - Why was it developed?
   - What indicators are used to measure HDI?
   - Who can name three countries with the highest / lowest HDI?

Further class and homework activity

Ask students to find out the HDI (figure and rank) for Malawi. They should use the information in the table on page 202 to explain Malawi's HDI.

Development dilemmas

answers

1 a GDP:
Strengths — it provides a straightforward method of comparing countries; giving figures as PPP allows direct comparison.
Weaknesses — can be misleading as countries with a high GDP can have a very unequal distribution of wealth, so many people are still poor.

b HDI:
Strengths — it is a broader measure than GDP as it is an average of four indicators.
Weaknesses — still closely linked to GDP so the poorest countries for GDP also have a low HDI.

2 a Wealthier countries can afford to spend more on health and education.

b Better health means people are more able to work. Better education provides a more highly qualified workforce able to do more highly skilled jobs – again contributing to a country's economy and wealth.

3 a and b Answers will vary depending on the countries chosen.

---

4 a Exam-style question *Describe two features of the countries with the highest HDI. (4 marks)*

This question is point marked. It requires two developed statements for 2 marks each, or 3 marks (maximum) for a well-developed description.

Suggested features include:

- All 'more developed' / 'High Income' Countries (HICs) — not just 'developed' (1).
- Any two economic indicators indicating a high level of development e.g. high GDP, low proportion of GDP or labour working in agriculture, high proportion working in services (2 marks maximum).
- Any two social indicators indicating a high level of development e.g. high literacy, long life expectancy, high numbers of doctors per 1000 people, low infant mortality (2 marks maximum).
- Plus other indicators on merit.

b *Suggest one reason why countries with the lowest HDI score poorly on this indicator. (2 marks)*

This question is point marked. It requires one developed explanation which must demonstrate a link to the meaning of HDI — such as GDP, education (literacy rates or length of schooling) or life expectancy.

Appropriate reasons include:

- GDP — with development e.g. 'so these countries have low HDI (1) as they all have very low GDP (1) — do not allow 'are poor', 'are less developed'.
- Literacy rates / short length of time spent in schooling — with development e.g. 'so these countries have low HDI as they all have very low literacy rates (1) — do not allow 'have no schooling', 'have poor schools'.
- Life expectancy / 'infant mortality' — with development e.g. 'so these countries have low HDI (1) as they all have very low levels of health care (1) — do not allow 'have poor education'.

12.3 The development gap

Section in brief

In this section students learn about the global development gap identified in 1980 in the Brandt Report, and how the world has changed since then.

In the activities, students:

- explain the differences between key terms;
- explain how the world has changed since 1980, and whether there is still a North-South Divide;
- answer an exam-style question to explain what is meant by the global development gap.

Key ideas

- The Brandt Report in 1980 identified differences in terms of GDP and quality of life between two major groups of countries as the North-South Divide.
- In the 1980s rapid economic development in Latin America created a group of Middle Income Countries (MICs).
- In the 1990s rapid development in South-East Asia led to the development of Newly Industrialising Countries (NICs).
- Rapidly Industrialising Countries (RICs) in the 2000s included China and India.
- In 1980, the world's poorest countries were almost entirely in Africa — they still are today.

Key vocabulary

global north; High Income Countries (HICs); global south; Low Income Countries (LICs); Middle Income Countries (MICs); Newly Industrialising Countries (NICs); Rapidly Industrialising Countries (RICs)

Skills practised

Geographical skills: explaining geographical terms; use data to explain how the world has changed in development terms

PLTS: independent enquiry

Section outcomes

By the end of this section, most students should be able to:

- define or explain the terms given in 'Key vocabulary' above;
- recognise the North-South divide identified in the 1980s on a world map;
- explain how the world has changed in development terms since 1980;
- explain what is meant by the global development gap.

Ideas for a starter

1 Recap development – what it is and how it is measured from sections 12.1 and 12.2. Then brainstorm: 'What is the global development gap?'

2 Show students a photo of Rio de Janeiro, Brazil, on the whiteboard. What do students know about Brazil? How developed do they think it is?

Ideas for plenaries

1 Ask students to spend two minutes with a partner to think of an interesting question about the development gap, which has not been covered in this lesson. This could provide a good enquiry question for the class to follow through.

2 Ask students to write a statement based on the work in this section and read them out to the class. Some should be true, others false. Students should identify the false ones.

Further class and homework activity

Ask students to find out about Malawi's exports and imports ready for the next section. They can use the CIA World Factbook online.

Development dilemmas

answers

1.
   - 'Global north': wealthy countries — mainly in the northern hemisphere — identified in the Brandt report.
   - 'Global south': much poorer countries — mainly in the southern hemisphere — identified in the Brandt report.
   - MICs: Middle Income Countries e.g. Brazil, Peru, and Chile, in which rapid economic development took place in the 1980s.
   - NICs: Newly Industrialising Countries of South-East Asia, where rapid development took place in the 1990s.
   - RICs: include China and India which saw rapid industrialisation in the 2000s.
   - BRICs: Brazil, Russia, India and China are collectively known as the BRICs. Russia is another emerging economy.

2. b Since 1980 a number of countries which were LICs and included in the 'global south' have experienced rapid development. This has created different groups of countries, such as the MICs of Latin America, the NICs of south-east Asia, the RICs of India and China, and the BRICs including Russia.

   c The North-South divide identified in 1980 does not exist in the same way today. Many countries in the 'global south' have experienced rapid economic development — although many of the world's poorest countries in 1980 are still the poorest today.

3. **Exam-style question** *Using examples; explain what is meant by the global development gap. (6 marks)*

   This question is marked using levels. The key to this question is the command word 'explain' — a Higher Tier command word. Purely descriptive points by Higher Tier candidates get no marks. Foundation Tier students may answer the alternative question:

   Using examples; describe the main features of the global development gap.

   In this case, replace references to 'explanations' in the mark scheme with 'descriptions'. Cap answers at the top of Level 2 (4 marks) which do not include named countries, or specific indicators of development.

   Suitable explanations could include:

   - General explanation e.g. 'a global disparity between more and less developed / low income and high income countries' — plus development e.g. 'caused by wide differences in GDP' — or well-developed e.g. 'which is caused by low economic growth'.
   - Reference to specific socio-economic indicators e.g. life expectancy, literacy rates, numbers of doctors, infant mortality, GDP, levels of trade — plus development which explains their meaning e.g. 'which means that the world's less developed countries have low literacy rates compared to the more developed' — or well-developed e.g. 'caused by lack of spending on education because of low government incomes'.

Level	Descriptor
0	No rewardable content
1 (1-2 marks)	Simple or very basic statements using little or no subject vocabulary.
2 (3-4 marks)	Generalised explanations but with some use of geographical terms Up to two developed statements as shown by examples above.
3 (5-6 marks)	Detailed statements with clear explanations using geographical terms. e.g. 'The global development gap means differences between low income and high income countries, caused by low economic development, trade and lack of industry'. Three developed or two well-developed points as shown by examples above.

12.4 Barriers to progress in sub-Saharan Africa

Section in brief

In this section students learn about recent development in Malawi, and the barriers which are holding Malawi back — its location, poor infrastructure, the impact of HIV/AIDS, and trade.

In the activities, students:

- draw a spider diagram to show the problems facing Malawi, and decide which is the greatest;
- list the advantages and disadvantages of different projects to help Malawi develop, and decide which they would choose;
- answer an exam-style question to describe the barriers that prevent the progress of one country in sub-Saharan Africa.

Key ideas

- Malawi has made some development progress, but there are barriers to its further development.
- Malawi's landlocked location is a barrier to trade.
- Malawi's government cannot afford to improve its infrastructure.
- HIV/AIDS has a number of impacts, and is a major economic problem.
- Malawi is only likely to develop if it increases trade.

Key vocabulary

landlocked; infrastructure

Skills practised

Geographical skills: analyse development data; draw spider a diagram to show problems facing Malawi

PLTS: creative thinking; team-working

Literacy skills: write extended answer justifying their choice of project

Section outcomes

By the end of this section, most students should be able to:

- define or explain the terms given in 'Key vocabulary' above;
- explain why Malawi is stuck in a cycle of poverty;
- draw a spider diagram to show the problems Malawi faces;
- decide on one project to help Malawi develop, and justify their choice.

Ideas for a starter

1. Ask students to look at the map of Malawi, and the photo of the train on a single track railway on pages 208 and 209. Ask students: 'How does Malawi's landlocked location, and its single track railway affect its ability to develop?'
2. Recap what students learnt about Malawi from section 12.1 — its location, level of development and development indicators.

Ideas for plenaries

1. Use question 2 from page 209 of the students' book, as a plenary activity.
2. Play 'Just a minute'. The topic is 'Barriers to progress in Malawi.' Students have up to a minute to talk on the topic without hesitation or repetition.

Further class and homework activity

Tell students that Malawi's biggest export commodity is tobacco, representing 53% of Malawi's exports. Ask them what problems this could create for Malawi's export earnings.

Development dilemmas

answers

1 a Students' spider diagrams should include:
- *Infrastructure*: one single-track railway line to the coast; unreliable power supply; water shortages; poor telecommunications; lack of money to improve infrastructure.
- *HIV/AIDS*: 20% of adults affected; creates poverty for those affected and unable to work; many of those dying are in their 20s and 30s (normally the most economically active age group); orphans live with grandparents who are then less able to work.
- *Trade*: trade still creates problems; tariffs mean that companies importing coffee want to import raw beans rather than roasted beans, meaning Malawi earns less money.

b Answers will vary.

2 a
- **Faster rail link to coast:** *Advantages* — more goods could be exported more quickly, increasing earnings for Malawi. *Disadvantages* — goods would still have to go through Mozambique.
- **Programme to treat everyone with HIV:** *Advantages* — deaths would be reduced, and life expectancy would increase; number of economically active workers would increase; people would have more money.
- **Build factories to roast and process coffee beans:** *Advantages* — Malawi would earn more from exports. *Disadvantages* — power supply still unreliable; water shortages still occur.

b Answers will vary.

---

3 Exam-style question *Using examples from one country in sub-Saharan Africa, describe the barriers that prevent its progress. (6 marks)*

Cap answers at the top of Level 2 (4 marks) which do not include:
- examples from a named country in sub-Saharan Africa e.g. Malawi;
- descriptions of how a features are barriers to progress.

Suitable descriptions could include:
- Any description of the cycle of poverty shown on page 208 e.g. 'because the government gets little tax, it can't afford to provide education for everyone' — plus development e.g. 'to help it cope with its huge debt so that people aren't affected so badly by austerity' — or well-developed e.g. 'and trying to prevent the banking crisis from spreading and causing collapse'.
- It's landlocked (plus a definition) — with development e.g. 'which means that it is costly to get to the coast by road or rail / it depends politically upon another country to export its goods' — or well-developed e.g. 'which is a barrier as this would make its goods expensive'.
- Health barriers e.g. HIV-AIDS — with development e.g. 'which weakens those affected and makes them less able or likely to work' — or well-developed with further expansion e.g. 'which lowers the country's economic production'.

Level	Descriptor
0	No rewardable content
1 (1-2 marks)	Simple or very basic statements using little or no subject vocabulary.
2 (3-4 marks)	Generalised explanations but with some use of geographical terms. Up to two developed statements as shown by examples above.
3 (5-6 marks)	Detailed statements with clear explanations using geographical terms.

12.5 How do countries develop?

Section in brief

In this section students learn about two theories of development regarding how societies develop over time.

In the activities, students:

- decide which stage of Rostow's model different countries are at, and label them on the model;
- research imports and exports for five countries and mark the countries on Frank's model;
- decide whether Rostow or Frank put forward the better theory to explain development;
- answer an exam-style question to describe Rostow's theory about how countries develop over time.

Key ideas

- Rostow's model of economic development is based on the experience of Europe, North America and Australasia – that all countries should pass through five stages of development.
- Rostow's theory is also known as modernisation theory, as it was a way for countries to modernise.
- Frank's dependency theory is based on the idea that development was about two types of global region – core (developed countries) and periphery (developing countries).
- In Frank's theory, the periphery depends on the core for a market for its products.
- Frank believed that historical trade was what made countries poor in the first place.

Key vocabulary

Rostow's theory, Frank's dependency theory, core, periphery

Skills practised

Geographical skills: analysing a table of development data; describing how countries develop over time

PLTS: independent enquiry

Section outcomes

By the end of this section, most students should be able to:

- define or explain the terms given in 'Key vocabulary' above;
- describe Rostow's theory about how countries develop over time;
- describe Frank's dependency theory about development;
- identify examples of countries at different stages of Rostow's model;
- identify countries in the different regions of Frank's model.

Ideas for a starter

1. Recap section 12.4 – Malawi's recent development and the barriers to its progress.
2. Ask students to work in pairs. Invite one of the pair to the front of the class to look at the graph of Rostow's model of economic development for 20 seconds. They should return to their partner and draw as much of the model as they remember. Repeat this with the other students. Use this as an introduction to development theories.

Ideas for plenaries

1. Use question 4 from page 211 of the students' book as a plenary activity, and ask students to work in small groups to compare answers. Whose answer does the group think is best? How could the others be improved?
2. Ask students if they found anything difficult about the work in this section. What could help to make it less difficult?

Further class and homework activity

Ask students how far they believe that Malawi's poverty is due to its past relationships with other countries.

Development dilemmas

answers

1 a
- Stage 1: Mali — most people work in farming; very low GDP
- Stage 2: Sri Lanka – shift from farming to manufacturing; low GDP but growing quickly
- Stage 3: Chile — GDP increasing rapidly; more people work in manufacturing than farming.
- Stage 4: Singapore — few people in farming; high overall GDP
- Stage 5: Australia — over 20% in manufacturing; high GDP; high spending on education and health.

2 The countries should be positioned as follows: Mali and Sri Lanka – periphery; Chile – semi-periphery; Australia and Singapore – core.

3 Students should notice that Australia doesn't quite match expectations – it exports raw materials e.g. coal, iron ore, wool, wheat — a characteristic of periphery countries.

4 Answers will vary.

5 Exam-style question *Describe Rostow's theory about how countries develop over time. (6 marks)*

This question is marked using levels. With 'describe' as a command word, it is suitable for all candidates. If you wish to differentiate, Higher Tier students may answer the alternative question:

Explain Rostow's theory about how countries develop over time. (6 marks)

In this case, replace the term 'descriptions' in the table below with 'explanations'. Remember, therefore, that in this case purely descriptive points by Higher Tier candidates get no marks. However, as the examples below show, it is difficult to separate description and cause (i.e. explanation) in this question, so you may decide to leave the question as it is.

Suitable descriptions of Rostow's theory could include:

- An overview of the whole model e.g. 'it has five stages from a traditional subsistence society to a highly developed economy' — plus development e.g. 'at each stage a country's level of industrialisation increases' — or well-developed e.g. 'which means that more people have better paid jobs.
- Any of the stages in detail e.g. 'stage 3 is where fastest growth occurs — plus development e.g. 'which is where new investment brings many new industries' — or well-developed e.g. 'which produce consumer goods sold as exports to bring increased wealth'.

Level	Descriptor
0	No rewardable content
1 (1-2 marks)	Simple or very basic statements using little or no subject vocabulary. May be a descriptive or basic list of points e.g. 'Rostow's model shows countries becoming better off over time'.
2 (3-4 marks)	Generalised explanations but with some use of geographical terms e.g. 'Rostow's model shows countries becoming better off over five stages of growth, from subsistence farming to a consumer economy'. Up to two developed statements as shown by examples above.
3 (5-6 marks)	Detailed statements with clear explanations using geographical terms. e.g. 'Rostow's model shows countries becoming better off over five stages of growth, from subsistence farming with only just enough food, to a consumer economy in which people are wealthy and have enough wealth to pay for health and education'. Three developed or two well-developed points as shown by examples above.

12.6 Investigating India

Section in brief

In this section students learn how levels of development vary within India. While India's economic growth has created wealthy core regions, those on the periphery remain poor.

In the activities, students:

- use data to make up statements to show that Maharashtra is part of India's 'core', and Bihar part of its periphery;
- draw a cycle of poverty to show what happens when circumstances change;
- draw spider diagrams to show the circumstances in Bihar;
- answer an exam-style question to describe how levels of development can vary within a country.

Key ideas

- Levels of development and wealth are very uneven within India.
- India's economic growth has created a 'multiplier effect' leading to the development of core regions such as Maharashtra.
- Regions away from the core receive less investment, produce less wealth, and are on the periphery e.g. Bihar.
- Farmers in the rural periphery become trapped in a cycle of poverty.

Key vocabulary

multiplier effect, core region, caste-based society, subsistence farming, cycle of poverty

Skills practised

Geographical skills: interpreting multiplier effect and cycle of poverty diagrams; describing how levels of development vary within a country

PLTS: independent enquiry

Literacy skills: writing statements about Maharashtra and Bihar

Section outcomes

By the end of this section, most students should be able to:

- define or explain the terms given in 'Key vocabulary' above;
- describe how levels of development vary within India;
- write statements to show that Maharashtra is part of India's core, and Bihar is part of its periphery;
- explain why farmers in the rural periphery become trapped in a cycle of poverty.

Ideas for a starter

1. Give students an idea of India's size by showing them a map of India and then superimposing it over a map of Europe. Tell them it isn't just India's size that is big, and read out the bullet points on page 212 of the students' book.
2. Play a video clip about India as students enter the room for the lesson. The clip should give students a flavour of India and convey something of the size and scale of the country. Look for a suitable clip or use the BBC's 2012 series Welcome to India.

Ideas for plenaries

1. Ask students to work in pairs to write a paragraph about varying levels of development in India. They should include these terms: multiplier effect; core region; caste-based society; periphery.
2. Create a graffiti of students' learning from this lesson.

Further class and homework activity

Ask students to find out about the Green Revolution. They should find out what it was, and the impacts it had on India.

Development dilemmas

answers

1 a Maharashtra (core): growth has attracted investment and service jobs with large TNCs; Mumbai has large manufacturing industries such as clothing, steel, engineering and food processing and the world's largest film industry (Bollywood).

b Bihar (periphery): 86% rural population, mostly working in farming; low annual incomes; little investment in the region; only 59% of Bihar's population has electricity; high rates of illiteracy; school attendance is poor; high fertility rate due to early marriage.

2 a Family member falls ill → unable to work → income would decline further forcing the family further into poverty.

b Family member gets into debt → spare income is used to pay the debt → may lead to eventual starvation.

c Family member goes to Mumbai to work → sends home wages → money to invest in land improvement, machinery or materials → more crops produced and sold → family income increases.

3 a Little investment in machinery or fertiliser; land is worked by hand under a system called share-cropping; there is no surplus to sell.

b Lack of education results in low literacy rates; uneducated women marry and have children early, rarely own land and work as low-wage labourers.

c Caste-based society; children are needed to work on the land.

---

4 Exam-style question *Using examples, describe how levels of development may vary within a country. (6 marks)*

This question is marked using levels. With 'describe' as a command word, it is suitable for all candidates. Cap answers at the top of Level 2 (4 marks) which do not include:

- examples of the detailed ways in which wealth varies e.g. core and periphery;
- named countries / regions where variation can be seen.

Suitable descriptions could include:

- An overview of the core and periphery model e.g. 'countries have regions of high and low — plus development e.g. a description of a core region using the model on page 211.
- Examples of core and periphery in a named country e.g. Maharashtra and Bihar in India — plus development e.g. characteristics of Maharashtra as a core region — or well-developed e.g. characteristics of Bihar as a peripheral region.

Level	Descriptor
0	No rewardable content
1 (1-2 marks)	Simple or very basic statements using little or no subject vocabulary.
2 (3-4 marks)	Generalised explanations but with some use of geographical terms e.g. 'India has differences in wealth like Maharashtra with industries, and rural areas like Bihar which is much poorer'. Up to two developed statements as shown by examples above.
3 (5-6 marks)	Detailed statements with clear explanations using geographical terms. e.g. 'India has differences in wealth like Maharashtra with industries and the port of Mumbai, compared to the rural state of Bihar which is much poorer as incomes are only a third of the Indian average'. Three developed or two well-developed points as shown by examples above.

12.7 Which way now?

Section in brief

In this section students learn about two different types of development in India – top-down and bottom-up, with examples of each.

In the activities, students:

- explain the difference between top-down and bottom-up development projects;
- complete a table to compare top-down (HYV) and bottom-up (biogas) development projects and decide which is best for national interests and local communities;
- answer an exam-style question to describe the differences between top-down and bottom-up development.

Key ideas

- In top-down development projects, decisions are made by governments or large private companies.
- The Green Revolution (a top-down development project) offered High Yielding Variety (HYV) seeds which produced more grain than traditional rice.
- HYVs have had mixed impacts.
- In bottom-up development, experts work with communities to identify their needs and give people control in improving their lives.
- The biogas development project is an example of bottom-up development using intermediate technology.

Key vocabulary

top-down development, bottom-up development, biogas, intermediate technology

Skills practised

Geographical skills: defining geographical terms; comparing development projects

PLTS: independent enquiry

Section outcomes

By the end of this section, most students should be able to:

- define or explain the terms given in 'Key vocabulary' above;
- complete a table to compare the HYV (top-down) and biogas (bottom-up) development projects;
- decide which development project is best for national interests and which for local communities.

Ideas for a starter

1. If students completed the Further activity from section 12.6, ask several of them to feedback what they found out to the class.

2. Show students the two drawings of rice from page 214 of the students' book — the traditional and new (HYV) varieties. Then read out the text in the 'On your planet' bubble about the lack of straw for cattle. Discuss with students about how the lack of involvement of the farmers resulted in this situation.

Ideas for plenaries

1. Provide students with a map of India. Ask them to annotate the map with 5 points about top-down development (HYV) and five points about biogas (bottom-up development).

2. Ask students to think back over the lesson and write down two questions related to what they have learnt. Ask some of the other class members to answer.

Further class and homework activity

Ask students to answer the exam-style question for homework.

Development dilemmas

answers

1 Top-down development — decisions are made by governments or large private companies who identify needs or opportunities at a national level; experts help to plan the changes, and they are then imposed on people. Bottom-up development — experts work with communities to identify their needs, and assist with progress; local people have control in improving their own lives.

2 a

	Top-down project (HYV)	Bottom-up project (Biogas)
Size and scale	Large, national scale	Small, community scale
Aims of the project	To produce enough rice to feed the population and avoid hunger	To reduce the time spent collecting fuel
Who pays for it	Government and large private companies. Farmers have to pay for new seed each year.	Development project and local community
Who makes the decisions about what's needed	Government and large private companies	Development project and local community
Raw materials and technology required	New seeds required every year. Irrigation water, fertiliser and pesticide needed. High level of technology used by scientists to develop seeds.	Cow dung – produced by cows already owned by community. Intermediate technology used – a simple technique using local materials.
Who benefits	Mainly the private companies and wealthy farmers.	Local communities.

b i Top-down developments suit national interests best.
  ii Bottom-up developments suit local communities best.

---

3 Exam-style question *Using examples, describe the differences between top-down and bottom-up development. (6 marks)*

This question is marked using levels. Cap answers at 4 marks which do not include:

- examples of either precise differences between the two models of development, or named countries / regions where each is found;
- comparisons of the differences between top-down and bottom-up development — a single comparative word or phrase e.g. 'whereas' or 'however' validates the whole answer.

Suitable explanations could include:

- A general comparison e.g. 'top-down is where large companies or governments make decisions, compared to bottom-up development which involves local people and their own needs' — plus a brief description of each type of project and how it works.
- Examples e.g. the 'Green Revolution' in India compared to the development of biogas — plus development e.g. characteristics of the Green Revolution and who made the decisions — or well-developed e.g. biogas as a product of the ASTRA project.

Level	Descriptor
0	No rewardable content
1 (1-2 marks)	Simple or very basic statements using little or no subject vocabulary.
2 (3-4 marks)	Generalised explanations but with some use of geographical terms. Up to two developed statements as shown by examples above.
3 (5-6 marks)	Detailed statements with clear explanations using geographical terms. Three developed or two well-developed points as shown by examples above.

12.8 A top-down project: The Narmada River Scheme

Section in brief

In this section students learn about a top-down development project – the Narmada River Scheme. The dam will bring benefits and cause problems for different groups of people.

In the activities, students:

- complete a table to show the economic, social, and environmental benefits and problems of the Sardar Sarovar Dam;
- identify the local benefits and those which are further away;
- explain whether top-down schemes should be built if they cause problems;
- answer an exam-style question to explain the benefits and problems of a top-down development project.

Key ideas

- Over much of India, rainfall is seasonal and unreliable.
- Demand for water is rising as India's population increases and the economy grows.
- The Indian government has embarked on a major programme of dam building to store water, including the Sardar Sarovar Dam on the Narmada River.
- The Sardar Sarovar Dam will benefit some groups of people.
- Other groups will lose out as a result of the dam being built.

Key vocabulary

irrigation

Skills practised

Geographical skills: classifying benefits and problems of the Sardar Sarovar Dam as economic, social and environmental; identifying greatest benefits and problems

PLTS: independent enquiry

Section outcomes

By the end of this section, most students should be able to:

- explain the term given in 'Key vocabulary' above;
- explain why the Indian government is building dams;
- classify the benefits and problems of the Sardar Sarovar Dam as economic, social and environmental;
- identify the greatest benefits and problems;
- explain whether dams like the Sardar Sarovar should be built if they cause major problems.

Ideas for a starter

1. Recap top-down and bottom-up development from section 12.7 with students. Ask: 'What is the difference between them?'
2. Ask students to describe the rainfall distribution shown on the map from the top of page 216 of the students' book. Explain that India's rainfall is seasonal, its population is increasing and its economy is booming. What issues could this cause and how could they be solved?

Ideas for plenaries

1. Hold a class discussion. Is the Sardar Sarovar Dam an engineering marvel, or a disaster?
2. Hot seat! Ask several students to take on the roles of Indian government ministers. The rest of the class should take on the roles of either people who will benefit from the new dams, or those who have been forced from their homes as a result of dam building. Students should ask the ministers sensible questions about their reasons for building the dams.

Further class and homework activity

Ask students to complete a dictionary of key terms for this chapter.

Development dilemmas

answers

1 a and **b** (*local* points are in italics)

Economic: Benefits — provides electricity for industry; encourages economic development. Problems — silt reduces dam's capacity.

Social: Benefits — provides drinking water; provides electricity for people. Problems — *234 villages drowned, 320 000 people forced out; villages cannot afford the electricity; religious and historical sites flooded.*

Environmental: Benefits — provides water to irrigate farmland in driest parts of states. Problems — *good quality farmland submerged; irrigation increases salinity, making soil less useable; sediment deposited during flooding will be lost; dam could trigger earthquakes.*

c Social and economic benefits are greatest — they are all further away.

d Social and environmental problems are greatest — they are all local.

e Students' responses may vary, but they should be aware that there needs to be some means of providing water and power for India's rapidly growing population and economy.

---

2 Exam-style question *For a top-down development project that you have studied, explain its benefits and problems. (8 marks)*

Foundation Tier students may answer the alternative question:

For a top-down development project that you have studied, describe the benefits and problems that it has brought. (6 marks)

In this case, replace the term 'explanations' in the table below with 'descriptions'. Cap answers at 6 marks (4 marks for the Foundation question) which do not include:

- named, specific examples e.g. the Sardar Sarovar Dam — not just 'in India'.
- *both* benefits and problems.

Suitable **benefits** of a project such as the Sardar Sarovar dam include:

- Its location and characteristics i.e. size, its multi-purpose nature etc — plus development e.g. 'providing electricity for India's cities as well as the local area — or well-developed e.g. 'and also provides piped supplies of drinking water'.

Suitable **problems** of a project such as the Sardar Sarovar dam include:

- A brief outline of those who may lose out e.g. 'those local people whose land has been flooded' — plus development e.g. 'especially as it was the most fertile land in the valley bottom which was flooded most' — or well-developed e.g. 'and their new land has become more saline making it less fertile for crops'.

Level	Descriptor
0	No rewardable content
1 (1-3 marks)	Simple or very basic statements using little or no subject vocabulary. May be a list or undeveloped description e.g. 'Top down projects such as dams in India have flooded people's land'.
2 (4-6 marks)	Generalised explanations but with some use of geographical terms e.g. 'A top-down project such as the Sardar Sarovar Dam in NW India has flooded fertile land and forced over 300 000 people to move'. Up to three developed statements as shown by examples above.
3 (7-8 marks)	Detailed statements with clear explanations using geographical terms. e.g. 'A top-down project such as the Sardar Sarovar Dam in NW India has flooded fertile land and forced over 300 000 people to move, often to worse land which is saline and less fertile'. Three developed points or two well-developed points are required for the top of Level 3 as shown by examples above.

13 The changing economy of the UK

About the chapter
These are the key ideas behind the chapter.
- There have been many changes in the UK's industrial structure, in both primary and secondary sectors, and tertiary and quaternary sectors.
- There are different ways of classifying jobs, and the type of employment in the UK has changed.
- Different regions of the UK have different industrial and employment structures.
- Deindustrialisation and economic change has environmental impacts.
- Economic development can include *greenfield development* and *brownfield regeneration* – but both have costs and benefits.
- The digital economy, education and research, and green employment, could all contribute to the future growth of the UK economy.
- The way people work is changing.

Chapter outline
Use this outline to provide your students with a brief roadmap of the chapter.

13.1 The UK's changing employment – 1
Changes in primary and secondary employment in the UK.

13.2 The UK's changing employment – 2
Changes in the UK's tertiary and quaternary industries.

13.3 It's all change in the jobs market
Classifying jobs, and why types of employment have changed.

13.4 Contrasting regions of the UK 1 – the North East
The UK's North East region, its industry and employment.

13.5 Contrasting regions of the UK 2 – the South East
Employment in the South East, and how it differs from the North East.

13.6 The impacts of changing employment
The impacts of deindustrialisation and economic change in Glasgow.

13.7 Where should future development take place?
The costs and benefits of greenfield development versus brownfield regeneration.

13.8 What kind of world...? 1
Three areas of possible growth for the UK economy.

13.9 What kind of world...? 2
How work is changing, and how people might work in future.

The changing economy of the UK

How is the specification covered?

This chapter covers Topic 5, Unit 2, People and the planet.

5.1 How and why is the economy changing?

5.2 What is the impact of changing work on people and places?

Key ideas	Detailed content	Pages in students' book
5.1a There have been many changes in the industrial structure of the UK economy in the past 50 years as a consequence of government policies and external forces such as globalisation.	Investigate the changes in primary and secondary industry to explain why: • employment has declined in many sectors • changes in output are more variable, with some growth areas e.g. vehicle manufacturing, but decline in others, e.g. footwear and clothing.	218-219
	Examine changes in tertiary and quaternary sectors, including the growth of retail, finance and business services and IT-related research.	220-221
5.1b There have been significant changes in the structure of the workforce in the past 50 years which vary from place to place within the UK.	Explore different methods of classifying employment and investigate why the balance of types of employment has changed in terms of average wages, full time/part time, temporary or permanent, male and female.	222-223
	Investigate two contrasting regions of the UK, e.g. the North East and the South East, to explain the differences in their industrial structure and workforce.	224-225, 226-227
5.2a Changing employment has environmental impacts, some of which are positive and some negative.	Assess the environmental impacts of de-industrialisation and economic diversification in one UK urban area.	228-229
	Examine alternative proposals for economic development by comparing the costs and benefits of a greenfield development and the regeneration of a brownfield site.	230-231
5.2b Employment is changing and will continue to change.	Examine the increasing contribution of the digital economy, education and research, the 'green' employment sector, and foreign workforce to the growth of the UK economy.	232-233
	Consider the impact of changing working practices including home working, teleworking, self-employment, flexible working and the impact of IT.	234-235

Chapter outcomes

By the end of this chapter, students should be able to:

- Describe changes in the UK's employment structure and suggest reasons for the changes.
- Compare jobs in different locations using different employment indicators and explain why changing employment patterns affect income.
- Describe the impacts of changing employment trends in the North East.
- Explain why there are more jobs and wealth in London and the South East, than in the North East.
- Assess whether deindustrialisation in Glasgow was worth the improved environment and job opportunities of today.
- Summarise the advantages and disadvantages of using brownfield and greenfield sites for new development.
- Outline three areas where economic growth might take place in future in the UK.
- Complete a table to show the advantages and disadvantages of different ways of working.

13.1 The UK's changing employment – 1

Section in brief

In this section students learn about changes in primary and secondary employment in the UK.

In the activities, students:

- explain how some factories are as productive as in the past, but with fewer people;
- consider the effect of changes on the community in Dagenham;
- research one of the top five car companies making cars in the UK;
- complete a table to show the advantages and disadvantages of clothing companies locating overseas;
- answer an exam-style question to suggest reasons for the changes in primary, secondary and tertiary employment in the UK.

Key ideas

- There have been major changes in the UK's employment structure over the last 30 years.
- Employment has declined in the primary and secondary sectors, but grown in the tertiary and quaternary sectors.
- The UK car industry has changed, enabling it to produce almost as many cars now as in the 1970s.
- In the clothing industry, most goods are now made overseas.

Key vocabulary

primary, secondary, tertiary, quaternary (employment), automated

Skills practised

Geographical skills: analysing a table of employment data;

PLTS: independent enquiry; creative thinking; team-working

Section outcomes

By the end of this section, most students should be able to:

- define or explain the terms given in 'Key vocabulary' above;
- describe the changes in the UK's employment structure;
- describe the effects on the community in Dagenham of reduced employment at the Ford factory;
- explain how some factories are as productive as in the past, but with fewer people;
- describe the advantages and disadvantages of clothing companies producing goods overseas, for different groups of people.

Ideas for a starter

1. Play students a trailer for the film 'Made in Dagenham' (you can find this on-line). Alternatives are 'Brassed Off' and 'Billy Elliott'. With all films you should check first in order to ensure that the language used is appropriate for the students you are teaching, and your school.

2. Brainstorm with students the definitions of primary, secondary, tertiary and quaternary employment, with examples of jobs in each sector. Section 11.2 of the students' book includes definitions for these terms.

Ideas for plenaries

1. Ask students to work in pairs to write a two minute news item with the title 'The UK's changing employment'.

2. Use question 4 from page 219 of the students' book as a plenary activity.

Further class and homework activity

Ask students to find out about the Green Revolution. They should find out what it was, and the impacts it had on India.

The changing economy of the UK

answers

1 Production is automated; robots and machinery assemble the products which requires fewer people.

2 a Unemployment would increase; people would have less money to spend in the local community, affecting local businesses.

b Young people would be forced to move away from the area to search for work elsewhere; less money would be spent in the local community.

3 Students could choose from: Nissan UK, Jaguar Land Rover, Toyota UK, Honda UK and Mini.

4 For the company: *Advantages* — cheap labour and reduced costs. *Disadvantages* — cannot label products as 'Made in Britain'.

For UK workers: *Disadvantages* — Job losses.

For consumers: *Advantages* — cheaper prices of goods; cannot support British industry, as goods are not made in Britain.

---

5 Exam-style question *Suggest reasons for the changes in primary, secondary and tertiary employment in the UK. (6 marks)*

This question is marked using levels. With 'suggest reasons for' as the command phrase, it is suitable for all candidates. As there are three foci for the question, you are technically looking for three developed explanations, one for each type of employment. However, a well-developed explanation for one can be used as evidence to help a student reach a higher level, even though another type of employment may be less well explained.

Suitable reasons for changes in **primary** employment include:

- A fall in the number of people working in e.g. coal mining — plus development e.g. 'because cheaper coal comes from overseas' — or well-developed with further expansion e.g. 'and has led to mines closing and people being put out of work'.

Suitable reasons for changes in **secondary** employment include:

- The fall in number of people in manufacturing in e.g. the clothing industry — plus development e.g. 'because labour costs are cheaper overseas' — or well-developed with further expansion e.g. 'which has led to companies opening factories overseas and closing down British clothing factories'.

Suitable reasons for changes in **tertiary** employment include:

- The steep increase in tertiary employment in e.g. IT — plus development e.g. 'to support the increase in the use of computers in manufacturing such as the car industry' — or well-developed with further expansion e.g. 'which has led to automated factories and the use of robots on production lines'.

Level	Descriptor
0	No rewardable content
1 (1-2 marks)	Simple or very basic statements using little or no subject vocabulary.
2 (3-4 marks)	Generalised explanations but with some use of geographical terms e.g. 'Many secondary companies have closed down factories and gone overseas where labour is cheaper'. Up to two developed statements as shown by examples above.
3 (5-6 marks)	Detailed statements with clear explanations using geographical terms. e.g. 'Many secondary industries such as clothing (e.g. Burberry) have closed down manufacturing and built new factories overseas where labour is cheaper'. Three developed or two well-developed points as shown by examples above.

13.2 The UK's changing employment - 2

Section in brief

In this section students learn about changes in the UK's tertiary and quaternary industries. They learn about the UK's knowledge economy and the growth of biotechnology industries.

In the activities, students:

- explain the difference between tertiary jobs, quaternary jobs and the knowledge economy;
- give examples of different types of tertiary and quaternary jobs;
- explain why some knowledge-based industries prefer to locate in city centres while others prefer out-of-town locations;
- brainstorm the reasons why office workers in Canary Wharf often work long hours;
- answer an exam-style question to describe the changes in tertiary and quaternary employment in the UK.

Key ideas

- Employment in tertiary and quaternary industries has risen over the last 30 years.
- The UK government had a policy to develop the tertiary and quaternary sectors.
- The knowledge economy is based on knowledge and intellectual skills.
- The number of people employed in biotechnology has doubled since 1985 to 2.3 million.

Key vocabulary

tertiary sector, quaternary sector, knowledge economy, biotechnology

Skills practised

Geographical skills: explaining geographical terms; explaining the location of knowledge-based industries; describing changes in tertiary and quaternary employment in the UK

PLTS: team-working

Section outcomes

By the end of this section, most students should be able to:

- define or explain the terms given in 'Key vocabulary' above;
- describe the changes which have occured in tertiary and quaternary employment in the UK;
- give examples of different types of tertiary and quaternary jobs;
- explain the rise in jobs in the knowledge economy.

Ideas for a starter

1. Show students a sequence of images of London on the whiteboard. End with a photo of Canary Wharf. Ask what jobs people in London do. You are looking to elicit that many people work in banking and investment. Tell students that each year over half of all the money in the world passes through London.

2. Recap section 13.1 - the changes to primary and secondary employment in the UK.

Ideas for plenaries

1. Use question 2 as a plenary activity, but brainstorm to see how many different jobs the class can come up with.

2. Ask students what types of jobs they would like to do in future. What sectors do these jobs fall into? How many think they will work in the knowledge economy?

Further class and homework activity

Ask students to investigate about 20 local jobs in preparation for section 13.3. How many are full-time, and how many are part-time? How many are permanent jobs and how many are temporary?

The changing economy of the UK

answers

1. **Tertiary jobs** —provide a service. They could be associated with manufacturing e.g. distribution or retailing, or people e.g. teaching, nursing.

   Quaternary jobs — provide information and expert help e.g. creative or knowledge-based industries, especially IT, biosciences, media etc.

   The knowledge economy —an economy based on knowledge and intellectual skills.

2. Students could come up with a range of tertiary and quaternary jobs within IT; finance and professional; scientific and technical sectors. Check their understanding of the difference between tertiary and quaternary jobs.

3. **City-centre locations** — close to other companies that they work with and which support them e.g banks and investment companies, insurance companies, IT companies.

   Out-of-town locations — they need more land for offices and research laboratories; which is cheaper in out-of-town locations e.g. biotechnology industries.

4. They are trading with colleagues around the world who work in different time zones, so they need to work long hours in order to do business with them.

5. **Exam-style question** *Using examples, describe changes in tertiary and quaternary employment in the UK. (6 marks)*

   This question is marked using levels. With 'describe' as a command word, it is suitable for all candidates or just for Foundation Tier. If you wish to differentiate, you can give Higher Tier students the question:

   Using examples, explain changes in tertiary and quaternary employment in the UK. (6 marks)

   In this case, replace the term 'descriptions' in the table below with 'explanations.' Purely descriptive points by Higher Tier candidates would get no marks. Cap answers at the top of Level 2 (4 marks) if they do not include examples of specific jobs, or types of company.

   Suitable changes for **tertiary** employment could include:

   - Growth of service jobs in cities such as London — plus development e.g. using data to illustrate growth from the data or the map on page 221 — or well-developed with further expansion e.g. 'with bio-technology companies which offer a lot of work in laboratories'.

   Suitable changes for **quaternary** employment could include:

   - Growth of banking and finance / the knowledge economy — plus development e.g. using data to illustrate growth from the table on page 221 — or well-developed with further expansion e.g. 'with companies such as HSBC in London's Docklands'.

Level	Descriptor
0	No rewardable content
1 (1-2 marks)	Simple or very basic statements using little or no subject vocabulary. May be a descriptive or basic list of points e.g. 'Tertiary employment has grown massively in cities like London'.
2 (3-4 marks)	Generalised description but with some use of geographical terms e.g. 'Quaternary employment has grown massively in London and the south-east e.g. there are 25 biotechnology companies near London'. Up to two developed statements as shown by examples above.
3 (5-6 marks)	Detailed statements with clear descriptions using geographical terms. e.g. 'Quaternary employment has grown massively in industries such as finance and bio-technology in London and South East England e.g. there are 25 biotechnology companies in the Home Counties and London'. Three developed or two well-developed points as shown by examples above.

13.3 It's all change in the jobs market

Section in brief

In this section students learn about different ways of classifying jobs, and why employment has changed. Dinnington, Rotherham and London's Canary Wharf are included as examples.

In the activities, students:

- explain why London has more professional and managerial jobs than Rotherham;
- explain why it is important if jobs are professional, skilled or semi-skilled;
- complete a table to compare jobs in Dinnington and Canary Wharf;
- explain why Dinnington would find it difficult to attract employers from the knowledge economy;
- answer an exam-style question using data to explain why average incomes in Rotherham are lower than in the rest of the UK.

Key ideas

- The balance of employment in the UK has changed in a number of ways.
- Employment can be classified in terms of the level of skill and responsibility involved, and whether it is full or part-time, permanent or temporary.
- The new economy is a service sector economy.
- Some jobs in the new economy are well paid, but the majority are at the lower end of the salary scale.

Key vocabulary

temporary, permanent, part-time, full-time

Skills practised

Geographical skills: comparing jobs using employment indicators

PLTS: independent enquiry

Numeracy skills: interpreting employment data

Section outcomes

By the end of this section, most students should be able to:

- define or explain the terms given in 'Key vocabulary' above;
- describe how the UK government classifies jobs (other than by job type);
- compare jobs in different locations using different employment indicators;
- explain how changing employment patterns affect income.

Ideas for a starter

1. If students completed the Further activity from section 13.2, ask a number of them to feedback their results to the class. How many of the jobs they found were full-time, and how many were part-time? How many were permanent jobs and how many temporary?

2. Find a video clip of the Dinington Colliery Band. Play this as students enter the room. Explain that Dinnington had one of the Yorkshire biggest collieries until 1992, when it was closed. During the twentieth century the town thrived along with the band. The miners have gone and employment has changed — but the band still thrives!.

Ideas for plenaries

1. Use the exam-style question on page 223 of the students' book.

2. Make a graffiti wall of students' learning from this lesson.

Further class and homework activity

Ask students to create either a poster, or presentation on employment changes in the UK. They should use information from sections 13.1, 13.2 and 13.3.

The changing economy of the UK

answers

1 London has many global companies which employ people in the knowledge economy / quaternary sector and need workers with high qualification and skill levels. In the past Rotherham's employment was based on primary sector employment, and has now shifted to the tertiary sector. Companies are attracted by cheap land and local labour, but many jobs are unskilled and need few qualifications.

2 The skill and responsibility level of jobs will determine income. More highly skilled jobs are also likely to be full-time and permanent.

3

	Dinnington	Canary Wharf
Level of qualification and skill	Many jobs unskilled, needing few qualifications	Highly skilled and highly educated (requiring degrees)
Full- or part-time	25% of jobs are part-time	Most jobs are full-time
Temporary or permanent	Many jobs are temporary, lasting just weeks or months	Many jobs are permanent, contract jobs are also available
Salary levels	Low (minimum wage or just above), with more for supervisor roles	High – depending on qualifications. New graduates can earn up to £60 000
Benefitting men or women?	Employees are both male and female, but more women than men	Employees are mostly male
Who benefits	In theory everyone should benefit. In fact it is the private companies and wealthy farmers who probably benefit most.	Local communities.

4 Dinnington is likely to find it hard to attract employers from the knowledge economy as those employers need workers with high qualification and skill levels — more likely to be found in large cities than in small towns.

---

5 Exam-style question *Using the table of data on the opposite page, explain why average incomes in Rotherham are lower than in the rest of the UK. (4 marks)*

This question is point marked. It requires two developed explanations for 2 marks each. Do not credit negatives e.g. 'there aren't as good jobs here as in London'.

Suitable reasons include:
- Rotherham has lower than UK / London for average professional and managerial employment (1) — plus development e.g. 'which pay higher than average incomes' (1).
- Higher than UK / London average semi- and unskilled employment (1) — plus development e.g. 'which pay lower than average incomes' (1).
- Lower than UK / London average full-time work (1) — plus development e.g. 'which would pay higher than part-time' (1) – or vice-versa.

13.4 Contrasting regions of the UK 1 – the North East

Section in brief

In this section students learn about the UK's North East region, its industry and employment.

In the activities, students:

- outline evidence to show that the North East is one of the UK's most deprived regions;
- draw a diagram to show how different industries are linked, and what happens when industry collapses;
- discuss whether the government should help companies relocating to the North East;
- answer an exam-style question to describe the impacts of changing employment trends on one UK region.

Key ideas

- The North East is England's most-deprived region.
- The North East has suffered from a 'domino effect' of collapsing industries and de-industrialisation.
- Manufacturing in the North East has declined and the tertiary sector has increased.
- There is a lack of high-salary jobs in the quaternary sector in the North East.

Key vocabulary

household income, public sector, domino effect

Skills practised

Geographical skills: outlining evidence; describing impacts of changing employment trends

PLTS: independent enquiry; team-working

Section outcomes

By the end of this section, most students should be able to:

- define or explain the terms given in 'Key vocabulary' above;
- give evidence to show that the North East is one of the UK's most deprived regions;
- draw a diagram to show what happened when the North East's manufacturing industries collapsed;
- list the advantages and disadvantages of the government helping companies relocate to the North East.

Ideas for a starter

1. Show students a photo of the Angel of the North. Ask: 'Who knows what this is. Where is it?' What can students tell you about the North East region of the UK?
2. Show students a map of the UK's 12 standard economic regions, but without the labels. Ask them to identify the North East and South East. Ask 'What are the differences between these two regions? How do they differ in terms of employment and industry? Are there any similarities?'

Ideas for plenaries

1. Make up eight statements based on what students have learnt in this section – some True, some False. Ask students to identify the false statements and correct them.
2. Ask students to tell their partner the single most important thing they have learnt in this lesson.

Further class and homework activity

Ask students to search for film clips about shipbuilding in the North East in the 1960s. They should be able to find some at the 'BBC Nation on film' website. Ask them to write a paragraph about changing industry and employment in the North East.

The changing economy of the UK

answers

1 a The North East suffers from: one of the highest unemployment rates in the UK; the worst indicators in England for deaths from smoking, heart disease, strokes and cancer; the lowest percentage of adults who eat healthily; the UK's lowest income region; over-crowded housing.

b Health can suffer due to lack of income to buy fresh, healthy produce; increase in smoking etc. due to stress.

2 a Students' diagrams should include these links: coal was used to produce steel; steel was used in engineering to manufacture ships engines which were built on the Tyne and Wear estuaries.

b The coal industry collapsed as it was expensive to mine; the steel industry fell because of globalisation and cheap overseas competition; engineering and shipbuilding collapsed when Asian countries began to build bigger ships with cheaper labour; shops and services would suffer as a result of job losses and lack of money in the local community.

3 Pros — Government help would revitalise the region with new jobs; increasing income in the local community; improving health and quality of life.

Cons — Huge expense to the taxpayer; other regions may suffer as a result.

---

4 Exam-style question *Describe the impacts of changing employment trends on one UK region you have studied. (6 marks)*

This question is marked using levels. With 'describe' as a command word it is suitable for all candidates. Cap answers at the top of Level 2 (4 marks) if they do not include:

- specific examples from a named UK region e.g. North-East England
- the impact of changing employment trends — not just a description of *how* employment is changing.

Suitable impacts for North-East England could include:

- **Economic:** England's most deprived region — developed with examples e.g. falling public sector employment — or well-developed e.g. lack of high salary jobs or new investment; lack of jobs in the high-income knowledge economy.
- **Economic:** collapse in employment opportunities in traditional jobs — developed with examples e.g. the domino effect of traditional industries collapsing as they close / move overseas — or well-developed e.g. most new employment is tertiary which pays less.
- **Social:** England's worst indicators for health — developed with examples e.g. smoking / early deaths from heart disease — or well-developed e.g. and lowest percentage of adults eating healthily as a result of low incomes.

Level	Descriptor
0	No rewardable content
1 (1-2 marks)	Simple or very basic statements using little or no subject vocabulary.
2 (3-4 marks)	Generalised descriptions but with some use of geographical terms e.g. 'Traditional industries have closed down in the North East region, causing high unemployment and low incomes'. Up to two developed statements as shown by examples above.
3 (5-6 marks)	Detailed statements with clear descriptions using geographical terms. e.g. 'Traditional industries such as coal and steel have closed down in the North East region, causing high unemployment and low incomes, due to fewer highly paid jobs'. Three developed or two well-developed points as shown by examples above.

13.5 Contrasting regions of the UK 2 – the South East

Section in brief

In this section students learn about employment in the South East of England and how it differs from the North East of England.

In the activities, students:

- describe the evidence to show that the South East region is more affluent than the North East;
- draw a diagram to show why there are many jobs and more wealth in the South East;
- explain the benefits that companies might get from moving to the North East, and suggest why few do move;
- answer an exam-style question to explain the employment trends in one UK region.

Key ideas

- The South East offers a high quality of life for many.
- London has many well-paid tertiary and quaternary jobs.
- While the North East has lost public sector jobs in the last few years, the South East gained them.
- The South East has many job opportunities and the unemployment rate is below average.
- The South East has a growing knowledge economy.

Key vocabulary

There is no key vocabulary in this section.

Skills practised

Geographical skills: use data as evidence; explain trends

PLTS: independent enquiry; creative thinking

Numeracy skills: interpret a table of employment data

Section outcomes

By the end of this section, most students should be able to:

- describe evidence to show that the South East is more affluent than the North East;
- describe the job opportunities available in London and the South East;
- draw a diagram to show why there are more jobs and wealth in the South East;
- explain how employment has changed in London and the South East since 1996.

Ideas for a starter

1. Recap section 13.4, and changes to industry and employment in the North East.
2. Ask students to look at the table on page 227 of the students' book. Ask students to describe the trends they can see.

Ideas for plenaries

1. If you used starter 2 from section 13.4, return to the ideas you recorded. Now that students have studied both the North East and the South East, do their initial ideas need amending?
2. Ask students, if they had a choice, where would they rather live – the North East, or South East? Take a class vote, and ask individuals to justify their choice on the basis of what they have learnt.

Further class and homework activity

Ask students to create a set of revision notes on the two contrasting regions of the UK they have studied. They should include:

- a map to show where the regions are,
- information on quality of life/deprivation,
- information on changes to industry and employment.

The changing economy of the UK

answers

1. The South East has a lower unemployment rate and higher average income (over 35% higher) than the North East; people in the South East spend the most on healthy foods and live on average 11 years longer than people in the North East; the North East has a lack of high-salary jobs in the quaternary sector or knowledge economy.

2. Students' should include things such as: well-paid jobs in both public and private sector; large numbers of jobs across a range of employment sectors; opportunities for promotion; high spending on R&D.

3. a Benefits of moving to the North East may include: a large available workforce; financial help from the government to move; lower salary costs; lower living costs.

   b Possible reasons why few companies actually move could include: higher quality of life in the South East; difficulty of attracting highly skilled people to quaternary jobs in the North East; the need to be close to other companies in the quaternary sector; the South East has easier communications with Europe.

4. **Exam-style question** *Explain the employment trends in one UK region you have studied.* (8 marks)

   This question is marked using levels. The key to this question is the command word 'explain' — a Higher Tier command word. Purely descriptive points by Higher Tier candidates get no marks. Foundation Tier students may answer the alternative question:

   Using named examples, describe the employment trends in one UK region you have studied. (6 marks)

   In this case, three developed or two well-developed descriptions are required for 6 marks.

   Cap answers at the top of Level 2 (6 marks) which do not include:
   - reference to a named UK region
   - explanations of specific employment trends e.g. 'rising employment in the knowledge economy because it's near to London' and not just 'more jobs'

   Suitable employment trends for the South-East include:
   - Rising employment opportunities in the knowledge economy (with examples) — plus development e.g. due to the location in the region of local biotechnology and IT companies — or well-developed e.g. which are expanding e.g. in research and development.
   - Increased employment opportunities in London (with examples) — plus development e.g. because it's the capital with many jobs in government or in company headquarters — or well-developed e.g. 'which are highly paid because many are senior posts'.

Level	Descriptor
0	No rewardable content
1 (1-3 marks)	Simple or very basic statements using little or no subject vocabulary.
2 (4-6 marks)	Generalised explanations but with some use of geographical terms. Up to three developed statements as shown by examples above.
3 (7-8 marks)	Detailed statements with clear explanations using geographical terms. e.g. 'there are increasing numbers of jobs in South-East England because London is nearby, where there are highly paid jobs in the knowledge economy and in industries such as banking'. Two well-developed points plus other developed statements are required for the top of Level 3 as shown by examples above.

13.6 The impacts of changing employment

Section in brief

In this section students learn about the economic, social and environmental impacts of deindustrialisation in Glasgow. Economic change, aided by government investment, has led to the expansion of tertiary and quaternary industries.

In the activities, students:

- explain why deindustrialisation can lead to social problems;
- create a diagram to show the economic effects of deindustrialisation and investment in Glasgow;
- create a poster to show Glasgow's docks and riverside before and after deindustrialisation;
- assess whether Glasgow's deindustrialisation was a price worth paying for the improved environment and job opportunities of today;
- answer an exam-style question to explain the environmental impacts of deindustrialisation and economic change.

Key ideas

- Deindustrialisation had enormous economic impacts, particularly on cities which depended on traditional heavy industries.
- Deindustrialisation caused serious social impacts in Glasgow in the 1980s.
- There are a range of environmental impacts associated with deindustrialisation, both negative and positive.
- Diversification, using government grants, has been used to try to create a cycle of economic growth in Glasgow.

Key vocabulary

cycle of decline, cycle of growth, diversification

Skills practised

Geographical skills: identifying the economic and environmental impacts of deindustrialisation and economic change

PLTS: independent enquiry; creative thinking

Section outcomes

By the end of this section, most students should be able to:

- define or explain the terms given in 'Key vocabulary' above;
- explain why deindustrialisation has social impacts;
- create a diagram to show the economic effects of deindustrialisation and investment;
- assess whether deindustrialisation in Glasgow was worth the improved environment and job opportunities of today;
- outline how investment has created a cycle of growth in Glasgow.

Ideas for a starter

1. Show students the photo from page 288 of the students' book. Ask: 'What is this an example of? (You are looking to elicit the idea of deindustrialisation.) What impacts does deindustrialisation have?'
2. Show 'before' and 'after' photos of Glasgow, e.g. shipbuilding yards in action and the docks or riverside today. Ask: 'Is this the same place? How has it changed? What caused the change?'

Ideas for plenaries

1. Use question 4 from page 229 of the students' book as the basis for a class discussion. Students can summarise the discussion in writing afterwards.
2. Ask students to close their books. Then ask them to draw a 'cycle of decline' diagram and a 'cycle of growth' diagram.

Further class and homework activity

Ask: 'Would private industries have invested in Glasgow if Scottish, UK and EU government grants had not kick-started the process?' Students should explain their answer.

The changing economy of the UK

answers

1. Deindustrialisation has resulted in high unemployment. As people lose their jobs, they have less disposable income and more time on their hands. This can lead to tensions within the family resulting in increased family breakdown. People may turn to crime to obtain things they can no longer afford to buy.

2. Negative economic effects of deindustrialisation in Glasgow: industries close — loss of personal income — loss of income in local area (for shops and services) due to people's lack of spending power — local economy declines — no new investment — loss of tax income for local and national government — rising demand for income support services — skilled workers move away.
Positive economic effects of investment in Glasgow: government helps new industries to locate in the area — jobs are created as a result of new industries — people have increased personal income — increased income for local shops and services — local economy grows; new investors are encouraged to move to the area — more people move to the region.

3. Answers will vary.

4. Answers will vary, but should take into account the social, economic and environmental impacts of deindustrialisation in Glasgow.

5. **Exam-style question** *Using examples, explain the environmental impacts of deindustrialisation and economic change. (8 marks)*

   This question is marked using levels. The key to this question is the command word 'explain' — a Higher Tier command word. Purely descriptive points by Higher Tier candidates get no marks. Foundation Tier students may answer the alternative question:

   Using examples, describe how deindustrialisation can have environmental impacts. (6 marks)

   Cap Higher Tier answers at the top of Level 2 (6 marks) which do not include:
   - named specific locations
   - an explanation of deindustrialisation *and* economic change

   Suitable **environmental** impacts based on Glasgow include:
   - Closure of industries has environmental impacts e.g. derelict land, closed shipyards or steelworks — plus development e.g. 'which makes the place look run down and gives it a bad image' — or well-developed with further impacts e.g. 'which costs a lot to improve and puts investors off creating new jobs'.
   - Other explained negative impacts as shown in the diagram at the foot of page 228.
   - Allow positive impacts e.g. less noise, or air / water pollution from industry.

Level	Descriptor
0	No rewardable content
1 (1-3 marks)	Simple or very basic statements using little or no subject vocabulary.
2 (4-6 marks)	Generalised explanations but with some use of geographical terms e.g. 'when industries close, the environment often deteriorates because of derelict land which puts investors off'. Up to three developed statements as shown by examples above (or two well-developed points for Foundation Tier answers).
3 (7-8 marks)	Detailed statements with clear explanations using geographical terms. e.g. 'when industries like steel closed in Glasgow, the environment deteriorated because of the derelict land and run-down buildings. This puts investors off because they cost too much to improve'. Two well-developed points plus other developed statements are required for the top of Level 3 as shown by examples above.

13.7 Where should future development take place?

Section in brief

This section looks at the costs and benefits of 'greenfield development' versus 'brownfield regeneration'.

In the activities, students:

- outline the likely problems faced by Birmingham after the collapse of its traditional industries;
- choose regeneration ideas that would bring the greatest benefits to Birmingham, and present their ideas to the class;
- identify which regeneration options Fort Dunlop have done well;
- complete a table of the advantages and disadvantages of using brownfield and greenfield sites for new development;
- answer an exam-style question to compare the benefits of brownfield and greenfield urban development.

Key ideas

- Deindustrialisation can lead to land dereliction and brownfield sites.
- Brownfield sites provide a number of regeneration options.
- Redeveloping brownfield sites does have some disadvantages.
- Fort Dunlop has been regenerated to provide employment and leisure, and also improve the local environment.
- Greenfield sites have both advantages and disadvantages in terms of development.

Key vocabulary

brownfield sites, greenfield sites

Skills practised

Geographical skills: identifying advantages and disadvantages of brownfield and greenfield sites for new development

PLTS: independent enquiry; creative thinking; team-working; effective participation

Section outcomes

By the end of this section, most students should be able to:

- define or explain the terms given in 'Key vocabulary' above;
- explain how deindustrialisation can lead to brownfield sites;
- choose three regeneration options for brownfield sites in Birmingham and justify their choices;
- outline how Fort Dunlop has been regenerated;
- summarise the advantages and disadvantages of using brownfield and greenfield sites for new development.

Ideas for a starter

1. Ask students: 'What are brownfield sites?' Are there any in your local area? If so, have they been redeveloped? Show students photos of the sites before and after redevelopment. If they have not been redeveloped what could they be used for?
2. Show the before and after photos of Fort Dunlop from page 231 of the students' book on the whiteboard. Ask students what benefits can regenerating brownfield sites bring?

Ideas for plenaries

1. Ask students to make a set of revision notes to help them remember the Fort Dunlop case study of the costs and benefits of regenerating brownfield sites.
2. Ask students to tell their neighbour the two most important things that they have learnt today. Then ask them to tell them another two things which are interesting but less important.

Further class and homework activity

Use the exam-style question on page 231 of the students' book as a homework activity. Students can use their responses to question 4 to help them answer this question.

The changing economy of the UK

answers

1. Answers should include a range of economic, social and environmental problems e.g loss of employment, family breakdown, crime, derelict contaminated land (brownfield sites), empty buildings and associated vandalism.

2. Answers will vary.

3. The Fort Dunlop scheme has provided: new commercial sites for office space; a mixed use development; cafes and restaurants; retail space — a good example of how a brownfield site can be regenerated to provide employment, and improve the local environment.

4. **Brownfield sites:** Advantages — existing infrastructure makes it suitable for development; provides a range of regeneration options e.g. retail use, residential use, office space, mixed use, recreational use and so on. Disadvantages — can be more expensive than developing greenfield sites, because of clean-up costs; not always in areas where housing demand is highest; some brownfield land provides important wildlife habitats or public spaces.

   Greenfield sites: Advantages — no clean-up costs; no existing infrastructure to consider. Disadvantages — valuable farmland is lost; negative impact on rural landscape; no existing infrastructure, so developers must pay for installation; many sites are on protected greenbelt land; may destroy important habitats.

5. **Exam-style question** *Using examples, compare the benefits of brownfield and greenfield urban development. (8 marks)*

   The key to this question is the command word 'compare' — so it is suitable for all students. However, for Foundation students, reduce the number of marks from 8 to 6; in this case, three developed or two well-developed descriptions are required for 6 marks.

   Cap answers at the top of 6 marks (or 4 marks for Foundation Tier) which do not include:
   - reference to a named place or specific benefits,
   - explanation of *both* brownfield and greenfield urban development,
   - a *comparison* of brownfield and greenfield development — a single comparative word e.g. whereas, validates the whole answer.

   Suitable benefits of **brownfield** urban development include:
   - It improves the previous environment such as derelict industrial land — plus development e.g. 'and there are already existing roads or services which are helpful for construction workers' — or well-developed e.g. 'and helps to clean up disused or polluted land'.

   Suitable benefits of **greenfield** urban development include:
   - A blank sheet for development so that developers can plan as they wish — plus development e.g. 'because there are no existing roads or services to take into account' — or well-developed e.g. 'which reduces some of the costs of development of housing or shopping centres'.

Level	Descriptor
0	No rewardable content
1 (1-3 marks)	Simple or very basic statements using little or no subject vocabulary.
2 (4-6 marks)	Generalised explanations but with some use of geographical terms. Up to three developed statements as shown by examples above.
3 (7-8 marks)	Detailed statements with clear explanations using geographical terms. e.g. 're-developing brownfield land in Fort Dunlop in Birmingham has cleaned up an old run-down factory and derelict land to provide a local shopping and business centre'. Two well-developed points plus other developed statements are required as shown by examples above.

13.8 What kind of world...? 1

Section in brief

This section looks at three areas of possible future growth for the UK economy.

In the activities, students:

- draw a spider diagram of jobs in the future economy and classify them as primary, secondary, tertiary and quaternary;
- discuss and summarise arguments in favour of, and against, companies employing highly skilled people from overseas;
- complete a table to show the advantages and disadvantages for the UK of a high percentage of young people going to university;
- answer an exam-style question outlining areas where economic growth might take place in the UK.

Key ideas

- The areas of possible growth for the UK economy include the digital economy, education and research, green employment.
- The digital economy is based on digital technology.
- The expansion of Higher Education is needed to create a highly educated workforce.
- Research and Development benefits the UK's economy.
- The green sector provides employment.
- Many jobs in the UK go to overseas migrants who are young and skilled.

Key vocabulary

digital economy, green employment

Skills practised

Geographical skills: classifying jobs; outline areas where economic growth will take place in the UK

PLTS: creative thinking; team-working

Section outcomes

By the end of this section, most students should be able to:

- define or explain the terms given in 'Key vocabulary' above;
- outline two areas where economic growth might take place in future in the UK;
- explain why Research and Development is important to the UK economy;
- give examples of the green sector and the employment it provides;
- summarise arguments, for and against, companies employing highly skilled people from overseas.

Ideas for a starter

1. Show students photos of a range of buildings in London's Olympic Park in 2012. Many of the buildings used less energy, recycled water, and were built from natural or recycled materials, e.g. the handball arena was coated in recycled copper, and the basketball stadium could be folded away and transported elsewhere. Explain that they are examples of the green sector, which is an area of future growth for the UK economy.

2. Ask students what R&D is. Why is it important to the UK economy?

Ideas for plenaries

1. Ask the class where the digital economy could expand next. How will entertainment and communication be affected?

2. Use the 'On your planet' bubble on page 232 as the basis for a class discussion. Will the high street be killed off, or will it evolve?

Further class and homework activity

Ask students to find out about one of the buildings from London's Olympic Park. They should find out what it was made from and how 'green' it is.

The changing economy of the UK

answers

1 a and **b** Answers will vary.

2 a Arguments in **favour** of companies employing highly skilled people from overseas include: they meet skills shortages; they help to balance the UK's ageing population; companies don't have to pay to train workers.

b Arguments **against** companies employing highly skilled people from overseas include: young people from UK might lose out on jobs and training; young graduates from the UK may have to move abroad for jobs.

3 Advantages include: more people become highly educated and skilled; more people to fill skills shortages in the knowledge economy and quaternary sector.

Disadvantages include: fewer people available to fill less-skilled jobs in the tertiary sector; fewer people in the workforce aged 18-21.

---

4 Exam-style question *Using examples, outline two areas where economic growth might take place in the UK. (6 marks)*

This question is marked using levels. With 'outline' as a command word, you can use this for all students. If you wish to challenge more able students, you can use the question:

Using examples, explain why two areas of the economy are likely to grow in future.

In this case, replace the term 'descriptions' in the table below with 'explanations'. Purely descriptive points by Higher Tier candidates get no marks. Cap answers at the top of Level 2 (4 marks) which do not include:

- named specific areas of the economy e.g. Green employment,
- reference to *two* areas of the economy

Suitable areas of the economy could include:

- The digital economy, with example e.g. home-based internet shopping or health care — plus development e.g. 'which is likely as superfast broadband spreads' — or well-developed with further expansion e.g. 'and saves people a lot of time e.g. in having to go to the doctor's surgery when they could use Skype'.

- Green employment, with example e.g. making more products from recycled materials — plus development e.g. 'which saves landfill or current materials such as plastic going to waste' — or well-developed with further expansion e.g. 'and reduces landfill costs and environmental impacts near landfill sites'.

Level	Descriptor
0	No rewardable content
1 (1-2 marks)	Simple or very basic statements using little or no subject vocabulary. May be a descriptive or basic list of points e.g. 'there will be more need for education and research so new things can be discovered'.
2 (3-4 marks)	Generalised descriptions but with some use of geographical terms e.g. 'Education and research in universities will expand because the knowledge economy is growing'. Up to two developed statements as shown by examples above.
3 (5-6 marks)	Detailed statements with clear description using geographical terms. e.g. 'Education and research in universities will expand because the knowledge economy is growing in areas of biotechnology such as GM seeds'. Three developed or two well-developed points as shown by examples above.

13.9 What kind of world...? 2

Section in brief

In this section students learn how the shift in the UK's economy means that work is changing, and the way people might work in future is also changing.

In the activities, students:

- explain the differences between different ways of working and give examples of each;
- complete a table to show the advantages and disadvantages of different ways of working for employers and employees;
- answer an exam-style question to explain the impacts of changing working practices on different groups of people.

Key ideas

- The change in the UK's economy affects the way people work now, and how they will work in the future.
- IT is an important part of people's working life.
- Tele-working (working from home) is becoming increasingly common.
- New technology allows employees to work flexibly, which has both advantages and disadvantages.
- It is increasingly common for tele-workers to become self-employed freelancers.

Key vocabulary

tele-working, flexible working, out-sourcing, freelancing, self-employed

Skills practised

Geographical skills: explaining key terms; explaining impacts of changing working practices on different groups of people

PLTS: independent enquiry

Section outcomes

By the end of this section, most students should be able to:

- define or explain the terms given in 'Key vocabulary' above;
- explain why the way people work is changing;
- give examples of jobs in these categories: tele-working, self-employment, out-sourcing, flexible working;
- complete a table to show the advantages and disadvantages of different ways of working (for employers and employees).

Ideas for a starter

1. Recap the changes to the UK's economy. Brainstorm: How do students think these changes will affect the way people work?

2. Hold a class survey if appropriate. What kind of work do students' parents do? Which employment sector does it fall into? Do parents work in offices, or from home? Are they employed by companies, or are they self-employed? Record students' responses on the whiteboard.

Ideas for plenaries

1. Ask students for their response to question 1b. How many different jobs have students come up with? Are these the kind of jobs which students would like to do in the future?

2. Ask students to create an acrostic. They should write 'THE CHANGING ECONOMY OF THE UK' down the side of a page and make each letter the first letter of a word, phrase or sentence about the UK's changing economy.

Further class and homework activity

Ask students to create a poster or presentation about the UK's changing economy, and how people might work in the future using information from 13.8 and 13.9.

The changing economy of the UK

answers

1 a **Tele-working** — working from home: enabled because of the increase in use of IT. **Self-employed** — people who are not employed by one company, but work freelance for a range of companies or organisations on different jobs. **Out-sourcing** — involves sending work outside the company e.g. to people who are self-employed. If companies out-source work they do not need to employ as many full-time staff. **Flexible working** — when work is done in different places e.g. from home, and at different times of the day or night.

b Answers will vary

2 The example of **flexible working**:

Advantages — employees are healthier and less stressed; parents can work from home; better for disabled people and those who want to work part-time; less absenteeism and lower staff turnover for employers; better productivity.

Disadvantages — less contact with boss; isolation from colleagues; motivation may be difficult; employees may find it difficult to separate work and home life.

3 Exam-style question *Using examples, explain the impacts of changing working practices on different groups of people. (8 marks)*

The key to this question is the command word 'explain'. Purely descriptive points by Higher Tier candidates therefore, get no marks. Foundation Tier students may answer the alternative question:

Using examples, describe the changing ways in which different groups of people now work. (6 marks)

In this case, three developed or two well-developed descriptions are required for 6 marks. Cap answers which do not include:

- examples of specific working practices or jobs e.g. tele-working or self-employment,
- explanations of the impacts upon different groups of people e.g. men and women, or younger / older people.

Suitable impacts include:

- On those who are / are not computer literate; with examples of jobs where computers are needed — plus development e.g. 'because so many jobs now require computer literacy people with these skills will be able to work anywhere' — or well-developed e.g. 'so those without these skills will lose out e.g. gain less career promotion / will earn less'.

- On work location; with future opportunities more likely for those who are flexible about where they live, compared to those who dont want to move — plus development e.g. 'because they'll be able to work with anyone in any country, on different projects' — or well-developed e.g. 'and will have greater opportunities than those who have to be in a fixed location such as an office or factory'.

Level	Descriptor
0	No rewardable content
1 (1-3 marks)	Simple or very basic statements using little or no subject vocabulary.
2 (4-6 marks)	Generalised explanations but with some use of geographical terms. Up to three developed statements as shown by examples above.
3 (7-8 marks)	Detailed statements with clear explanations using geographical terms. e.g. 'there'll be fewer jobs for life as companies outsource. Those who have skills might become self-employed, setting up businesses e.g. knowledge workers in IT. Two well-developed points plus other developed statements are required as shown in the examples above.

14 Changing settlements in the UK

About the chapter
These are the key ideas behind the chapter.

- There are economic, social, political and demographic reasons why some urban areas have grown and others declined.
- There are variations in the quality of urban residential areas and levels of multiple deprivation within urban areas.
- Rising demand for urban residential areas has environmental, social and economic impacts.
- Different strategies such as regeneration and rebranding, can be used to improve urban areas.
- Rural settlements in the UK have changed and new types of settlement have developed.
- Contrasting rural regions vary in terms of quality of life and levels of deprivation.
- Rural development projects can be used to stimulate growth in the rural economy and to stop out-migration.
- Green belts and National Parks can conserve landscapes and allow some economic development.

Chapter outline
Use this outline to provide your students with a brief roadmap of the chapter.

14.1 The UK's changing urban areas
The reasons why some urban areas such as London, grow, while others, such as Liverpool, have declined.

14.2 London contrasts
Variations in the quality of urban residential areas and levels of multiple deprivation.

14.3 Environment under pressure
The impacts of the rising demand for more residential areas.

14.4 Improving urban areas
Evaluating the success of the 2012 Olympic Games in improving Newham.

14.5 Changing rural settlements
How and why rural settlements have changed – a commuter village and a retirement village.

14.6 Contrasting rural regions
Investigating South-west England and the Scottish Highlands – quality of life and deprivation.

14.7 Making rural regions sustainable – 1
The success of two rural development projects – the Eden Project and Combined Universities in Cornwall.

14.8 Making rural regions sustainable – 2
Evaluating how successful green belts and National Parks are in making rural regions sustainable.

Changing settlements in the UK

How is the specification covered?

This chapter covers Topic 6, Unit 2 People and the planet.

6.1 How and why are settlements changing?

6.2 How easy is it to manage the demand for high quality places to live?

Key ideas	Detailed content	Pages in students' book
6.1a There have been many changes in urban areas in the UK in the past 50 years as a consequence of government policies, in addition to economic, social and demographic changes.	Investigate the contrasting economic, social, political and demographic processes that have transformed urban areas in the UK with some e.g. London experiencing significant economic growth with rapid population growth while others have experienced economic and population decline e.g. Liverpool.	236-237
	Examine how these processes have led to variations in the quality of urban residential areas (including housing, services, amenities and recreational areas), and the levels of multiple deprivation within large urban areas.	238-239
6.1b Rural settlements in the UK have changed greatly in the past 50 years and new types of settlement have developed in that time.	Identify different types of rural settlement, including remote rural communities in upland areas, retirement communities, and commuter villages, and explain how these have developed.	244-245, 246-247
	Investigate two contrasting rural regions in the UK, e.g. the Highlands of Scotland and East Anglia to explain the variations in the quality of life and levels of deprivation.	246-247
6.2a Current demand for some urban residential areas in the UK is rising, placing pressures on the environment.	Examine the environmental, social and economic impacts of rising demand for residential areas in one urban area in the UK.	240-241
	Evaluate the success of strategies to improve urban areas, e.g. 'rebranding' and urban regeneration.	242-243
6.2b Different strategies can be used to improve the quality of settlements in rural regions of the UK to make them sustainable.	Examine the role of rural development schemes and larger projects, e.g. the Eden Project in stimulating growth in the rural economy and arresting outmigration.	248-249
	Evaluate the success of planning policies such as 'green belts' and National Parks in both conserving valuable landscapes, and allowing economic development.	250-251

Chapter outcomes

By the end of this chapter, students should be able to:

- Identify the reasons why London's population is rising rapidly, and Liverpool has suffered decline.
- Complete a table to show how Richmond upon Thames and Canning Town differ in terms of housing, education, health and jobs.
- Draw a Venn diagram to show the environmental, social and economic impacts of the rising demand for more homes around London.
- Evaluate how successful the Olympics were in regenerating Newham.
- Describe the reasons why different types of settlement e.g. commuter villages and retirement villages have developed.
- Describe the problems facing remote rural regions in the UK, and how these can lead to a low quality of life.
- Explain how far one rural development project has helped to create sustainable development in South-west England.
- Assess how well green belts and national parks conserve the landscape and allow economic development.

14.1 The UK's changing urban areas

Section in brief

In this section students investigate the reasons why some urban areas grow, while others decline.

In the activities, students:

- design a spider diagram to show why London's population is rising rapidly, and classify the reasons as economic, social, political and demographic;
- explain why well-qualified young people are in demand for jobs in London;
- design a spider diagram to explain why Liverpool is not booming;
- answer an exam-style question to outline one economic and one demographic process that has led to population increase in a city they have studied.

Key ideas

- There are a number of demographic reasons for London's rising population.
- London acts as an economic hub, attracting people and investment.
- In the first half of the twentieth century Liverpool was booming, but population began falling in the late 1930s.
- A number of social, political and economic processes caused Liverpool to decline.
- Liverpool's population has started to rise, but it still faces a number of problems.

Key vocabulary

demographic, economic hub

Skills practised

Geographical skills: classifying reasons for a growing population; outline the economic and demographic processes leading to a population increase

PLTS: independent enquiry

Section outcomes

By the end of this section, most students should be able to:

- define or explain the terms given in 'Key vocabulary' above;
- identify and classify the reasons why London's population is rising rapidly;
- explain why London attracts well-qualified young people;
- produce a spider diagram to show the reasons why Liverpool is not booming in the same way as London;
- describe the problems Liverpool faces today.

Ideas for a starter

1. Show students photos of Liverpool and London. Ask them which one of these cities is booming and why.
2. Ask students to look at the population graph of Ealing and the UK on page 236. Ask students how Ealing's population structure might affect population growth?

Idea for a plenary

Discuss as a class the reasons why Liverpool is not booming in the same way as London. Ask students to complete question 3.

Further class and homework activity

Ask students to find out about life in Anfield in Liverpool. They should Google 'Anfield ward profile' and find out about the following:

- Population (rising or falling?)
- Average household income
- Average unemployment
- Housing (what type)
- Crime rate (above or below average)
- Health (good or poor)
- Education (attainment levels)

Students should create a table of their results and comment on what the figures show.

Changing settlements in the UK

answers

1 Reasons for London's population growth are:

Economic — London acts as an economic hub; over 3 million people work in service industries; over half the UK's top 100 companies have their headquarters in central London; media companies are concentrated there; tourism and entertainment are big employers.

Social — many migrants are in their 20s and 30s and start families; boroughs such as Ealing have a much higher than average percentage of people in the 25-44 age group; many people in this age group are well educated and skilled.

Political — central government departments employ large numbers of people (120 000 civil servants).

Demographic — migration from within, and outside, the UK; rapidly rising birth rate.

2 London has many job opportunities. Over 3 million people work in service industries, as civil servants, in the UK's top companies, in media, tourism and entertainment. Many of these jobs require well-qualified people.

3 Reasons why Liverpool is not booming include:

Economic — manufacturing declined the 70s and 80s and fewer ships passed through the port; jobs were lost; low level of new business start-ups; low average incomes; high percentage of part-time employment.

Social — unemployment is high; Liverpool has five of the ten poorest communities in England.

Political — slum clearances resulted in people moving into high rise flats and housing estates on the outskirts of the city.

Demographic — people left the city because of the decline in jobs.

---

4 Exam-style question *Outline one economic and one demographic process that has led to population increase in a city you have studied. (4 marks)*

This question is point marked. It requires two developed explanations for 2 marks each. One *economic* and one *demographic* process must be outlined. Cap answers which do not include a named city at 3 marks. Each outlined process must be directly linked to the reason for a population increase, so 'which creates jobs' is not correct, whereas 'which means that people move there for jobs' is.

Suitable **economic** processes (illustrated by London from pages 236-237) include:

- London's economy is huge — with some illustrative measure e.g. GDP size (1) — plus development e.g. 'which means more jobs for people so they move there' (1).

- Many companies have their headquarters / offices in London (1) — plus development e.g. 'which brings many people to London for work' (1).

Suitable **demographic** processes (illustrated by London from pages 236-237) include:

- Migration to London from within the UK (1) — plus development e.g. 'which increases the population' (1).

- Migration to London from overseas (1) — plus development e.g. 'which increases the population' (1).

- A rapidly rising birth rate (1) — plus development e.g. 'which causes natural increase' (1).

14.2 London contrasts

Section in brief

In this section students look at how the quality of urban residential areas varies in the same city.

In the activities, students:

- complete a table to show how Richmond and Canning Town differ;
- describe how have people in Richmond benefitted from London's economic growth;
- explain why people in Canning Town are less likely to benefit from London's growth;
- describe how Canning Town might have benefitted from the Olympic Games;
- answer exam-style questions to describe the patterns of deprivation in London, and how residential areas of a city vary.

Key ideas

- Different areas of the same city can vary in terms of the quality of residential areas.
- Different causes of deprivation can be grouped together to produce an Index of Multiple Deprivation.
- Canning Town is in Newham — one of London's most deprived boroughs.
- Richmond upon Thames is one of London's least deprived areas but has problems related to poor health, provision of health and social services, and lack of affordable housing.

Key vocabulary

Index of Multiple Deprivation, negative multiplier

Skills practised

Geographical skills: using a map to describe patterns of deprivation; comparing urban residential areas

PLTS: independent enquiry

Literacy skills: extended writing (Further activity)

Section outcomes

By the end of this section, most students should be able to:

- define or explain the terms given in 'Key vocabulary' above;
- use a map to describe the patterns of deprivation in London;
- complete a table to compare Canning Town and Richmond;
- explain why problems in places like Canning Town can lead to a downward spiral of decline;
- describe the problems which Richmond has.

Ideas for a starter

1. Show students the photo of Canning Town from page 238 of the students' book, and one of Richmond upon Thames, e.g. showing the riverside. How many words can students come up with to describe the photos?
2. Recap the reasons for London's growth from section 14.1. Ask: 'Who can remind me why London is booming?'

Ideas for plenaries

1. With books closed, ask students to draw a spiral of decline (or negative multiplier) to show how one problem in places like Canning Town can lead to another.
2. Use exam-style question 3a as a plenary activity. Allow students 3 minutes (if they are approaching their exam) to complete it. Once students have finished, ask them to work in small groups to compare answers. Which do they think is the best, and why?

Further class and homework activity

Ask students to do an internet search for 'Regeneration projects in Newham'. Ask them to find out what plans there are to transform the borough, and to write a 300 word report on what they find out.

Changing settlements in the UK

answers

1 **Canning Town:** *Housing* — cheaper than Richmond, but still too expensive for people on low incomes, and more expensive than UK average. *Education* — 43% of working-age adults have no qualifications. *Health* — 21% of population have poor health. *Jobs* — many people work in low paid, unskilled jobs.

Richmond upon Thames: *Housing* — high quality but very expensive. *Education* — people are highly qualified. *Health* — only 18% of the population has poor health. *Jobs* — a high proportion of skilled workers.

2 a Richmond has high levels of skilled and highly qualified workers, ideal for London's growing service industries.

b Nearly half of all working age adults in Canning Town have no qualifications so are less able to take advantage of the high-skilled, well-paid jobs available.

c The Olympic Games provided jobs for Canning Town's residents. The borough as a whole will benefit from the creation of the Queen Elizabeth Olympic Park including; jobs, housing, a new commercial centre, sports facilities and environmental improvements.

3 a **Exam-style question** *Describe the patterns of deprivation in London using the map on page 238. (3 marks)*

This question requires three identified patterns (1 mark each). There is no credit for developed points, but allow up to 1 mark for exceptions as illustrated below.

Correct patterns include:

- The most deprived areas are north of the river / in east London / in north-east London (1)
- The least deprived / wealthiest areas are on the outskirts of the city (1) except for two boroughs to the west and north (1)
- Inner London is more deprived than outer (1)

3 b *Using named examples, describe how residential areas of a city vary. (6 marks)*

This question is marked using levels. Cap answers at the top of Level 2 (4 marks) which do not include an examples of a specific city e.g. London, or boroughs within it.

Suitable variations could include:

- **Housing:** Cost of housing — with examples e.g. data on house prices comparing Richmond and Newham — or well-developed e.g. 'especially for detached and semi-detached houses'.
- **Level of education / employment:** Fewer educational qualifications — developed with examples — or well-developed e.g. which leads to variations in employment.
- **Ethnicity:** Canning Town / Newham has high concentrations of ethnic minorities — plus development e.g. 'many of whom do low-paid jobs' — or well-developed e.g. 'so live in London's cheapest areas of housing'.

Level	Descriptor
0	No rewardable content
1 (1-2 marks)	Simple or very basic statements using little or no subject vocabulary.
2 (3-4 marks)	Generalised descriptions but with some use of geographical terms Up to two developed statements as shown by examples above.
3 (5-6 marks)	Detailed statements with clear descriptions using geographical terms. Three developed or two well-developed points as shown by examples above.

14.3 Environment under pressure

Section in brief

In this section students consider how the rising demand for urban residential areas is putting pressure on the environment, and having social and economic impacts.

In the activities, students:

- explain the terms urban sprawl and rural-urban fringe;
- complete a table to compare the advantages and disadvantages of living in London and Chelmsford;
- draw a Venn Diagram to show the environmental, social and economic impacts of the rising demand for more homes around London;
- answer exam-style questions to describe the effects that rising demand for housing can have on people and the environment, and explain how the rising demand for residential areas has affected one urban area.

Key ideas

- The increasing demand for urban residential areas has a range of environmental, social and economic impacts.
- The Thames Gateway Project will have environmental impacts, but also develop brownfield sites, drain marshland for new housing, provide jobs and improve transport links.
- London's expansion is driving up the demand for, and price of, land for housing and business.
- As urban areas sprawl, the rural-urban fringe comes under more pressure.

Key vocabulary

brownfield sites, urban sprawl, rural-urban fringe

Skills practised

Geographical skills: defining geographical terms; drawing a Venn Diagram to show impacts of rising demand for homes

PLTS: independent enquiry;

Section outcomes

By the end of this section, most students should be able to:

- define or explain the terms given in 'Key vocabulary' above;
- complete a table to compare the advantages and disadvantages of living in London and Chelmsford;
- describe the effects that rising demand for housing can have on the environment;
- draw a Venn Diagram to show the environmental, social and economic impacts of the rising demand for more homes around London.

Ideas for a starter

1. Tell students that it is estimated that about 230 000 new homes are needed in England every year. Ask why they think so many new homes are needed.
2. Give students (in pairs) a photo of a modern housing estate. Ask them to annotate the photo with the impacts that building so many new homes will have on the environment.

Ideas for plenaries

1. 'As the demand for urban residential areas increases: habitats are destroyed...' Go round the class asking students to add to the list, without hesitation or repetition.
2. Ask students to prepare five statements for their partner based on this section. Some true, others false. Students should identify the false statements and correct them.

Further class and homework activity

Ask students to find out about plans for new housing developments in your area. Are they on brownfield sites, or on the rural-urban fringe? Ask students to classify the impacts as environmental, social and economic.

Changing settlements in the UK

answers

1 **Urban sprawl** — the growth of towns and cities into the surrounding countryside.
Rural-urban fringe — the area where the town/city meets the countryside.

2 **Living in London, working in London:**
Advantages — close to work, so less time and money spent travelling. *Disadvantages* — high cost of housing.

Living in Chelmsford, working in London:
Advantages — cheaper housing; excellent transport links to central London. *Disadvantages* — extra time / cost of travelling to work.

3 Venn diagrams should include the following (note that some will be in the overlapping sectors of the diagram):
Environmental — countryside is lost; open space and habitats destroyed; marshland drained; traffic and pollution increase; pressure on water resources; increase in quarrying. *Social* — provides new housing; improved transport links; rising prices of land and housing; time and cost of travel; traffic and pollution increase; services decline; people dependent on cars. *Economic* — rising price of houses and land; cost of travel.

These two questions help students to understand the difference between writing separate points (point-marking) compared to extended writing (level-marking). They may use similar examples for both.

4 a Exam-style question *Describe the effects that rising demand for housing can have on people and the environment. (4 marks)*

This question is point marked: it requires two developed effects (2 marks each). Cap answers at 3 marks which only include one well-developed effect *and* do not refer to *both* people *and* environment.

Suitable effects on **people** include:
- Rising cost of housing / land (1)
- Many people have to commute long distances to work (1)

Suitable effects on the **environment** include:
- Loss of countryside as the city expands (1)
- Urban sprawl (1)
- Loss of habitats (1) or open space (1)

4 b Exam-style question *Using examples, explain how the rising demand for residential areas has affected one urban area. (6 marks)*

Cap answers at the top of Level 2 (6 marks) which do not include named examples of specific places or effects. Examples may be at city scale e.g. Chelmsford, or part of a city e.g. Thames Gateway.

Suitable effects include:
- Demand causes rising house / land prices — plus development e.g. which means that many people cannot afford to live in London — or well-developed e.g. so they are forced to live outside London putting further pressure on towns / transport.
- Loss of countryside as London expands — plus development e.g. especially on the edge around cities like Chelmsford — or well-developed e.g. 'which leads to loss of habitats and farmland'.

Level	Descriptor
0	No rewardable content
1 (1-2 marks)	Simple or very basic statements using little or no subject vocabulary.
2 (3-4 marks)	Generalised explanations but with some use of geographical terms. Up to two developed statements as shown by examples above.
3 (5-6 marks)	Detailed statements with clear explanations using geographical terms. Two well-developed points or three developed explanations are required as shown by examples above.

14.4 Improving urban areas

Section in brief

In this section students evaluate how successful the 2012 Olympic Games were in improving Newham. It looks at the problems Newham has, and some of the improvements which the Games brought to Newham.

In the activities, students:

- evaluate how successful the 2012 Olympics were in regenerating Newham by scoring the improvements, writing a report, and suggesting how further improvements could be made to areas of east London;
- answer an exam-style question to explain how urban areas can be improved.

Key ideas

- In 2005, when London won the bid to host the Olympic Games, Newham was one of London's most deprived areas.
- The intention was that the Olympic Games would help to regenerate and rebrand the area, creating a positive multiplier effect.
- London's 2012 Games were planned with various sustainable principles in mind.
- Newham had problems related to jobs, housing and the environment.
- The Olympics brought improvements in jobs, housing and environment.

Key vocabulary

regeneration, rebranding, positive multiplier effect, quality of life

Skills practised

Geographical skills: evaluating the success of the Olympics in regenerating Newham

PLTS: independent enquiry; creative thinking; self managing

Literacy skills: writing a short report

Section outcomes

By the end of this section, most students should be able to:

- define or explain the terms given in 'Key vocabulary' above;
- describe the problems Newham has in relation to jobs, housing and the environment;
- score the improvements the Olympics brought to Newham;
- evaluate how successful the Olympics were in regenerating Newham;
- suggest further improvements which could be made to east London.

Ideas for a starter

1. Show footage from the 2012 Olympic Games as students enter the classroom. Tell students that before the Games, much of the site was rundown and derelict. How do they think the Olympics has helped to improve the area?
2. Show students the downward spiral of decline diagram from page 239 of the students' book. Ask: 'What needs to happen to change this into an upward spiral of improvement?'

Ideas for plenaries

1. Explore the website for the Queen Elizabeth Olympic Park http://noordinarypark.co.uk/ to see how the park has been transformed.
2. Ask students to write two sentences to summarise the lesson. They should include all the terms listed under Key vocabulary.

Further class and homework activity

Ask students to find out about a retirement village in preparation for the next lesson. If there is nothing suitable locally, ask them to find out about Roseland Parc, in Tregony, Cornwall. Students should find out: where the retirement village is; what type of properties the village has; what the village offers its residents.

Changing settlements in the UK

answers

1 a, b and **c** Answers will vary.

---

2 Exam-style question *Using examples, explain how urban areas can be improved. (6 marks)*

This question is marked using levels. The key to this question is the command word 'explain' — a Higher Tier command word. Remember, therefore, that purely descriptive points by Higher Tier candidates get no marks. If you wish to differentiate, you can give Foundation Tier students the question:

Using examples, describe how urban areas can be improved. (6 marks)

In this case, change 'explanations' in the mark scheme below to 'descriptions'.

Cap answers at the top of Level 2 (4 marks) which do not include a named location. These may be at the scale of a city or part of a city, or small town – anything that might reasonably be described as 'urban'.

Suitable improvements — using the example of the Olympic Park on pages 242-243 in the student textbook — include:

- Regeneration of an urban area e.g. around the Olympic Park — plus development e.g. to generate jobs / create a positive multiplier — or well-developed with further expansion e.g. creating more jobs and housing in the area.
- Environmental improvements, with examples e.g. the creation of a new park / Olympic Park — plus development e.g. which cleaned up abandoned / derelict land — or well-developed with further expansion e.g. 'and removed polluted land / soil'.
- Plus other explanations on merit.

Level	Descriptor
0	No rewardable content
1 (1-2 marks)	Simple or very basic statements using little or no subject vocabulary. May be a list e.g. 'London has been improved because of the new housing and parks there'.
2 (3-4 marks)	Generalised explanations but with some use of geographical terms e.g. 'Newham has been improved because of new housing and the Olympic Park which have made a better environment for people'. Up to two developed statements as shown by examples above.
3 (5-6 marks)	Detailed statements with clear explanations using geographical terms. e.g. 'Newham in east London has been regenerated with new housing around the new Olympic Park, which has made a better environment and is close to work for people'. Two well-developed points or three developed explanations are required for the top of Level 3 as shown by examples above.

14.5 Changing rural settlements

Section in brief

In this section students investigate why, and how, rural settlements in the UK have changed. They also look at a commuter village and a retirement village, and how these have developed.

In the activities, students:

- identify the advantages and disadvantages of living in Terling, compared to London or Chelmsford;
- research a retirement village and prepare a presentation;
- answer an exam-style question to describe the reasons why two types of rural settlement have developed.

Key ideas

- Rural villages originally developed because most people worked in farming or associated industries.
- Rural settlements in the UK have seen major changes.
- The change in the type and nature of settlements and land use as you move away from large cities and towns, is called the rural-urban continuum.
- Commuter villages develop because of their location and transport links.
- Retirement villages develop to cater for the needs of older people.

Key vocabulary

counter-urbanisation, suburbanised villages, second homes, holiday lets, services, rural-urban continuum, commuter village, retirement village

Skills practised

Geographical skills: identifying advantages and disadvantages of living in a commuter village; describing the reasons why different rural settlements developed

PLTS: independent enquiry, team-working

Section outcomes

By the end of this section, most students should be able to:

- define or explain the terms given in 'Key vocabulary' above;
- draw a spider diagram to show the changes which rural settlements in the UK have experienced;
- describe the reasons why commuter villages and retirement villages have developed;
- identify the advantages and disadvantages of living in Terling compared to London or Chelmsford.

Ideas for a starter

1. If students completed the Further Activity from section 14.4, ask a number of them to feedback what they found out to the class.
2. Show students a photo of a boarded up village pub or shop, similar to the one on page 244 of the students' book, on the whiteboard. Ask: 'Why has this pub/shop closed?' You are looking to elicit ideas about the changes in rural settlements e.g. people using services in nearby towns instead of local shops/pubs etc.

Ideas for plenaries

1. With students' books closed, give students a 'heads and tails' exercise to match the key vocabulary with the definitions from this section.
2. Ask students to prepare an odd-one-out for their partner based on what they have learnt in this section.

Further class and homework activity

Ask students to draw a spider diagram to show what might be different about Terling's residents, housing and services, if it were located many more miles from a major city on the rural-urban continuum.

Changing settlements in the UK

answers

1 Living in Terling: *Advantages* compared to living in London or Chelmsford — good communications; easy access to London; pleasant rural environment. *Disadvantages* compared to living in London or Chelmsford — local services declining/closing; housing is expensive (but may be cheaper than London), so local people can't afford to buy; have to spend time and money travelling to work in London; people are dependent on cars; little local employment.

2 Answers will vary.

---

3 Exam-style question *Using examples, describe the reasons why two types of rural settlement have developed. (6 marks)*

This question is marked using levels. With 'describe' as a command word, you use this for all candidates; effectively, 'describe the reasons' is the same as 'explain'! Cap answers at the top of Level 2 (4 marks) which do not include:

- Specific, rural locations
- Two different *types* of rural location — the examples in the student textbook (pages 244-245) are Terling and Roseland Parc respectively; the mark scheme below is based on these examples.

Suitable reasons for **commuter villages** include:

- Location close to large cities e.g. London, or to easy transport to such cities — plus development e.g. 'which leads to demand for housing in villages such as Terling from people who work in the city' — or well-developed with further expansion e.g. 'which means that new housing grows around the traditional village'.

Suitable reasons for **retirement villages** include:

- An ageing population which has increased demand for sheltered housing — plus development e.g. 'which consists of smaller sheltered / secure flats for elderly people' — or well-developed with further expansion e.g. 'and which consists of its own facilities such as entertainment or a restaurant'.
- Plus other reasons on merit.

Level	Descriptor
0	No rewardable content
1 (1-2 marks)	Simple or very basic statements using little or no subject vocabulary. May be a descriptive or basic list of points e.g. 'More older people has led to retirement villages'.
2 (3-4 marks)	Generalised description but with some use of geographical terms e.g. 'Longer life expectation has led to retirement villages like Roseland Parc which consists of flats'. Up to two developed statements as shown by examples above.
3 (5-6 marks)	Detailed statements with clear descriptions using geographical terms. e.g. 'Longer life expectation has led to separate retirement villages like Roseland Parc in Cornwall which consists of flats and separate amenities such as restaurants for those who live there'. Three developed or two well-developed points as shown by examples above.

14.6 Contrasting rural regions

Section in brief

In this section students investigate two contrasting rural regions – South West England and the Scottish Highlands.

In the activities, students:

- draw a spider diagram to show why quality of life can be low in rural regions;
- explain the reasons for different trends in remote rural areas, and problems this might cause;
- answer exam-style questions to describe the distribution of fragile areas and explain why remote rural areas can be described as 'fragile'.

Key ideas

- South West England has one of the UK's fastest growing populations.
- Remote rural parts of South West England have a number of problems.
- The Scottish Highlands have one of the lowest population densities in the UK.
- Kinloch Rannoch is a remote upland village in the Scottish Highlands, with a number of problems.
- The Scottish Highlands and South West England both suffer from deprivation.

Key vocabulary

fragile areas

Skills practised

Geographical skills: describing distribution shown on map; explaining reasons for trends

PLTS: independent enquiry

Section outcomes

By the end of this section, most students should be able to:

- define or explain the term given in 'Key vocabulary' above;
- draw a spider diagram to show why quality of life can be low in rural regions.
- describe and explain recent trends in remote rural regions: young people leave; there are few jobs; poor access to services;
- describe the distribution of fragile areas shown on a map of the Scottish Highlands.

Ideas for a starter

1. Tell students that Rannoch station is 18 miles from Kinloch Rannoch. It took 5000 men five years to build the 101 mile long railway line. There are now regular rail links with Glasgow, but it takes over an hour to get to Fort William. The first train doesn't arrive until 9:45am, so it's almost impossible to commute to work because of the time and cost involved.

2. Show students a map of the UK with the South West and Scottish Highlands regions highlighted. Ask students to describe their locations. What problems might these regions face?

Ideas for plenaries

1. Ensure that students are clear about what the map on page 247 shows, and the link between fragile areas and deprivation.

2. Make a graffiti wall of students' learning in this lesson.

Further class and homework activity

Students should answer the following question as an exam-style question worth 6 marks. 'Using examples, explain why some areas in rural regions are growing, while others are declining'.

Changing settlements in the UK

answers

1 Students' spider diagrams should include:
- Low incomes due to: remoteness; decline in agricultural jobs; mainly seasonal, low-paid and part-time jobs.
- Housing is expensive; local people can't afford it.
- Access to services is poor e.g. shops, pubs, health and education services.
- Communications can be difficult e.g. frequency of public transport, poor internet connectivity.
- High unemployment.

2 a Young people leave, often due to education or employment opportunities. The local population could become unbalanced as the remaining population become more elderly.

b Large companies are reluctant to locate there (isolated from major centres); full-time jobs in industries such as farming, fishing and mining have declined; people migrate to other areas or suffer a very low quality of life.

c Remote rural areas are attractive to people who want to buy houses, either as second homes or as holiday lets, driving up the price of housing; local residents are unable to afford to buy their own home; they may leave the area.

3 a **Exam-style question** *Describe the distribution of 'fragile areas' shown on the map. (3 marks)*

This question is point marked; it requires three identified points – 1 mark for each. Correct points include:
- Most fragile areas tend to be in central Scotland (1) or the north (1) together with some islands in the west / south-west (1).
- Least fragile areas are around the east coast / Inverness (1) and around Fort William (1)
- Plus other descriptions on merit.

3 b **Exam-style question** *Using examples, explain why remote rural areas can be described as 'fragile'. (4 marks)*

This question is point marked. It requires two developed explanations for 2 marks each; exceptionally, a well-developed effect can achieve a maximum of 3 marks. Examples need not be located, but should explain specific indicators.

Suitable explanations include:
- They have few opportunities for people (1) — plus development e.g. jobs (1) or 'they have long-term unemployment'.
- They suffer population decline (1) — plus development e.g. 'because of low wages / lack of job opportunities' (1).
- They have few services (1) — plus development e.g. 'which can't always survive because there isn't the demand / trade' (1) – or expanded further e.g. 'which gets worse as more people leave and population falls'.
- Plus other points on merit.

14.7 Making rural regions sustainable – 1

Section in brief

In this section students look at two rural development projects — the Eden Project and Combined Universities Cornwall (CUC) — in South West England, and assess their success.

In the activities, students:

- complete a table to compare the benefits brought by the Eden Project and CUC;
- explain how far has each project helped to create sustainable development in the South West;
- answer an exam-style question to describe how a rural development project can help to bring economic benefits to an area.

Key ideas

- Sustainable development projects can help to stimulate growth in the rural economy and stop out-migration.
- The Eden Project opened in 2001 and is a year-round attraction.
- The Eden Project has brought many economic, social and environmental benefits to Cornwall.
- CUC is a partnership of six universities and colleges working together to enable students to study in higher education in Cornwall and to transform the local economy.
- CUC has brought many economic benefits to Cornwall and the South West.

Key vocabulary

sustainable development, Gross Value Added (GVA)

Skills practised

Geographical skills: classifying benefits as economic, social and environmental; explaining how far a project has helped to create sustainable development

Section outcomes

By the end of this section, most students should be able to:

- define or explain the terms given in 'Key vocabulary' above;
- identify the benefits brought by the Eden Project and CUC;
- classify the benefits brought by the Eden Project and CUC as economic, social and environmental;
- explain how far one of the projects has helped to create sustainable development in the South West.

Idea for a starter

Show students photos of the Eden Project on the whiteboard. Ask if they know what, and where, this is. Explain that the Eden Project opened in 2001, and in its first 10 years had 13 million visitors. Record the benefits brought by the Eden Project as a spider diagram.

Ideas for plenaries

1. Tell students that Vivien Prideux runs a B&B in Fowey, near Eden. She said 'In the past we closed in winter, but the Eden Project has enabled us to stay open most of the year.' Ask students to explain why.
2. If you used starter 1 return to the spider diagram. Ask students what they need to amend on the diagram as a result of what they have learnt in this lesson.

Further class and homework activity

Ask students to find out about Local Enterprise Partnerships (LEP). They should find out what they are, what the funding they provide is used for, and about a project which the Cornwall and Isles of Scilly LEP has contributed to.

282

Changing settlements in the UK

answers

1 Eden Project benefits:
Economic — people who visit tend to stay for an average of 5 days, spending money in the local economy; 2500 local businesses have benefitted from supplying the Eden Project; over £1.1 billion earned for the local economy; enabled hotels and B&Bs to stay open for most of the year.
Social — in 2011, 574 people employed; since opening 3000 jobs have been created.
Environmental — has transformed an old clay pit and local area.

CUC benefits:
Economic — helping to transform the local economy into a knowledge economy; places like Falmouth have benefitted from rise in student numbers, particularly landlords and pubs and clubs; total value added to the economy by 2011 was over £70 million.
Social — students no longer have to leave Cornwall to study in higher education; 60% of graduates found jobs in the South West; 500 graduate jobs created.

2 Eden Project — has created jobs at the Project itself (and many are permanent), it has sustained 3000 jobs locally and benefitted 2500 businesses. It has been a major boon to the local economy. The creation of the Eden Project also transformed the environment.

CUC — has enabled students to study in higher education in Cornwall rather than leave to study elsewhere. 60% of graduates have found jobs in the south-west, helped by the creation of 500 jobs thanks to the 'Unlocking Cornish Potential' project. However, some graduates still leave Cornwall as they cannot afford the high cost of housing.

---

3 Exam-style question *Using examples, describe how a rural development project can help to bring economic benefits to an area. (4 marks)*

This question is point marked. It requires two developed explanations for 2 marks each; exceptionally, a well-developed effect can achieve 3 marks (though not 4).

Examples must be located, and should describe specific ways in which they stimulate growth.

Suitable descriptions for the *Eden Project*:
- Has provided over 400 full-time jobs (1) — plus development e.g. 'as well as additional jobs in supply industries which provide the cafes etc. with food' (1).
- Has provided a boost for other forms of tourism – including an example such as gardens (1) — plus development e.g. 'which has allowed hotels and B&Bs to stay open for longer / all year' (1).

Suitable descriptions for *CUC*:
- Helps to develop the knowledge economy with research and degree qualifications (1) — plus development e.g. 'as well as providing a boost for local pubs, clubs and student accommodation' (1).
- Plus other points on merit.

283

14.8 Making rural regions sustainable - 2

Section in brief
In this section students evaluate the success of green belts and National Parks in making rural regions sustainable.

In the activities, students:

- complete a table to score how well green belts and the Cairngorms National Park conserve landscapes and allow economic development;
- decide how successful green belts and National Parks are in making rural regions sustainable;
- answer an exam-style question to explain how either green belts or National Parks can help to make rural areas sustainable.

Key ideas

- Green belts are areas of open land around cities where development is restricted.
- Green belts are under constant threat from housing and road building.
- There are concerns that blocking developments on green belts will harm the economy.
- The Cairngorms are protected as they are part of a national park.
- One of the National Park's aims is to promote the social and economic development of the area's communities.

Key vocabulary
green belts

Skills practised
Geographical skills: interpreting a map and photo of green belts; evaluating the success of green belts and National Parks in making rural regions sustainable

PLTS: independent enquiry

Section outcomes
By the end of this section, most students should be able to:

- define the term given in 'Key vocabulary' above;
- describe the functions of green belts;
- describe the threats facing green belts;
- assess how well green belts and the Cairngorms National Park conserve the landscape and allow economic development;
- describe how successful green belts and National Parks are in making rural regions sustainable.

Ideas for a starter

1. Show students the photo of London and its green belt from the air, from page 250. Ask students what they think green belts do.
2. Show photos of some of the businesses in the Cairngorms National Park which support the ski resorts e.g. ski and snowboard hire shops etc. Tell students that many businesses operate in National Parks. Are they surprised?

Ideas for plenaries

1. Hold a class discussion. The topic is 'Green belts should never be built on'.
2. Asks students to work in pairs to write a paragraph on making rural regions sustainable.

Further class and homework activity

Ask students to find out: where their nearest area of green belt is (England only), how big it is, and what it is used for. They can find the information they need from a guide to 'Green belts in England' available to download from the CPRE website (search for green belts in England).

Changing settlements in the UK

answers

1. **a** and **b** Students should use the information in the text to help them complete the table. They should give a reason for their scores.

2. Students should use the table to decide how successful green belts and National Parks are in making rural regions sustainable. They should explain their answer using the reasons they gave in **1b**.

---

3. **Exam-style question** *Explain how either green belts or National Parks can help to make rural areas sustainable. (6 marks)*

   This question is marked using levels. The key to this question is the command word 'explain' — a Higher Tier command word. Purely descriptive points by Higher Tier candidates get no marks. Foundation Tier students may answer the alternative question:

   Describe ways in which National Parks can help to make rural areas more sustainable.

   In this case, change 'explanations' in the mark scheme below to 'descriptions'.

   Cap answers at the top of Level 2 (4 marks) which do not include:

   - reference to *either* green belts *or* National Parks,
   - a clear link to sustainability.

   Suitable points about **green belts** include:
   - They help to prevent the loss of open space by making it illegal to build there — plus development e.g. 'which helps preserve farmland and food supplies' — or well-developed with explicit link to sustainability e.g. 'which preserves that land and open space for future generations'.

   Suitable points about **National Parks** include:
   - They help to conserve / protect outstanding landscapes from development / tourism — plus development e.g. 'such as the Cairngorms where there are pressures from skiing and hotel development' — or well-developed with explicit link to sustainability (e.g. 'which preserves the landscape and open space for the future'.
   - Plus other explanations on merit.

Level	Descriptor
0	No rewardable content
1 (1-2 marks)	Simple or very basic statements using little or no subject vocabulary. May be a list e.g. 'national parks help to preserve landscapes'.
2 (3-4 marks)	Generalised explanations but with some use of geographical terms e.g. 'national parks such as the Cairngorms help to preserve special landscapes such as mountain regions and protect them from development'. Up to three developed statements as shown by examples above.
3 (5-6 marks)	Detailed statements with clear explanations using geographical terms. e.g. 'national parks such as the Cairngorms help to preserve special landscapes such as mountain regions and protect them from pressures caused by skiing and tourist development which could damage the landscape'. Three developed or two well-developed points as shown by examples above.

15 The challenges of an urban world

About the chapter
These are the key ideas behind the chapter.
- Urbanisation varies globally and across different regions.
- Cities grow as a result of migration and natural increase (internal growth).
- The economic activities, spatial growth and population of megacities varies in the developed and developing world.
- Cities in the developed world face challenges which lead to concentrated resource consumption.
- Eco-footprints vary for different cities, but can be reduced.
- It is possible to reduce a city's eco-footprint by developing more sustainable transport.
- Cities in the developing world face challenges which can lead to low quality of life.
- Self-help schemes, the work of NGOs and urban planning can improve quality of life in developing world cities.
- Attempts to develop less-polluted cities have advantages and disadvantages.

Chapter outline
Use this outline to provide your students with a brief roadmap of the chapter.

15.1 Urbanisation
How urbanisation varies around the world, and why cities grow.

15.2 Megacities
Contrasts between megacities in the developed and developing worlds.

15.3 Urban challenges in the developed world
Some of the challenges faced by cities in the developed world.

15.4 Reducing the environmental impact of cities – 1
Why eco-footprints vary from city to city, and how London is reducing its eco-footprint.

15.5 Reducing the environmental impact of cities – 2
How London is reducing its eco-footprint by developing a more sustainable transport system.

15.6 Urban challenges in the developing world
Some of the challenges that lead to low quality of life in the developing world.

15.7 Managing challenges in developing world cities – 1
How a self-help scheme has improved quality of life.

15.8 Managing challenges in developing world cities – 2
Examples of the work of NGOs and urban planning projects in improving quality of life.

15.9 Managing challenges in developing world cities – 3
Two different attempts to develop less-polluted cities – Mexico City and Masdar City.

The challenges of an urban world

How is the specification covered?

This chapter covers Topic 7, Unit 2, People and the planet.

7.1 How have cities grown and what challenges do they face?

7.2 How far can these challenges be managed?

Key ideas	Detailed content	Pages in students' book
7.1a The world is increasingly urbanised as cities grow due to different processes.	Examine urbanisation trends globally and across different regions, including reasons for growth (migration and internal growth).	252-253
	Contrast the economic activities, spatial growth and population of megacities in the developed and developing world.	254-255
7.1b Cities face a range of social and environmental challenges resulting from rapid growth and resource demands.	Examine urban challenges in the developed world including food, energy, transport and waste disposal demands that may lead to concentrated resource consumption.	256-257
	Examine urban challenges in the developing world including slum housing, the informal economy, and urban pollution, that lead to low quality of life.	262-263
7.2a Cities in the developed world have huge potential for reducing their environmental impact (eco-footprint).	Investigate why eco-footprints vary from city to city and assess how one named city in the developed world is lessening its eco-footprint by reducing energy consumption and waste generation.	258-259
	Analyse the potential for more sustainable transport in a named city in the developed world.	260-261
7.2b Different strategies can be used to manage social and environmental challenges in developing world cities.	Consider the success of strategies to improve quality of life in cities in the developing world: self-help schemes, the work of NGOs, urban planning, e.g. Curitiba.	264-265, 266-267
	Evaluate the advantages and disadvantages of attempts to develop less-polluted cities, e.g. Masdar City, Mexico City.	268-269

Chapter outcomes

By the end of this chapter, students should be able to:

- Describe the rates of urbanisation in different regions of the world, and explain the reasons for the growth of cities.
- Contrast the economic activities, spatial growth, and population of megacities in the developed and developing world.
- Explain some of the challenges faced by cities in the developed world.
- Describe how one city in the developed world is lessening its eco-footprint by reducing energy consumption and waste generation.
- Describe how transport can be made more sustainable in a city in the developed world.
- Outline the challenges which can lead to low quality of life in cities in the developing world.
- Explain how far different strategies have improved quality of life in developing world cities.
- Evaluate the advantages and disadvantages of attempts to develop less-polluted cities.

15.1 Urbanisation

Section in brief

In this section students find out what urbanisation is, how it varies around the world and why cities grow.

In the activities, students:

- use a map to describe the distribution of the world's urban population;
- explain why a migrant is unlikely to return to a rural area to live;
- explain why industrial growth usually leads to urban growth and rural-urban migration;
- explain how migrants affect the rate of population increase in cities;
- answer an exam-style question to describe the rate of urbanisation in different regions of the world.

Key ideas

- Urbanisation is the rise in the percentage of people living in urban areas, in comparison with rural areas.
- In 2007 the world's population balance changed, and more people lived in urban areas than rural areas.
- Urbanisation has happened later, and faster, in developing countries, than it did in developed countries.
- Rates of urbanisation vary in different regions of the world.
- Cities grow as a result of urbanisation and natural increase (internal growth).

Key vocabulary

urbanisation, rural-urban migration, natural increase, internal growth

Skills practised

Geographical skills: using a map to describe population distribution
PLTS: independent enquiry
Numeracy skills: interpreting graphs

Section outcomes

By the end of this section, most students should be able to:

- define or explain the terms given in 'Key vocabulary' above;
- describe the distribution of the world's urban population;
- explain why industrial growth usually leads to urban growth and rural-urban migration;
- describe the rate of urbanisation in different regions of the world;
- explain how migrants affect the rate of population increase in cities.

Ideas for a starter

1. Show students the map from page 252. Ask them to describe: the distribution of countries with an urban population of over 50%; the distribution of the largest cities (those with a population of 10 million or more).

2. Show students the graph from page 253 showing the increase in the world's urban population. In 2007 the world's population balance changed, and for the first time more people, lived in urban areas than rural. Ask: 'Why do people leave the countryside and move to towns?'

Ideas for plenaries

1. Ask students to summarise what they have learnt in this lesson in 50 words or less.

2. Make up 5-10 statements (some true, some false) based on what students have learnt about urbanisation in this lesson. Students should identify the false ones, and give you the correct version.

Further class and homework activity

Ask students to create a diagram to show the push and pull factors to explain why people leave rural areas and move to cities.

The challenges of an urban world

answers

1 a Over 50% — North and South America, Europe, the Middle East, China and the Far East, Russia, along with Australia and New Zealand. African countries include Libya, Algeria and South Africa.

b Many countries in Africa have an urban population of under 50% along with countries in central and southern Asia.

2 Sunita is likely to stay in Mumbai as her family are likely to have left the countryside as a result of poverty and lack of jobs. Mumbai will offer more in the way of jobs for her family, along with better educational and health facilities, if they can afford them.

3 a Industrial growth leads to urban growth as workers are needed for the growing industries. Migrants to the cities are often young and start families when they are settled. The city grows as a result of natural increase or internal growth.

b Rural areas often have few jobs and many people living in poverty. Industrial growth provides jobs in the cities and attracts workers from rural areas hoping for an improved life, and so leading to rural-urban migration.

4 a Most migrants are young as it is easier for younger people without families to move to cities.

b They get married in the city rather than at home as they tend to migrate in their 20s and 30s before they marry.

c They often start families once they have settled; increasing the birth rate and population in cities (internal growth).

---

5 Exam-style question *Using the graph above, describe the rate of urbanisation in different regions of the world. (4 marks)*

This question is point marked; it requires four identified patterns — 1 mark per correct pattern. There is 1 mark maximum for the use of data, but remember that the sting on this question is '*rate of*' urbanisation' – so focus on the ability of students to pick out 'rapid rate', 'slow rate' etc. or comparatives e.g. 'fastest' / 'slowest'.

Correct patterns include:

- Oceania has the slowest rates of growth (1)
- North America Europe / Oceania were fast (1) but have slowed down / are now steady (1)
- The fastest rate(s) are in Africa and Asia (1) though Africa is speeding up (1) / Asia is slowing down (1)
- Regions which were fastest in the 1950s are now slowest / vice-versa (1)
- Plus other points on merit.

15.2 Megacities

Section in brief

In this section students explore the differences between megacities in the developed and developing worlds. They contrast the economic activities, size and spatial growth, and population of Mumbai — a developing world megacity, and Los Angeles — a developed world megacity.

In the activities, students:

- plot megacities on a world map — identifying those in the developed and developing worlds;
- describe what the map shows about the distribution of the world's megacities;
- draw two spider diagrams to contrast the economic activities, growth and population of developed and developing world megacities;
- answer an exam-style question to explain how economic activities can lead to the population growth and spatial growth of megacities.

Key ideas

- Megacities are cities with a population of over 10 million people.
- There are differences between the megacities in the developed and developing worlds in terms of:
  - Spatial growth
  - Economic activities
  - Population.

Key vocabulary

megacities, spatial growth, conurbations, informal economy, formal economy, hyperurbanisation

Skills practised

Geographical skills: plot megacities on world map; describe the distribution of megacities; draw spider diagrams to contrast megacities in developed and developing worlds

Numeracy skills: interpret graph of megacities

Section outcomes

By the end of this section, most students should be able to:

- define or explain the terms given in 'Key vocabulary' above;
- describe the distribution of the world's megacities;
- draw two spider diagrams to contrast the economic activities, growth and population, of developed and developing world megacities;
- explain how economic activities can lead to the population growth and spatial growth of megacities.

Ideas for a starter

1. Recap urbanisation and the reasons why cities grow from section 15.1.
2. Show students photos of some of these cities: Tokyo, Mumbai, Mexico City, Shanghai, Buenos Aires, Los Angeles, Cairo, and Paris. Can students identify any of them? Ask: 'What have these cities got in common?' They are all megacities with a population of over 10 million people.

Ideas for plenaries

1. Ask students to write a paragraph to summarise the lesson. They should use all the key vocabulary from this section.
2. Ask students to work in pairs for question 2 from page 255 of the students' book. One student can create a spider diagram for developed world megacities and their partner can create the diagram for developing world megacities.

Further class and homework activity

Ask students to find out what an eco-footprint is, and how it is measured, in preparation for the next section.

The challenges of an urban world

answers

1 **a** and **b** Students' maps should show that most of the world's megacities are in developing countries.

2 If students want to use specific examples on their spider diagrams they can use the information on Mumbai and Los Angeles on page 255. Remind them that 'contrast' means they should look for differences.

3 **Exam-style question** *Using examples, explain how economic activities can lead to the population growth and spatial growth of 'megacities'. (8 marks)*

This question is marked using levels. The key to this question is the command word 'explain' — a Higher Tier command word. Foundation Tier students may answer the alternative question: *Using examples, give reasons for the population growth and spatial growth of megacities. (6 marks)*

In this case, three developed or two well-developed descriptions are required for 6 marks.

Cap answers at the top of Level 2 (6 marks) which do not include:

- named locations from developed or developing world cities,
- specific economic reasons — e.g. 'the increase in manufacturing has led to factory jobs in Mumbai' and not just 'there are more jobs in cities',
- an explanation of the link between population growth and spatial growth.

Suitable reasons for how economic activities can lead to **population growth** include:

- Rapid growth in population due to employment in cities, with examples e.g. Mumbai — developed with reasons or types of employment e.g. film industry — or well-developed with further expansion e.g. which leads to growth due to migration from other parts of the country.

Suitable reasons for how economic activities can lead to **spatial growth** include:

- Population growth has led to the sprawl of cities, with examples e.g. Tokyo or LA — developed with reasons e.g. land is cheaper so both housing and workplaces spread outwards — or well-developed with further expansion e.g. which has led to cities merging / the growth of conurbations.
- Similar, but developed with data e.g. physical size of LA as shown on page 255.

Level	Descriptor
0	No rewardable content
1 (1-3 marks)	Simple or very basic statements using little or no subject vocabulary. May be a list e.g. 'there are many jobs in LA so people move there'.
2 (4-6 marks)	Generalised explanations but with some use of geographical terms e.g. 'there are many jobs in LA such as the film industry so people move there which has led to population growth'. Up to three developed statements as shown by examples above.
3 (7-8 marks)	Detailed statements with clear explanations using geographical terms. e.g. 'there is a wide variety of employment in LA, such as its port and the film industry, so people move there which has led to massive growth in the size of the city'. Two well-developed points plus other developed statements are required for the top of Level 3 as shown by examples above.

15.3 Urban challenges in the developed world

Section in brief

In this section students look at some of the challenges faced by cities in the developed world.

In the activities, students:

- calculate their own eco-footprint and explain their score;
- explain why cities consume more resources than rural areas;
- design a questionnaire, and carry out a survey, to find out what people recycle in school and the local area;
- decide on a programme of changes needed in the local area, and in London, to reduce eco-footprints;
- answer an exam-style question to explain some of the challenges faced by cities in the developed world.

Key ideas

- The early development of cities depended on the ability of surrounding rural areas to provide their needs.
- As cities have grown they have become places of concentrated resource consumption.
- An eco-footprint measures the area of land needed to provide all the resources and services consumed, and absorb all the waste produced.
- London's growing population creates challenges in terms of food and energy consumption, use of transport, and waste produced.
- London could solve its waste problem by prevention and recycling.

Key vocabulary

concentrated resource consumption, eco-footprint, global hectares per person (gha)

Skills practised

Geographical skills: calculate and compare eco-footprints

PLTS: independent enquiry; creative thinking; team-working

Section outcomes

By the end of this section, most students should be able to:

- define or explain the terms given in 'Key vocabulary' above;
- calculate their own eco-footprint;
- explain why cities consume more resources than rural areas and some of the problems this leads to;
- suggest a programme of changes to reduce eco-footprints in London.

Ideas for a starter

1. Show students the photo of London at night, from page 256 of the students' book. How many words can they come up with to describe it? What challenges does a city like London create (ask them to think about resources)?
2. Show a large image of a footprint on the whiteboard. If students completed the further activity from 15.2, ask them to feedback what they have found out. Write students' ideas within the footprint on the whiteboard.

Ideas for plenaries

1. Ask: 'Why should we be concerned about the size of our eco-footprints?'
2. Hold a class discussion on how sustainable London is as a city.

Further class and homework activity

Remind students that half of London's waste is sent to landfill. The remaining waste which is not recycled, is incinerated. Ask students to research the arguments for and against both landfill and incineration. They should come up with four arguments in each category presented in a table.

The challenges of an urban world

answers

1. Students need to use a search engine to find an eco-footprint calculator and calculate their own eco-footprint. They should explain their scores.

2. The growing populations of cities require vast amounts of resources from all over the world. London consumes 6.9 million tonnes of food a year, 81% of which comes from outside the UK. It consumes 13.2 million tonnes of oil equivalent, and all of London's energy is imported.

3. **and 4** Answers will vary.

---

5. **Exam-style question** *Using examples, explain some of the challenges faced by cities in the developed world. (8 marks)*

   This question is marked using levels. The key to this question is the command word 'explain' — a Higher Tier command word. Purely descriptive points by Higher Tier candidates get no marks. Foundation Tier students may answer the alternative question:

   Using examples, describe some of the challenges faced by cities in the developed world. (6 marks)

   In this case, three developed or two well-developed descriptions are required for 6 marks.

   Cap answers at the top of Level 1 (3 marks) if they do not include examples from *developed* cities. The answer requires development of points to reach Level 2. Level 3 (7 or 8 marks) should be awarded only where at least one of these is well-developed. If the student provides only developed statements, the answer is capped at the top of Level 2 (6 marks).

   Suitable challenges include:

   - Eco-footprint (with definition) — developed with reason, such as why London's eco-footprint is so great e.g. resource / food consumption — or well-developed with further expansion e.g. data which illustrates its eco-footprint from page 256.
   - Waste, with some description of its extent / volume from page 257 in the student textbook — plus development e.g. how to manage its disposal and the impact on areas outside the city — or well-developed with further expansion e.g. which leads to the challenge of how to reduce this through recycling.
   - Plus other explanations on merit.

Level	Descriptor
0	No rewardable content
1 (1-3 marks)	Simple or very basic statements using little or no subject vocabulary.
2 (4-6 marks)	Generalised explanations but with some use of geographical terms e.g. 'cities like London face the challenge of waste disposal, because landfill in south-east England will soon be full'. Up to three developed statements as shown by examples above.
3 (7-8 marks)	Detailed statements with clear explanations using geographical terms. e.g. 'cities like London face the challenge of waste disposal, because landfill in south-east England will soon be full, and the city has to face choices about how to increase waste prevention and recycling'. Two well-developed points plus other developed statements are required for the top of Level 3 as shown by examples above.

15.4 Reducing the environmental impact of cities – 1

Section in brief

In this section students investigate why and how eco-footprints vary from one place to another. It looks at cities in the UK with the largest and smallest footprints and considers how London is reducing its eco-footprint.

In the activities, students:

- use a graph to suggest reasons why Winchester's eco-footprint is higher than Salisbury's;
- research the BedZED scheme, and explain how energy consumption has been reduced;
- discuss the ideas that people should be fined for not recycling, and that every house should be built to BedZED standards;
- answer an exam-style question to describe how one urban area is reducing its eco-footprint.

Key ideas

- Eco-footprints vary from city to city.
- The consumption of goods and resources (including energy), plus transport use, all affect a city's eco-footprint.
- London is reducing its eco-footprint by reducing energy consumption and reducing waste generation.
- BedZED in south London, is an example of a sustainable community that promotes energy conservation.

Key vocabulary

retro-fitting

Skills practised

Geographical skills: use a graph to suggest reasons for differences in eco-footprints; interpret a table of data on eco-footprints;

PLTS: independent enquiry; creative thinking; team-working; effective participators

Section outcomes

By the end of this section, most students should be able to:

- explain the term given in 'Key vocabulary' above;
- suggest reasons why Winchester's eco-footprint is higher than Salisbury's;
- describe how London is reducing its energy consumption;
- describe how London is reducing its waste generation;
- explain how energy consumption has been reduced in BedZED.

Ideas for a starter

1. Recap: 'What does the term eco-footprint mean? How do we measure it? What contributes to it?'
2. Show the two tables from page 258 on the whiteboard. Remind students what the term eco-footprint means, and discuss what these tables show.

Ideas for plenaries

1. If students have completed question 2 from page 259 of the students' book, then use question 3 (the class discussions) as a plenary activity.
2. Tell students that in the USA in 2007 the average eco-footprint per person was 6.7gha. In a study of 18 cities, New York had the lowest eco-footprint (6.1gha) per person, and Seattle had the highest eco-footprint (7.4gha) per person. How do those figures compare with the eco-footprints for British cities?

Further class and homework activity

Ask students to write a letter to Winchester City Council suggesting two main ways in which the city could reduce its eco-footprint.

The challenges of an urban world

answers

1. Incomes in Winchester are higher than Salisbury, so people probably have larger houses (which require more energy), and consume more. People in Winchester commute further to work. In Salisbury, a higher percentage of workers walk, cycle or use public transport to get to work.

2. The BedZED scheme only uses energy from renewable sources — including solar panels and tree waste to produce electricity and heating; houses are triple glazed with high thermal insulation; rainwater is collected and reused; water-efficient appliances have been installed as standard; residents are encouraged to join an on-site car-sharing club; some parking spaces have charging points for electric cars.

3. Answers will vary. Note that it would be beneficial if students had completed question 2 before attempting this class discussion.

4. **Exam-style question** *Using examples, describe how one urban area is reducing its eco-footprint. (6 marks)*

   This question is marked using levels. With 'describe' as a command word, you use this for all candidates or just for Foundation Tier. Higher Tier students may answer the alternative question:

   Using examples, explain the ways in which urban areas are reducing their eco-footprint. (6 marks)

   In this case, replace the term 'descriptions' in the level descriptions below with 'explanations'. Purely descriptive points by Higher Tier candidates get no marks.

   Cap answers at the top of Level 2 (4 marks) which do not include examples which are specific to a named city. Suitable methods (based on London in page 259 in the student textbook) include:

   - Reducing waste consumption e.g. reducing energy consumption in buildings — plus development e.g. building insulation — or well-developed with further expansion e.g. or creating low-carbon zones where energy emissions are reduced.
   - Reducing waste generation e.g. re-using waste — plus development e.g. by developing waste burning power stations — or well-developed with further expansion e.g. which use household waste to generate electricity in areas such as London's Olympic Park.
   - Plus other descriptions on merit.

Level	Descriptor
0	No rewardable content
1 (1-2 marks)	Simple or very basic statements using little or no subject vocabulary. May be a descriptive or basic list of points e.g. 'London needs to reduce its energy consumption and stop wasting as much energy'.
2 (3-4 marks)	Generalised descriptions but with some use of geographical terms e.g. 'London is reducing its energy consumption by planning new low-carbon zones where less energy will be used in buildings'. Up to two developed statements as shown by examples above.
3 (5-6 marks)	Detailed statements with clear descriptions using geographical terms. e.g. 'London is reducing its energy consumption by planning 10 new low-carbon zones where less energy is used in buildings, such as using solar panels and insulating buildings'. Three developed or two well-developed points as shown by examples above.

15.5 Reducing the environmental impact of cities – 2

Section in brief
In this section students look at how London is reducing its eco-footprint by developing a more sustainable transport system.

In the activities, students:
- identify the benefits of making London's transport more sustainable;
- complete a table to show the advantages and disadvantages for different schemes to make London's transport sustainable;
- draw a spider diagram to show how the schemes could be developed, and whether their local town or city should develop a congestion charge;
- answer an exam-style question to describe the possibilities for making transport more sustainable in a developed world city.

Key ideas
- London is aiming to reduce its eco-footprint by making transport more sustainable.
- London is encouraging the use of clean technology in vehicles in the city.
- High polluting vehicles have been discouraged with the Low Emission Zone.
- The congestion charge was introduced to reduce congestion and pollution.
- A cycle hire scheme and building cycle superhighways is encouraging cycling in London.

Key vocabulary
Low Emission Zone, congestion charge

Skills practised
Geographical skills: identifying advantages and disadvantages of London's transport schemes; describing possibilities for making transport more sustainable

PLTS: independent enquiry; creative thinking; team-working

Section outcomes
By the end of this section, most students should be able to:
- define or explain the terms given in 'Key vocabulary' above;
- explain how making London's transport more sustainable will reduce its eco-footprint;
- identify the benefits for people, the environment, and the economy of making London's transport more sustainable;
- complete a table to show the advantages and disadvantages for each scheme to make London's transport sustainable;
- describe how the schemes could be developed further.

Ideas for a starter
1. Show students one of London's traffic jam cameras live on the interactive whiteboard. Use this link http://www.bbc.co.uk/travelnews/london/trafficcameras#roadCameras Choose a camera showing congestion. Then click on 'Live incidents' to see the problem's London's traffic is facing today.
2. Show students a short film about the new London bus and how it has been developed. Use this link http://www.london.gov.uk/priorities/transport/investing-transport/buses/new-bus-london — scroll down and click on the 'New bus for London' clip.

Idea for a plenary
Use question 3 as a plenary. Open up a discussion to find out what other students think about the ideas suggested.

Further class and homework activity
Ask students to find out about London's plans to increase the number of people walking in London. They can find the information they need on www.london.gov.uk — click on Transport at the bottom of the screen, then 'Making walking count'.

The challenges of an urban world

answers

1 a Benefits for **people** include: improved air quality; improvements in London's transport; improvements in health.

 b Benefits for the **environment** include: improved air quality; reduction in use of fossil fuels; reduction in greenhouse gas emissions.

 c Benefits for the **economy** include: transport is cheaper to run; money from congestion charge used to improve London's transport; less congestion means less time / money wasted for businesses.

2 Encouraging clean technology: *Advantages* — new hybrid buses will be cleaner, more fuel-efficient and quieter; electric vehicles are easier to charge. *Disadvantages* — high cost of replacing buses; number of vehicles may increase.

Discouraging high-polluting vehicles: *Advantages* — air quality should improve. *Disadvantages* — costly for businesses operating vehicles which either need to be altered to meet emissions standards, or pay to enter the zone.

Reducing congestion and pollution: *Advantages* — congestion charge has increased bus passengers; money which has been raised is used to improve London's transport. *Disadvantages* — congestion is now back to the level it was before the charge was introduced; expensive for businesses travelling within the congestion zone; could lead to increase in traffic outside the congestion zone.

Encouraging cycling: *Advantages* — green, clean and healthy way to get around the city; should reduce number of cars on the roads. *Disadvantages* — new 'cycle superhighways' reduces the width of roads, possibly slowing down other traffic and leading to more congestion.

3 Answers will vary.

4 Exam-style question *Using examples from a named city in the developed world, describe the possibilities for making transport more sustainable. (8 marks — or 6 marks for Foundation Tier students)*

This question is marked using levels. Foundation Tier students require three developed or two well-developed descriptions for 6 marks. Cap answers at the top of Level 1 (3 marks) which do not include examples which are specific to a named city in the *developed* world.

Suitable possibilities for London include:

- Using clean technology on buses — plus development e.g. electric vehicles or hybrid engines using both fuel- and electric-power sources — or well-developed with further expansion e.g. which are quieter and reduce noise / have lower CO_2 emissions.
- Introducing a congestion charge — plus development e.g. 'which involves making a charge on all vehicles entering central London' — or well-developed e.g. 'and is designed to discourage people from using their cars and use public transport instead'.

Level	Descriptor
0	No rewardable content
1 (1-2 marks)	Simple or very basic statements using little or no subject vocabulary.
2 (3-4 marks)	Generalised explanations but with some use of geographical terms e.g. 'London is introducing cleaner buses which use electric motors to reduce CO_2 emissions and are quieter'. Up to three developed statements as shown by examples above.
3 (5-6 marks)	Detailed statements with clear explanations using geographical terms. e.g. 'London is introducing cleaner buses which use hybrid electric- and fuel-powered engines to reduce CO_2 emissions, as well as more charging points for electric cars'. Two well-developed points plus other developed statements are required for the top of Level 3 as shown by examples above.

15.6 Urban challenges in the developing world

Section in brief

In this section students examine some of the challenges which lead to low quality of life in the developing world.

In the activities, students:

- list and classify the challenges faced by Mumbai and its residents;
- explain whether Mumbai's problems are mainly economic, social or environmental;
- explain why cities such as Mumbai, experience pollution;
- discuss and present ideas about different ways to make improvements to cities;
- answer an exam-style question to describe two differences between the formal and informal economy.

Key ideas

- Many of the problems people face in developing world cities lead to low quality of life.
- Many people in developing world cities work in the informal economy.
- In India, a lack of tax revenue means city authorities cannot afford to provide services for everyone.
- Some slums are well-established, while others are more temporary with poor quality housing.
- Rapid urbanisation and industrialisation in developing countries has created environmental problems, including water and air pollution.

Key vocabulary

quality of life, informal economy, water pollution, air pollution

Skills practised

Geographical skills: classifying challenges as economic, environmental and social; defining geographical terms

PLTS: independent enquiry; creative thinking; team-working

Literacy skills: extended writing

Section outcomes

By the end of this section, most students should be able to:

- define or explain the terms given in 'Key vocabulary' above;
- list the challenges faced by Mumbai and its residents;
- classify the challenges as economic, environmental, or social;
- explain why developing world cities experience pollution;
- present different ideas about how improvements can be made to cities.

Ideas for a starter

1. Play students a clip from the BBC TV series 'Welcome to India'. There is one from Episode 2 on shipbreaking http://www.bbc.co.uk/programmes/p00zbjwl which shows the dirty and dangerous work which some people in developing countries do.

2. Show students a photo of rag-picking in Mumbai. Tell them this is a way of making money from other people's rubbish, and is an important part of the informal economy. Ask: 'Who can remind me what the informal economy is?'

Idea for a plenary

Tell students that Mumbai has banned diesel as a fuel in all of its taxis. Many of the city's 58 000 taxis now use compressed natural gas instead as a way of reducing air pollution. What other ideas can students come up with to cut air and water pollution in Mumbai?

Further class and homework activity

Ask students to design a poster to raise awareness of the problems people face in developing world cities which lead to a low quality of life.

The challenges of an urban world

answers

1 a The challenges for Mumbai's residents revolve around:
  - the informal economy — up to 60% of people work in the informal economy, with no regular wage, no job security, no health and safety protection and no pension provision.
  - lack of services — including clean water, sewerage etc.
  - poor housing — lacking sanitation, overcrowded, polluted.
  - pollution — air and water.

b and **c**
Students should explain how these problems overlap and that many of Mumbai's' problems are social.

2 Mumbai's pollution is a result of rapid urbanisation and industrialisation. Rapid urbanisation results in people arriving in the city faster than the authorities can provide services in terms of things like sewerage — which may be too expensive. Rapid industrialisation and economic growth means more electricity is needed — often generated by burning fossil fuels like coal — which results in air pollution. Rivers are often used as dumping grounds for industrial waste resulting in water pollution.

3 a and **b**
Students can use the information in this section, and their own thoughts, to come up with ideas about whether India's government should increase tax on companies to pay for improvements to cities — and how far local people should club together to start city improvement schemes.

---

4 Exam-style question *Describe two differences between the formal and informal economy.*
(4 marks)

This question is point marked. It requires a developed definition of each of the formal and informal economy, for 2 marks each, or exceptionally 3 marks for a well-developed description. However, a comparison must be stated using a connective such as 'whereas' so that the *difference* is clear; cap any answer which simply provides two statements without linking them at 3 marks.

- The **formal** economy means jobs with contracts of employment and more security, plus example e.g. a teacher or mechanic.
- The **informal** economy means jobs that are not official and have little security i.e. they may not know if they will have much work to do from one day to the next, plus example e.g. a street trader.

15.7 Managing challenges in developing world cities – 1

Section in brief

In this section students investigate how a self-help scheme has improved the quality of life in Rocinha, Brazil's largest favela.

In the activities, students:

- find, and annotate photos of Rocinha, to show what quality of life is like;
- explain the advantages and disadvantages of 'self-help' as a way of improving housing in Rocinha;
- design a spider diagram to explain why geographers study crime;
- explain why crime affects quality of life and the economy, and why it needs to be reduced before the 2016 Olympic Games;
- answer an exam-style question to describe two challenges faced by cities in the developing world.

Key ideas

- Rocinha, is Brazil's largest favela and is home to up to 210 000 people.
- The authorities in Rio set up self-help schemes to improve the favelas.
- Quality of life in Rocinha has improved due to the self-help schemes.
- Rocinha's crime problem is being tackled by the government.
- Police Pacification Units are used to take control of neighbourhoods and to reduce crime.

Key vocabulary

favela

Skills practised

Geographical skills: annotating photos; explaining advantages and disadvantages of self-help

PLTS: independent enquiry; team-working

Section outcomes

By the end of this section, most students should be able to:

- define the term given in 'Key vocabulary' above;
- annotate a photo to show what quality of life is like in Rocinha;
- explain the advantages and disadvantages of 'self-help' as a way of improving housing in Rocinha;
- describe how quality of life in Rocinha has improved as a result of self-help schemes;
- explain how crime in Rocinha affects people's quality of life.

Ideas for a starter

1. Show students a video clip from the Rio 2016 website entitled 'Passion and Transformation'. Rio wants its games to be better than London's in 2012 — but first of all it has some big problems to deal with — including crime.

2. Tell students that in the UK around 500 people are murdered a year. Can anyone guess how many are murdered in Rio de Janeiro each year, and why? The answer is around 6000 people and many of them die as a result of drug-related crime.

Idea for a plenary

Use the exam-style question on page 265 as a plenary activity.

Further class and homework activity

Ask students to find a map of Rio de Janeiro showing the location of Rocinha, and another map showing the location of the Olympic venues (they can use the official Rio Games website for this http://www.rio2016.org.br. Which venues will be close to Rocinha? How might this cause a problem for the authorities?

The challenges of an urban world

answers

1. **a** and **b** Answers will vary.

2. **Advantages** of the self-help schemes: authorities pay for building materials; residents build their own permanent homes with water and electricity; improved water and sanitation creating healthier living conditions; more school — improved education opportunities and people can get better jobs.

   Disadvantages of the self-help schemes: still located in the same overcrowded, steep location; they don't deal with the issue of crime.

3. Reasons include: crime impacts on quality of life; crime can cluster in certain geographical locations; high crime rates may determine the location of other activities.

4. **a** Crime can make Rocinha a dangerous place to live, especially drug-related crime.

   b Crime will impact adversely on the economy. Businesses are less likely to locate in high crime areas.

   c Rocinha is very close to the main site for the 2016 Olympic Games. High levels of crime may deter visitors to the Games.

5. **Exam-style question** *Using examples, describe two challenges faced by cities in the developing world. (6 marks)*

   This question is marked using levels. Higher Tier students may answer the alternative question:

   Using examples, explain the challenges faced by cities in the developing world. (8 marks)

   8 mark answers require at least two well-developed points plus other developed explanations. Purely descriptive points by Higher Tier candidates get no marks.

   Cap answers at the top of Level 2 (4 marks) which do not include:

   - examples which are specific to a named city in the developing world e.g. Rio de Janeiro or Rocinha within it,
   - two well-developed descriptions which focus upon challenges.

   Suitable challenges (based on Rocinha in pages 264-265 in the student textbook) include:

   - **Housing:** Description of housing conditions with an example e.g. housing materials — plus development e.g. without sanitation or clean water — well-developed with an identified challenge e.g. 'which creates health problems and the spread of disease'.

   - **Crime:** Description of the nature of crime e.g. drug trafficking or gangs — plus development e.g. which have taken control of some neighbourhoods which have become very dangerous — and well-developed with an identified challenge e.g. which means that providing security and safety for the 2016 Olympics will be very difficult.

Level	Descriptor
0	No rewardable content
1 (1-2 marks)	Simple or very basic statements using little or no subject vocabulary. May be a descriptive or basic list of points e.g. 'housing in Rocinha is very poor quality'.
2 (3-4 marks)	Generalised descriptions but with some use of geographical terms e.g. 'housing in Rocinha is high density and mostly poor quality, without services such as sewerage'. Up to two developed statements as shown by examples above.
3 (5-6 marks)	Detailed statements with clear descriptions using geographical terms. e.g. 'housing in Rocinha is high density, mostly poor quality, and does not have services such as sewerage, which creates a major health risk for residents there'. Three developed or two well-developed points as shown by examples above.

15.8 Managing challenges in developing world cities – 2

Section in brief

In this section students look at how the work of NGOs and urban planning can improve quality of life in developing world cities.

In the activities, students:

- judge the success of attempts to improve quality of life for people living in Rocinha, Dhaka and Curitiba;
- write a report on the project they think has been most successful;
- describe and explain two targets that they would give each project to work on;
- answer an exam-style question to explain how far different projects have improved quality of life in developing world cities.

Key ideas

- 40% of Dhaka's population live in slums and lack basic services.
- NGO projects in Dhaka have improved the lives of female slum dwellers and a local community using small-scale, sustainable projects.
- Curitiba in Brazil faced environmental and social problems as a result of rapid growth and industrialisation.
- Quality of life in Curitiba has been improved as a result of urban planning.

Key vocabulary

non-governmental organisations (NGOs), maternal death, tube wells, urban planning

Skills practised

Geographical skills: evaluating the success of attempts to improve quality of life

PLTS: independent enquiry; creative thinking

Literacy skills: writing a report

Section outcomes

By the end of this section, most students should be able to:

- define or explain the terms given in 'Key vocabulary' above;
- describe one NGO project to improve quality of life in a developing world city;
- describe how Curitiba's government improved quality of life as a result of urban planning;
- evaluate the success of attempts to improve the quality of life for people living in Rocinha, Dhaka and Curitiba.

Ideas for a starter

1. Challenge students to be the first one to find out something about life in Dhaka, Bangladesh. Share the information students find out with the rest of the class.

2. Ask: 'Does anyone know what the term non-governmental organisation means?' Who can give me an example of one? What kind of work do they do, and where?' You are looking to elicit the fact that NGOs develop small-scale, sustainable solutions to local problems in developing countries. Oxfam, the Red Cross and WaterAid are examples of NGOs.

Ideas for plenaries

1. Ask students to write down the biggest insight they have gained from this lesson.

2. Ask students to spend two minutes with a partner to think up one interesting question about managing the challenges in developing world cities. Ask other members of the class to answer the best questions.

Further class and homework activity

Ask students to find out about Masdar City in preparation for the next lesson. They should find out where it is, and how it is different to other cities.

The challenges of an urban world

answers

1 a Students should complete a table for each project they have studied in Rocinha, Dhaka and Curitiba. For each aspect given in the table students should score it out of 5 and give a reason for their score.

b Students should add up the scores for each project and decide which they think has been most successful in improving the quality of life of those affected, and write a report.

c Answers will vary.

---

2 Exam-style question *Using examples of projects you have studied, explain how far they have improved the quality of life in cities in the developing world. (8 marks)*

This question is marked using levels. Foundation Tier students may answer the alternative question:

Using a named urban project in the developing world, describe how it has improved the quality of life in a city. (6 marks)

In this case, three developed or two well-developed descriptions are required for 6 marks.

Cap answers at the top of Level 1 (3 marks) which do not include specific projects from a named city in the *developing* world. Cap answers at the top of Level 2 (6 marks) which do not include an evaluation of improvements to quality of life i.e. 'it is better because …', not just an explanation of how the project has worked.

Suitable improvements to quality of life in Dhaka (page 266 in the student textbook) or Curitiba (page 267) include:

- The Manoshi project, with a brief description — plus development e.g. which helps women with ante-natal and new-born care — and well-developed with an evaluation of an identified improvement to quality of life e.g. 'which has resulted in better quality of life through improved health for mothers and children'.

- Improved transport in Curitiba, with a brief description — plus development e.g. which has involved greatly increasing bus services across the city — well-developed with an evaluation of identified improvement to quality of life e.g. 'which has resulted in lower traffic congestion and it is easier for people to get to work'.

Level	Descriptor
0	No rewardable content
1 (1-3 marks)	Simple or very basic statements using little or no subject vocabulary. May be a list e.g. 'new tube wells have been built in Dhaka'.
2 (4-6 marks)	Generalised explanations but with some use of geographical terms e.g. 'new tube wells have been built in Dhaka to a point deep in the water table where water is clean'. Up to three developed statements as shown by examples above.
3 (7-8 marks)	Detailed statements with clear evaluation using geographical terms. e.g. 'new tube wells have been built in Dhaka to a point deep in the water table where water is clean, meaning that quality of life is better with less time spent collecting water and improved health'. Two well-developed points plus other developed statements are required for the top of Level 3 as shown by examples above.

15.9 Managing challenges in developing world cities – 3

Section in brief

In this section students evaluate two attempts to reduce pollution in cities. They look at attempts to improve Mexico City's environment, and the building of a new sustainable city — Masdar City in the United Arab Emirates.

In the activities, students:

- complete tables to show the advantages and disadvantages of Mexico City and Masdar City's attempts to reduce pollution;
- decide which city seems to be more sustainable;
- answer an exam-style question to explain how far one city has been successful in trying to reduce pollution.

Key ideas

- Mexico City's rapid growth and size have created major environmental problems.
- Mexico City has tackled its pollution by moving heavy industry out of the city and implementing a 'Green Plan', with key changes to transport.
- Despite the improvements, Mexico City still has below average air quality.
- Masdar City is a totally new planned settlement designed on sustainable principles.
- There are still issues facing the development of Masdar City.

Key vocabulary

There is no key vocabulary on this spread.

Skills practised

Geographical skills: evaluating attempts to reduce pollution in cities

PLTS: independent enquiry; creative thinking

Section outcomes

By the end of this section, most students should be able to:

- describe the reasons why Mexico City was so polluted;
- identify the advantages and disadvantages of Mexico's City's attempts to reduce pollution;
- identify the advantages and disadvantages of Masdar City's attempts to reduce pollution;
- decide which city seems to be more sustainable.

Ideas for a starter

1. If students completed the Further activity from section 15.8 ask a number of them to feedback what they found out to the class.

2. Show photos of Mexico City shrouded in smog, and a bike from Mexico City's bike rental scheme (called Ecobici) on the whiteboard. Ask: 'What is the link between these two images?' In 1992 Mexico City 'won' the title of most polluted city on the planet. Since then it has made major efforts to manage its pollution including making changes to transport systems — one of which was the introduction of a bike rental scheme.

Ideas for plenaries

1. Have a class debate. The motion is 'We should make existing cities sustainable, rather than build new cities.'

2. Make a graffiti wall of what students have learnt in this chapter on 'The challenges of an urban world'.

Further class and homework activity

Ask students to use the ideas in this section, along with further research, to design a sustainable city. They can locate it anywhere in the world.

The challenges of an urban world

answers

1 a **Advantages** of Mexico City's attempts to reduce pollution: moving heavy industry out of the city means that cleaner services now dominate economic activity; implementation of the Green Plan has made improvements to water supply, transport, climate and waste management; changes to transport have reduced air pollution and driven down CO_2 emissions.

Disadvantages of Mexico City's attempts to reduce pollution: cars still remain a major form of transport; it's expensive – US$1 billion is spent a year on the Green Plan.

b **Advantages** of Masdar City's attempts to reduce pollution: designed on sustainable principles — planned to be free of carbon, waste and pollution; designed with the hot desert in mind; most transport will be provided by a rapid transit system, leaving streets free for pedestrians; energy will be provided from renewable sources.

Disadvantages of Masdar City's attempts to reduce pollution: building it is very expensive — up to US$20 billion; scarce water is being used to cool the air; there is debate about whether it would be better to make existing cities more sustainable, rather than building new ones; there is concern that only the wealthy will benefit from the new city.

c Answers will vary

2 **Exam-style question** *Using examples, explain how far one city you have studied has been successful in trying to reduce pollution. (8 marks)*

Foundation Tier students may answer the alternative question:

Using examples, describe how a city you have studied is trying to reduce pollution. (6 marks)

Foundation Tier answers require three developed or two well-developed descriptions for 6 marks. Cap answers at 3 marks which do not include specific examples from a named city.

Cap answers at 6 marks (4 marks for Foundation Tier answers) which do not:

- clearly state the ways in which pollution is reduced e.g. 'reducing CO_2 emissions and air pollution', not just 'reducing pollution'
- evaluate how far the city has been successful i.e. 'it has been successful because …', not just an explanation of how the attempt has worked.

Suitable attempts for Mexico City or Masdar City include:

- The Green Plan in Mexico City with a brief description — plus development e.g. which has tried to cut car use and air pollution by introducing a rapid bus transit system — and well-developed with an evaluation of the attempt e.g. 'which has been successful because it has led to huge reductions in CO_2 emissions'.
- Plans to make Masdar City free of carbon, waste or pollution — plus development e.g. by using wind towers to draw cool air into homes from the roof — and well-developed with an evaluation of the attempt e.g. 'which has been successful because it has led to reduced need for air conditioning which uses a lot of energy'.

Level	Descriptor
0	No rewardable content
1 (1-3 marks)	Simple or very basic statements using little or no subject vocabulary.
2 (4-6 marks)	Generalised explanations but with some use of geographical terms Up to three developed statements as shown by examples above.
3 (7-8 marks)	Detailed statements with clear evaluation using geographical terms. Two well-developed points plus other developed statements are required for the top of Level 3 as shown by examples above.

16 The challenges of a rural world

About the chapter
These are the key ideas behind the chapter.
- The rural economy in the Lake District includes commercial farming systems and tourism.
- The Lake District's rural population faces challenges related to employment, isolation, declining services and the effects of counter-urbanisation.
- Farmers in the developed world can diversify to generate extra income.
- Rural areas in the developing world face many challenges including rising costs, drought, the impact of rural-urban migration and isolation.
- The rural economy in Malawi varies – including cash-crop plantations, tobacco tenants and smallholders.
- Different groups are involved in rural development projects in developing countries.
- Farming in developing countries can benefit from Fairtrade schemes and intermediate technology.
- Development projects in rural areas in developing countries, are designed to improve opportunities and quality of life.

Chapter outline
Use this outline to provide your students with a brief roadmap of the chapter.

16.1 Life in the Lake District
The varied rural economy in the Lake District.

16.2 Challenges facing the Lake District
The challenges facing the Lake District's rural population.

16.3 How can farmers diversify?
How farmers in the developed world often diversify to earn extra income.

16.4 Life in rural Malawi
How rural areas in northern Malawi face different challenges.

16.5 Malawi's rural economy
How the rural economy varies in Malawi.

16.6 Getting Malawi's economy moving
Some of the different groups involved in rural development projects.

16.7 Looking to a rural future 1
How farming in Malawi can benefit from Fairtrade schemes and intermediate technology.

16.8 Looking to a rural future 2
Development projects which are designed to improve quality of life.

The challenges of a rural world

How is the specification covered?

This chapter covers Topic 8, Unit 2 People and the planet.

8.1 What are the issues facing rural areas?

8.2 How might these issues be resolved?

Key ideas	Detailed content	Pages in students' book
8.1a Rural areas have contrasting economic characteristics.	Explore the varied rural economy in the developed world, including commercial farming systems, employment and service provision in rural areas.	270-271
	Explore the varied rural economy in the developing world, including cash-crop farming for export versus subsistence farming.	278-279
8.1b Rural areas in the developed and developing world face a number of challenges.	Examine rural challenges in a named rural area in a developed country including: rural isolation, changes to rural services, the decline of farm employment, tourist pressures, and the effects of counter-urbanisation.	272-273
	Examine rural challenges in a named rural area in a developing country including: isolation, changing farm economy and landholdings, the impact of rural-urban migration, natural hazards.	276-277, 278-279
8.2a Livelihoods and opportunities for people in rural areas in developing countries can be improved.	Examine the role of different groups involved in development projects in rural areas: national and local government, Non-Governmental Organisations (NGOs), Intergovernmental Organisations (IGOs), local communities.	280-281
	Evaluate initiatives in contrasting rural areas in the developing world designed to improve opportunities and quality of life, e.g. micro-finance, mobile health services and education.	284-285
8.2b The farming economy of rural areas needs to adapt to be economically and environmentally more sustainable.	Explore how developed world farms can diversify to generate new income streams, e.g. specialist crops and food, organic farming, recreation and leisure.	274-275
	Explore how developing world farming can benefit from fair-trade schemes and intermediate technology to reduce soil erosion, improve water supply and raise yields.	282-283

Chapter outcomes

By the end of this chapter, students should be able to:

- Describe how rural economies can vary in the developed world.
- Explain the challenges facing rural areas in a developed country.
- Give examples of the ways in which farmers in the developed world can diversify to generate new income.
- Outline the challenges faced by farmers in a developing country.
- Describe how the rural economy varies in a developing world country.
- Explain how different groups are involved in rural development projects in developing countries, and describe one project.
- Describe how Fairtrade and intermediate technology can benefit farmers in the developing world.
- Outline how a rural development project in a developing country can improve opportunities and quality of life.

16.1 Life in the Lake District

Section in brief

In this section students learn about the varied rural economy in the Lake District.

In the activities, students:

- research and produce a presentation of images of the Lake District, including the advantages and disadvantages of the Lake District as a place to live;
- suggest reasons why there is little manufacturing and few quaternary jobs in the Lake District;
- complete a farm systems diagram for a commercial sheep farmer;
- outline two reasons why there has been a decline in farm employment in the Lake District;
- answer an exam-style question to describe how the rural economy can vary in the developed world.

Key ideas

- The Lake District is one of the UK's most popular National Parks, and home to 45 000 people.
- Most employment in the Lake District is in the tertiary sector, with tourism providing 33% of jobs.
- Only 2% of people work in farming, but farming dominates the landscape.
- A farm system is made up of inputs, processes and outputs.
- The Lake District provides challenges to farming in terms of its relief, soils and climate.

Key vocabulary

farm system, inputs, processes, outputs

Skills practised

Geographical skills: interpreting maps and photos; creating a systems diagram

PLTS: independent enquiry

Section outcomes

By the end of this section, most students should be able to:

- define or explain the terms given in 'Key vocabulary' above;
- suggest reasons why there are few secondary and quaternary jobs in the Lake District;
- describe the rural economy in the Lake District;
- complete a farm systems diagram for a commercial sheep farmer in the Lake District;
- outline the challenges facing farming in the Lake District.

Ideas for a starter

1 Ask students: 'Where is the Lake District? Who can tell me three things about it? What kind of jobs might people do there?'

2 Show students a photo similar to that of Langdale on page 270 of the students' book, on the whiteboard. Ask: 'How does this landscape affect farming? Think about the relief, climate, and so on.'

Ideas for plenaries

1 Ask students why so many people visit the Lake District. What do they do there?

2 Ask students to create a mind map around the phrase 'Life in the Lake District'. How many ideas can they come up with in two minutes?

Further class and homework activity

Ask students to work in pairs to create a spider diagram about the problems that people living in a rural area like the Lake District might face. If they need ideas suggest that they think about things like employment, housing, transport and services such as buses, shops, hospitals etc.

The challenges of a rural world

answers

1. Advantages and disadvantages of the Lake District as a place to live could include: outstanding scenery, lack of highly paid jobs, the climate.

2. a There is little manufacturing in the Lake District due to its relative remoteness and its distance from main markets and sources of labour.

   b Quaternary jobs such as business and financial services tend to cluster in large cities and centres with universities, high levels of population and good transport and communication networks e.g. South East England.

3. Students diagrams should include:

   Inputs: *Physical* — steep slopes; poor soils; cool and wet climate. *Human* — rent / bank loan; labour required; cost of machinery, vet's bills, livestock.

   Processes: *Jobs* — shearing; lambing; taking animals to market. *Physical challenges* — related to weather. *Human challenges* — changes in market price and demand for goods

   Outputs: *Products for sale* — animal produce e.g. lamb, wool, sheep milk. *Products for use on farm* — manure; young livestock.

4. It is cheaper to hire contractors, so the number of full-time jobs has fallen. The physically challenging environment makes it difficult to earn a living, as it is really only suitable for sheep farming.

5. **Exam-style question** *Using examples, describe how the rural economy can vary in the developed world. (6 marks)*

   This question is marked using levels. Cap answers at the top of Level 1 (2 marks) which do not include specific locations in a developed country e.g. the Lake District – not just 'the UK'.

   This answer is looking for examples of variety in the economy. Suitable points include:

   - **Farming:** Brief outline of type of farming e.g. hill sheep farming — plus development e.g. suited to the upland landscape — or well-developed with further expansion e.g. 'with some crop growing on the valley floors'.

   - **Tertiary employment:** Brief outline of tourism e.g. in shops and restaurants — plus development e.g. use of information from page 270 to show its importance — or well-developed with further expansion e.g. with some manufacturing such as nuclear reprocessing at Sellafield.

   - Plus other descriptions on merit.

Level	Descriptor
0	No rewardable content
1 (1-2 marks)	Simple or very basic statements using little or no subject vocabulary. May be a descriptive or basic list of points e.g. 'Tourism and farming are really important in the Lake District.
2 (3-4 marks)	Generalised descriptions but with some use of geographical terms e.g. 'Tourism is important in the Lake District, making up a third of all jobs'. Up to two developed statements as shown by examples above.
3 (5-6 marks)	Detailed statements with clear descriptions using geographical terms. e.g. 'Tourism is important in the Lake District, making up a third of all jobs, including those working in hotels and shops, and also in supply industries such as food'. Three developed or two well-developed points as shown by examples above.

16.2 Challenges facing the Lake District

Section in brief

In this section students learn about the challenges facing the Lake District's rural population. Some of these challenges relate to employment, tourism, isolation, declining services and the cost and availability of housing.

In the activities, students:

- compile a table of the benefits and problems of tourism in the Lake District;
- score the benefits and problems to decide whether the benefits outweigh the problems;
- discuss whether counter-urbanisation is good or bad for the Lake District and draw a spider diagram of their ideas;
- answer an exam-style question to explain the challenges facing rural areas in a developed country.

Key ideas

- Tourists bring many benefits to the Lake District.
- The number of full-time, tourism jobs is small, and unemployment is a problem.
- The Lake District is isolated and it is difficult to live there without a car.
- Some services in the Lake District are declining.
- Counter-urbanisation and second homes have led to rapidly rising house prices.

Key vocabulary

counter-urbanisation

Skills practised

Geographical skills: identifying and evaluating benefits and problems of tourism

PLTS: independent enquiry; team-working

Section outcomes

By the end of this section, most students should be able to:

- define the term given in 'Key vocabulary' above;
- list the benefits and problems tourism creates for the Lake District;
- describe the problems that the isolated nature of the Lake District causes for people who live there;
- explain why some services are declining in the Lake District;
- decide whether counter-urbanisation is good or bad for the Lake District.

Ideas for a starter

1. If students completed the Further Activity from section 16.1 ask a number of them to feedback what they found out to the class.
2. Show students a video clip of the Lake District National Park so that they can get a sense of the landscape. You should be able to find something suitable the Lake District National Park website. Once they have seen the clip ask students what challenges the people who live in this rural landscape face.

Ideas for plenaries

1. Tell students to imagine that they live in Ambleside. They should write a letter to the local newspaper expressing their views about the challenges of living in the Lake District.
2. Give students eight minutes to answer the exam-style question in the students' book.

Further class and homework activity

Tell students they should imagine that they own a second home in Ambleside. They should write a letter to the local newspaper responding to criticisms that they cause a problem for residents of the Lake District.

The challenges of a rural world

answers

1 a Students tables should include the following, as well as anything else they have found as a result of their own research.

Benefits of tourism in the Lake District:

- Income for the local economy — tourists spend money on. accommodation, food and drink, recreation, shopping and transport.
- Jobs — 55% of jobs in Windermere and Keswick come from tourism.
- Tourists help to support local services — such public transport, shops, cafes etc.
- Car park charges generate money for local councils.
- Farmers benefit by selling local produce and providing accommodation.
- Second homeowners spend a lot with local builders and suppliers.

Problems of tourism in the Lake District:

- High seasonal unemployment — many jobs in tourism are only available in the summer month and are low-paid / part-time.
- Traffic congestion as most tourists arrive by car.
- High demand for second homes have pushed up house prices, which are now unaffordable for local people.
- Second home owners are often not there, meaning businesses may close in winter, and communities are destroyed.

b and **c** Answers will vary.

2 Answers will vary depending upon students' point of view.

3 Exam-style question Using examples, explain the challenges facing rural areas in a developed country. (8 marks)

Foundation Tier students may answer the alternative question:

Using examples, describe the challenges facing rural areas in a developed country. (6 marks)

In this case, three developed or two well-developed descriptions are required for 6 marks.

Cap answers at 3 marks which do not include specific locations in a developed country. Cap answers at 6 marks which do not specify the *challenges* faced.

Suitable challenges include:

- A description of challenges posed by tourism, with examples e.g. types of employment in the Lake District — developed with reasons e.g. most jobs are temporary because they only occur in summer — or well-developed e.g. many people don't benefit as jobs in hotels and restaurants are also low paid / part-time.
- Problems facing rural services, with examples e.g. buses, roads or weather — developed with reasons e.g. 'many roads suffer summer congestion caused by tourist traffic' — or well-developed e.g. 'which can create problems for emergency vehicles if someone needs to get to hospital'.

Level	Descriptor
0	No rewardable content
1 (1-3 marks)	Simple or very basic statements using little or no subject vocabulary.
2 (4-6 marks)	Generalised explanations but with some use of geographical terms. Up to three developed statements as shown by examples above.
3 (7-8 marks)	Detailed statements with clear explanations using geographical terms. e.g. 'Winter weather can be a challenge in the Lake District because snow can block country roads, and can drift on the hills. Children face problems in getting to school and farmers lose sheep'. Two well-developed points plus other developed statements are required for the top of Level 3 as shown by examples above.

16.3 How can farmers diversify?

Section in brief

In this section students learn how farmers in the developed world diversify to earn extra income. Diversification activities can be either farm-based, or non-farm based.

In the activities, students:

- list the problems that farmers in the Lake District face;
- list the things needed to develop a business such as Low Sizergh Barn;
- put together a plan to persuade a bank to lend money for a business;
- explain the benefits that Low Sizergh Barn and Holmescales can bring;
- decide which business best suits the Lake District and the people who live there;
- answer an exam-style question to explain how farmers in the developed world can diversify to generate new income.

Key ideas

- Farmers sometimes find their income threatened by events outside their control.
- Farmers diversify — widen the range of goods and services they offer — in order to reduce the risks their businesses face.
- Some diversification consists of farm-based activities — based around the business of farming.
- Some diversification consists of non-farm based activities — which use farmland, but for different purposes.

Key vocabulary

diversify

Skills practised

Geographical skills: identify the problems that farmers face; explaining the benefits that diversification activities can bring

PLTS: independent enquiry; creative thinking; team-working

Section outcomes

By the end of this section, most students should be able to:

- define the term given in 'Key vocabulary' above;
- identify the problems that farmers in the Lake District face;
- explain the difference between farm-based and non-farm based diversification activities;
- explain the benefits that different types of diversification activities can bring to farmers, the local community and the Lake District.

Ideas for a starter

1. Recap the challenges farmers in the Lake District face from section 16.1.
2. Show photos similar to those in this section of farm diversification, i.e. quad biking, children feeding a calf, paintballing etc. Ask: 'What have these activities go to do with farming?'

Ideas for plenaries

1. Ask students to work in small groups to think of other ways in which farms could diversify. How many different activities can they come up with?
2. Use question 3b as a plenary activity. Take a class vote on which business students think best suits the Lake District and the people who live there. Complete a spider diagram of the reasons why students think the business suits the Lake District.

Further class and homework activity

Ask students to complete the exam-style question as a homework activity.

The challenges of a rural world

answers

1 The problems farmers in the Lake District face include: poor soils; tough climate; poor relief. Many events are also outside their control e.g. weather, Chernobyl explosion, high cost of animal feed, low incomes.

2 a Get planning permission; get a loan from the bank; convert a barn for the business; produce information for the barn; create a farm trail; source goods for the gift shop; prepare food for the café and shop.

b Answers will vary.

3 a i The farmer: Low Sizergh Barn and Holmescales have expanded their business and increased turnover, making farming more secure.

ii The local community: may gain employment; other businesses may also benefit from increasing visitor numbers to the area.

iii Lake District: increased visitor numbers — attracting people in the winter months as well as the summer.

b Answers will vary.

---

4 Exam-style question *Using examples, explain how farmers in the developed world can diversify to generate new income. (8 marks)*

Foundation Tier students may answer the alternative question:

Using examples, describe ways in which farmers in the developed world can use their farms to create new income. (6 marks)

In this case, three developed or two well-developed descriptions are required for 6 marks.

Cap answers at the top of Level 1 (3 marks) which do not include named locations in the developed world. Cap answers at the top of Level 2 (6 marks) which do not include specific activities– e.g. 'using land for leisure purposes such as renting out campsites' — not just 'they make money from tourism'.

Suitable examples of diversification include:

- Farm-based activities, with examples e.g. a farm shop and café — developed with reasons e.g. 'which helps to increase value-added on farm products such as vegetables or meat' — or well-developed with further expansion e.g. 'which can expand to making higher-value ready meals'.

- Non-farm-based activities, with examples e.g. 'adventure challenges such as paintballing' — developed with reasons e.g. 'for urban companies on team-building days' — or well-developed with further expansion e.g. 'and family activities like off-roading or mountain biking'.

Level	Descriptor
0	No rewardable content
1 (1-3 marks)	Simple or very basic statements using little or no subject vocabulary. May be a list e.g. 'farmers have many ways of making extra money such as farm shops'.
2 (4-6 marks)	Generalised explanations but with some use of geographical terms e.g. 'farmers can diversify to make extra income from meat or vegetables such as farm shops'. Up to three developed statements as shown by examples above.
3 (7-8 marks)	Detailed statements with clear explanations using geographical terms. e.g. 'farmers can diversify to make extra income from farm-based activities such as selling meat or vegetables in their own farm shop, which adds extra value to their produce'. Two well-developed points plus other developed statements are required for the top of Level 3 as shown by examples above.

16.4 Life in rural Malawi

Section in brief

In this section students learn about some of the challenges facing rural areas in northern Malawi.

In the activities, students:

- explain why good roads and improved telecommunications are important if rural Malawi is to develop;
- list the ways in which a farm system in Malawi is different to a hill farm in the UK;
- complete a table to show the impacts of climate change on small farmers in northern Malawi;
- list the benefits and problems for a rural family if a husband/father leaves to work in the city;
- answer an exam-style question to outline one challenge faced by farmers in a developing country.

Key ideas

- Many farmers in Malawi suffer from problems of rising costs and falling prices.
- Climate change in Malawi is resulting in lower rainfall and drought.
- Male family members in rural areas often move to towns or cities to find work and send remittance payments home.
- Much of rural northern Malawi is isolated with poor infrastructure and telecommunications.

Key vocabulary

remittance payments, infrastructure

Skills practised

Geographical skills: classify impacts of climate change

PLTS: independent enquiry

Section outcomes

By the end of this section, most students should be able to:

- define or explain the terms given in 'Key vocabulary' above;
- outline three challenges faced by farmers in rural northern Malawi;
- classify the potential impacts of climate change on farmers in northern Malawi;
- list the benefits and problems for a rural family if a husband/father leaves to work in the city;
- explain why good roads and improved communications are important if rural Malawi is to develop.

Ideas for a starter

1. Ask students: 'Who can be the first to find Malawi on a world map, or in an atlas? Who can describe its location?'
2. Tell students some information about Malawi to introduce this section. It is one of the world's most densely populated and least developed countries. 80% of the population live in rural areas. Agriculture accounts for one-third of GDP and 90% of export revenue. Tobacco is hugely important and makes up more than half of all exports.

Ideas for plenaries

1. Discuss question 1 on page 277 of the student's book as a class. Students can write up the answer later.
2. Make a graffiti wall of what students have learnt from this section.

Further class and homework activity

Ask students to find out about tobacco farming in Malawi. They should find out:

- how much tobacco is produced,
- how much the tobacco is worth,
- tobacco estates and smallholders,
- the use of child labour in tobacco farming.

The challenges of a rural world

answers

1. **a** Malawi is very dependent on tobacco exports, and needs to be able to transport tobacco via road from the farmers in rural areas, to market towns and then onwards for export. Improved roads are important therefore for the transport of tobacco and higher export earnings. The more easily it can be transported the more likely it is rural Malawi will be able to develop.

   b Telecommunications are needed for the communication of ideas and information. Without improved telecommunications rural Malawi will find it difficult to develop.

2. Mozesi's farm is different in terms of:

   a **Inputs:** *Physical* — small farm, only 2 hectares; *Human* — labour and hand tools; fertiliser (high cost).

   b **Processes:** *Jobs done* — ploughing; sowing; harvesting. *Challenges* — drought and water shortages / reduced rainfall; very heavy rain destroying crops.

   c **Outputs:** *To feed family* — maize; *For sale* — tobacco.

3. Potential impacts of climate change on small farmers in Malawi include:

   Economic impacts: crops fail due to drought; crop yield reduced due to heavy rain.

   Social impacts: loss of income; flooding destroys homes; food shortages; water shortages.

   Environmental impacts: drought; variable rainfall; flooding; increased desertification.

4. Potential impacts on a rural family if the husband / father leaves to work in the city:

   Benefits: money sent home (remittance payments); increased family income; money can help to pay for medical and school fees.

   Problems: women, young children and elderly are left behind; fewer people are left to work the land which makes farming harder; yields fall, so there is less to eat or sell; land is under-used; families are less likely to afford new farming techniques.

---

5. **Exam-style question** *Outline one challenge faced by farmers in a developing country. (3 marks)*

   This question is point marked. It requires one developed description of a challenge for 2 marks plus a located example of a developing country. A country must be named; cap any answer which does not name one at 2 marks.

   Suitable challenges include:

   - Rising prices of products such as fertilisers (1) — plus development e.g. 'which means that the farmer has to either has to pay more or use less (1) — with an added location (1).
   - Rural-urban migration of younger people (1) — plus development e.g. 'which means there are few young, energetic people to work the land' (1) — with an added location (1).
   - Plus other points on merit.

16.5 Malawi's rural economy

Section in brief

In this section students learn how the rural economy varies in Malawi.

In the activities, students:

- complete diagrams to show the problems that farmers face, what decisions affect them, who is making the decisions and where they are being made;
- explain how farmers lives are linked to the lives of people in the UK;
- research, and write a letter about the use of child labour in Malawi;
- answer an exam-style question to describe how the rural economy can vary in a developing country.

Key ideas

- Over 80% of Malawi's population works in farming and the country depends on cash crops for its exports.
- Cash crop plantations grow tea, coffee and tobacco, and many estates are British owned.
- Almost all adult tobacco growers work as tobacco tenants for tobacco companies.
- Malawi has high levels of child labour working in the tobacco industry.
- Most farmers are smallholders working small plots - many are subsistence farmers.

Key vocabulary

subsistence farming

Skills practised

Geographical skills: describe the varied rural economy in a developing country

PLTS: independent enquiry; creative thinking; team-working; effective participation

Literacy skills: writing a letter

Section outcomes

By the end of this section, most students should be able to:

- explain the term given in 'Key vocabulary' above;
- complete diagrams to show the problems farmers in Malawi face, what decisions affect them, who is making the decisions and where they are being made;
- explain how farmers lives are linked to the lives of people in the UK;
- write a letter to explain their view about the use of child labour.

Ideas for a starter

1. Recap section 16.4 – life in rural Malawi and the different challenges people face.
2. Read the text box 'The other face of tobacco' from page 278 of the students' book aloud to students. What is their reaction to Chisomo's story?

Ideas for plenaries

1. Ask students to put themselves in Chisomo's shoes and write a diary entry for a day in her life.
2. Use the 'What do you think?' bubble on page 278 to start a class discussion about child labour.

Further class and homework activity

Ask students to create a mind map about Malawi's rural economy, based on the information in this section.

The challenges of a rural world

answers

1 a Students' diagrams should include the information given in the table below.

	Cash crop plantations	Tobacco tenants	Smallholders
Problems faced	Landless labourers and subsistence farmers work on plantations. They face the problem of low wages.	Many workers are children. Workers lack medication, housing, safe water and food. Tenants lose money on tobacco grown.	Lack of investment. Costs of fertiliser, oil and transport have all risen. Many farmers are only subsistence farmers.
What decisions are being made?	Decisions about wages and employees terms and conditions.	Decisions about the cost of seed and fertiliser affects farmers' profits.	Decisions about what to grow and how to grow it.
Who is making the decisions and where?	Decisions are made by large companies, TNCs, including those in British ownership. Decisions may be made overseas.	Decisions are made by tobacco estate owners (large companies, such as British American Tobacco), probably in Malawi.	Farmers make own decisions.

b Many large estates are owned by British TNCs e.g. 'Unilever' which produces PG tips; people in the UK buy the tea, coffee and tobacco grown and picked by farmers working on the plantations; people in the UK may own shares in companies that own large estates and employ tobacco tenants; rising prices in the UK may result in additional income for smallholders in Malawi.

2 a and **b** Answers will vary.

3 Exam-style question *Using examples, describe how the rural economy can vary in a developing country you have studied. (6 marks)*

This question is marked using levels. Cap answers at the top of Level 1 (2 marks) which do not include examples from developing countries e.g. Malawi.

Suitable descriptions include:

- **Variations in farm holdings:** Differences described between cash crop plantations and another form of farming, such as smallholdings — with brief definitions e.g. 'large foreign-owned estates' / 'which consists mainly of subsistence farmers' — plus development e.g. 'often owned by large multi-national companies' / 'often owned by individual families' — well-developed with expansion.

- **Variations in farm products:** Differences described between types of crops produced e.g. tobacco / tea, and maize / rice — plus development eg. on large / small farms — well-developed with expansion e.g. 'which are sold mainly for export' / 'which are grown mainly by subsistence farmers for their own consumption'.

Level	Descriptor
0	No rewardable content
1 (1-2 marks)	Simple or very basic statements using little or no subject vocabulary.
2 (3-4 marks)	Generalised descriptions but with some use of geographical terms. Up to two developed statements as shown by examples above.
3 (5-6 marks)	Detailed statements with clear descriptions using geographical terms. e.g. 'Many farmers work on plantations which are large estates growing tea and tobacco for export, whilst others are subsistence farmers producing food crops for themselves'. Three developed or two well-developed points as shown by examples above.

16.6 Getting Malawi's economy moving

Section in brief

In this section, students look at how two kinds of organisations — governments and non-governmental organisations — can kick-start rural development projects in developing countries like Malawi.

In the activities, students:

- complete a table about the two rural development projects included in this section;
- decide which of the two projects they would recommend for solving rural poverty and families affected by HIV/AIDS;
- answer an exam-style question to explain how one organisation has helped to develop rural areas.

Key ideas

- Development projects can be funded by governments, international or inter-governmental organisations (IGOs) and non-governmental organisations (NGOs).
- The Sustainable Livelihoods Programme is funded by the UNDP and is promoting mushroom growing.
- The mushroom growing scheme is cheap and sustainable, and has been a success.
- NGO 'World Vision' supports a project to develop fish farming with rural families affected by HIV/AIDS.
- The fish farming project has had wide-ranging benefits.

Key vocabulary

micro-loans, inter-governmental organisations (IGOs), non-governmental organisations (NGOs)

Skills practised

Geographical skills: identifying and classifying benefits of projects

PLTS: independent enquiry; creative thinking

Section outcomes

By the end of this section, most students should be able to:

- define or explain the terms given in Key vocabulary above;
- understand that development projects can be funded in different ways;
- complete a table to show the benefits and spin-off effects of two rural development projects;
- decide which of the two projects they would recommend for solving rural poverty and families affected by HIV/AIDS.

Ideas for a starter

1. Remind students about Mozesi Katsonga, the farmer from section 16.4. Tell them that global anti-smoking campaigns have reduced the demand for his tobacco. What ideas can students come up with to help farmers like Mozesi, and improve Malawi's rural economy?

2. Ask students what these terms mean: inter-governmental organisations (IGOs) and non-governmental organisations (NGOs). What do they do? Who can give you some examples of each?

Ideas for plenaries

1. Ask students to work in pairs to write two paragraphs (one each) about how development projects can improve the economy in rural Malawi.

2. Ask students to think back over this section and write down two questions related to what they have learned. Ask other members of the class to try to answer them.

Further class and homework activity

Ask students to complete a pyramid review of this lesson. They should arrange the following in the shape of a pyramid:

- one question they have,
- two points they are not sure of,
- three points they have learned.

The challenges of a rural world

answers

1 a

	MUSHROOM FARMING	FISH FARMING
Type of project (e.g. NGO or government)		
	IGO (Malawian government plus UNDP)	NGO (World Vision)
How is the project financed?		
	Government using UNDP money to: provide training; offer micro-loans to buy the first mushroom compost; pay for an advertising programme.	Farmers are helped by World Vision to dig small ponds. Fish are fed on farm and kitchen waste.
Economic benefits		
	Micro-loans are rapidly repaid. Mushrooms provide an alternative source of income.	Provides a regular income for farmers. The project has doubled the income of 1200 households.
Social benefits		
	Mushrooms are high in protein and have medicinal properties. Income is used to fund other developments.	Fish is highly nutritious for HIV/AIDS patients increasing life expectancy by up to 8 years. Child malnutrition has been reduced by 30%.
Environmental benefits		
	Mushroom growers use waste from other crops as raw material for the mushroom compost.	The ponds provide water for crops during droughts. Farms with ponds are 20% more productive than those without. Pond bottom sediment provides fertiliser.
Additional benefits		
	Villagers have started other businesses e.g. raising hens (for eggs), fruit juices, vegetable oil, honey, bakeries.	Fish and vegetable consumption has increased among rural communities. The project has helped women who form 30% of those taking part.

b i Both projects have been successful in solving rural poverty.

ii The fish farming project is the best for families affected by HIV/AIDS.

---

2 Exam-style question *Using examples, explain how one organisation has helped to develop rural areas. (8 marks)*

Cap answers at 6 marks which do not include the name of a specific organisation and the country in which it operates. Suitable organisations and their work include:

- Malawi's Sustainable Livelihoods Programme, mushroom growing in Ndawambe —developed with reasons e.g. 'which involves training farmers in growing mushrooms as a cash crop' — or well-developed 'which is financed by micro-loans which are cheap and easily paid off'.

- The work of World Vision in Malawi, with example e.g. fish farming — developed with explanation e.g. 'which involves villagers digging out rain-fed ponds in which fish can be kept' — or well-developed 'which is cheap and can produce up to 1.5 tonnes of fish per year'.

Level	Descriptor
0	No rewardable content
1 (1-3 marks)	Simple or very basic statements using little or no subject vocabulary.
2 (4-6 marks)	Generalised explanations but with some use of geographical terms. Up to three developed statements as shown by examples above.
3 (7-8 marks)	Detailed statements with clear explanations using geographical terms. Two well-developed points plus other developed statements as shown by examples above.

16.7 Looking to a rural future 1

Section in brief

In this section students find out how farming in rural Malawi can benefit from intermediate technology and Fairtrade schemes.

In the activities, students:

- design a flow chart to show the causes, processes and impacts of soil erosion;
- explain how a photo showing contour ploughing could be used to help train farmers;
- design a poster to show the different methods being used by the COVAMS project;
- complete a table to show the impacts of Fairtrade on Middle Shire;
- answer an exam-style question to describe how Fairtrade can benefit farmers in the developing world.

Key ideas

- Deforestation in Malawi has resulted in soil erosion.
- A Malawian and Japanese IGO is working on a project (COVAMS) involving local people using intermediate technology to conserve the soil and replant trees.
- The Kasinthula Cane Growers Project was set up to provide income for subsistence farmers.
- The Project was certified for Fairtrade, earning extra money which has been spent on community development projects.

Key vocabulary

soil erosion, inter-governmental organisation (IGO), intermediate technology, Fairtrade

Skills practised

Geographical skills: design flow diagrams; classify impacts

PLTS: creative thinking; team-working

Section outcomes

By the end of this section, most students should be able to:

- define or explain the terms given in 'Key vocabulary' above;
- design a flow diagram to show the causes, processes and impacts of soil erosion;
- design a poster to show the different methods being used by the COVAMS project;
- complete a table to show the economic, social and environmental impacts of Fairtrade on Middle Shire.

Ideas for a starter

1. Show a photo of soil erosion similar to that on page 282 of the students' book on the whiteboard. Ask: 'What is happening here? What is causing this? What impacts does this have?'
2. Ask students what they know about Fairtrade. How does it help people in developing countries? Use this opportunity to explore the Fairtrade website www.fairtrade.org.uk on the interactive whiteboard, and to answer any questions students might have.

Ideas for plenaries

1. Discuss as a class how soil conservation can help rural areas in poorer countries to develop.
2. Use the exam-style question on page 283 of the students' book as a plenary.

Further class and homework activity

Ask students to find out about the Grameen Bank in preparation for the next lesson. They should find out what it is, where it operates and who benefits from it.

The challenges of a rural world

answers

1 Causes: Deforestation — as more land is needed to grow crops/food for a growing population, and tobacco to maintain export income.

Processes: Heavy rain runs down deforested hillsides and removes soil.

Impacts: Rivers and lakes silt up, reducing water flow and HEP output; potential for eco-tourism is threatened; decline in crop yields.

2 By ploughing around the hillside (i.e. contour ploughing) before planting crops, farmers can reduce surface runoff and soil erosion.

3 Answers will vary.

4

Economic impacts	Social impacts	Environmental impacts
Fairtrade sales provide higher income for subsistence farmers. Cash payments have enabled farmers to replace sugar cane plants and machinery.	Boreholes provide clean water, and taps are being installed in farmers' homes. Electricity has been provided. Secondary school built. Health clinic opened with four bicycle ambulances.	Poor land has been converted into productive sugar cane plots.

5 Exam-style question *Using examples, describe how Fairtrade can benefit farmers in the developing world. (6 marks)*

This question is marked using levels. Cap answers at the top of Level 1 (3 marks) which do not include examples from the developing world. Examples must be at most at a national scale, e.g. Malawi, but preferably the name of a project e.g. the Kasinthula Cane Growers Project. Suitable methods include:

- *Farming* benefits e.g. higher prices for sugar-cane farmers — plus development e.g. 'by working as a co-operative to buy and sell sugar' — or well-developed with further expansion e.g. 'and sells sugar at a guaranteed price which makes a good living for farmers'.
- *Community* benefits e.g. using profits to fund community projects — plus development e.g. 'a secondary school and health clinic' — or well-developed with further expansion e.g. 'together with clean water boreholes and electricity'.

Level	Descriptor
0	No rewardable content
1 (1-2 marks)	Simple or very basic statements using little or no subject vocabulary. May be a descriptive or basic list of points e.g. 'Fairtrade has given farmers a good price for their crops.'
2 (3-4 marks)	Generalised descriptions but with some use of geographical terms e.g. 'The Kasinthula Cane Growers Project is a Fairtrade project which gives farmers a fair price for their sugar crops'. Up to two developed statements as shown.
3 (5-6 marks)	Detailed statements with clear descriptions using geographical terms. e.g. 'The Kasinthula Cane Growers Project is a Fairtrade project which gives farmers a guaranteed fair price for their sugar and allows them to fund schools for village children'. Three developed or two well-developed points as shown by examples above.

16.8 Looking to a rural future 2

Section in brief

In this section students explore development projects designed to improve quality of life for poor communities in developing countries.

In the activities, students:

- complete a table to show the benefits of each of the projects;
- decide which project has the greatest benefits for the local economy, for people and communities, and overall;
- decide which project is the best for long-term development and how far they would suit Malawi;
- answer an exam-style question to explain how a rural development project can improve opportunities and quality of life.

Key ideas

- Poor communities often need small, affordable development projects over which they have some control, in order to improve quality of life.
- India's biogas plants have created 200 000 permanent jobs and brought a range of other benefits to Indian villages.
- The Grameen Bank is a micro-finance bank in Bangladesh which makes small loans to the rural poor.
- Mobile health clinics in South Africa, developed by 'Anglo-American', bring free health services to remote rural areas.

Key vocabulary

There is no key vocabulary in this section.

Skills practised

Geographical skills: classifying benefits of development projects; explaining how rural development projects can improve quality of life

PLTS: independent enquiry; team-working

Section outcomes

By the end of this section, most students should be able to:

- Identify the social, economic and environmental benefits of the development projects;
- decide which project has the greatest benefits for the local economy, for people and communities, and overall;
- decide which project would be best for long-term development;
- explain how a rural development project can improve opportunities and quality of life.

Ideas for a starter

1. If any students completed the Further Activity from section 16.7, ask them to present what they found out about the Grameen Bank to the rest of the class.

2. Recap India's big development project – the Sardar Sarovar Dam from section 12.8. Ask students what benefits big projects like this bring, and what problems they cause. Then explore the idea that what lots of poor communities need are, small affordable projects over which they have some control.

Ideas for plenaries

1. One of the benefits of biogas plants in India is that girls have more time to go to school. Discuss as a class why this is important, and the impacts it can have.

2. Ask students to tell their partner the three most important things they have learnt from this section. Now ask them to tell them another two things which are interesting, but less important.

Further class and homework activity

Ask students to choose one of the development projects and to create a thirty second soundbite for a radio programme about it.

The challenges of a rural world

answers

1 a i Biogas plants

Short-term: *Social* — time saved as women/girls no longer have to gather fuel.

Medium-term: *Social* — better health; less disease from cattle dung; water pumped by electricity generated by biogas; electricity provides light at night.

Long-term: *Social* — girls can go to school. *Economic* — 200,000 permanent jobs; increased incomes (families are now able to produce 3 crops a year). *Environmental* — land improves due to better fertiliser; cattle graze in compounds, so woodland can regenerate.

ii Grameen bank

Medium-term: *Social* — people not dependent on aid. *Economic* — loans repaid in short period.

Long-term: *Social* — communities benefit e.g. from wells, farm equipment and livestock. *Economic* — people develop business skills; people earn more and are lifted out of poverty.

iii Mobile health clinics

Short-term: *Social* — medical help can improve some conditions immediately.

Medium-term: *Economic* — people are more likely to be able to work if healthy.

Long-term: *Social* — long term health will improve due to treatment.

b i The Grameen Bank — small loans encourage people to start small businesses, increasing spending in the local economy.

ii The biogas plants — benefit more people in terms of saved time, improved health, easier dung collection, regeneration of woodland, provision of electricity and water for the village.

iii Answers will vary.

c and **d** Answers will vary.

---

2 Exam-style question *Using examples, explain how a rural development project can improve opportunities and the quality of life. (8 marks)*

Foundation Tier students may answer the alternative question:

Describe how a named rural development project you have studied can improve quality of life for people. (6 marks)

In this case, three developed or two well-developed descriptions are required for 6 marks.

Cap answers at the top of Level 2 (6 marks) which do not include: details of a project from a named location, and improvements in *opportunities* and *quality of life.*

Suitable links to **improved opportunities** include:

- The Grameen Bank in Bangladesh — plus development of its impacts e.g. 'micro-loans given to women to buy livestock' — or well-developed e.g. 'which allows them to earn their own income and repay the loan quickly'.

Suitable links to **quality of life** include:

- The example of biogas in India, with brief outline — plus development of its impacts e.g. 'it frees women and girls from the burden of collecting firewood' — or well-developed with further expansion e.g. 'which allows girls to attend school and achieve an education'.

Level	Descriptor
0	No rewardable content
1 (1-3 marks)	Simple or very basic statements using little or no subject vocabulary.
2 (4-6 marks)	Generalised explanations but with some use of geographical terms. Up to three developed statements as shown by examples above.
3 (7-8 marks)	Detailed statements with clear explanations using geographical terms. Two well-developed points plus other developed statements are required for the top of Level 3 as shown by examples above.

Unit 3

17 Making geographical decisions

Introduction to Unit 3

Unit 3 poses perhaps the greatest change to the Geography GCSE B specification. It is the Unit about which teachers are most concerned. This chapter gives some guidance on how to prepare students for the examination.

The examination differs from its predecessor in that it has no specific content that students can learn or revise. There is no pre-release booklet. Instead, the exam consists of an unseen Resource Booklet which requires geographical skill in interpreting new material, and geographical knowledge and understanding from Units 1 and 2 in order to answer the exam questions for Unit 3.

The Key Ideas

Six 'Key Ideas' form the specification for Unit 3. These are printed in the student textbook on pages 286-287. They are largely about sustainability. Students need to know and understand the meaning of these. They are not intended to be taught discretely — teachers should integrate and highlight these throughout the course. It is therefore important that teachers help students to:

- understand links between the compulsory topics *within* each of Units 1 and 2, i.e. Chapters 1-4 and 9-12 in the student textbook,
- understand links *between* the compulsory topics Units 1 and those in Unit 2,
- know the six Key Ideas in Unit 3,
- ensure that students realise that specific knowledge and understanding from Units 1 and 2 will be assessed in the examination for Unit 3.

Teaching and preparing students for Unit 3

There are several ways in which teachers can prepare students for the examination in Unit 3:

- Teach Unit 1 and 2 topics alternately. For example, Restless Earth and Changing climate (Unit 1), could be followed by, Population dynamics and Consuming resources (Unit 2). This has the advantage of helping students to learn elements of physical and human Geography, and to develop awareness of the breadth of the subject, but in itself, it is not sufficient to prepare students for Unit 3.
- Allow more teaching time for teaching the second Unit that you teach from Units 1 and 2. For example, if you teach Unit 1 first, allow more time for Unit 2 topics. The purpose of this is to 'refer back' at appropriate points. This has the benefit of ensuring revision of previous topics as well as linkages between topics, but again, in itself, it will not be sufficient to guarantee adequate preparation for Unit 3.

Making geographical decisions

More successful is likely to be two mutual approaches to curriculum planning:

Teach **content** linked to Unit 3 Key Ideas:

- Plan a skeletal teaching programme for each of Units 1 and 2, including indicative examples, to ensure coverage.
- Identify potential linkages between topics in each Unit.
- Review the Key Ideas in Unit 3. Identify opportunities in which to focus upon these and make them explicit to students, via linkages between topics in Units 1 and 2.
- Develop a teaching programme which contains examples where students can see explicit links between Units 1 and 2, and which enables them to develop awareness and understanding of the Key Ideas in Unit 3.

Teach **geographical skills** relevant to Unit 3:
Knowledge and understanding via specification coverage is not sufficient in itself to prepare students fully for the examination. In addition, students need to gain:

- **Skills in interpreting geographical sources** e.g. a range of photographs, maps, data, graphs and text.
- Experience in **handling unseen materials**, in lessons as well as in timed examination conditions. A single 'mock' examination will not provide sufficient experience, so develop an approach where you confront students with unseen geographical sources and ask students to interpret these.
- Insight into **issues with geographical dimensions**, i.e. where there are issues with controversial causes, and where there may be several possible proposals for their resolution.
- Experience in which students **describe and analyse secondary sources** e.g. data, text and spatial distributions.
- Experience in **justifying a choice of a possible solution** to resolve an issue, including the use of extended writing.

Example: Planning a case study of a large water management project

- In teaching Unit 1, Topic 4 'Water world' *(Costs and benefits of a large-scale water management scheme)*, make links with Unit 2 Topic 4 'Development dilemmas' *(Evaluate the impact of one large top-down project on different groups of people in a developing country)*.
- Develop teaching resources which will ensure that you meet the specification requirements of each of these Topics, i.e. teach costs and benefits, and assess impacts.
- Introduce Key Idea 1 from Unit 3 in teaching your case study for these Topics *('Examine contrasting ways of judging whether development is sustainable socially, economically or environmentally')*. Provide a framework by which students assess impacts of the water management project.
- Support this approach by referring also to Key Idea 3 in Unit 3 *('Consider how pressures on resources are likely to increase in the future, due to population growth and increasing affluence through development and globalisation and how this can lead to conflict between different individuals and organisations')* in order to assess how far dams are a widespread phenomenon around the world. In this way, you'll broaden student perspectives outside their chosen case study.

325

Opportunities for teaching the Key Ideas

Key Idea 1 — Sustainable development is an important concept.

- Investigate the 'Brundtland' definition of sustainable development – 'whether current social and economic needs can be met while protecting the environment and its resources for future generations'.
- Ways of judging whether development is sustainable socially, economically or environmentally by comparing small scale bottom-up projects using intermediate technology, with large scale, top-down approaches.

Examples in this book which could help you prepare for this include:

- Section 3.5 – threats to the Biosphere.
- Sections 4.7 and 4.8 – solutions to the water crisis in developed and developing countries.
- Section 12.7 – biogas and sustainable development in rural India.

Key Idea 2 — Since the 1990s environmental sustainability has become increasingly important.

- Investigate attitudes towards environmental sustainability e.g. those of TNCs, governments, NGOs and pressure groups such as Greenpeace.
- Explore reasons why these organisations have different attitudes towards environmental sustainability and adopt different polices, e.g. no-growth and switching to renewable resources.

Examples in this book which could help you prepare for this include:

- Section 3.4 – conflicts of interest in St Lucia.
- Section 11.6 – who wins and loses from Globalisation?
- Section 12.7 – the debate about GM crops and sustainable development.

Key Idea 3 — Demand for resources is rising globally but resource supply is often finite which may lead to conflict.

- Investigate how pressure on resources can lead to environmental and social problems, at a range of scales, e.g. the exploitation of forests, energy and water resources.
- Consider how pressures on resources are likely to increase, due to population growth and affluence through development and globalisation — and how this leads to conflict between individuals and organisations, e.g. oil drilling in Nigeria and conflicts between TNCs, governments, local people and NGOs.

Examples in this book which could help you prepare for this include:

- Section 2.5 – how human activity can change the atmosphere and may be a cause of climate change.
- Section 9.1 – the rising global population.
- Section 10.1 and 10.2 – increasing global demands on resources.

Making geographical decisions

Key Idea 4 — Balancing the needs of economic development and conservation is a difficult challenge.

- Investigate how governments try to meet economic and social needs but also protect the environment, e.g. conservation areas and greenbelts versus urban and industrial development.
- Investigate how global organisations e.g. the United Nations, have become more important in managing environmental threats, and why national governments have differing attitudes to global agreements e.g. Kyoto Protocol.

Examples in this book which could help you prepare for this include:

- Section 3.7 – ways of conserving the biosphere e.g. RAMSAR.
- Section 4.8 – the development of small-scale solutions to problems of water supply.
- Section 10.7 – how governments encourage the development of renewable energies.

Key Idea 5 — Achieving sustainable development requires funding, management and leadership.

- Examine the management and funding challenges for governments trying to achieve sustainable development both locally and nationally, e.g. renewable national energy targets and recycling.
- Investigate the role of NGOs in achieving sustainable development, e.g. the impact of environmental groups on deforestation or the campaign to promote fair trade.

Examples in this book which could help you prepare for this include:

- Section 2.9 – how Egypt is threatened by climate change.
- Section 3.8 – encouraging the sustainable management of ecosystems.
- Section 10.10 – the development of renewable energies and technologies.

Key Idea 6 — Physical processes and environmental changes increasingly put people at risk.

- Examine trends in population and urbanisation to understand why increasing numbers of people, property and livelihoods are vulnerable to tectonic hazards and the impacts of climate change.
- Investigate why managing risks is challenging due to the rising demand for places to live and the uncertain and unpredictable nature of risks.

Examples in this book which could help you prepare for this include:

- Sections 1.7 and 1.8 – living with the threat of earthquake hazards and how these can be managed.
- Section 2.8 and 2.9 – the changing climate, and risks posed to the UK and to the African continent.
- Section 4.4 – living with chronic water shortage in the Sahel.

Foundation Tier Mark Schemes
(for questions on P296 of the student textbook)

Section 1 (8 marks)

a **1 mark** Answer: New Zealand.

b **1 mark** Answer: The Southern hemisphere.

c **2 marks** This question is point marked. It requires two single features for 1 mark each; no development is required. Suitable features include:
- Clustered in a line (1)
- The earlier ones are inland (1) and later ones nearer the coast / in Christchurch (1)
- There are far more smaller ones than large ones (1)
- Plus other points on merit.

d **4 marks** This question is point marked. It requires two single reasons for 1 mark each; no development is required. Suitable reasons include:
- They were located closer to Christchurch city (1)
- More people lived in that area (1).
- Much damage had already been done in the earlier earthquake (1) which meant that many buildings had already been weakened (1).
- Plus other points on merit.

Section 2 (10 marks)

a **1 mark** Answer: Conservative.

b **3 marks** This question is point marked. Marks can be awarded for three separate points for 1 mark each (bullet points would be acceptable) or one well-developed explanation. Correct ways include:
- As plates move they rub against each other (1) — plus development e.g. causing friction (1) — plus further expansion e.g. which causes the plates to move in a series of jolts (1)
- Plus other relevant points on merit.

c **2 marks** This question is point marked. Marks can be awarded for two separate points for 1 mark each (bullet points would be acceptable) or one developed explanation. Suitable reasons include:
- The plate boundary extends through most of the South Island (1) or close to North Island (1)
- Plus other relevant points on merit.

d **4 marks** This question is point marked. It requires two developed descriptions, or exceptionally one well-developed description for 3 marks (not 4). Four separate un-developed points are not acceptable – cap any list of separate points at 2 marks. Suitable ways include:
- Regular earthquake drills (1) — plus development e.g. 'such as how to protect yourself by getting under a table' (1) — or well developed with further expansion e.g. 'which means that people know how to behave if there's an earthquake' (1)
- Develop the skills of the emergency services (1) — plus development e.g. 'so they can go into action straight away if an earthquake happens' (1)
- Develop intelligent building design (1) — plus development e.g. 'by introducing counter-balance weights' (1) — or well developed with further expansion e.g. 'which means that buildings move and flex in an earthquake and don't collapse' (1)
- Plus other relevant points on merit.

Making geographical decisions

Section 3 (10 marks)

a 4 marks This question is point marked. It requires two developed descriptions, or exceptionally one well-developed description for 3 marks (not 4). Four separate un-developed points are not acceptable — cap any list of separate points at 2 marks. Suitable ways include:

- Damage to buildings (1) — plus development e.g. 'which means that they probably had nowhere to go to work' (1)
- Damage to transport systems (1) — plus development e.g. 'which meant they couldn't get to work or go shopping' (1)
- Possible danger from after-shocks (1) — plus development e.g. 'so they could have been injured by falling buildings' (1)
- Plus other relevant points on merit.

b 2 marks This question is point marked. It requires one developed explanation for 1 mark per point. Two separate points are not acceptable and should be capped at 1 mark maximum. Suitable reasons include:

- They weren't built with earthquake-resistant design / proofing in mind (1) — plus development e.g. 'which means they collapsed instead of flexing' (1)
- Plus other relevant points on merit.

c 4 marks This question is point marked. It requires two developed points — one on each of economic and social impacts — for 2 marks each. A well-developed point can be credited with 3 marks (but not 4). Cap answers at 3 marks which do not include both an economic and a social impact.

Suitable **economic** impacts include:

- The cost of damage, with some data illustration (1) — plus development e.g. 'caused by building collapse' (1)
- Many workplaces destroyed, with example e.g. Canterbury TV building (1) — plus development e.g. 'which would have caused a recession' (1)
- Plus other relevant points on merit.

Suitable **social** impacts include:

- Many injuries and deaths (1) — plus development e.g. 'which would have caused grief for many families / people' (1)
- Plus other relevant points on merit.

Section 4 (5 marks)

a 1 mark This question is point marked. It requires a single reason for 1 mark; no development is required. Suitable reasons include:

- Because of the likelihood of aftershocks (1)
- Because it's close to (NOT on) a plate margin (1)
- Scientists say there's a 72% chance there'll be another one before the end of 2013 (1).

b 4 marks This question is point marked. It requires two developed points for 2 marks each; exceptionally, a well-developed point can be credited with 3 marks (but not 4). Suitable features include:

- Close to the River Avon (1) — plus development e.g. 'between the city centre and the coast' (1)
- East / North-east of the city centre (1) — plus development with example e.g. 'in the suburbs of Avonside/Dallington' (1).

Foundation Tier Mark Schemes continued

Section 5 (8 marks)

a **1 mark** Answer: Development which is decided by government and other large organisations.

b **1 mark** This question is point marked, and requires a single feature for 1 mark; no development is required. Suitable features include:

- Identifying the needs of communities by asking them (1)
- Local people contribute ideas to what they need (1)
- Local people have control over decisions (1)
- Experts help people out but the people decide what happens (1)
- Plus other suitable features on merit.

c **6 marks** This question is marked using levels. The answer requires development of points to reach Level 2. The top of Level 3 (6 marks) should be awarded where three descriptions are either developed, or two are well-developed.

As the question asks for differences, separate descriptions which do not actually state differences are capped at the top of Level 2 (4 marks). Differences must use a comparative term such as 'whereas', or 'compared to'. However, a single comparison validates the whole answer.

Suitable points include:

- Top-down plan: Formed by the New Zealand government and Christchurch City Council — plus development e.g. 'who have a new plan for the whole of the city centre' — or well-developed with further expansion e.g. 'to develop a knowledge economy'.
- Bottom-up plan: Put together by local people — plus development e.g. 'who want housing as opposed to businesses as the priority' — or well-developed with further expansion e.g. 'with parks and places to create a good quality of life'.
- Plus other descriptions on merit.

Level	Descriptor
0	No rewardable content
1 (1-2 marks)	Simple or very basic statements using little or no subject vocabulary. May be a descriptive or basic list of points e.g. 'the bottom-up plan is for local people'.
2 (3-4 marks)	Generalised descriptions but with some use of geographical terms e.g. 'the bottom-up plan has been put together by local people because they want housing as a priority'. Up to two developed statements as shown by examples above.
3 (5-6 marks)	Detailed statements with clear descriptions using geographical terms. e.g. 'the bottom-up plan has been put together by local people who want housing and parks, with good public transport, as a priority, instead of the top-down plan which is mainly about business'. Three developed or two well-developed points as shown by examples above.

Making geographical decisions

Section 6 (9 marks)

9 marks This question should be marked as a whole, i.e. parts **a** and **b** together, using levels. The key to this question is the command words 'explain' and 'outline'. Remember, therefore, that purely descriptive points and those which are undeveloped do not progress beyond Level 1.

All three options should give the opportunity for students to write at length. Any could be chosen; all are 'real'. Credit negative points as well as positives; e.g. Option 1 'although re-planning the CBD should not be a priority, people in Christchurch do need work now and in the long term'.

Points should be developed for an answer to reach Level 2 or 3. One developed statement takes a student to the top of Level 1. Further developed points take them to mid-high Level 2, but at least one of these must be well-developed for Level 3. A single well-developed point takes a student into Level 2. Look for three well-developed points to award a top Level 3.

Guidance on options:

Option 1 — Accept the top-down plan

Advantages of Option 1 include:

- It would bring jobs to the city centre.
- It would make sure that buildings are much safer.
- The jobs would be high-earning jobs which would create further jobs e.g. in shops, restaurants and hotels.
- It might develop the reputation of Christchurch as a city, major business centre etc.
- It includes essential services e.g. emergency services.

Disadvantages of Option 1 include:

- It does nothing about the issue of housing shortage.
- It could make the housing problem worse as people will have to be moved out to make way for businesses.

Option 2 — Accept the bottom-up plan

Advantages of Option 2 include:

- It gives priority to housing which is the greatest need for the greatest number of people.
- It is fairer for people rather than for business.
- It helps to develop quality of life by providing parks and areas of leisure for people to enjoy.
- It's more sustainable because it relies less on cars and more on walking, cycling and public transport.

Disadvantages of Option 2 include:

- It does not guarantee that there'll be enough work in the city.
- It does not focus on essential services.

Option 3 — Abandon Christchurch

Advantages of Option 3 include:

- It may be the cheapest option.
- The earthquake problem will not go away.

Disadvantages of Option 3 include:

- Loss of jobs to the city and to New Zealand.
- Loss of a city's heritage.

Level	Descriptor
0	No rewardable content
1 (1-3 marks)	Simple or very basic statements using little or no subject vocabulary. May be a list e.g. 'Option 1 would be a good thing for Christchurch as there'd be jobs'.
2 (4-6 marks)	Generalised explanations but with some use of geographical terms e.g. 'Option 1 would bring jobs and develop a highly paid knowledge economy'. Up to three developed statements as shown by examples above.
3 (7-9 marks)	Detailed statements with clear explanations using geographical terms. e.g. 'Option 1 would bring employment and develop a highly paid knowledge economy, which would have the advantage of developing a demand for other services like a positive multiplier'. Two well-developed points plus other developed statements are required for the top of Level 3 as shown by examples above.

Higher Tier Mark Schemes
(for questions on P297 of the student textbook)

Section 1 (8 marks)

a 2 marks This question is point marked. It requires two single points for 1 mark each; no development is required. Suitable points include:
- In New Zealand (1)
- On the east coast (1) of South Island (1)
- In Canterbury region (1).

b 2 marks This question is point marked. It requires two single features for 1 mark each; no development is required. Suitable descriptions include:
- Clustered along a line (1) running east-west (1)
- The earlier ones are inland (1) and later ones nearer the coast / in Christchurch (1)
- There are more smaller ones than large ones (1)
- Plus other points on merit.

c 4 marks This question is point marked. It requires two developed points for 1 mark each, but a comparison must be given for 4 marks. Two independent descriptions without comparison should be capped at 3 marks. Suitable points include:
- Those in 2011 were located closer to Christchurch city (1) but were smaller in intensity – with use of data (1)
- Those in 2010 were inland (1) and were larger in intensity – with use of data (1)
- The damage in 2011 was greater (1) as much had already been done in the earlier earthquake (1) which meant that many buildings had already been weakened (1)
- Plus other points on merit.

Section 2 (7 marks)

a 1 mark Answer: Conservative.

b 2 marks This question is point marked. Marks can be awarded for two separate points for 1 mark each (bullet points would be acceptable) or one developed explanation. Correct explanations include:
- The plate boundary extends through most of the South Island (1) or close to North Island (1)
- As plates move they rub against each other (1) — plus development e.g. causing friction (1) / which causes the plates to move in a series of jolts (1)
- Plus other relevant points on merit.

c 4 marks This question is point marked. It requires two developed explanations, or exceptionally one well-developed explanations for 3 marks (not 4). Four separate un-developed points are not acceptable. Cap any list of separate points at 2 marks. Suitable explanations include:
- Regular earthquake drills (1) — plus development e.g. 'which means that people know how to behave if there's an earthquake' (1)
- Rehearse emergency service procedures (1) — plus development e.g. 'so they can go into action straight away if an earthquake happens' (1)
- Develop intelligent building design such as counter-balance weights (1) — plus development e.g. 'which means that buildings move and flex in an earthquake and don't collapse' (1)
- Plus other relevant points on merit.

Making geographical decisions

Section 3 (10 marks)

a 4 marks This question is point marked. It requires two developed descriptions for 2 marks each; exceptionally 3 marks may be awarded for a well-developed point (but not 4). Suitable points include:

- Most violent shakes were in / close to the city centre (1) except where the epicentre was in Lyttleton (1)
- Damage was less intense away from the city towards the outskirts (1) / away from the coast / further inland (1).

b 6 marks This question is marked using levels. The answer requires development of points to reach Level 2. The top of Level 3 (6 marks) should be awarded where three descriptions are either developed, or two are well-developed. Cap answers at the top of Level 2 (4 marks) which do not include both economic and social impacts of the earthquakes.

Suitable **economic** impacts include:

- The cost of damage (with some data illustration) — plus development e.g. 'caused by building collapse'
- Many workplaces destroyed — plus development e.g. Canterbury TV building — plus further expansion e.g. 'which would have caused a recession'.

Suitable **social** impacts include:

- Many injuries and deaths (with use of data) — plus development e.g. 'which would have caused grief for many families / people'.

Level	Descriptor
0	No rewardable content
1 (1-2 marks)	Simple or very basic statements using little or no subject vocabulary. May be a descriptive or basic list of points e.g. 'many housing areas were destroyed in the earthquakes'.
2 (3-4 marks)	Generalised descriptions but with some use of geographical terms e.g. 'social impacts included the destruction of many housing areas and many people having to be rehoused'. Up to two developed statements as shown by examples above.
3 (5-6 marks)	Detailed statements with clear descriptions using geographical terms. e.g. 'social impacts included the destruction of residential areas close to the city centre, and many people having to be rehoused as damage made houses unsafe to live in'. Three developed or two well-developed points as shown by examples above.

Section 4 (6 marks)

a 2 marks This question is point marked. It requires a single developed reason for 2 marks. Suitable reasons include:

- Because of the likelihood of aftershocks (1) — plus development e.g. which are likely to damage the city further
- Because it's close to (NOT on) a plate margin (1) and means that earthquakes can never be predicted (1)
- Earthquakes occur in swarms (1) — plus development e.g. 'and scientists say there's a 72% chance there'll be another one before the end of 2013' (1).

b 4 marks This question is point marked. It requires two developed reasons for 2 marks each; exceptionally, a well-developed point can be credited with 3 marks (but not 4). Suitable reasons include:

- The cost of rebuilding is so high (1)
- The areas shown are those which suffered worst damage in the earthquake (1) — plus development e.g. 'so they would be most expensive' (1)
- The areas were closest to the epicentre in 2011 (1) — plus development e.g. 'which means that quakes are almost certain to happen again' (1)
- New 'earthquake proof' buildings would be needed (1) — 'which would be hugely expensive'.

Higher Tier Mark Schemes continued

Section 5 (7 marks)

a 1 mark This question is point marked. It requires a single point for 1 mark; no development is required. Suitable points include:

- Development which is decided by government and other large organisations (1)
- Decisions imposed on people / people do not have a say (1)
- The kind of development that involves building infrastructure / examples e.g. road, rail (1)
- Development where wealth or benefits trickle down to people (1).

b 6 marks This question is marked using levels. The answer requires developed explanations to reach Level 2. The top of Level 3 (6 marks) should be awarded where three explanations are developed, or two are well-developed. Purely descriptive points do not get above Level 1 (max. 2 marks).

As the question asks for differences between top-down and bottom-up viewpoints, separate descriptions which do not actually state differences are capped at the top of Level 2 (4 marks). Differences must use a comparative term such as 'whereas', or 'compared to'. However, a single comparison validates the whole answer.

Suitable points include:

- Top-down viewpoints: Plan for CBD formed by the New Zealand government and Christchurch City Council — plus development e.g. 'because they want to generate economic growth / want to ensure success for the new plan for city centre' — or well-developed with further expansion e.g. 'because they think a knowledge economy will bring most wealth to Christchurch'.
- Bottom-up plan: Promoted by local people who want housing — plus development e.g. because they believe in people's priorities coming first / put social values above economic — or well-developed with further expansion e.g. and environmental values / putting parks and quality of life above economic development.
- Plus other explanations on merit.

Level	Descriptor
0	No rewardable content
1 (1-2 marks)	Simple or very basic statements using little or no subject vocabulary. May be purely descriptive or basic list of points e.g. 'the bottom-up plan is for local people who want parks'.
2 (3-4 marks)	Generalised explanations with some use of geographical terms e.g. 'the bottom-up plan has been put together by local people who believe housing should be the priority because so many were made homeless'. Up to two developed statements as shown by examples above.
3 (5-6 marks)	Detailed statements with clear descriptions using geographical terms. e.g. 'the bottom-up plan is being promoted by local protestors who believe housing should be the priority because so many were made homeless, and they believe social values are more important than economic'. Three developed or two well-developed points as shown by examples above.

Making geographical decisions

Section 6 (12 marks)

12 marks This question is marked using levels. The key to this question is the command word 'justify', which requires explanation for the chosen option. Remember, therefore, that purely descriptive points and those which are undeveloped do not progress beyond Level 1.

All three options should give the opportunity for students to write at length. Any could be chosen; all are 'real'. Credit negative explanations as well as positives e.g. 'although re-planning the CBD, Option 1 should not be a priority as the growth of the knowledge economy is not going to help anyone except the highly paid'.

Points should be developed points for an answer to reach Level 2 or 3. 1-2 developed explanations take a student to the top of Level 1. Further developed points take them to mid-high Level 2, but at least one of these must be well-developed to get into Level 3. One single well-developed point takes a student into Level 2. Look for 3-4 well-developed points to award a top Level 3.

Guidance on options:

Option 1 — Accept the top-down plan

Advantages of Option 1 include:
- It would bring jobs to the city centre.
- It would make sure that buildings are much safer.
- The jobs would be high-earning jobs which would generate other jobs in shops, restaurants and hotels.
- It might develop the reputation of Christchurch as a city, major business centre etc.
- It takes essential services into account.

Disadvantages of Option 1 include:
- It does nothing about the issue of housing shortage.
- It could make the housing problem worse as people will have to be moved out to make way for businesses.

Option 2 — Accept the bottom-up plan

Advantages of Option 2 include:
- It gives priority to housing which is the greatest need for the greatest number.
- It makes plans for the future fairer for people rather than for business.
- It helps to develop quality of life by providing parks and areas of leisure.
- It's more sustainable because it relies less on cars and more on walking, cycling and public transport.

Disadvantages of Option 2 include:
- It does not guarantee that there'll be enough work in the city.
- It does not focus on essential services.

Option 3 — Abandon Christchurch

Advantages of Option 3 include:
- It may be the cheapest option.
- The earthquake problem will not go away.

Disadvantages of Option 3 include:
- Loss of jobs to the city and to New Zealand.
- Loss of a city's heritage.

Level	Descriptor
0	No rewardable content
1 (1-4 marks)	Simple or very basic descriptive statements using little or no subject vocabulary. May be a list e.g. 'Option 1 would be a good thing for Christchurch as there'd be jobs for people'. 1-2 simply developed explanations required for the top of Level 1.
2 (5-8 marks)	Generalised explanations but with some use of geographical terms e.g. 'Option 1 would bring jobs and develop a highly paid knowledge economy which would increase the number of well-paid people'. Up to 4 developed explanations required for the top of Level 2 as shown by examples above.
3 (9-12 marks)	Detailed statements with clear coherent explanations using geographical terms. e.g. 'Option 1 would bring employment and develop a highly paid knowledge economy. This has the advantage of developing a demand for other services like a positive multiplier, placing Christchurch at the heart of the New Zealand economy'. 3-4 well-developed explanations are required for the top of Level 3 as shown by examples above.

Spelling, Punctuation and Grammar (SPaG)

Marks for Spelling, Punctuation and Grammar (SPaG) are awarded in the final question (Section 6) of Unit 3, not across the whole paper. This is done in order to give students a chance to be rewarded for their SPaG in the question offering the best opportunity for extended writing. Use the following levels as follows to give an extra mark out of 3 for SPaG. In this way you'll end up with a mark out of 53 for the Unit 3 examination.

Level	Descriptor
0 (0 marks)	Errors severely hinder the meaning, or candidates do not spell, punctuate or use the rules of grammar properly.
1 (1 mark)	Work is spelt and punctuated with some accuracy and rules of grammar are sound. The meaning of the answer is fairly clear. A small range of specialist subject terms.
2 (2 marks)	Work is spelt and punctuated with considerable accuracy and the rules of grammar are good. The meaning of the answer is clear. A good range of subject specialist terms.
3 (3 marks)	Work is spelt and punctuated with consistent accuracy and the rules of grammar are very good, enhancing the meaning of the answer. A wide range of subject specialist terms used accurately.

Unit 4

18 Controlled Assessment

Introduction to Unit 4

Unit 4 is known as the controlled assessment; it replaces traditional written GCSE coursework. Like the other three units, it counts for 25% of the final GCSE grade. Unlike the others, it is a common assessment for all students – with no separate tiers. It can be completed successfully and submitted for June entry in either year of the course. The main considerations are logistical, e.g. when it is appropriate for fieldwork to be carried out in your school. There is no evidence to say that students suffer by completing enquiries of this sort in Year 10 as opposed to Year 11. Chapter 18 of the students' book provides guidance for students in setting out the report. Each year Edexcel will publish eight new task titles from four themes in the course, giving schools a choice of controlled assessment topics and therefore fieldwork locations. Teachers are free to select more than one focus (and therefore location), although a separate internal moderation would be needed for each sample. The fieldwork titles are based on four different themes, each derived from the four small-scale options in Units 1 and 2. There will be two titles for each theme.

- River environments – one title will usually be physical in nature, while the second will focus more on people-environment relationships (e.g. flooding and pressures on the landscape).
- Coastal environments – like rivers, one title will usually be physical in nature, while the second will focus more on people-environment relationships (e.g. coastal protection).
- Rural environments – which may include tourism.
- Urban environments – which may include residential, quality of life, etc.

The titles for each cohort of students are released two years in advance, so that teachers can plan which they consider best for their students or for their course. Titles last for a given cohort of students over the whole two-year period, so that any one cohort will have two opportunities for entry with the same titles (June in Year 10 and again in Year 11). Any re-sits are done on the same topics, with amendments made by students; a complete new study is not required. The total length of work required is approximately 2000 words or equivalent (e.g. using PowerPoints, videos, web-pages, etc.).

The stages of controlled assessment

Controlled assessment is based on fieldwork on a set title, or task. The idea of 'control' is to ensure degrees of teacher supervision throughout, so that the work can be easily authenticated as students' own. Students prepare a 'final report', which can be completed and presented as:

- a written report of about 2000 words
- a PowerPoint presentation
- a video/DVD
- a GIS presentation
- a web page.

Whichever is selected, it should be the equivalent of a final report of 2000 words. The report could provide a combination of outcomes, i.e. combine different types, such as a written report with a video or short PowerPoint presentation.

Each task will consist of guidance from Edexcel, known as a 'task brief'. The brief will outline guidance on how to undertake the work, including pre-fieldwork, research, analysis, etc. Guidance on timings is also suggested, along with headings for candidates to follow. Candidates can use a range of 'write-up' options, e.g. PowerPoint presentations.

Completing the controlled assessment takes place in a series of five stages, which follow the enquiry process (see a to e in the diagram). In the text boxes, the assumption is that teachers have two hours per week for each class.

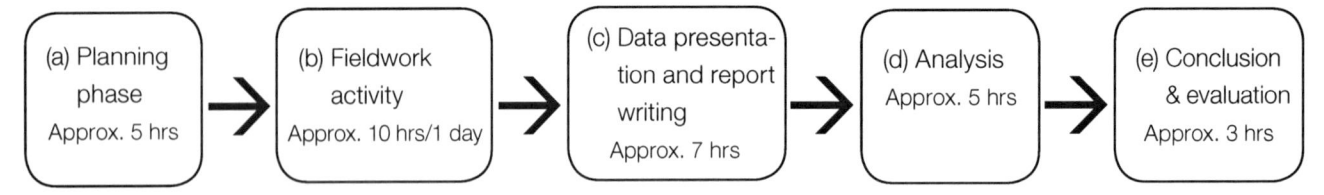

(a) Planning phase — Approx. 5 hrs → (b) Fieldwork activity — Approx. 10 hrs/1 day → (c) Data presentation and report writing — Approx. 7 hrs → (d) Analysis — Approx. 5 hrs → (e) Conclusion & evaluation — Approx. 3 hrs

Although there is flexibility, the whole process should take about 20 hours, i.e. 10 teaching weeks – plus about one day's fieldwork. The total of ten hours set aside for fieldwork is longer than the school day to take account of extra research that may be done by students, e.g. for secondary data or sources.

Levels of control

'Control' refers to the degree of supervision necessary at each stage of the enquiry. By implementing different levels of control, it is hoped that the work of candidates can be better authenticated as their own, i.e. no parental involvement or plagiarism from sources such as the Internet or past projects.

There are three levels of control: limited, moderate and high.

Levels of control are designed to ensure that teachers know that the completed project is each student's own work. The degree of supervision – or control – increases as the work progresses, and includes marking and moderation of completed samples.

Investigating geography

LIMITED CONTROL: introduction, planning and fieldwork	• Students work in open classrooms, with discussion and sharing ideas. • Teachers can help to introduce the topic and discuss fieldwork methods openly with students. Students can write an introduction based on this. • In the field, students complete work under limited supervision. • Students can work collaboratively (in groups/pairs) to collect data and share ideas about good websites away from direct supervision.
MODERATE CONTROL: collective researching, collating data, and all presentation of results	• This stage is classroom based, in a resource area or other appropriate environment; the teacher/supervisor is present. • Some collaborative work can be undertaken, e.g. collective researching and collation of results. • Work carried out under moderate control may be part of the final report. • Data presentation is completed in this way, with the teacher on hand to assist in organising work, suggest possible choices about how data might be presented, or respond to ICT queries – but unable to instruct students about how to present data. • Students leave work in a secure folder at the end of each lesson. They can plan further stages of work at home but cannot transfer work between home and school.
HIGH CONTROL: the main writing stage – analysis, conclusions and evaluation	• This stage is classroom based, or in an environment where close supervision is possible. • Close supervision does not mean working under exam conditions or in silence, but it does mean that tight control is needed to ensure that no work is transferred between home and school. • Students can plan work or practise writing analytically at home; teachers can provide guidance on what constitutes good analysis, or on how to write a conclusion or evaluation. But any work practised in this way cannot be transferred to school. • No other new materials should be introduced at this stage. • The use of ICT is encouraged, but there must be controlled access to external websites, or to the school VLE, to prevent work being downloaded from home, e.g. through the VLE or e-mail attachments. • All students' work should be completed independently; no collaboration is allowed.
MODERATE CONTROL: teacher marks the work	• The teacher marks the work, based on Edexcel's mark scheme. • Internal moderation takes place between teachers of different sets, or between teachers who may have taught different topics. • Edexcel administration forms are completed and sent off to a moderator with a sample. • The work is moderated by an external examiner. • Marks are approved or adjusted, with a feedback report completed and sent when results are issued.

Selecting titles

The titles are actually statements or hypotheses. The conclusion to the controlled assessment is that each student should identify the extent to which their investigation helps to accept or reject the hypothesis. Example statements could include:
'The channel characteristics of a river change along its course.'
'Recent changes in inner urban areas have brought many challenges.'

Each statement may contain possible (but not compulsory) mini-investigations within it, which could be used as part of a group exercise. For instance, for a river investigation, some students could investigate how the width and depth change downstream, while another group could investigate changes in river velocity.

Organising the report

The report should be structured into sections, as follows:
- Introduction and aims
- Methods of data collection
- Data presentation
- Analysis
- Conclusion
- Evaluation

This structure should be used, irrespective of the presentational format selected by the student. Students within the same centre might have a different focus based on the title, and a different presentational format. For example:

	Focus (within task)	Chosen format
Student A	Changes in width and depth	DVD and accompanying commentary/transcript
Student B	Changes in the river speed with progression downstream	PowerPoint and accompanying 'script' or notes
Student C	Changes in a river's load	Traditional written report

It is also possible to 'mix and match' formats. For example, the final report could include a short piece of edited DVD footage – for instance, to film and evaluate the methodologies used, or to present some of the results – as well as written work. The only condition is that it must be 2000 words long or the equivalent. The nature of the sections means that few words will be used for data presentation (annotations or tables of data are not included in the word count); the majority will be used for analysing the data.

Getting the most out of students

Given that the report is marked out of 50, it is worth understanding the mark scheme to help students access the highest marks. Note that data presentation and analysis/conclusions are worth 29 marks out of the total 50, i.e. nearly 60% of the total and 15% of the whole GCSE qualification. The following is intended to help you maximise the support you can give to students in letting them know what is required.

Group — Low level of control: 26 marks
- Planning the topic for study, including background research
- Establishing the aims of the enquiry & describing the location
- Planning methods of data collection
- Fieldwork, group data collation & sharing of results
- Data presentation – deciding on which methods to use

+

Individual — High level of control: 24 marks
- Interpretation and analysis of results, including description and explanation
- Discussion of conclusion(s) linking back to original aims and any links between different data sets
- Evaluation of findings by reflecting on the fieldwork

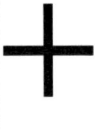

Investigating geography

Data presentation

As well as traditional graphs and maps, there are some additional ways in which data can be presented. These include:

Annotated photographs	• An effective method of presenting geographical information. • They can be used to show and justify the choice of equipment, location of sites and site description, and geographical processes. • Technology can help, e.g. Microsoft MovieMaker can be used to stitch together a series of photographs into an illustrated (DVD) transect through a town/city.
Written description	Geographical 'prose'. Drawing the reader into a photograph, map or other resource can be achieved through a written *geographical* description of the item.
Highlighting and coding	This can be used as a way of both presenting and analysing data. It is well suited to written data, such as leaflets, websites and longer interviews.
'Storyboard'	Just as in film-making, a series of pictures or cartoons can illustrate processes or sets of data, e.g. how a place changes along a transect.
Mind-maps	A geographical diagram can be used to represent ideas, themes or processes. Usually words (or pictures) are arranged around a central theme. Connections between different elements of information can also be shown by using arrows for example. Thicker arrows may indicate stronger connections.
Flow diagrams	These can be used as a graphical representation of a process that may have been tested during the investigation, e.g. the development of a town or resort, or the way in which river processes operate. Different symbols can also be used.

Given the controls over the latter stages of controlled assessment, and the likely pressures that will result on ICT facilities in schools, it is worth noting that work can be hand written throughout. Individual cartography, field sketching, etc. are strongly encouraged. However, the use of computers to access GIS is very much in the ethos of fieldwork and research, and there is an advantage in using ICT to collate group data, present results, as well as record findings in the field, e.g. podcasts, digital photos, or a DVD.

Writing the analysis

Good analysis is critical to a good report. Its purpose is to:
- describe the data patterns and findings
- explain these findings and patterns
- look for interrelationships between different sets of data.

In total, the analysis should be about 1200–1400 words in length. The table on the next page shows examples of high- and low-level indicators, based on the mark scheme.

High-level indicators	Low-level indicators
• Logical and well structured into sections • Patterns are described • Uses evidence of data in the text to support observations • Offers explanations for what the data show • Uses basic statistical tools (e.g. scatter graphs or correlation) to help describe and explain the data • Identifies and explains links and relationships between different data	• Weak ordering or sequencing • Largely descriptive • Does not use data to illustrate patterns, so statements remain generalised rather than specific • Little or no explanation or links between the data sets

Conclusion and evaluation

The conclusion and evaluation should each be about 300 words.

The **conclusion** should:

- Return to the original question or aim, or hypothesis.
- Draw together all the threads of the analysis. Whereas analysis will focus upon each of the sets of results, the conclusion will look at the aims of the study and overall findings.
- Show how far the conclusion is definite, or tentative. Students who use phrases such as 'In some ways', 'my conclusion is definite because ….', 'whereas in other ways I am less sure because ….' will probably fare better because they will recognise shortcomings as well as firm findings.

The **evaluation** should:

- Also return to the original question or aim, and say how valid they think their conclusions are. For example;
  - If you studied a river to see how its channel or landforms changed downstream, were your own results true for the river as a whole?
  - Did you or your teacher just select parts of the river that fitted your aim, or did you look at lots of variations?
  - Did river velocity always increase downstream or were there places where it didn't? Were these due to your results or to odd circumstances at these places?
- Think about the strengths and weaknesses of the fieldwork investigation. A diagram with simple columns is a good way to summarise findings, e.g. a SWOP table (Strengths / Weaknesses / Opportunities / Problems). Here the accuracy and reliability of the data can be discussed. Were there enough data? Would the study produce different findings if it were repeated on other days of the week, or times of year?
- Show how the study could be improved if it were to be repeated. This could include suggesting other avenues of enquiry.
- Suggest who might find the study useful, and why. Would a marketing organisation find your study useful for a shopping centre, for example?

Understanding the mark scheme

Given that the controlled assessment report is worth 25% of the whole GCSE, it is worth teachers understanding the mark scheme in order to help students access the highest marks. The table below sets out the marks for each section and the criteria that help towards Level 3 in the mark scheme. The marks reflect the amount of support given to individual, as opposed to supported, work.

Section	Part of task	Criteria for success	Marks
1	Planning	• Aim of study is clearly stated. • Context and geographical background given to the study. • Location maps clearly show the study area locally, regionally, nationally.	6
2	Methods of data collection	• Data required are listed clearly. • Reasons for data collection methods are briefly described. • Methods used are briefly described and photographed. • Any problems encountered are outlined. • Description of ways in which any problems encountered were dealt with, in order to make data collection as reliable as possible.	9
3	Data presentation	• A range of data presentation techniques. • Data are presented geographically – e.g. pie charts or other graphs are located to show where their location. • Good quality annotations describe the data. • Methods chosen are appropriate for the data collected.	11
4	Analysis and conclusions	Analysis • General trends are described and data used to support statements. • Links between sets of data are identified and explained e.g. on a river, between velocity and the width or depth of the river. • Geographical theory is used where relevant. Conclusions • Clear, and linked to the original aim or statement. • Evidence is used to support conclusions. • The wider geographical significance of the work is recognised.	9
5	Evaluation	• Describes realistic limitations of the fieldwork process. • Shows how the study could be extended or developed further. • Shows who might find the study significant or of use. • Links how effectively the findings of the study answer the task question or statement.	9
6	Planning and Organisation	• Students must be within the word limit (2000 words) to achieve top marks. • Organised and well-structured. • Diagrams integrated into text. • Appropriate sub-headings. • SPaG has been checked. • Clear accurate use of geographical terminology.	6

Quality of Written Communication

Throughout, Quality of Written Communication (QWC) is important; reflecting how well students structure their work, together with spelling, punctuation and grammar. The use of geographical terminology is also taken into account. Marks for QWC are included within each section of the mark scheme. Students should bear in mind:

- legibility
- that all diagrams, maps, graphs are best called Figures, and should be referenced
- the pagination and organisation of their work – how easy is it to navigate?
- cartographic and graphical standards, e.g. labelling axes and titles on graphs
- providing a contents section, together with a bibliography and acknowledgements.

Below are the answers to section 18.3.

answers

1. Canary Wharf – 3780. Liverpool Street station – 3381.
2. Canary Wharf – 374803. Liverpool Street station – 332818. Answers may vary slightly, according to students' judgement.
3. a 11.2 cm = 5.6 km   b 9.5 cm = 4.75 km
4. a WNW (west northwest)   b E (east)
5. *No written answer.*
6. Answers could include: Street names (as they are superimposed by Google); colour of the Millennium Dome and its support towers; boats on the river; individual residential buildings with gardens; actual colours of the river, land and buildings. If they have increased the scale beyond that of the OS map, they may mention finer details such as footpaths and landforms in the park areas and individual rail tracks.
7. *No written answer.*
8. Answers should exemplify the differences between the three areas and may include the following:
   Canary Wharf is within the meander of a river, and is intersected by waterways, docks, that lead back out to the Thames. Buildings are tall office blocks, suggesting its function as a business centre.
   Shadwell appears to be a more residential area, with blocks of terraced housing and outdoor garden areas. Some larger buildings suggest shopping areas, office blocks or schools.
   Victoria Park is a large outdoor space with at least two lakes, criss-crossed by footpaths, but also intersected by roads. Area used for recreation and leisure.